An important collected work that brings together some of the broader, social and criminological perspectives on cybercrime in its broadest sense. A welcome victim-centric perspective is prevalent throughout and should provide food for thought for both scholars in the area but also, perhaps more importantly, those who deal with these problems in their professional lives.

Andy Phippen, *Professor of Social Responsibility in IT, Plymouth Graduate School of Management and Plymouth Business School, Plymouth University, UK*

Cybercrime and its Victims is a welcome, victim-centred addition to the growing literature on cybercrime. Cybercrime is complex to understand, detect, and combat, and is constantly evolving. But what is even harder is protecting those millions of innocent victims who are affected by it, in one form or another. Through this collection, Martellozzo and Jane show how both adults and children are victimised online. Regardless of where they live, at some point of their lives, anyone may be subjected to cyberbullying, online sexual grooming, or online racial discrimination, or they may be targeted as a result of personal information they have shared online. It is our responsibility as researchers and professionals to continue to explore the ever-changing world of cyber space and to ensure the findings have an impact on policy, education and possibly behaviour.

Massimiliano Frassi, *CEO, Prometeo, Bergamo, Italy*

In *Cybercrime and its Victims* Elena Martellozzo and Emma Jane bring together a coherent collection of academic contributions that engage head-on with the ugly side of human behaviour on the internet. This collection uniquely focuses upon the cybercrime victim and in so doing, extinguishes the romance of technology by exposing the many callous ways in which cybercriminals can use it to exploit their victims.

David S. Wall, *Professor of Criminology at the Centre for Criminal Justice Studies, School of Law, University of Leeds, UK*

Cybercrime and its Victims

The last twenty years have seen an explosion in the development of information technology, to the point that people spend a major portion of their waking life in online spaces. While there are enormous benefits associated with this technology, there are also risks that can affect the most vulnerable in our society but also the most confident. *Cybercrime and its Victims* explores the social construction of violence and victimisation in online spaces and brings together scholars from many areas of inquiry, including criminology, sociology, and cultural, media, and gender studies.

The book is organised thematically into five parts. Part I addresses some broad conceptual and theoretical issues. Part II is concerned with issues relating to sexual violence, abuse, and exploitation, as well as to sexual expression online. Part III addresses issues related to race and culture. Part IV addresses concerns around cyberbullying and online suicide, grouped together as 'social violence'. The final part argues that victims of cybercrime are, in general, neglected and not receiving the recognition and support they need and deserve. It concludes that, in the volatile and complex world of cyberspace, continued awareness-raising is essential for bringing attention to the plight of victims. It also argues that there needs to be more support of all kinds for victims, as well as an increase in the exposure and punishment of perpetrators.

Drawing on a range of pressing contemporary issues such as online grooming, sexting, cyberhate, cyberbullying, and online radicalisation, this book examines how cyberspace makes us more vulnerable to crime and violence, how it gives rise to new forms of surveillance and social control, and how cybercrime can be prevented.

Elena Martellozzo is a criminologist and senior lecturer at Middlesex University, UK. She is also an Associate Senior Researcher for the Centre for Trauma and Abuse Studies. She works extensively with children and young people, sex offenders and practitioners. Her research includes exploring children and young people's online behaviour, the analysis of sexual grooming, online sexual exploitation and police practice in the area of child sexual abuse.

Emma A. Jane is a Senior Research Fellow and Senior Lecturer at the University of New South Wales, Australia. Misogyny online, cyberhate, internet mobs, digital vigilantism ("digilantism"), and non-legislative interventions for technology-related crime are the current foci of her ongoing research into the social and ethical implications of emerging technologies. In 2016, the public benefit of her research into misogyny online was recognised when she was named the Anne Dunn Scholar of the Year.

Routledge Studies in Crime and Society

19 **Men, Masculinities and Violence**
An ethnographic study
Anthony Ellis

20 **Order and Conflict in Public Space**
Edited by Mattias De Backer, Lucas Melgaço, Georgiana Varna and Francesca Menichelli

21 **Policing, Port Security and Crime Control**
An Ethnography of the Port Securityscape
Yarin Eski

22 **Organised Crime in European Businesses**
Edited by Ernesto Savona, Michele Riccardi and Giulia Berlusconi

23 **Regulation and Social Control of Incivilities**
Edited by Nina Peršak

24 **Skinhead History, Identity, and Culture**
Kevin Borgeson and Robin Valeri

25 **Homicide, Gender and Responsibility**
Edited by Sandra Walklate and Kate Fitz-Gibbon

26 **Cybercrime Through an Interdisciplinary Lens**
Edited by Thomas J. Holt

27 **Domestic Violence in International Context**
Edited by Diana Scharff Peterson and Julie A. Schroeder

28 **Child Trafficking in the EU**
Policing and Protecting Europe's Most Vulnerable
Pete Fussey and Paddy Rawlinson

29 **Resettlement of Sex Offenders after Custody**
Circles of Support and Accountability
David Thompson and Terry Thomas with Susanne Karstedt

30 **Cybercrime and its Victims**
Edited by Elena Martellozzo and Emma A. Jane

31 **Gender, Technology and Violence**
Edited by Marie Segrave and Laura Vitis

32 **Money and the Governance of Punishment**
A Genealogy of the Penal Fine
Patricia Faraldo Cabana

Cybercrime and its Victims

Edited by Elena Martellozzo and
Emma A. Jane

LONDON AND NEW YORK

First published 2017
by Routledge

2 Park Square, Milton Park, Abingdon, Oxfordshire OX14 4RN
52 Vanderbilt Avenue, New York, NY 10017

Routledge is an imprint of the Taylor & Francis Group, an informa business

First issued in paperback 2019

Copyright © 2017 selection and editorial matter, Elena Martellozzo and Emma A. Jane; individual chapters, the contributors

The right of Elena Martellozzo and Emma A. Jane to be identified as the authors of the editorial matter, and of the authors for their individual chapters, has been asserted in accordance with sections 77 and 78 of the Copyright, Designs and Patents Act 1988.

All rights reserved. No part of this book may be reprinted or reproduced or utilised in any form or by any electronic, mechanical, or other means, now known or hereafter invented, including photocopying and recording, or in any information storage or retrieval system, without permission in writing from the publishers.

Notice:
Product or corporate names may be trademarks or registered trademarks, and are used only for identification and explanation without intent to infringe.

British Library Cataloguing in Publication Data
A catalogue record for this book is available from the British Library

Library of Congress Cataloging in Publication Data
A catalog record for this book has been requested

ISBN: 978-1-138-63944-7 (hbk)
ISBN: 978-0-367-22670-1 (pbk)

Typeset in Times New Roman
by Wearset Ltd, Tyne and Wear, Boldon

To our children: Alice, Leonardo and Lorenzo, future 'netizens' of cyberspace.

Contents

List of contributors xi
Foreword xiv
Acknowledgements xvi

Introduction: victims of cybercrime on the small 'i' internet 1
EMMA A. JANE AND ELENA MARTELLOZZO

PART I
Conceptual issues 25

1 **Victims of cybercrime: definitions and challenges** 27
  NICOLE A VINCENT

2 **Theorising power online** 43
  CHRIS BRICKELL

PART II
Sexual violence, abuse, and exploitation 59

3 **Gendered cyberhate, victim-blaming, and why the internet is more like driving a car on a road than being naked in the snow** 61
  EMMA A. JANE

4 **Sexting in context: understanding gendered sexual media practices beyond inherent 'risk' and 'harm'** 79
  AMY SHIELDS DOBSON

Contents

5	Victims of sex trafficking and online sexual exploitation KRISTINE HICKLE	94
6	Online sexual grooming: children as victims of online abuse ELENA MARTELLOZZO	108

PART III
Race and culture 129

7	Online racial hate speech JAMIE CLELAND	131
8	Malign images, malevolent networks: social media, extremist violence, and public anxieties RAMASWAMI HARINDRANATH	148

PART IV
Social violence 165

9	Bullying in the digital age ROBIN M. KOWALSKI AND GARY W. GIUMETTI	167
10	Internet suicide and communities of affirmation RONALD NIEZEN	187

PART V
Conclusions 207

11	Beyond law: protecting victims through engineering and design NICOLE A VINCENT AND EMMA A. JANE	209

Index 224

Contributors

Elena Martellozzo is a criminologist and senior lecturer at Middlesex University, London. Elena works extensively with children and young people, sex offenders and practitioners. Her research includes exploring children and young people's online behaviour, the analysis of sexual grooming, online sexual exploitation and police practice in the area of child sexual abuse. The findings of her research inform police and other agencies' strategies and practice. She works closely with the media and provides regular expert advice to a number of key agencies. She is the author of *Online Child Sexual Abuse* (2012) and has published widely in a number of international journals.

Emma A. Jane (formerly Emma Tom) is a Senior Research Fellow at the University of New South Wales in Sydney, Australia. Misogyny online is the focus of her ongoing research into the social and ethical implications of emerging technologies. In 2016, Emma received the Anne Dunn Scholar Award for excellence in research about communication and journalism. This followed her receipt, in 2014, of a three-year government grant to study gendered cyberhate and digital citizenship. Prior to her career in academia, Emma spent nearly 25 years working in the print, broadcast, and electronic media during which time she won multiple awards for her writing and investigative reporting. Her ninth book – *Misogyny Online: A Short (and Brutish) History* – was published by Sage in 2017.

Nicole A Vincent obtained her PhD in 2007 from the University of Adelaide in Australia. She is Associate Professor of Philosophy, Law, and Neuroscience at Georgia State University, and holds honorary appointments at Macquarie University in Australia and Technische Universiteit Delft in The Netherlands. The concept of responsibility occupies centre stage in her work in the fields of neuroethics, neurolaw, ethics, philosophy of tort and criminal law, and political philosophy.

Chris Brickell is Associate Professor in Gender Studies at Otago University, Dunedin, New Zealand. A sociologist by training, he has published extensively on the sociology and history of sexuality, masculinity, adolescence and affect in such journals as *The Sociological Review, Journal of the History of*

Sexuality, Rethinking History, Visual Anthropology, Gender, Place & Culture and *Journal of Social History*. His books explore New Zealand history in its international context: *Mates & Lovers: A History of Gay New Zealand* (2008), and *Teenagers: The Rise of Youth Culture in New Zealand* (2017).

Amy Shields Dobson holds a University of Queensland Postdoctoral Fellowship in the Institute for Advanced Studies in the Humanities, where her work focuses on youth, gender politics, and social media. Amy's projects include research into gender and cyber-safety education, sexting in schools, and female genital cosmetic surgery in Australia, including the role of social media practices. Her book *Postfeminist Digital Cultures* (2015) is published by Palgrave Macmillan. With leading girl studies scholar Anita Harris, Amy has recently co-edited a special issue of *Continuum: Journal of Media and Cultural Studies* on 'Post-girlpower: globalized mediated femininities'.

Kristine Hickle is a Lecturer in Social Work at University of Sussex. Previously, she was a researcher and clinical social worker in the USA, where she worked primarily with adults and young people victimised by sexual exploitation and other forms of sexual violence. Research interests include child sexual exploitation and human trafficking; trauma-informed approaches to practice and group-based interventions. Current research projects include interdisciplinary research exploring police responses to CSE in the UK, and a national study in England evaluating the implementation and impact of a multi-agency model for practice with children and young people affected by child sexual exploitation.

Jamie Cleland is a Senior Lecturer in the Management School at the University of South Australia. He is the author of *A Sociology of Football in a Global Context* (Routledge, 2015) and co-author of *Football's Dark Side: Corruption, Homophobia, Violence and Racism in the Beautiful Game* (Palgrave, 2014) and has published widely on contemporary culture and identity, particularly focusing on communication, sexuality, race, and active supporter mobilisations within the field of football.

Ramaswami Harindranath is Professor of Media at the University of New South Wales, Sydney, Australia. His research interests include global media, economy and culture; diasporic media and identity; multicultural arts and cultural citizenship; South Asian politics and culture; and postcoloniality. His major publications include *Approaches to Audiences, The 'Crash' Controversy, Perspectives on Global Cultures, Re-imagining Diaspora*, and *Audience-Citizens*. He is currently completing a manuscript entitled *Southern Discomfort*, which re-assesses contemporary forms of political, economic, and cultural inequality.

Robin M. Kowalski is a Trevillian professor of psychology at Clemson University. Her research focuses primarily on aversive interpersonal behaviours, most notably complaining, teasing, and bullying, with a particular focus on cyber bullying. She is the author or co-author of several books including *Complaining, Teasing, and Other Annoying Behaviors*, *Aversive Interpersonal Behaviors, Behaving Badly*, and *Cyber Bullying: Bullying in the Digital Age*. Dr. Kowalski has received several awards including Clemson's Award of Distinction, Clemson's Award for Excellence in Undergraduate Teaching, the Phil Prince Award for Excellence and Innovation in the Classroom, and Clemson's College of Business and Behavioral Science Senior Research Award. She was also selected as a finalist for the 2013 and 2014 South Carolina Governor's Professor of the Year Awards.

Gary W. Giumetti is an Associate Professor of Psychology at Quinnipiac University. Gary holds a Bachelor's and Master's degree in Psychology from Villanova University and a PhD in Industrial-Organizational Psychology from Clemson University. Gary also has over five years of human resources consulting experience, working with many Fortune 500 organisations to develop and validate their selection systems for hiring new employees. Additionally, Gary has published research on such topics as cyberbullying, cyber incivility, and fairness perceptions among applicants, and his research appears in such journals as *Psychological Bulletin*, the *Journal of Occupational Health Psychology*, the *Journal of Applied Psychology*, and the *International Journal of Selection and Assessment*.

Ronald Niezen is the Katharine A. Pearson Chair in Civil Society and Public Policy in the Faculty of Law and Department of Anthropology at McGill University. He has a PhD from Cambridge University and has done research on Islamic reform in West Africa, justice campaigns in Aboriginal communities in northern Canada and on the international movement of indigenous peoples in the United Nations. His books include: *The Origins of Indigenism: Human Rights and the Politics of Difference* (University of California Press, 2003) and *Truth and Indignation: Canada's Truth and Reconciliation Commission on Indian Residential Schools* (University of Toronto Press, 2013).

Foreword

The novelist William Gibson – credited with first coining the term 'cyberspace' in 1984 – offered the following reflection more than 20 years later:

> 'Cyberspace' as a term is sort of over. It's over in the way that, after a certain time, people stopped using the suffix '-electro' to make things cool, because everything was electrical. 'Electro' was all over the early 20th century, and now it's gone. I think 'cyber' is sort of the same way. The things that *aren't* cyberspace seem to comprise a smaller set than things that are.
>
> (In Phillips 2016: 189)

Elena Martellozzo and Emma A. Jane would, I think, be inclined to agree with Gibson. One of the crucial starting points for their book is an appreciation that what was once met with amazement and perplexity (the emergence of the internet, the World Wide Web, and the forms of networked communication they enable) are now increasingly ordinary, part-and-parcel of the furniture of everyday life. Those confronting the initial explosion of these technologically-driven innovations can perhaps be forgiven for viewing them as harbingers of a radical transformation of the very texture and fabric of social reality itself (captured most clearly in the language of 'virtual reality', a parallel universe supposedly existing apart from the material world with which we have been accustomed). However, time and more sober reflection have shown that the 'cyber' is in fact part of a continuum of social experience and is deeply-entwined with familiar social structures and processes – one of the most remarkable things about 'life online' is just how thoroughly *unremarkable* (in the sense of familiar and recognisable) it usually is. Exactly the same observation can be made about 'cybercrime' (and its variants or counterparts, such as 'cyber-deviance', 'cyber-exploitation', 'cyber-terrorism', 'cyber-conflict', 'cyber-war', and so on); far from being unprecedented, patterns of online law- and rule-breaking behaviour need to be seen as reconfigurations and extensions of offline behaviours and relationships. As Martellozzo and Jane are at pains to point out, this is not to simply dismiss the changes and challenges presented by crimes occurring in the online environment (these are very real), but rather to appreciate that any attempt to form an adequate criminological account about them needs to appreciate their embeddedness in the wider world of social institutions, practices, divisions and hierarchies. One of the important features of the collection they've assembled is the sensitivity to such complex inter-relations that is exhibited by the authors. In a reversal of Occam's Razor, it seems to me that this volume is oriented by an appreciation that, when it comes to social interactions and processes, simple answers are seldom the right ones, and that a healthy degree of reflexivity about commonplace assumptions is paramount if our explanations and interpretations of online crime are to be adequate to the task.

A second important characteristic of this book is clearly addressed in its title – it aims to reorient the 'cyber-criminological gaze' in the direction of victims. Reflecting on the development of this field of inquiry over the past 20 or so years (and including my own contributions to that development), it strikes me that it may have unintentionally fallen into some of the same blind spots that characterised the wider field of criminology for many decades. Specifically, the focus upon categorisation (creating typologies of crimes), measurement (gauging the scope and scale of crimes) and aetiology (explaining how and why crimes occur and who perpetrates them) left victims (including their social and cultural characteristics, their experiences, and their needs) if not entirely neglected then certainly in the background. However, just as the rise of critical victimology within criminology created a much-needed visibility for, and sensitivity to, the 'targets' of crime, so this volume aims to correct any one-sided focus upon the perpetrators of cybercrime, their motivations, criminal careers, punishment, potential for 'desistance' and suchlike. However, this task requires a delicate balancing act. On the one hand, there is a need to recognise and explore how online victimisation is bound-up with wider patterns of gendered and racialised inequality, exploitation and oppression; on the other, the definitions and boundaries of victimhood and victimisation – and the very usefulness of the category of 'victim' in itself – need to be subject to ongoing critical reflection, lest they become reified and static. Again, it is to the credit of all involved that the papers assembled here, taken together, manage to trace a nuanced path through these competing demands. The result is a book that pushes forward the boundaries of interdisciplinary and international research about online crime; that provides an important focus upon the study of victims and victimisation; and that reflects the growing depth and maturity of the field of cybercrime studies. As such, it is a welcome contribution to one of the most lively and topical areas of contemporary criminology, and is sure to stimulate further research and discussion over the coming years.

Majid Yar, Professor of Criminology, Lancaster University, UK

Reference

Phillips, P.A. (ed.) (2016) *Conversations with William Gibson.* Jackson, MS: University of Mississippi Press.

Acknowledgements

We would like to express our gratitude to the committed scholars who contributed to this book: it has been a pleasure working with you and learning from you.

We would like to thank the Routledge team for their support and for enabling us to publish this fascinating collection.

Emma A. Jane would like to thank the Australian Research Council (ARC) for her Discovery Early Career Research Award (DECRA Project ID: DE150100670) which allowed her the time for writing and editing of this book.

Above all we would like to thank our families who supported and encouraged us in spite of all the time it took us away from them.

Introduction

Victims of cybercrime on the small 'i' internet

Emma A. Jane and Elena Martellozzo

Two decades ago, academic texts about The Internet usually started with some solid 'ooh-ing' and 'ahh-ing'. 'My goodness!' late 1990s Elena Martellozzo and Emma A. Jane might have gushed. 'The novelty, possibility, and sheer size of the thing! Whoever can believe it?!' Before long, however, we would have moved onto the important business of 'oh no!-ing'. 'Don't start celebrating too early,' we would have warned. 'This place of limitless possibility has *a dark side*.' Cue the scholarly equivalent of Macaulay Culkin's screaming face from the *Home Alone* franchise (this was the late 1990s, after all). Then, as we walked you through the futuristic new world of 'computer crime', you might well have wondered how any of these cutting edge offences could ever possibly be understood, regulated, or prosecuted using existing apparatus because they were occurring in that hallucinogenic parallel universe known as The Cybersphere.

We'll talk more about these bipolar swings in thinking about cyberspace (it's all good/it's all bad) in a moment. For the time being, we draw your attention to the fact that something extraordinary has happened: the place that was once thought to have the power to both fix and break everything has become ordinary. In 2011, the communications professor Klaus Bruhn Jensen observed that – in stark contrast to early notions of the internet as an extraordinary place full of identity experiments, avant-garde artworks, and innovative business models – the cybersphere was in the process of 'becoming ordinary' (2011, p. 47). More recently, the technology writer Nilay Patel marvelled at the way the 'research science pipe dream' of networking all the world's computers had become 'a necessary condition of economic and social development, from government and university labs to kitchen tables and city streets' (2014). Given that the network is interwoven into every moment of our lives, Patel's neat point is that we no longer do things on the internet, we just do things (2014).

In fact, the internet has become so run-of-the-mill, so what's-all-the-fuss-about, that – after a lengthy, linguistic tug-of-war – it is gradually succumbing to the irresistible force of decapitalisation. While 'Internet' is still deployed in contexts requiring formal and prescriptive usage, the linguist Susan C. Herring notes that the use of the capital 'I' in such cases can make a writer or publication appear 'stuffy and out-of-date' (2015). Her view is that the lower-case version will 'eventually win the day … driven by age-old principles of language change' (ibid.). We concur. What's more, we think this process of decapitalisation – so closely linked to the process of 'ordinary-fication' – also works well as a metaphor for the changing nature of scholarly research into crime and victimisation online.

In the early years of internet studies, many scholars in many disciplines seemed struck by both shock and awe when they cast their concepts and their research questionnaires around the cybersphere (Barker and Jane 2016, p. 463). Indeed, it may be hard for digital natives – that is, those who have always known the internet – to understand just how revolutionary these new digital technologies were to those of us who grew up in households without a computer, let alone a computer connected to everyone else's computers. (Jane, for instance, started her career as a cadet journalist at a time when people in open plan offices smoked cigarettes at their desks, and newsrooms still contained some actual typewriters and rotary dial phones.) The 'shock of the new' posed by cyberspace helps explain why so much early thinking about the internet – particularly thinking about regulation, crime, and victimisation on the internet – see-sawed so wildly between cyber-utopianism and cyber-dystopianism.

For an example of the cyber-utopian view, we can look to John Perry Barlow's 'A declaration of the independence of cyberspace'. This famous/infamous manifesto from 1996 introduced cyberspace as 'the new home of Mind', a place where all could enter 'without privilege or prejudice accorded by race, economic power, military force, or station of birth'. It was to be a world 'where anyone, anywhere may express his or her beliefs, no matter how singular, without fear of being coerced into silence or conformity'. Firmly throwing down the gauntlet to industrial governments, Barlow declared that traditional regulators had no moral right to rule online, and no methods of enforcement cyberspace dwellers had true reason to fear:

> You are not welcome among us. You have no sovereignty where we gather.... You claim there are problems among us that you need to solve. You use this claim as an excuse to invade our precincts. Many of these problems don't exist. Where there are real conflicts, where there are wrongs, we will identify them and address them by our means. We are forming our own Social Contract. This governance will arise according to the conditions of our world, not yours. Our world is different.
>
> (Barlow 1996)

The optimism/naiveté is striking. In the context of this edited collection, it is also interesting to note who and what are being framed as the victims here. Barlow's implication is that it is traditional regulators – those 'weary giants of flesh and steel' – who have become antiquated and atrophied, outwitted by virtual citizens connected via the hive mind. They are presented as victims of their own hubris and materiality. Yet another set of victims in this scenario are those citizens in the offline world who have fallen foul not only of the putative legislative overreach of the weary giants, but of the race, gender, and class inequities that would supposedly be eliminated online. In this view of the cybersphere, e-citizens are not victims but agents empowered via the dual forces of self-governance and virtuality.

Compare Barlow's idealistic vision of a problem-free, self-regulating cybersphere to one presented around the same time in a book on cybercrime called *I-Way Robbery: Crime on the Internet* (Boni and Kovacich 1999). The foreword of this volume, by Professor Emeritus John P. Kenney, begins with a textbook version of the 'ooh-ing' and 'ahh-ing' described in the first paragraph of our introduction. Kenney marvels at the profound impact of the 'global Internet or "I-Way"' on personal relationships, international politics, and business (Kenney in Boni and Kovacich 1999, p. ix). He notes that the internet is user-friendly for many people 'from children and housewives in the home … to corporate managers and farmers'. Kenney quickly warns, however, that in addition to the exploits of 'hackers, phreakers, and crackers', 'ominous' new crimes and criminal enterprises mean most industrial nations have become 'vulnerable to the ravages of techno-terrorists and cyber-criminals employing the "I-Way" to wreak havoc' (Kenney in Boni and Kovacich 1999, p. ix). The book goes on to offer, among much else, a chapter which profiles the various 'miscreants' one may encounter while using the I-Way for business or government purposes (Boni and Kovacich 1999, pp. 69–100).

Two decades or so later, neither the utopian nor the dystopian framings of cyberspace pass the 'Goldilocks standard' of seeming quite right. Barlow was correct about its revolutionary nature, as well as about the issue of 'sovereignty' (as it relates to jurisdictional issues) and the relative impotence of traditional regulators in online domains. Sadly, he was wrong to imagine this would be a place free from 'real' problems like crime or structural discrimination. Contrary to his idealistic vision, violence and victimisation are occurring online in ways which directly mirror or are very similar to the offline world, and have not been solved in-house. Indeed, as Jane discusses in her chapter of this book, some internet dwellers are making things much worse for people who have already been victimised online. Books such as *I-Way Robbery*, meanwhile, were right to identify the threats posed by various bad actors online (even if language such as 'ominous', 'ravages', and 'miscreants' seems somewhat overblown). Yet they fail to capture the fact that most internet transactions are notable only for their absolute lack of note-ability.

Without wishing to underplay the very real harms caused by crime and victimisation online, it is important to remember that the vast bulk of online engagement and interactions are banal, often taking forms such as shopping, banking, making small talk with friends, and reminding significant others to please pick up some tofu on their way home from work. Just as Hollywood's canon of serial killer movies can give a false impression of the true extent of Hannibal Lecterism, the 'shock horror' media coverage given to the most extreme examples of cybercrime can obscure the fact that most of our time online is positive and problem-free. In curating this book, therefore, we have done our best to offer nuanced contributions that are neither overly triumphalist nor sensationally alarmist in tone. We proceed from the view that the online world is much the same as the offline one: mostly fine, but occasionally profoundly *not* fine (with members of traditionally marginalised, excluded, and oppressed groups far more likely to be victimised than those with greater privilege).

One obvious advantage of the 'ordinary-fication' of the internet is that the increasing familiarity of the territory is lending itself to more textured scholarly work less reliant on unhelpful binaries such as the cyber-utopian versus cyber-dystopian framings discussed above. This is certainly the type of scholarship we have aimed to showcase in this volume. That said, we note that familiarity presents its own research challenges. For instance, certain features of the cyber-sphere can quickly seem so natural and indisputable that it is assumed these features always have and always will be part of the cyberscape. Writing on Google and 'the culture of search', for instance, Ken Hillis, Michael Petit, and Kylie Jarrett note that to search has become 'so natural and obvious a condition of using the Web, and the Web such a natural and obvious feature of the internet, that the specific contingency of these everyday practices has become obscured' (2013, p. 2). This is the flipside of overemphasis, exaggeration, and sensationalisation.

Consider, for example, the proliferation of hate speech online, and the way many users have learned to 'see but not see' the graphic misogynist, racist, and homophobic comments that now swamp comment sections (Barker and Jane 2016, p. 463). Such habituated blindness may well assist internet users navigate the internet efficiently, but it can also result in the downplaying or overlooking of significant social problems (Jane 2015, p. 73). As we in academia recover from being shocked by the new, therefore, we must also ensure we are not blinded by the obvious – or to assume that all the important questions about the internet have already been answered (or, indeed, *asked*).

With regard to knowledge gaps, for instance, we note that while there is now a great deal of awareness about the internet's role in giving rise to potentially empowering new forms of self-identity and social relationships, the ways in which online social relationships are engendering new forms of violence and victimisation are less clearly understood. Certainly the general topic of the intersection of the internet and law could do with more attention. In Matthew Lippman's *Contemporary Criminal Law: Concepts, Cases, and Controversies* (2013), for example, 'computer crime' and related terms appear on only nine pages (this includes cyberstalking and cyberbullying). The other main topics covered are copyright infringements, trespass (unauthorised access to computers), and causing computers to malfunction. And this is in a text book for college students with 560 pages not including notes or index!

Fortunately, other texts are emerging which respond not only to the urgent need for greater scholarly coverage of cybercrime, but to the necessity of constantly updating this coverage. In the preface to the second edition of *Cybercrime and Society*, for example, Majid Yar, acknowledges the 'perishable' nature of books on internet crime (2013). He notes that the 2005 edition of his text made no mention of Facebook because the social media platform was then in its infancy. As we know, baby platforms can grow up fast in the cybersphere. These days, Facebook is a behemoth and well on the way to – as one writer puts it – 'eating the internet' (Lafrance 2015). In late 2016, there were more than 1.71 billion monthly active Facebook users, with 300 million photos uploaded every day and five new profiles created every second ('The top 20 valuable Facebook statistics – updated September 2016' 2016).

Like Yar, we acknowledge that there is only so much a book about the internet can do to remain up-to-date (especially if that book also happens to be made out of dead trees). Literature relating to the cybersphere inevitably dates extremely quickly and it is easy for a text such as this to seem embarrassingly outdated to student readers who are constantly exploring new platforms and apps online. Indeed, some internet insiders joke that internet years are like dog years in that each single year sees about seven years' worth of change (Bland 2016). This would mean we have been working on this book for nearly two decades! Aware that new legislation and platform changes are occurring constantly, we have attempted to make this volume as time-resistant as possible, partly by focusing on the sorts of broad trends and principles we believe will continue to have relevance over time, even if the examples best used to illustrate them change.

Our aim is to help fill knowledge gaps relating to victimisation online by exploring the social construction of violence and victimisation in online spaces in three key ways. First, we examine the ways in which the unique social structures, spaces and interactions that have taken shape in cyberspace over the past two decades have engendered distinctive forms of problematic behaviour, violence and victimisation. Second, we show how social processes of violence and victimisation in online spaces are tied into broader social formations of crime and violence. Third, we consider new and enhanced approaches to the prevention of violence, crime, and victimisation in online spaces.

To achieve these ends, we adopt a transnational and interdisciplinary perspective, exploring cybercrime, and violence and victimisation in a range of international settings. Our intentions are to foreground the experiences of victims and targets, to offer insight into emerging criminal practices, and to model the usefulness of interdisciplinary perspectives and interdisciplinary conversations in this area. The tricky balancing acts we undertake include attempting: to avoid being alarmist without facilitating complacency; to offer a big picture perspective without losing sight of individual experiences and case studies; and to balance empirical and prevalence data and statistics with the human faces of cybercrime. At all times, we endeavour to avoid unhelpful extremes. That is, we avoid framings of the cybersphere which are either overly utopian or overly dystopian, which formulate discrete divisions between the online and offline, or which buy into all-or-nothing approaches to intervention. This recognises that the internet is not all safety or all danger; all risk or all possibility. Instead, like any other place where humans congregate, it involves shades of grey rather than stark blacks and whites.

Rather than being prescriptive, or offering simplistic solutions, therefore, we wish to propose a series of open-ended questions that prompt readers to contemplate the complexity of cybercrime. These include (but are by no means limited to):

- Does cyberspace make us more or less vulnerable to crime and violence?
- Under what circumstances might 'cyber*wrong*' (see Chapter 1) be a better term than 'cyber*crime*'?
- In what ways does cyberspace challenge prejudice and the stereotyping of marginalised groups, and in what ways does it reproduce, reinforce and amplify these offline phenomena?
- In what ways (if any) should online regulatory interventions differ from the offline variety? That is, are there special circumstances relating to crime on the web or should cyberspace be considered as just another jurisdiction or criminal context?
- How much regulation online is too much or too little?
- What are some of the competing values involved in questions around regulation online? For example, when should freedom of speech and expression be protected at the expense of those suffering abuse, harassment and victimisation? Is the free speech defence being misused? Or is it not being given adequate consideration by regulators?
- Given the increasing public pressure on states to act, is there a danger of ad hoc, knee-jerk policy making that is not fit-for-purpose, or which rapidly dates? How might we best avoid this type of policy making?
- Where should the role of state regulation end and the role of communities, schools, and individual users begin?
- Should platform managers be held responsible for the activities of their users?
- How do crime and violence in online spaces give rise to new forms of surveillance and social control?
- What role might technology design have in preventing crime and violence online in the future?

The complexity of crime online

To understand the perspective of the victims of cybercrime (as well as the victims of what Nicole A Vincent in Chapter 1 calls cyber*wrongs*) it is first necessary to understand the offences; how they occur, and how the internet may enable perpetrators to commit them. Again, the dynamism of the cybersphere makes this task daunting given the dizzying speeds at which platforms and usage patterns materialise and de-materialise. (At the time of writing, for instance, Jane's nine-year-old daughter was fixing her mother with a withering look of techno-contempt while explaining that the term 'muser' referred to a user of the app 'musical.ly' ['*duh*, mum'] which happened to be 2016's answer to 'Dubsmash' and whose intricacies could not possibly be comprehended by anyone as ancient as her parent.)

The internet and its multitude of interconnected devices are indeed singular in terms of speed and uptake. For example, it took broadcast radio 38 years and television 13 to clock up their first 50 million users, while the web achieved this number in just four years (Naughton 2014). This makes the internet the fastest growing medium ever recorded. In 2016, around 40 per cent of the world's population had an internet connection (compared to less than 1 per cent in 1995), and there were nearly three-and-a-half billion internet users across the globe ('Internet Users' n. d.). As the stop watch-style counter at www.internetlivestats.com/internet-users/ demonstrates so graphically, this figure was continuing to rise at a rate of knots (for want of a more digitally savvy metaphor).

New technologies have always posed a challenge for regulators at the state level (police and policy makers) as well as those presiding over domestic jurisdictions (in the form of parents and caretakers). (For example, Martellozzo, in her chapter, observes that children and young people are often more techno-savvy than their caregivers, as well as being more physically mobile, in that they are able to use internet-enabled devices in potentially riskier contexts outside of home environments.) Yet while new modes of criminality are indeed coming into being far faster than various regulators are able to keep pace with them, many instances of online crime bear striking resemblances to offline variations – and vice versa. The Australian Crime Commission (now part of the Australian Criminal Intelligence Commission), lists a number of traditional crimes and their cybercrime equivalents ('Cyber and technology enabled crime' 2013, p. 2). These include: fraud (the cybercrime equivalents being online fraud, and mass marketed fraud including auction fraud, advance free fraud, and phishing[1]); burglary and malicious damage (online hacking, denial of service attacks, viruses); child sex offences (online grooming, child pornography websites); money laundering (through online payment systems and e-cash); and theft (identity theft, bank website phishing, and movie, music and software piracy).

Stalking, bullying, and domestic violence have also developed distinct online versions, including various forms of technology-facilitated and technology-amplified abuse, harassment, and coercion. There is, for example, emerging research into the links between online abuse and offline domestic violence against women. The UK organisation Women's Aid, notes that 48 per cent of UK women who suffer violence at the hands of a partner experience harassment or online abuse during their relationship as well as once they have left it, with 38 per cent of women being stalked online after they leave their relationships (Smith 2014). Such figures also demonstrate the way violent partners and ex-partners are able to use the internet to incite others to join their attacks: in effect, to crowdsource harassment. There have also been increases in the use and abuse of new communication and surveillance technologies to stalk, intimidate, harass, humiliate, and coerce intimate partners, particularly girls and women (Ostini and Hopkins 2015). This includes: using electronic means to remove women's access to their bank account funds; preventing friends and family members from being able to reach women via their phones and computers; installing GPS trackers on women's vehicles; and circulating false and/or intimate information about women online (Ostini and Hopkins 2015). Understanding these sorts of offences requires thinking beyond a simple and arguably overly narrow framework of 'cybercrime' and understanding their overlap with more traditional offences and wrongs, as well as their reflection of broad, structural inequalities.

A useful case study which provides insights into some of the key features of – and regulatory challenges posed by – cybercrime concerns the online trade of illicit drugs. Intriguingly enough, the world's first commercial transaction online is said to have been a drug deal. Students at Stanford University used Arpanet accounts to arrange the sale of 'an undetermined amount of marijuana' to their counterparts at Massachusetts Institute of Technology (John Markoff cited in Power 2013b). Since then, vast quantities of recreational drugs have been traded on encrypted sections of the net using the untraceable online currency Bitcoin (Martin 2014; Ball 2013). Indeed, one 2013 survey suggests that nearly a quarter of all users are buying drugs online, making the internet a rival to laneways and street corners as a place to buy illicit drugs (Ball 2013). These purchases often occur via channels such as Silk Road which has been dubbed an 'eBay for drugs' and has been closed down multiple times by multiple authorities (Ball 2013). The online drug trade poses challenges for regulators in that the substances available online are often technically legal because their chemical compounds are very similar to illicit substances yet are different enough to bypass existing laws (Power 2013a, 2013b). Without wishing to take sides in the heated debate about whether adult drug users constitute 'victims', it is worth noting that the unknown and unpredictable formulations in what are known as 'synthetic' drugs can make them potentially very dangerous for users (Barker and Jane 2016, p. 185). Again, however, it is important not to over-inflate the risks associated with new drugs being sold in new domains given that substances purchased in offline contexts may also be cut with unknown and potentially harmful substances.

The trade of illicit (and illicit*ish*) drugs online also draws attention to the nature and significance of what is known as the 'deep web'. This term refers to the fact that only about four per cent of the information available on the internet can be accessed using commercial search engines. The other 96 per cent of content comprises what is known as the deep web (Bradley 2014). Given that nearly five billion pages are available in the visible, surface or clear web, the size of this hidden dimension is truly extraordinary (Barker and Jane 2016, p. 492). It is important to remember, however, that most of this content in this part of the web is banal in that it includes material such as user databases, webmail pages, registration-required web forums, pages behind paywalls and website pages that have been created but are yet to go 'live' (Egan 2015).

There is, however, a subsection of the deep web known as the 'dark web'. Material here cannot be found using traditional search engines. Access, therefore, requires a degree of cyber savvy as well as the use of browsers such as The Onion Router (Tor) which obscure physical locations, as well as permitting access to sites that might otherwise be blocked (Bradley 2014). While there has been no shortage of sensational media reports drawing attention to those sectors of the dark web used for the trade of drugs, child abuse images, weapons, and criminal services, people are also making use of this intriguing – and currently extremely understudied – sector of the internet for political reasons. In 'closed, totalitarian societies' the dark web can be used to communicate with the outside world (Egan 2015). Internet users are also said to be moving their communication onto the dark web in the light of 'recent revelations about US and UK government snooping on web use' (Egan 2015).

The deep and dark web offer rich directions for future scholarly inquiry as very little academic research has been conducted on these aspects of the internet. An exception is the work of Robert W. Gehl (2014) who conducted an ethnographic study of a social networking site only accessible to web browsers equipped with Tor. Gehl's conclusions about the Dark Web Social Network (DWSN) are that its norms and ideals have much in common with the early days of the internet in participants' rejection of state-based intervention and call for disembodied communication dissociated from putatively superficial identity markers such as race or gender. Unlike the pioneers of the early internet, however, this political stance is being taken not in opposition to the offline world but to the intensely corporatised and surveilled 'clear web' (Barker and Jane 2016, p. 493).

While many crimes online do have similarities with those committed offline, some aspects of digital spaces are singular in nature. As such, offences committed online may have elements and idiosyncrasies which their offline counterparts do not. Consider, for instance, the 'always-on', omni-connected aspects of contemporary existence. As various contributors to this collection show, the reach enabled by technology combined with the 'always-on' nature of modern life means perpetrators have the potential to tyrannise targets in new and perfidious ways.

A cogent example is sextortion – an emerging criminal practice in which perpetrators gain remote access to computers to obtain intimate or compromising footage of targets who are then blackmailed into performing sex acts (thereby becoming entrapped even further). The US coder Luis Mijangos, for instance, hacked into hundreds of computers and installed sophisticated, antivirus software-resistant malware that allowed him to track targets' keyboard activity, to search their hard drives, and to remotely operate their web cams (Kushner 2012). Wheelchair-bound and living at home with his mother in California, Mijangos – later dubbed a candidate for the title 'world's creepiest hacker' – spent days on end watching multiple targets on up to four web cams at once – each spying on a different victim (Kushner 2012). He boasted to his peers that he had found a way to control up to 600 computers simultaneously and spread the word that his services were available to others wishing to spy on girlfriends, wives, or unsuspecting strangers (Kushner 2012). When US law enforcement agents finally arrested Mijangos in March 2010, he had more than 15,000 webcam-video captures, 900 audio recordings, and 13,000 screen captures associated with around 230 women and teenaged girls from around the world – 44 of whom were minors and one of whom lived as far away as New Zealand (Wittes *et al.* 2016, p. 2).

The case study of sextortion shows the way a single offender is able to use technology to victimise large numbers of people located anywhere in the world.

It also demonstrates the fact that new modes of online violence and victimisation may not fit easily into pre-existing criminal categories such as 'theft', 'sexual assault', or 'stalking'. Sextortion, for instance, can involve elements of stalking, home invasion, theft, blackmail, paedophilia, domestic violence, sexual exploitation, harassment, and abuse, and organised crime. This creates obvious problems for police and prosecutors, and has resulted in regrettable inconsistencies with regards to sentencing. In a 2016 report analysing 78 sextortion cases, researchers from the Brookings think tank note that – given no crime of 'sextortion' exists in the US – cases in that nation have proceeded under a 'hodgepodge' of state and federal laws including 'actions under the most dimly-related of statutes' (Wittes *et al.* 2016, pp. 4–5). This has produced what the researchers condemn as 'indefensible' disparities in sentencing (Wittes *et al.* 2016, p. 5). Mijangos, for instance, was sentenced to six years' imprisonment which is 'dramatically lighter' than he would have received for multiple physical attacks on even a fraction of the number of people he was accused of victimising (Wittes *et al.* 2016, pp. 2, 5). In another case analysed by Brookings Institution, a perpetrator received only three years in prison for victimising up to 22 young boys (Wittes *et al.* 2016, p. 5).

Like many other emerging crimes in digital spaces, sextortion is dramatically under-studied. Brookings' researchers note that while sextortion is an acknowledged problem within law enforcement and among private advocates, no government agency or private advocacy group publishes data on its prevalence, and the subject lacks a body of academic literature (Wittes *et al.* 2016, p. 4). The lack of understanding about new forms of violence and victimisation online is due, in part, to various issues of visibility. The crimes themselves may be invisible if they are so new they are yet to register on the public's radar (let alone be written into law). If arrests are not being made, and offenders are not being processed by the courts, neither will such crimes be visible to the public. Further, as Brookings points out in relation to sextortion, the frequency with which offences are occurring cannot be measured to determine prevalence.

There are, however, some paradoxical elements relating to the issue of cybercrime and visibility. While some violence and victimisation online is urgently in need of *more* attention and exposure, certain offences involve victims who desperately want *less* eyes on their situations. Two examples are the victims of revenge porn (a term used to describe the malicious circulation of intimate images without the consent of the subject) and doxing (the circulation of targets' personal details online, sometimes accompanied by an incitement to others to attack targets online or offline). If a victim is a child, their case may be kept out of the limelight for their own protection. In such instances, concealing aspects of a crime makes sense. Other invisibility issues are, however, more insidious. Sometimes victims do not come forward because they want to avoid further shame and embarrassment. As Martellozzo explains in her chapter, victims of online child sexual abuse may never come forward because they do not realise that what they have experienced *is* abuse. Sometimes victims *do* report their experiences to police, but no action is taken because they are not believed or taken seriously.

Introduction   11

In other cases, victims are invisible because they are not recognised *as* victims. Consider women targeted for revenge porn. As with offline sexual violence, it is often implied or stated explicitly that such women are to blame for their experiences because they trusted the wrong men, posed for the wrong photos, and so on (see Chapter 3). Victim-blaming also occurs when the targets of various cybercrimes are framed as being insufficiently tech savvy, as overreacting or being too sensitive to the rough and tumble of online life, or as being opposed to the ideals of free speech. Often they are accused of not being able to take a joke, or of not appreciating the edgy humour of the cybersphere. In these ways, targets are recast not only as the problem but as the solution to the problem, in that they are encouraged to undertake do-it-yourself (DIY) measures to remedy their situations. This is profoundly unfair, is inconsistent with the rule of law, and ignores the fact that different internet users have different resources available for self-help in this regard.

Failing to act with regard to online violence and victimisation may also strengthen extrajudicial cultures online as manifest in digital vigilantism – or 'digilantism' – tactics such as 'hacktivism',[2] 'scam-baiting',[3] 'denial-of-service attacks',[4] and 'naming and shaming' (Jane 2016a, 2016b, 2017). Like offline vigilantism, online versions of vigilantism cannot (by definition) be legally justified. They can, however, be morally *justified*, and possibly even morally *demanded* if there exists a social need alongside deficiencies in the state security system (Jane 2016b, 2017). That said, our view is that such actions should be regarded as *diagnostic of* rather than *solutions to* state security deficits. This is because – again, like offline vigilantism – digilantism has many risks and downsides. Consider, for instance, the rapid formation of vicious online mobs whose public shaming of individuals might be disproportionate to or even worse than the originally objectionable behaviour or action.

Cogent, here, is the case of the PR professional Justine Sacco who, in 2013, tweeted the following comment shortly before boarding a flight to South Africa: 'Going to Africa. Hope I don't get AIDS. Just kidding. I'm white' (cited in Ronson 2015b). Sacco has always insisted the comment was intended to parody American ignorance about HIV, but the wider public viewed it as offensively racist. As a result, Sacco disembarked from her 11-hour flight from Heathrow to Cape Town to discover that mob attacks on her online had rendered her 'the number-one worldwide trend on Twitter' (cited in Ronson 2015a, p. 65). Sacco was subsequently sacked. Reflecting on this and other similar public shaming cases, the author Jon Ronson notes the disconnect between 'the severity of the crime' – frequently some poorly considered joke on social media – and the 'gleeful savagery' of the vigilante mob punishment (2015b).

Different but related to digilantism is the problem of corporate exploitation of people who have been targeted for violence and victimisation online. Danielle Keats Citron and Mary Anne Franks, for instance, note the existence of web sites which publish revenge porn and then charge the pictured individuals to have the material removed (2014). A 28-year-old San Diego man, Kevin Bollaert, ran a revenge porn site called ugotposted.com featuring the sexually explicit photographs, full names, location details, and Facebook profiles of thousands of women and men ('Revenge porn kingpin Kevin Bollaert jailed' 2015). Bollaert also ran a companion 'takedown' site called changemyreputation.com which charged up to $350 for the removal of photos. In 2015, he was jailed for 18 years in what was described as the first case of its kind in US criminal history ('Revenge porn kingpin Kevin Bollaert jailed' 2015). The importance of possessing a positive online reputation has also led to a proliferation of professionals who charge clients for cyber 'makeovers' which involve promoting positive content while attempt to bury negative search engine results (Barker and Jane 2016, p. 488). While such businesses are neither illegal nor comparable to the unscrupulous business ventures conducted by individuals such as Bollaert, they do show the vulnerability of those victimised online, as well as the fact that the ability to buy oneself out of reputational strife is not an option equally available to all. Such options costs upwards of US$1,000 a month (Lock 2013) and are therefore only feasible for those with the means to pay.

There also exists a regrettable – and deeply unfair – tendency to suggest that victims of cybercrime are not *real* victims because the offences occur in a virtual domain and therefore cannot possibly involve 'real' harm. Heated debates about the differences between 'harm' and 'offense' have a long history, particularly with regard to how they should impact law-making and freedom of expression. These issues will be addressed in the conclusion of this book where we appraise various regulatory and non-regulatory responses to cybercrimes and cyber-wrongs. While it is beyond the scope of this book to deal with the subject in any depth, we also note advances in neurophysiology and cellular biology which show that cognition, emotion, and social context can be even more influential than tissue damage in terms of producing physical pain (Moseley 2007; Moseley 2011; Moseley *et al.*, 2012; Butler and Moseley 2013). This complicates the ability to make neat distinctions between 'embodied' injuries that cause physical pain, and 'disembodied' injuries that cause what might be dismissed as different and/or lesser sorts of suffering. In particular, the 'medicosociolegal' nature of the modern world (Moseley *et al.* 2012, p. 37) means such findings are becoming increasingly relevant in legal contexts involving the consideration of harms or injuries that are not visible to the naked eye or apparent in medical scans (see: Jane 2017, p. 66; Davis 2016).

In addition to this research, there is good evidence to show that many victims of attacks in online domains suffer real, material harms in the offline world. This is starkly demonstrated by the impact statements of victims of sexually violent crimes online. The Brookings researchers who studied sextortion, for instance, underline the fact that this is a crime of often 'unspeakable brutality' (Wittes *et al.* 2016, p. 3). The prosecutor in the Mijangos case, for instance, noted that some of Mijangos' victims thoroughly feared him and continued to be traumatised by his criminal conduct on an ongoing basis. One victim reported feeling 'terrorised' and did not leave her dorm room for a week after the episode (Wittes *et al.* 2016, p. 2). Other victims demonstrated signs of immense psychological stress. Disturbingly, the Brookings researchers noted that perpetrators seemed to revel in the desperate pleas of their scared and under-aged victims:

> In multiple cases we have reviewed, victims contemplate, threaten, or even attempt suicide – sometimes to the apparent pleasure of their tormentors. At least two cases involve either a father or stepfather tormenting children living in his house. Some of the victims are very young. And the impacts on victims can be severe and likely lasting. Many cases result, after all, in images permanently on the Internet on multiple child pornography sites following extended periods of coercion.
>
> (Wittes *et al.* 2016, p. 5, internal references omitted)

We can see that the suffering of victims of crimes such as sextortion and revenge porn is unlikely to end just because a perpetrator is arrested and even imprisoned. In addition to the ongoing impact of the initial degradation and trauma, it is all but impossible to stop intimate images and footage circulating once such material makes its way onto the internet. This is the sort of evil genie that is impossible to return to its bottle and the psychological harm caused to victims aware that their images are freely travelling around the web is severe. Similarly, sexual offences against children and young people recorded on video or in still photographs may be kept for personal gratification, like trophies sitting on a dusty shelf, or may be distributed online to other abusers. Further, producing, downloading, storing, and viewing such material can increase the demand and, as the result, the continuation of the cycle of victimisation (Martellozzo 2012, p. 76). It is well rehearsed in the literature, for instance, that re-victimisation occurs each time an image of child abuse is downloaded and/or shared (Taylor and Quayle 2003, p. 24).

The harms caused by reputational damage online can also be severe and ongoing. Findings from the Pew Research Center, for instance, show that of those people targeted for physical threats and sustained harassment online, about a third feel their reputations have been damaged (Duggan 2014, p. 7). Citron's research, meanwhile, reveals that female teachers and government employees have been fired after naked photos of them appeared on revenge porn sites or were otherwise circulated publicly (2014b). To understand how the harm in such situations is not just a one-off affair, consider the fact that nearly 80 per cent of employers consult search engines to collect intelligence on job applicants, and about 70 per cent of applicants are rejected because of these findings (Citron 2014c). Common reasons for not interviewing and hiring applicants include concerns about 'lifestyle', 'inappropriate' online comments, and 'unsuitable' photographs, videos, and information (Citron 2014b). These aspects of cybercrime and cyberwrongs underline the fact that – as various contributors argue throughout this collection – criminal law may be of limited use to victims.

Why, then, consider legal remedies at all? Our case is that while law is only one element of what must be a multifaceted approach to cybercrime, it is, nonetheless, an important element. Many states are becoming increasingly sophisticated about how the physical infrastructure of the internet is monitored and controlled (Suzor 2016). Yet the atmosphere in many online domains remains one of impunity. As the Australian legal scholar Nicolas Suzor, puts it:

many parts of the open internet are, to put it mildly, not nice places. The infrastructure we've built allows everyone to speak, but all-too-often drowns out and silences voices from the more vulnerable groups in our societies. It is used as a highly effective tool to direct abuse and hate against minorities, to invade the privacy of those who speak out, and to enable violence, chilling threats, and coordinated attacks.

(2016)

As simplistic as it may sound, a critical first step in bringing perpetrators to account is to identify perpetrators *as* perpetrators. Among other problems, the victim-blaming narratives and tendencies described above contribute to the invisibilising and exculpation of bad actors online. After all, if people who are attacked or scammed online are also blamed for being attacked or scammed, perpetrators are neatly written out of the narratives. Offenders are also invisibilised when the cybersphere is framed as either a lawless Wild West or as inherently dangerous – that is, a place where trouble should be expected, and people should only visit if they have thick skins, or special training. Once again, these frontier-style framings facilitate victim-blaming in that targets are chastised for having gone to the 'wrong' places, for engaging in the 'wrong' sort of behaviour online, for clicking 'reply' on the wrong sort of email, and so on. At the same time, perpetrators are exculpated and permitted to continue offending without fear of punishment because the danger is linguistically located in the landscape rather than in the harm-producing human agents who inhabit this landscape (see Chapter 3).

An increased understanding about and focus on the perspective of victims is necessary to help provide immediate relief for those people who are currently being attacked or abused and who may need assistance extricating themselves from volatile situations that have the potential to rapidly worsen in a way that can have ongoing and potentially irreversible impacts. To work towards a culture of accountability online, a culture that reinforces the ideals of fairness, justice, and equity of access, victim-blaming needs to stop and, where feasible and appropriate, the punishing of perpetrators needs to start. These punishments might include the loss of certain online privileges, or they might include fines, community service, and/or imprisonment. A range of potential remedies and interventions for cybercrimes and cyberwrongs will be discussed throughout this volume, and particularly in the conclusion.

Like our contributors, we acknowledge that addressing cybercrime is no easy task. As discussed earlier in this introduction, such offences are notoriously difficult to investigate and prosecute because they play out in domains where perpetrators are often difficult to identify, where victims may be reluctant (or may not even realise it is an option to) report offences, and where police often lack the requisite resources and the techno-savvy to act. On those occasions where police are successful in making a cybercrime-related arrest, it may be discovered that an act is legally liminal or not covered by existing legislation – not least because prosecutors in many nations are relying on laws drafted for a pre-internet age. In the UK, the chief constable responsible for fighting digital crime,

Stephen Kavanagh, has admitted that the 'unimagined scale of online abuse' threatens to overwhelm the police service (cited in Laville 2016). Noting that existing laws include one dating back to the nineteenth century, Kavanagh has called for new and more simplified legislation in the hope of achieving justice for tens of thousands of targets (cited in Laville 2016).

Without wishing to point fingers, we agree that – while the contours of the cybersphere are indeed novel and constantly changing – there is validity in activist claims that police, policy makers, and platform managers could be working faster and more effectively to assist targets and victims in online environments. Rather than continuing to drag their collective metaphorical feet, we believe these bodies should move faster and more effectively. They must acknowledge the vertiginous pace of developments in communications technology, take it for granted that new forms of criminality will continue to emerge fast and furiously, and plan – and act – accordingly. As various authors featured in this collection argue, community groups, schools, technology designers, online groups, and individual users also have important roles to play.

On targets, victims, and 'victims'

Different contributors to this book are more comfortable with the use of the term 'victim' than others. Jane, for instance, explains in her chapter that she prefers the term 'target', although she does refer to 'victim-blaming' for idiomatic reasons. In her disciplinary areas, there is an emphasis on the tremendous power of words to either enhance or distract from people's agency, and their ability to not only survive but to thrive after even indubitably dreadful experiences. That said, she notes that the keenness of some cultural studies scholars to emphasise agency and empowerment may inadvertently overlook or underplay the real suffering and harm of those targeted for cybercrime and cyberwrongs.

Martellozzo, meanwhile, in her chapter more readily uses 'victim' terminology in reflection of its legal meaning, that is, 'a natural person who has suffered harm, including physical, mental or emotional harm or economic loss which was directly caused by a criminal offence' (www.cps.gov.uk). She purposely deploys the term 'victim' to emphasise the harms children and young people suffer if they are targeted, groomed, and victimised online. Like other contributors in this book, she recognises that developing effective interventions requires looking closely at the empirical evidence that reveals some of the harsh realities of what occurs in the intangible and somewhat obscure word of cyberspace.

Regardless of the different terminology used, however, together we are interested in exploring a textured, mid-ground approach. This is not intended to underplay or overlook the violence involved in cybercrime and cyberwrongs, but to acknowledge that targets and victims are not necessarily forever violated, but potentially able to engage in healing and resistance that might permit them to move on.

Our nuanced approach is also designed to recognise that robust public disagreement exists about who should and should not be categorised as a victim with regards to emerging social problems online. Consider, as just one prominent example, public dispute over the case of Edward Snowden. In 2013, the former National Security Agency (NSA) analyst leaked classified information showing the full extent of American domestic and global surveillance, specifically, that American spies now have the ability to track the activities and movements of anyone almost anywhere in the world. Snowden's actions kickstarted highly charged debates about – among many other issues – how best to balance freedom and security in the post-9/11 era. While it seems indubitable that Snowden broke US laws relating to espionage, whether or not he should be seen as a victim or a victimiser is hotly debated. His detractors, for example, see his actions as unforgivably traitorous and guilty of treason that put US troops at risk and worked to the advantage of terrorists. To supporters, however, Snowden is a patriot and courageous whistleblower who sacrificed his career and his life in the US (at the time of writing he was living in exile in Russia) in order to draw attention to America's 'digital totalitarianism' (Sigmar Gabriel cited in Koepf 2013). The Snowden case study shows that the victim/victimiser distinction is not always clear cut.

Further, some individuals who seem more like perpetrators make dubious claims to victim status. An apt example involves the origins of GamerGate – the term for the series of extraordinary and ongoing attacks on, among others, female video gamers, journalists, academics, and social justice activists from 2014. GamerGate began when a software developer named Eron Gjoni posted a 10,000-word blog impugning the personal and professional reputation of his former girlfriend, Zoë Quinn. He implied, for instance, that she had slept with a games journalist in order to obtain positive reviews for a game she had designed – a claim he later withdrew, saying it was a typographical error (Jane 2017, pp. 29–30). Gjoni's behaviour was extremely questionable. As Quinn later testified in a Boston court while obtaining a restraining order (that Gjoni was to breach on multiple occasions), he had deliberately besmirched her professional reputation as well as coaching and egging on a 'hate mob' (cited in Jason 2015). Members of the latter had circulated personal details such as Quinn's phone number and home address, alongside photos of her naked (Quinn cited in Jason 2015). Gjoni, however, continues to insist that *he* is the victim – a survivor of Quinn's 'emotional abuse' no less (Gjoni 2014). An addendum to his initial blog apologises if other emotional abuse survivors find his story triggering, and provides a link to a domestic violence hotline (Gjoni 2014).

Another scenario in which the victim/victimiser line is murky involves the *en masse* leak, in July 2015, of the details of users of a Canada-based website which facilitates cheating in marriage and whose logo is 'Life is short. Have an affair'. A total of 30 gigabytes of Ashley Madison data (Zetter 2015) – including names, phone numbers, and other personal details – were published online in what one journalist called 'the most appallingly intimate internet leak of the modern age' (Lamont 2016). Schadenfreude reigned as media and other commentators said they felt no pity for the individuals exposed, not least because of the 'stupidity factor' involved in signing up for such a site (Ellen 2015). Others, however, saw these millions of users as victims because they had been assured that their use of the service would be 'anonymous' and '100% discreet'. It was reported that resignations, divorces, and even suicides followed the *exposé* (Lamont 2016). Further, apparently, 1,200 of the leaked email addresses had suffixes indicating that users lived in Saudi Arabia, a country where adultery is punishable by death (Girl on the Net 2016). In Alabama, meanwhile, a newspaper decided to print all the names of people from the region who appeared on Ashley Madison's database (Lamont 2016). In addition to illustrating the aforementioned risks associated with digilante tactics, the Ashley Madison case study shows the special problems facing those targets who do not fit the stereotype of the 'perfect' victim.

Overview of approaches and chapter breakdown

Violence and victimisation in online spaces are of considerable interest to scholars from many areas of inquiry, including sociology, criminology, and cultural, media, and gender studies. As such, we believe one of the strengths of this book is its interdisciplinarity. Martellozzo's background is in criminology and her particular interests include exploring children and young people's online behaviour, and the analysis of online sexual grooming, sexual exploitation, and police practice in the area of child sexual abuse. Jane comes predominantly from a cultural, media, and gender studies background, but now works with an increasing focus on philosophy – especially with regard to *aretaic* or 'virtue' ethics. In addition to formulating concrete interventions for cybercrime in a practical sense, she is also interested in more abstract ideas relating to the ethics of online engagement, and how best to cultivate a culture of accountability online.

Some of the challenges we faced in assembling this book are challenges which also arise in addressing the very problems about which we write. A lack of communication between scholars from different disciplines working in the field, for instance, can contribute to the rise of unhelpful knowledge 'silos'. We have, however, attempted to turn these challenges to our advantage by deliberately seeking contributions from a range of disciplines, and inviting contributors to 'translate' discipline-specific terms and paradigms. We believe that conversations between scholars from different departments and nations are important for tackling the broader problem of violence and victimisation online, just as dialogue between institutions (for example, between police, policy makers, platform managers, community groups, and schools) is also essential.

As mentioned earlier (and explored in detail in Chapter 1), many of the cases discussed in this volume are legally liminal or better referred to as 'cyberwrongs' – that is, they cannot be classified as 'cybercrimes' in an uncomplicated way. Again, we believe this is one of the strengths rather than one of the limitations of the book. One of our aims is to stimulate thinking and debate about how best to classify emerging practices online. As such, we invite readers to consider the problematic acts discussed in this book as belonging to two broad categories. The first are those acts which are currently recognised as crimes, and perhaps which have non-computer-related analogues (such as unauthorised trespass/ access, damage, theft, and so on). A second group contains those acts which are currently not recognised as crimes or are on the penumbra. In relation to this second group, we can see that there exists a wrong and perhaps we can also see that these acts involve harms to victims. But either they are not currently recognised as crimes and/or they do not have simple analogues in non-computer-related domains. A key dilemma identified by this book is how the slow-moving and largely victim-disregarding criminal law might respond to acts located in this second category.

The book is organised thematically into five main sections. The first aims to address some broad conceptual issues and contains two chapters. Chapter 1 sets the scene for this collection. In it, Vincent offers crucial definitions and critically presents two groups of reasons as to why victims of cybercrime are marginalised by the criminal law. Furthermore, she provides some theoretical background to and perspectives on the many hurdles and needs outlined by other contributors to this collection. In Chapter 2, Chris Brickell presents three theoretical frameworks to help us think systematically about power in relation to the internet, particularly in relation to 'digital sexuality'.

The focus of Part II – which contains four chapters – is concerned with issues relating to sexual violence, abuse, and exploitation, as well as to sexual expression online. Chapter 3 looks at the problem of gendered cyberhate such as rape threats and revenge porn. Through the use of current case studies, Jane provides an overview of the common manifestations and significant harms of contemporary misogyny online and explains how the inadequate responses of police, policy makers, and platform managers are contributing to the proliferation of those crimes. In Chapter 4, Amy Dobson explores the growing issue of 'sexting' media practices within a gendered social, cultural, historical, and technological context. Her contribution unpacks the ways in which the 'risks' and 'harms' of sexting media practices, frequently understood as inherent to digital sexual image exchange, are socially and culturally determined.

Chapters 5 and 6 examine issues surrounding the sexual exploitation of adults, children and young people. Kristine Hickle, in Chapter 5, looks at the current research on internet-facilitated commercial sexual exploitation, and explains how cyberspace provides a new terrain for traffickers to recruit, blackmail, exchange, and advertise victims to potential sex buyers who are also complicit in the victimisation of both children and adults. It also explores how new technologies play a crucial part in creating new opportunities to exploit people and facilitating exploitation. In Chapter 6, Martellozzo focuses on online sexual grooming, types of online groomers, and some of the risk factors affecting the likelihood of children and young people becoming victims of online sexual abuse.

The third, pivotal section of the book addresses issues related to race and culture. In Chapter 7, Jamie Cleland looks at online racial hated speech and the way in which virtual spaces may act as platforms for racial discriminatory discourses.

Ramaswami Harindranath, in Chapter 8, examines relatively recent concerns regarding the use of the internet and social media for alleged recruitment and propaganda purposes by Islamic extremists, and the ways in which this has contributed to increasing public anxieties, especially in Europe, the US, and Australia. His case is that media and official discourse on counter-radicalisation can impact negatively on minorities of colour, resulting in a double victimisation of such minorities: first by acts of terror and then by policies to counter radicalisation.

The two final chapters of the collection address cyberbullying and online suicide – topics we group together as 'social violence'. In Chapter 9, Robin Kowalski and Gary Giumetti provide an overview of cyberbullying, including how cyberbullying is typically defined, the prevalence rates of cyberbullying across varying demographics, and antecedents and consequences of involvement in cyberbullying. Chapter 10 looks at how some distinctive features of the internet have allowed the formation of close-knit communities meeting in online forums to discuss matters related to suicide. In this chapter, Ronald Niezen argues that suicide forums tend to be rigorous, rational, and instrumentally effective when it comes to exchanging information on the techniques of self-inflicted death. He explores the possibility that the internet facilitates a normalisation of suicide, looking at whether and under what circumstances the cybersphere might encourage or provoke, and/or discourage and hedge against acts of self-destruction.

In the fifth and concluding section of this book, Vincent and Jane argue that victims of cybercrime are, in general, neglected and not receiving the recognition and support they need and deserve. They argue that although continued awareness-raising and education are important for bringing attention to the plight of victims in online spaces, they do not constitute a sustainable solution to the problems targets and victims face daily. Further, they argue that while law might offer some benefits for some victims of some cybercrimes/cyberwrongs in some jurisdictions, a multitude of non-legislative responses must also be adopted in order to truly make a difference.

The aspiration of this book

As with the ugliest corners of the offline world, the cybersphere contains many dark shadows which are unregulated and unmonitored, and where people have the ability to behave in ways that cause real suffering to others. We sincerely hope that this book will draw some much-needed attention to the various forms of harms that can be inflicted online. In our conclusion, we argue that there needs to be an increase in support of all kinds for victims, as well as an increase in the exposure and punishment of perpetrators. We discuss the role which could be played by not only increased legislation, but by novel approaches such as value sensitive design and 'nudge' techniques. Going forwards, we hope this collection feeds into and helps inform policing and policy-making in multiple jurisdictions, as well as inspiring others to engage in more research, especially of an interdisciplinary nature.

Notes

1 While definitions of 'phishing' vary, it usually refers to a form of online identity theft that allows the stealing of personal identity data and financial account credentials. This might take the form of sending forged emails to recipients mimicking a legitimate institution and requesting details such as credit card numbers or bank account passwords (Dunham et al. 2009, p. 128).
2 'Hacktivism' – a portmanteau of 'hacking' and 'activism' – refers to the unauthorised access to and disruption of computer systems in the name of socio-political agendas.
3 Scam-baiting' is the practice of turning the tables on internet scammers by scamming them back.
4 A 'denial-of-service' (DoS) or 'distributed denial-of-service' (DDoS) attack results in a computer or online network becoming unavailable to users.

References

Ball, J. 2013, 'Internet drug dealing on the rise, survey finds', *The Guardian*, 18 April, viewed 28 June 2016, www.theguardian.com/world/2013/apr/18/internet-drug-dealing-survey-guni=Article:in%20body%20link

Barker, C. and Jane, E.A. 2016, *Cultural Studies: Theory and Practice*, 5th edition. Sage, Los Angeles, London, New Delhi, Singapore, Washington DC, Melbourne.

Barlow, J.P. 1996, 'A declaration of the independence of cyberspace', *Electronic Frontier Foundation*, 8 February, viewed 28 July 2016, www.eff.org/cyberspace-independence

Bland, J. 2016, 'Expert interview: what the internet and dog years have in common', *TechnologyAdvice*, 13 January, viewed 15 October 2016, http://technologyadvice.com/blog/marketing/expert-interview-what-the-internet-and-dog-years-have-in-common/

Boni, W.C. and Kovacich G.L. 1999, *I-Way Robbery: Crime on the Internet*. Butterworth Heinemann, Boston, Oxford, Auckland, Johannesburg, Melbourne, New Delhi.

Bradley, P. 2014, 'Data, data everywhere', *Legal Information Management*, vol. 14 no. 4, pp. 249–252.

Butler, D. and Moseley, L. 2013, *Explain Pain*, 2nd edition. Noigroup Publications, Adelaide.

Citron, D.K. 2014a, *Hate Crimes in Cyberspace*. Harvard University Press, Cambridge, MA, London.

Citron, D.K. 2014b, '"Revenge porn" should be a crime in U.S.', *CNN*, 16 January, viewed 5 August 2016, http://edition.cnn.com/2013/08/29/opinion/citron-revenge-porn/

Citron, D.K. 2014c, 'How cyber mobs and trolls have ruined the internet – and destroyed lives', *Newsweek*, 19 September, viewed 5 August 2016, www.newsweek.com/internet-and-golden-age-bully-271800

Citron, D.K. and Franks, M.A. 2014, 'Criminalizing revenge porn', *Wake Forest Law Review* vol. 49, 19 May, pp. 345–391, viewed 4 July 2016, http://digitalcommons.law.umaryland.edu/cgi/viewcontent.cgi?article=2424&context=fac_pubs

'Cyber and technology enabled crime' 2013, *Australian Crime Commission*, July, viewed 24 July 2016, https://crimecommission.gov.au/sites/default/files/CYBER%20AND%20TECHNOLOGY%20ENABLED%20CRIME%20JULY%202013.pdf

Davis, K. 2016, 'Personal injury lawyers turn to neuroscience to back claims of chronic pain', *ABA Journal*, 1 March, viewed 5 June, www.abajournal.com/magazine/article/personal_injury_lawyers_turn_to_neuroscience_to_back_claims_of_chronic_pain

Dunham, K. (ed.) 2009, *Mobile Malware Attacks and Defense*. Syngress, Burlington, MA.

Duggan, M. 2014, 'Online harassment', *Pew Research Center*, 22 October, viewed 5 August 2016, www.pewinternet.org/2014/10/22/online-harassment/

Egan, M. 2015, 'What is the Dark Web? How to access the Dark Web. What's the difference between the Dark Web and the Deep Web', *PC Advisor*, 20 August, viewed 23 August 2015, www.pcadvisor.co.uk/how-to/internet/3593569/what-is-dark-web-how-access-dark-web/

Ellen, B. 2015, 'Ashley Madison has a stupidity factor – men', *The Guardian*, 23 August, viewed 5 August 2016, www.theguardian.com/commentisfree/2015/aug/23/ashley-madison-men-sex-women-dating-adultery

Gehl, R.W. 2014, 'Power/freedom on the dark web: a digital ethnography of the Dark Web Social Network', *New Media & Society*, doi: 10.1177/1461444814554900

Girl on the Net 2015, 'Ashley Madison hack: do victims "deserve" to be punished?', *The Guardian*, 24 August, viewed 5 August 2016, www.theguardian.com/science/brain-flapping/2015/aug/24/ashley-madison-hack-victims-deserve-punished

Gjoni, E. 2014, *thezoepost*, 16 August, viewed 14 October 2016, https://thezoepost.wordpress.com/

Herring, S.C. 2015, 'SHOULD YOU BE CAPITALIZING THE WORD "INTERNET"?', *Wired*, 19 October, viewed 24 July 2016, www.wired.com/2015/10/should-you-be-capitalizing-the-word-internet/

Hillis, K., Petit, M. and Jarrett, K. 2013, *Google and the Culture of Search*. Routledge, New York.

'Internet Users' (n.d.), *Internet Live Stats*, viewed 13 October 2016, www.internetlivestats.com/internet-users/

Jane, E.A. 2015 'Flaming? What flaming? The pitfalls and potentials of researching online hostility', *Ethics and Information Technology*, vol. 17, no. 1, pp. 65–87.

Jane, E.A. 2016a, ' "Dude … stop the spread": antagonism, agonism, and #manspreading on social media', *International Journal of Cultural Studies*, pp. 1–17, doi: 10.1177/1367877916637151

Jane, E.A. 2016b, 'Online misogyny and feminist digilantism', *Continuum: Journal of Media & Cultural Studies*, vol. 30, issue 3, pp. 284–297, doi: 10.1080/10304312.2016.1166560

Jane, E.A. 2017, *Misogyny Online: A Short (and Brutish) History*. Sage, London.

Jason, Z. 2015, 'Game of fear', *Boston Magazine*, May, viewed 28 December 2015, www.bostonmagazine.com/news/article/2015/04/28/gamergate/

Jensen, K.B. 2011, 'New media, old methods – internet methodologies and the online/offline divide', in M. Consalvo and C. Ess (eds), *The Handbook of Internet Studies*, Wiley-Blackwell, Oxford.

Koepf, P.H. 2013, 'Against digital totalitarianism', *The Atlantic Times*, 23 August, viewed 14 April 2015, www.the-atlantic-times.com/index.php?option=com_content&view=article&id=1396%3Aagainst-digital-totalitarianism&catid=86%3Aaugust-2013-politics&Itemid=65

Kushner, D. 2012, 'The hacker is watching', *GQ*, 11 January, viewed 4 August 2016, www.gq.com/story/luis-mijangos-hacker-webcam-virus-internet

Lafrance, A. 2015, 'Facebook is eating the internet', *The Atlantic*, 29 April, viewed 15 October 2016, www.theatlantic.com/technology/archive/2015/04/facebook-is-eating-the-internet/391766/

Lamont, T. 2016, 'Life after the Ashley Madison affair', *The Guardian*, 28 February, viewed 5 August 2016, www.theguardian.com/technology/2016/feb/28/what-happened-after-ashley-madison-was-hacked

Laville, S. 2016, 'Online abuse: "existing laws too fragmented and don't serve victims"', *The Guardian*, 5 March, viewed 13 April 2016, www.theguardian.com/uk-news/2016/mar/04/online-abuse-existing-laws-too-fragmented-and-dont-serve-victims-says-police-chief

Lippman, M. 2013, *Contemporary Criminal Law: Concepts, Cases, and Controversies*, 3rd edition. Sage, California, London, New Delhi, Singapore

Lock, C. 2013, 'Is online reputation management worth the money?', *Forbes*, 26 July, viewed 5 August 2016, www.forbes.com/sites/learnvest/2013/07/26/is-online-reputation-management-worth-the-money/#f2eef6a480d7

Martellozzo, E. 2012, *Online Child Sexual Abuse: Grooming, Policing and Child Protection in a Multi-Media World*. Routledge, Oxon, New York.

Martin, J. 2014, 'Digital refugees flee via Silk Road to black markets in drugs', *The Conversation*, 10 October, viewed 28 June 2016, https://theconversation.com/digital-refugees-flee-via-silk-road-to-black-markets-in-drugs-31465

Moseley, G.L. 2007, *Painful Yarns: Metaphors & Stories to Help Understand the Biology of Pain*. Dancing Giraffe Press, Canberra.

Moseley, G.L. 2011, 'Why things hurt', *TEDxAdelaide*, 21 November, viewed 4 June 2016, www.youtube.com/watch?v=gwd-wLdIHjs

Moseley, G.L., Butler, D.S., Beames, T.B. and Giles, T.J. 2012, *The Graded Motor Imagery Handbook*. Noigroup Publications, Adelaide.

Naughton, J. 2014 '25 things you might not know about the web on its 25th birthday', *The Guardian*, 9 March, viewed 28 June 2016, www.theguardian.com/technology/2014/mar/09/25-years-web-tim-berners-lee

Ostini, J. and Hopkins, S. 2015, 'Online harassment is a form of violence', *The Conversation*, 8 April, viewed 5 August 2016, https://theconversation.com/online-harassment-is-a-form-of-violence-38846

Patel, N. 2014 'The internet is fucked (but we can fix it)', *The Verge*, 25 February, viewed 24 July 2016, www.theverge.com/2014/2/25/5431382/the-internet-is-fucked

Power, M. 2013a, *Drugs 2.0: The Web Revolution That's Changing How the World Gets High*. Portobello Books, London.

Power, M. 2013b, 'Online highs are old as the net: the first e-commerce was a drugs deal', *The Guardian*, 19 April, viewed 28 June 2016, www.theguardian.com/science/2013/apr/19/online-high-net-drugs-deal

'Revenge porn kingpin Kevin Bollaert jailed' 2015, *news.com.au*, 4 April, viewed 5 August 2016, www.news.com.au/world/revenge-porn-kingpin-kevin-bollaert-jailed/news-story/08657722ae61ca3d32b0e58ba51401f8

Ronson, J. 2015a, *So You've Been Publicly Shamed*. Picador, New York.

Ronson, J. 2015b, 'How one stupid tweet blew up Justine Sacco's life', *The New York Times Magazine*, 12 February, viewed 5 August 2016, www.nytimes.com/2015/02/15/magazine/how-one-stupid-tweet-ruined-justine-saccos-life.html?_r=0

Smith, L. 2014, 'Domestic violence and online abuse: half uk survivors experience trolling in "tidal wave of hate"', *International Business Times*, 1 March, viewed 5 August 2016, www.ibtimes.co.uk/domestic-violence-online-abuse-half-uk-survivors-experience-trolling-tidal-wave-hate-1438420

Suzor, N. 2016, 'Governing the internet: the rule of law in decentralized regulation', *Medium*, 26 May, viewed 5 August 2016, https://medium.com/dmrc-at-large/governing-the-internet-the-rule-of-law-in-decentralized-regulation-c9af23d28f6b#.fyv1m3a09

Taylor, M. and Quayle, E. 2003, *Child Pornography: An Internet Crime*. Brunner-Routledge, Hove.

'The top 20 valuable Facebook statistics – updated September 2016' 2016, *Zephoria*, September, viewed 14 October 2016, https://zephoria.com/top-15-valuable-facebook-statistics/

Wittes, B., Poplin, C., Jurecic, Q. and Spera, C. 2016, 'Sextortion: cybersecurity, teenagers, and remote sexual assault', *Brookings Institution*, May, viewed 4 August 2016, www.brookings.edu/wp-content/uploads/2016/05/sextortion1-1.pdf

Yar, M. (2013), *Cybercrime and Society*, 2nd edition. Sage, London.

Zetter, K. 2015, 'Ashley Madison hackers release an even bigger batch of data', *Wired*, 20 August, viewed 14 October, www.wired.com/2015/08/ashley-madison-hackers-release-even-bigger-batch-data/

Part I
Conceptual issues

1 Victims of cybercrime
Definitions and challenges

Nicole A Vincent

Introduction

This chapter highlights two groups of reasons why victims of cybercrime are overlooked by the criminal law. First, and perhaps most surprisingly to many readers, victims and their harms are at best of only marginal interest to the criminal law. Second, core features of criminal law doctrine are conceptually incompatible with recognizing and adjudicating cybercrimes. Consequently, for largely doctrinal and conceptual reasons, criminal law makes a very poor ally for victims of cybercrime.

Drawing on contemporary work in Anglo-American jurisprudence, I highlight key features of the notions of "crime" and "criminal law." These include that crimes: are defined within jurisdictions; involve specific recognized offenses; need not involve harms, nor be morally troublesome, nor even have victims; have specific *mens rea* requirements such that a given act will not even count as a crime unless the offender committed it with the requisite intention or knowledge of wrongdoing; are committed by identifiable offenders, in precise geographical locations; and are committed against the state, which reserves an exclusive right to determine whether to initiate criminal prosecution.

Next, I explain how these generic features of the criminal law, when combined with generic features of online interactions and some features of the technology involved, create special hurdles for recognizing, thinking about, and responding to cybercrime. These hurdles include: where the conduct occurs (which impacts on whether it qualifies as a crime in that jurisdiction); who committed the crime (especially given online anonymity, impermanence of online evidence, and the law's high standards of proof for securing criminal convictions); and difficulties in establishing causation and *mens rea* in cases that often involve multiple and diffuse perpetrators and victims.

The aim of this chapter is to provide some theoretical background and perspective on the many hurdles and needs outlined by contributors to this collection. It paves the way for the argument – made in detail in the conclusion of this book – that non-legal responses might ultimately hold more promise for helping cybercrime's victims in a timely, sensitive, and effective manner.

Victims and their harms are not the criminal law's central concern

The main aim of this section is to describe features of the criminal law in virtue of which victims in general (not just victims of cybercrime) and the harms that they suffer are not of central concern to the criminal law. In pursuit of this aim I will make two main points.

The first of these two points is that, as peculiar as it may sound, crimes need not necessarily involve victims, nor harms, nor even moral wrongs.

For instance, consider unsuccessful criminal attempts (Lippman 2013, pp. 161–196; Yaffe 2014), like when one person attempts to kill another – e.g. by sprinkling deadly poison over their dinner plate – but fails because the victim, who doesn't know their food is poisoned, decides they no longer feel hungry and leaves their plate untouched. There is, luckily, no victim in this scenario, but yet it is still an offense to unlawfully attempt to kill someone, regardless of whether you succeed or fail. And if the attempted offense is discovered, the state will prosecute regardless of whether there is a victim or not.[1] Furthermore, even if someone else decides to have seconds and eats the poisoned food and consequently dies, the fact that there would now be a victim whose harm could be fixated on would not make the original criminal attempt disappear. Rather, the offender might now be charged with not just one offense – i.e. the unsuccessful attempt to poison the original person – but also with a second crime, like manslaughter or reckless endangerment of human life.

There is also the vast category of so-called "victimless crimes" (Bergelson 2013) which includes a potentially staggering range of acts, ostensibly between consenting parties, and even self-regarding[2] acts, that the state treats as criminal offenses. Even though the parties involved do not deem themselves to have been harmed or victimized by the legally prohibited interaction, and even though they may indeed be more likely to view themselves as victims of the state's unwelcome intrusion. Typical examples, depending again on the jurisdiction in question since not all jurisdictions criminalize the following conduct, include prostitution, homosexual sex, use of certain recreational drugs, use of some prescription medications in non-prescribed ways, gambling, provision of euthanasia, other consented-to killings, and even suicide.[3] It may be tempting to view the existence of such victimless criminal offenses merely as vestiges of an outdated morality, of prudishness-turned-criminal-offense, or even of the tyranny of a majoritarian approach to law-making where what sticks out from what is considered normal by the majority becomes liable to criminal prosecution. However, to see why this would be too quick, consider some of the reasons why victimless crimes might exist and are kept in place. For instance, because it may be too difficult to establish whether consent was present in a given case (e.g. in euthanasia, especially after a patient has been euthanized). Or perhaps, we might reason, that although a blanket ban on euthanasia prevents some people from legitimately taking their own lives with someone else's assistance to avoid a slow and painful death, it also ensures that a greater evil won't occur by deterring greedy and unscrupulous relatives from killing off their vulnerable dying relatives. In other words, policy considerations regarding what state of affairs we would like to avoid, not individual judgments regarding specific instances of actual behavior, may underpin the creation and retention of such victimless crime categories.[4]

Lastly, there is the issue of whether moral wrongness should be a deciding factor in whether something should be classified as a criminal offense. Intuitively, it may seem like it should. On reflection, though, there is reason to resist this intuition. To see why, consider John Stuart Mill's famous "harm principle" that underlies much thinking about which conduct it is permissible to criminalize. Mill, whose work in ethics[5] and political philosophy[6] makes him one of the most influential nineteenth century British philosophers, argued that "the sole end for which mankind are warranted, individually or collectively, in interfering with the liberty of action of any of their number, is self-protection," and that "the only purpose for which power can be rightfully exercised over any member of a civilized community, against his will, is to prevent harm to others" (Mill 1859, I.9). As I comment in note 4, this raises the question of which conduct should be identified as "harmful," and here Mill thought that the state should defer to the judgments of those people whose interests would be affected in order to decide whether they would be harmed or not. He wrote that:

> neither one person, nor any number of persons, is warranted in saying to another human creature of ripe years, that he shall not do with his life for his own benefit what he chooses to do with it. He is the person most interested in his own wellbeing: the interest which any other person, except in cases of strong personal attachment, can have in it, is trifling, compared with that which he himself has; the interest which society has in him individually (except as to his conduct to others) is fractional, and altogether indirect: while, with respect to his own feelings and circumstances, the most ordinary man or woman has means of knowledge immeasurably surpassing those that can be possessed by anyone else.
>
> (Mill 1859, IV.4)

Because Mill thought that people are best-placed to know what is and what is not conducive to their own happiness[7] – after all, each person seems to have the most intimate acquaintance with their own interests, preferences, likes, and dislikes – he therefore supported siding with people's own judgments about what does and does not harm them. However, it also seems plausible that at least sometimes people can be mistaken about whether they are harmed or not, and this view finds equal support among *conservatives* (who typically favor criminalizing such things as sodomy, prostitution, adultery, and fornication) and *progressives* (who celebrate the de-criminalization of such things). After all, both sides fundamentally agree that people's moral views can be mistaken. If they did not agree on that (even if they disagree about the details of precisely who is mistaken), then they could not have a basis for claiming that someone else's view was wrong and that theirs was right, nor that some changes can be rightfully classified as instances of moral progress (Rachels 1999, pp. 21–23). Theoretical simplicity aside, the answer probably lies somewhere in between these two views. That is, in some cases it makes sense to defer to people's own judgments, but sometimes people are indeed mistaken. Nevertheless, the problem with this view, sensible as it might be, is that if we attempt to enact laws that enforce morality, then that will create long-lasting and intractable disputes over what, if anything, should be left in the sphere of private (as opposed to public) morality – i.e. that part of morality over which the law should not have a say in our lives.[8] For this reason, apart from the most serious moral wrongs about which people's views converge, the category of criminal offenses cannot be co-extensive with the category of moral wrongs.

This is not to say that victims are completely absent from criminal proceedings. However, the way in which they are present is not one that gives them, their harms, and their views about their own harms – in particular, about why they matter and about what should be done about them – much pride of place or authority. Victims appear on the witness stand, in gruesome photographs, when the defense of provocation is raised by the criminal offender (i.e. as potentially having brought the harm onto themselves), and when judges hand down judgments that formally acknowledge the wrong they suffered.[9] Victims also appear in victim impact statements, but even then this is a relatively recent innovation. In the US, it is only since the case *Payne v. Tennessee* (1991) that the Supreme Court allowed this to be presented as aggravating evidence, and even then only at the sentencing (not guilt determination) phase of a criminal trial – that is, only to decide upon the punishment, but not on the offender's degree of guilt.

However, if victims and their harms do not feature prominently in the criminal law, then who and what does? The short answer, which brings me to the second of the two main point of this section, is that offenders, the state, and offenses against it (not offenses against victims) are what features most prominently within the criminal law.

To understand why, it helps to note some general features of crimes and of the criminal law. Crimes are understood as acts or omissions defined as offenses within the criminal statutes of a given jurisdiction, that are prosecuted by the state and at the state's discretion, and where a finding of criminal guilt may result in the offender's being punished by the state (e.g. see Blackstone 1765; Kleinig 1978; Duff 2010). Furthermore, criminal offenses are defined by two elements – the "actus reus" and "mens rea" – and in order for a person to be convicted of having committed a specific criminal offense, both elements of that offense must typically be proven. The *actus reus* element (forbidden act) specifies what a person must have done or failed to do – e.g. unlawful killing of a human being, non-consensual sexual intercourse, or failing to come to another person's aid (the last of these being an example of an omission rather than a positive act). And the *mens rea* (guilty mind) element specifies the degree of intention with which that *actus reus* must have been committed – e.g. on purpose, with knowledge, recklessly, negligently, or in some cases regardless of intention (also known as "strict liability").[10]

"Crime" is thus a *technical* term that applies to very specific and specifically defined acts, with very specific mental state requirements, and what is or is not a crime is highly contingent on the precise jurisdiction in question. The upshots of these dry and technical-sounding points are very important. If two jurisdictions differ in what actions or omissions they list in their criminal statutes, or in how those actions or omissions are described, or in how key terms are understood, or if they require those actions or omissions to be performed with different degrees of intention to satisfy the criteria for committing the given criminal offense, then a person who performs the very same actions or omissions in three different places (i.e. under three different jurisdictions) may be guilty of committing one crime in one jurisdiction, another crime in another jurisdiction, and possibly no crime in the third jurisdiction. That was a long sentence, so now consider some examples. For instance, if a fetus of a specific age is recognized as a human being in a particular jurisdiction, then a physician who provides an abortion in the relevant jurisdiction could be found guilty of murder,[11] and similarly for physicians who provide terminally ill patients with euthanasia. If the abortion and euthanasia were performed in different jurisdictions, in which that conduct is not criminalized, there might be no criminal law ramifications. Inter-jurisdictional differences in what counts as "consent," whether "sexual intercourse" requires opposite sexes and penile penetration of a vagina, and how a person's gender is established, can also account for marked differences in such things as what counts as rape, and why in some jurisdictions assailants can only be found guilty of indecently assaulting transgender people but not of raping them.[12]

The immediately preceding discussion has two ramifications for this and the remaining chapters in the present book.

First, to the extent that the criminal law even cares about harms, those harms will only be recognized as criminal offenses in those jurisdictions in which they actually are *explicitly* recognized, and only to the extent allowed by their precise definition as criminal offenses. This is important for three reasons (the second and third of which will be elaborated on in the next section below). One, it further explains why the criminal law may not be adequately sensitive to harms suffered by victims – namely, because regardless of the moral wrongness of certain kinds of harms, unless they are explicitly defined as crimes and the offender-specific elements are also defined in such a way that their commission will be recognized as a criminal offense, then they simply may not even qualify as criminal offenses in a given jurisdiction. Two, and relatedly, even if each of the examples of things referred to as "cybercrimes" in this book is a criminal offense somewhere in the world (which is itself a further empirical question, to which the answer may plausibly be "no"), it is doubtful that all of them are recognized as (cyber)crimes everywhere in the world, in all jurisdictions. This matters because it means that in some places the examples of cybercrimes cited in this book's chapters may not even count as cyber*crimes* but at most only as something like cyber*wrongs*, and in virtue of this it may be technically imprecise to refer to them currently as cyber*crimes* and to expect the criminal law to respond to them (though having made this point, I shall henceforth adopt the convention used in this book and keep referring to them as cybercrimes). Three, several features of cybercrimes (e.g. lack of physical location-specificity for acts committed in the cybersphere, impermanence of digital data, and difficulties in establishing specific offenders' *mens rea* requirements) combined with the technical nature of what constitutes a criminal offense, may make it especially difficult to secure convictions of perpetrators of cybercrimes.

The second ramification of the above discussion is that the *offender's* role and state of mind *is* clearly of interest to the criminal law. After all, without an identifiable offender to commit a criminal offense – and, notably, with a specific degree of intention[13] – it is even difficult to say precisely what crime may have been committed, if any. Furthermore, the criminal law clearly also cares about what motives a criminal *offender* may have had, what they knew, what they intended, with what degree of intention they intended it, whether they were provoked, or suffered from a mental condition that undermined their ability to perceive and judge correctly or to control their actions in light of their decisions. The criminal law has a very clear interest in the *offender's* mind and mental state.

On the other hand, the *victim's* role or their state of mind is afforded none of these explicit recognitions. In *civil* litigation (see below) the impact of offenders' conduct on victims is clearly recognized, and the significance of the injurer's state of mind or personal circumstance is clearly played down. In a much-quoted passage, Oliver Wendell Holmes Jr. (1881, p. 108) argued that:

> If for instance, a man is born hasty and awkward, is always having accidents and hurting himself or his neighbours, no doubt his congenital defects will be allowed for in the courts of Heaven, but his slips are no less troublesome to his neighbours than if they [had] sprang from guilty neglect. His neighbours accordingly require him, at his proper peril, to come up to their standard, and the courts which they establish decline to take his personal equation into account.

The criminal law is, unfortunately for victims, mainly concerned with offenders and their minds. The criminal law is, in this sense, for offenders, not for victims.

Another way in which victims are marginalized by the criminal law can be gleaned by comparing it to civil litigation (Simons 2008; Duff 2014). In civil litigation, which falls into the category of "private law," victims (referred to as "plaintiffs") initiate legal action against their injurers (referred to as "defendants"), and a successful lawsuit often results in the payment of damages (i.e. compensation) by the defendant to the plaintiff. In civil litigation, the victim's presence is even noted explicitly in how cases are named – that is, "Plaintiff v. Defendant" is the general formula for naming civil cases. But this is distinctly not what we find in criminal law, which falls into the category of "public law." Criminal offenses are typically described as being committed against the state (not against who we might be inclined to identify as the victims). The state has discretion over whether to initiate criminal proceedings or not. The victim's assent is neither sought nor does it make a difference in any other way to whether the state will prosecute, nor does a victim's explicit objection to proceeding with prosecuting an accused even matter. And the punishment is again inflicted on the offender by the state not by the victim. Lastly, even the naming of criminal cases, like the above criminal case of *Payne v. Tennessee* (1991) where the defendant (Pervis Tyrone Payne) is pitted against the state (of Tennessee, in this case), fails to acknowledge that criminal offenses may have individual humans as their victims.

This marginalization of victims by the criminal law, in contrast to what happens in civil litigation, is not intended to be an expression of callousness or a lack of care for victims. Indeed, a number of important distinct reasons can be discerned for why this is so. For example, Antony Duff argues that one reason why criminal offenses are conceived of as being committed against the state rather than against specific identifiable human victims is that a

> liberal democracy's law is a "common" law, in the sense that it is the citizens' own law.... From this perspective, I am answerable for my (alleged crimes) to my fellow citizens [not to the individual victims in particular], since it is our law, and the values embodied in that law, that I have violated.
> (2004–5, p. 460)

Another reason why criminal offenses are conceived of as being committed against the state is that if a victim is killed, nobody may be left to prosecute the offender. Furthermore, because the justification for criminal punishment is typically distinguished from mere vengeance,[14] it makes little sense to either allow individual victims or aggrieved families to adjudicate when to prosecute an alleged offender. Finally, because what kind and degree of punishment is fitting to a given criminal offense depends on how the precise punishment will meet the criminal law's plural aims,[15] it also makes no sense to leave it up to the discretion of victims or their aggrieved families to set the punishment. However, because of this large number of aims that criminal punishment is meant to serve, sentencing judges must strike a compromise between how best to satisfy all or some subset of these aims with the very blunt instrument of (what is most often) a prison sentence of some duration. Viewed from this perspective, the criminal justice system has many masters – it tries to satisfy many competing aims – but only one tool with which to serve them, and this is another important reason why victims are marginalized in criminal law.

Features of cybercrime that create special difficulties for the criminal law

The previous section's purpose was to get across that the criminal law's marginalization of victims is not a personal matter between it and victims of *cybercrimes* specifically, but a systemic matter between it and *all victims*. However, there are also specific features of cybercrime that make it especially difficult for the criminal law to recognize this group of victims and their specific harms. The purpose of this section is thus to recount some of these features – which in many instances are simply generic features of online (inter)action or the technology involved – and to explain how they create significant hurdles for recognizing, thinking about, and responding to cybercrime.

First, as Susan W. Brenner (2006) explains, unlike conventional criminal offenses which typically occur in a specific physical location, when people interact on the internet it is difficult to say precisely *where* their interactions take place. After all, the victim may be in one country, the offender in another, and their interactions may take place on third-party servers located on yet another country's soil. Providers of fora can also host their operations with one company (in one country) one day, and move them to another hosting company (in another country) on the following day. And for certain types of internet-mediated interactions – e.g. email – servers in *many* locations collaborate with one another to look up domain names and progressively move a message along from server to server until it reaches its destination. This feature of online interactions – that there is no clear place where such interactions occur – creates distinct challenges to policing and enforcement, as well as conceptual, moral, and legal challenges.

For instance, unlike the pace and quantity of interactions that can occur in a given physical location, the internet makes it easy for many people to come into contact with one another very quickly. This means that new ways of interacting can arise quickly and spontaneously, with correlated new opportunities for inflicting harm. Harm can thus start to occur long before there is even a reasonable chance for a human (as opposed to, say, an automated system) to spot a troubling pattern of interaction – let alone to start monitoring or to intervene. Also, by the time a pattern is noticed, the troublesome conduct may have already shifted elsewhere. The speed with which things can change online, and the sheer volume of interactions, means that flesh-and-blood humans cannot reasonably be charged with the task of monitoring what goes on in online fora unless automated methods of monitoring can be developed. However, one problem here is just that what constitutes violent or harmful interaction is itself something that can be difficult enough for people to recognize and agree upon. For instance, what to one online user may seem like humor or irony, to another may seem like a racist or sexist comment, and to the public may engender a long and far from clear cut debate. Given the problems that humans have with recognizing and coming to agreement on problems of this sort, with current artificial intelligence technology it is unlikely that the quickly emerging novel forms of violent and harmful interaction could be automatically identified (e.g. see Hewitt *et al*. 2016; citing Jane 2014a, 2014b, 2015). But even if we limit the scope of monitoring to known, unambiguous, and un-disputed forms of violent and harmful interaction (assuming that these three qualifiers still even leave any interactions in that set), there would still be significant technical problems to overcome. For instance, a portion of interactions between users may be encrypted, or they may be buried under so many layers of data structure and algorithm[16] that for practical purposes they may as well have been encrypted, such that the task of monitoring all user interactions would again become intractable. These are some of the problems to which differences between physical-location-bound interactions and interactions in online environments give rise.

But notice that the question of *where* cybercrimes occur is not even one that yields to simple physical investigation, since it concerns a conceptual issue. Namely, when actions and interactions take place in a *virtual* place, is it even legitimate to point to any given physical location and say, "That is where those (inter)actions took place?" Plausibly, the answer is "no." A similar conceptual issue is encountered when we ask where a telephone conversation between two people on opposite sides of the Earth occurred. In one country? In the other? Or on the wires and satellites that carry the digital signals that encode their voices? Another example might be when a person located in one country sends a letter containing a pathogen like anthrax to someone in another country. Was the crime committed in the location from which the letter was posted, or at the destination where it was received? Perhaps the right answer is that the telephone conversation and anthrax attack happen on Earth, or even – to broaden the scope so that the physical location of telecommunication satellites is included – within the Earth's orbit, and thus to say something similar about the location of cybercrimes. But although in a sense that would be true – cybercrimes indeed happen within the borders of the Earth's orbit – this answer would raise a range of conceptual, moral, and legal problems.

For one, there is the already-noted unease about transposing the location of interactions that occur in virtual environments onto somewhere in the physical world, as if doing so did not result in a significant loss of meaning. For another, this would also overlook the myriad ways in which the cybersphere has created and sustains new ways of interacting and new interests, which in turn provide opportunities for novel ways of harming and being harmed. For instance, to invade privacy by searching another's web browser's history, to steal another's work without physically depriving them of it by making unauthorized copies, to impersonate another by creating a Twitter account with a similar-looking handle, for a jilted lover to humiliate their ex-partner by posting their intimate photographs onto "revenge porn" sites, or to cause significant upset by vandalizing deceased people's Facebook pages. To appreciate the significance of these interactions, it is crucial to understand the role of social media in people's lives, that these days people do not do things online but that doing things online is in many cases the norm for how things are done, and such things as that digital data, once posted online, may be practically impossible to eliminate from caches on numerous servers around the world.[17] But another fundamental problem with this answer – or, for that matter, with refusing to pinpoint any specific physical location for cybercrimes – is that crimes require a jurisdiction which is normally co-extensive with a physical place with physical borders. Without a concrete jurisdiction, it is not clear where the offense should be tried, nor whether and in what ways it even counts as a criminal offense.[18] On a more practical note, without adequate international cooperation and inter-jurisdictional agreements[19] – for instance, about which nation state or governing body will prosecute cybercrimes – there may simply be no institution to which such offenses can even be reported, let alone through which they could be investigated, pursued, and prosecuted.[20]

Second, the comparative ease with which anonymity can be secured on the internet, and the impermanence of online evidence, also presents steep challenges to securing criminal convictions. Given the high stakes for those accused of criminal offenses, to secure a conviction the criminal law has high evidentiary standards. The reason why the standard used in criminal law to secure a conviction is "beyond reasonable doubt," as opposed to the "more likely than not" standard used in civil cases, is because what's at stake in criminal cases for defendants is often significantly greater (e.g. a term in prison, or even execution) than in civil cases (e.g. liability, which may often even be covered by insurance). However, digital data is (at least in principle) infinitely malleable/modifiable, and modifications of digital content can leave little or no trace of when, how, or by whom the data was modified. Thus, unless backups are regularly taken and stored in a secure location, without fastidious record-keeping practices (which nobody has reason to engage in unless they suspect they may become a victim of cybercrime) this can make it difficult to either identify the offender or precisely what they did, let alone to do this with a sufficient degree of certainty to satisfy the criminal law's high evidentiary standards. And even if backups are taken, questions can still arise about how often backups should be taken, for how long they should be kept, and what records must be maintained to provide credible proof at an adequate standard for the criminal law that those backups had not themselves been tampered with. It could even be argued that until sufficient data security and integrity can be systematically assured on the internet, even if an internationally recognized jurisdiction were set up to investigate and prosecute cybercrimes,[21] many such laws may simply be un-enforceable.

Third, it is challenging enough in conventional crimes that occur in physical locations to establish an accused's motives or intentions in order to provide adequate evidence to satisfy the required *mens rea* element for the given criminal offense. Since we do not yet have direct ways of reading people's minds, a court must therefore rely on indirect evidence to reach a decision about their motives and intentions. One form of indirect evidence is by interrogating the accused in court. Alternatively, the fact that an accused might have acted in ways that are consistent with someone who is trying to cover their tracks, for instance, may be taken by a court to infer that the accused knew that what they were doing was wrong, which in turn helps to establish their *mens rea*. For instance, perhaps their actions occurred in the silence of night when typically nobody is watching, or perhaps they used cleaning products at the crime scene presumably to remove fingerprints. However, given the very generic but common features of online interaction and the implicated technologies that were mentioned above, even if we could identify the offender, they may be in another country and thus be unavailable for interrogation, and because of concerns about data impermanence, malleability, and integrity, we may have legitimate worries about relying on such data to infer what their intentions may have been. Moreover, because online environments make it simple for many people to get involved in a given interaction – e.g. online cyber-mobs harassing an individual – this creates at least problems of a greater magnitude vis à vis collective action than what is typically encountered in more conventional physical crimes.[22] It also creates additional problems with regards to establishing the *mens rea* element. Specifically, when many people each make an individually-small contribution to what collectively amounts to as a sustained cyber-attack on a victim, it would be contrived to attempt to disentangle each person's individual contribution to the overall outcome. Furthermore, whose *mens rea* should we even look at in such cases of fractured online collective action?[23]

Fourth, and lastly, the ease with which interactions can occur online, and the physical dislocation of offenders from their targets, has two further noteworthy upshots. One is just that because the number of such interactions can be great, and since offenders are physically removed from their victims, they may genuinely fail to become fully cognizant on any given occasion of the impact that their actions have on their victims. What may feel to them as a harmless dig at yet another faceless dumbass internet user, may to that user be yet another one of many small attacks that they have to endure. This gives at least *some* purchase to the defense that at least some offenders may fail to realize what their actions (together with those of others) contributed to doing to another person. It also means that a state that took seriously a commitment to criminalizing cyber-offenses could be up for substantial expense. After all, there may be a great many cases, and prosecuting any individual case may involve chasing up many offenders from many jurisdictions and gathering up much evidence on many micro-interactions.

The purpose of this section was to identify several features of cybercrimes (by contrast with conventional crimes) that make it especially difficult for the criminal law to recognize this group of victims and their specific harms. These included that cybercrimes do not occur in a clear physical location, the ease of remaining anonymous in online interactions, the impermanence and malleability of digital data, difficulties with establishing *mens rea* including in multi-agent interactions, and the relative ease and physical detachment from victims when engaging in cybercrime. And the point of that was to explain why, in addition to the criminal law's general lack of concern for victims and their harms, features of *cyber*crimes make it especially difficult for the criminal law to recognize cybercrime's victims and their harms, and to respond to them in a fitting way.

Conclusion

This chapter highlighted two groups of reasons why victims of cybercrime are overlooked by the criminal law. First, because the harms suffered by victims of any crimes are at best of only marginal interest to the criminal law. Second, because fairly generic features of online-mediated interactions and the technology that underpins them do not sit well with existing criminal law doctrine, categories, and requirements. This explains why the criminal law makes a very poor ally for victims of cybercrime, and provides important context for the various case studies that are detailed in subsequent sections of this book.

The purpose of this chapter has been to lay out some hard facts pertaining to the way law works (and, from the perspective of the victim, perhaps, the way law *fails* to work). Its aim has been to broadly map the lay of the land rather than to critique the topography found there. This should not, however, be read as a ringing endorsement of either the nature or the fairness of the status quo. Indeed, an understandably human response to the information laid out in this chapter might well be an outraged declaration that this state of affairs – while logistically understandable – seems monumentally unjust. Despair would be another reasonable response. Given the severe constrictions on law detailed in this chapter, we might well wonder what hope there is for the victims of exploitative, oppressive, and harmful practices online. Fortunately, the criminal law is just one tool among many at our disposal for addressing social problems. Indeed there is a persuasive case – and it is one made at length in the conclusion of this book – that some problems (especially those that stem from technological innovation) may be better addressed not mainly or solely through legislative responses, but through a pluralistic approach.

Notes

1 Discovery of the attempt may still leave the victim in fear or another unpleasant state, but that is not why we prosecute unsuccessful attempts. As Lippman (2013, pp. 175–211) points out, considerations of retribution and deterrence provide ample reasons to do so. And as Yaffe argues, "[u]nder ... the prohibition of an action is also an implicit prohibition of an attempt to engage in that action; a prohibition of causing a result is [also] an implicit prohibition of an attempt to cause that result" (2014, p. 131).
2 Self-regarding acts are, intuitively, things people do to themselves that do not involve another person – for instance, perhaps suicide, or manufacturing illicit drugs solely for one's own use. Given that nobody lives in a vacuum, though, it is debatable whether any act is truly self-regarding. After all, aren't the people that a person who commits suicide leaves behind affected in an adverse way? And mightn't society be harmed when its citizens impair themselves (e.g. by drug addiction)? In my view what such examples show is that although technically all actions can have some kind of impact on others, not all ways of being impacted upon are sufficiently important to warrant restricting our freedom to act as we see fit. Precisely where the line should be drawn between kinds of impact that should and shouldn't count as impacting on others in a significant way is an interesting question, but it is one that falls beyond the scope of this chapter.
3 Despite the fact that a successful suicide attempt leaves the offender beyond the reach of the law, suicide (and not just attempted suicide) was still a criminal offense in many jurisdictions until recently (e.g. see Sydney Criminal Lawyers 2016).
4 As Bergelson points out, "[s]ome argue that there is no such thing as 'victimless' crime: crime always has victims. For example, a drug user is a victim of his addiction and a prostitute is a victim of sexual exploitation" (2013, p. 4). However, as I discuss, such a claim rests on a definition of "victim" that raises contestable evaluations about who is and who is not harmed by given conduct – contestable because different people may see these matters differently – and some people identified as "victims" in this manner may staunchly object to being identified as such.

5 In particular, developing the utilitarian moral theory, according to which "actions are right in proportion as they tend to promote happiness, wrong in proportion as they tend to produce the reverse of happiness" (Mill 1879, Chapter 2). Though perhaps appearing tame by today's standards, Mill's (and his predecessor Jeremy Bentham's) humanism – i.e. placing human pleasures and sufferings, rather than divine authority or the demands of an abstract moral duty that exists independently from the humans to which it applies, for instance – is so significant that it underpins how contemporary governments formulate public policy to this day.

6 A significant portion of Mill's work in political philosophy was concerned with the topic of individual liberty: with explaining what it is, why it matters, and in particular with identifying the conditions under which a state may legitimately curtail it through the laws that it creates and enforces. This focus on individual liberty, and on demarcating the conditions of fair interaction among individuals (as well as between individuals and the state), makes him an ally of conservatives and progressives alike; whether it be to reject paternalism, to advocate free speech and minimalist government, or to defend equality and the freedom of individuals to experiment with non-conventional ways of life.

7 Setting aside children and others whom we deem not competent to make such decisions.

8 Commenting on the debate between Lord Patrick Devlin (1959) and H.L.A. Hart (1963) about the (de-)criminalization of prostitution and homosexuality, Gerald Dworkin summarized the (by then 35-year-old) entrenched stalemate in this debate and the stance of main players as follows:

> the question [in the debate] can be formulated as: Ought immorality as such be a crime? It is claimed that Mill and Hart say that the answer is "No"; it is said that Fitzjames Stephen and Devlin say "Yes." Contemporary liberal theorists such as Joel Feinberg, Thomas Nagel, and Ronald Dworkin are united in agreement with Mill and Hart that it is not a legitimate function of the state to punish conduct simply on the grounds that it is immoral.
>
> (1999, pp. 927–928)

9 Judges do this precisely because otherwise the criminal justice system, including the sentences handed down, holds very little comfort for victims (see comments in the second-last paragraph of this section for an explanation of why this is so).

10 These categories come from *Model Penal Code* as adopted at the 1962 Annual Meeting of the American Law Institute at Washington, D.C., May 24, 1962 (American Law Institute 1985, pp. 18–19), though the *Model Criminal Code* in Australia contains similar categories that include intention, knowledge, recklessness, negligence, strict liability, and absolute liability (Parliamentary Counsel's Committee 2009, pp. 13–15).

11 Assuming that the other *actus reus* and *mens rea* requirements are also satisfied, and that the accused does not raise a successful defense such as a recognized excuse or justification.

12 The example under discussion is highlighted by Human Rights Watch who write

> The inequality meshes with other discriminatory provisions in South Africa law. For instance, it means that female-to-male [sic] transgender people lack adequate protections against rape – since they are still legally male, under South Africa's confused Sexual Offences Act, non-consensual sex between two men is punishable only as the lesser crime of "indecent assault".
>
> (Human Rights Watch 2003, p. 206)

Presumably the reference was meant to be to "male-to-female" not "female-to-male" transgender people. Human Rights Watch also cite an interview with Wendy Isaack who observed "Many transgender people are abused or raped in their communities....

And the law won't say it is rape" (quoted in Human Rights Watch 2003, p. 206, note 492). In recent years, subsequent to legislative reform, in jurisdictions that have now recognized transgender people as belonging to the gender with which they identify, this situation has changed. Legislative reform has also often explicitly adopted gender-neutral language to recognize that men can also be victims of rape. However, exceptions still exist, including notably in India where Section 375 of the Indian Penal Code begins the definition of rape as "Rape – A man is said to commit 'rape' if he:" (Criminal Law Amendment Act 2013, Section 375).

13 See note 10 about the *mens rea* requirement and the text preceding that note.
14 Vengeance is sometimes referred to as "lex talionis," law of the claw, "eye for an eye, tooth for a tooth." For other justifications for punishment, see the list in the next note.
15 The list of aims includes retribution, deterrence, rehabilitation, reform, isolation of the criminal offender to protect the community, the expression of solidarity with victims and those close to them as well as of condemnation for the offender, a deeper communication with the offender (in which the aim is to encourage repentance, reform, and reconciliation, that ultimately results in the offender's re-integration into the community), and reasserting the law's authority subsequent to its having been publicly challenged.
16 For instance, a platform can be implemented in several different frameworks, which can be installed under a number of different operating systems, hosted on different virtual machines, that may run on different kinds of physical hardware.
17 Matthew Williams discusses "growing concerns over sub-criminal activity within increasing populated virtual environments[, in which] new forms of sociopathic behaviour, which present themselves in abundance, [are] disregarded due to their 'virtual status'" (2000, p. 95).
18 Williams similarly observes that "while the conventional 'high tech' crimes which rely on the presence of a physical space have been rapidly met with both social and legal responses, those which exist in virtual space escape any form of social or legalistic rationalization" (2000, p. 96).
19 In recognition of this difficulty, the Council of Europe (2001) set up Treaty No. 185, also known as the Budapest Convention on Cybercrime, that to-date has 49 nation state signatories. The Council of Europe subsequently published a report in 2008 which noted that "[o]ne of the biggest problems connected with cybercrime is jurisdiction. For this reason the CoC has established … some criteria in order to establish jurisdiction for the criminal offences" (Council of Europe 2008, p. 51). However, as a more recent report published by the Council of Europe (2014, p. 5) underscores, there are ongoing difficulties in securing coordination between jurisdictions that have adopted versions of earlier recommendations which "fail either adequately or altogether to cover international cooperation". Francesco Calderoni (2010) also discusses some of the challenges the EU has faced in regards to devising an effective response to cybercrime.
20 One possible solution to this problem could be to adopt a radically different governance model like Bruno S. Frey's and Reiner Eichenberger's (1996) Functional, Overlapping, and Competing Jurisdictions (FOCJ) in which institutions of governance "emerge in response to the 'geography of problems'" (1996, p. 317, emphasis omitted), not physical geography. I mention Frey's work not just because of its potential application to general governance problems, but because in another paper Frey (2001) explicitly discusses the application of FOCJ to internet-based challenges. A foreseeable difficulty, however, with Frey's proposed solution is that it requires whatever existing governmental structures are currently in place in the many jurisdictions that are to be coordinated to relinquish their power, and to an organization that may not even have location-specific allegiance. My aim here is not to ponder whether this would be a good idea or a bad idea, but just whether it is even realistic in a political climate where nationalistic sentiments seem to be on the rise in response to increasing globalization.
21 See note 19 for an example of how this has proven to be a very challenging problem for the EU.

22 For instance, see Saskia E. Polder-Verkiel's (2012) discussion of the collective responsibility issues raised by the online suicide of Abraham Biggs, which was witnessed and encouraged by many onlookers, and how it compares to issues raised in an analogous physical case.
23 These *mens rea* problems could be addressed by defining cybercrimes in such a way that they require a lower standard of intentionality than purpose or knowledge, perhaps negligence, or strict liability. The problem with doing this, however, is that the criminal law's coercive force could then be applied to people who were only just negligent or clueless but not intentionally malicious.

References

American Law Institute 1985, *Model Penal Code: Official Draft and Explanatory Notes*, Philadelphia, PA, USA.

Bergelson, Vera 2013, 'Victimless Crimes', in Hugh LaFollette (ed.) *The International Encyclopaedia of Ethics*, Blackwell Publishing Ltd., London, UK, pp. 5329–5337. doi: 10.1002/9781444367072.wbiee094

Blackstone, William 1765–1769, *Blackstone's Commentaries on the Laws of England* (1st edition), Book Four, First Chapter: Of the Nature of Crimes, And Their Punishment, Clarendon Press, Oxford, UK, viewed 16 July 2016, http://avalon.law.yale.edu/18th_century/blackstone_bk4ch1.asp

Brenner, Susan W. 2006, 'Cybercrime Jurisdiction', *Crime, Law, and Social Change*, vol. 46, no. 4, pp. 189–206.

Calderoni, Francesco 2010, 'The European legal framework on cybercrime: striving for an effective implementation', *Crime, Law, and Social Change*, vol. 54, no. 5, pp. 339–357.

Council of Europe 2001, *Convention on Cybercrime: Chart of Signatures and Ratifications of Treaty 185*, viewed 19 July 2016, www.coe.int/en/web/conventions/full-list/-/conventions/treaty/185/signatures

Council of Europe 2008, *National Legislation Implementing the Convention on Cybercrime – Comparative Analysis and Good Practices*, prepared by Lorenzo Picotti and Ivan Salvadori for Council of Europe, Strasbourg, France, viewed 17 July 2016, www.coe.int/t/dg1/legalcooperation/economiccrime/cybercrime/T-CY/DOC%20567%20study2-d-version8%20provisional%20%2812%20march%2008%29.PDF

Council of Europe 2014, *Cybercrime Model Laws: Discussion Paper Prepared for the Cybercrime Convention Committee (T-CY)*, prepared by Zahid Jamil for Council of Europe, Strasbourg, France, viewed 17 July 2016, https://rm.coe.int/CoERMPublic-CommonSearchServices/DisplayDCTMContent?documentId=0900001680303ee1

Criminal Law Amendment Act 2013 (Republic of India), viewed 19 July 2016, http://indiacode.nic.in/acts-in-pdf/132013.pdf

Devlin, Patrick 1959, *The Enforcement of Morals*, Oxford University Press, Oxford, UK.

Duff, R.A. 2005, 'Who is Responsible, for What, to Whom?', *Ohio State Journal of Criminal Law*, vol. 2, pp. 441–461.

Duff, R.A. 2010, 'Theories of Criminal Law', *Stanford Encyclopedia of Philosophy*, viewed 17 July 2016, http://plato.stanford.edu/archives/spr2010/entries/criminal-law/

Duff, R.A. 2014, 'Torts, Crimes, And Vindication: Whose Wrong Is It?', in Matthew Dyson (ed.) *Unravelling Tort and Crime*, Cambridge University Press, Cambridge, UK, pp. 146–173.

Dworkin, Gerald 1999, 'Devlin Was Right: Law and the Enforcement of Morality', *William & Mary Law Review*, vol. 40, no. 3, pp. 927–946.

Frey, Bruno S. 2001, 'A Utopia? Government without Territorial Monopoly', *Journal of Institutional and Theoretical Economics*, vol. 157, no. 1, pp. 162–175.

Frey, Bruno S. and Eichenberger, Reiner 1996, 'FOCJ: Competitive Governments for Europe, *International Review of Law and Economics*, vol. 16, pp. 315–327.

Hart, H.L.A. 1963, *Law, Liberty, and Morality*, Stanford University Press, Stanford, CA, USA.

Hewitt, S., Tiropanis, T., and Bokhove, C. 2016, 'The Problem of Identifying Misogynist Language on Twitter (and Other Online Social Spaces)', in Wendy Hall, Paolo Parigi and Steffen Staab (eds), *Proceedings of the 8th ACM Conference on Web Science*, ACM, New York, NY, USA, pp. 333–335, viewed 7 October 2016 http://dx.doi.org/10.1145/2908131.2908183

Holmes, Oliver W. 1881, *The Common Law*, Project Gutenberg EBook #2449, viewed 19 July 2016, www.gutenberg.org/files/2449/2449-h/2449-h.htm#link2H_4_0003

Human Rights Watch 2003, *More Than a Name: State-Sponsored Homophobia and Its Consequences in Southern Africa*, Human Rights Watch, New York, NY, USA, viewed 7 October 2016, www.hrw.org/reports/2003/safrica/safriglhrc0303.pdf

Jane, Emma A. 2014a, '"Your a Ugly, Whorish, Slut": Understanding E-bile', *Feminist Media Studies*, vol. 14, no. 4, pp. 531–546.

Jane, Emma A. 2014b, '"Back to the Kitchen, Cunt": Speaking the Unspeakable about Online Misogyny', *Continuum: Journal of Media & Cultural Studies*, vol. 28, no. 4, pp. 558–570.

Jane, Emma A. 2015, 'Flaming? What Flaming? The Pitfalls and Potentials of Researching Online Hostility', *Ethics and Information Technology*, vol. 17, no. 1, pp. 65–87.

Kleinig, John 1978, 'Crime and the Concept of Harm', *American Philosophical Quarterly*, vol. 15, no. 1, pp. 27–36.

Lippman, Matthew 2013, *Contemporary Criminal Law: Concepts, Cases, and Controversies*, 3rd edition, SAGE Publications Ltd., London, UK.

Mill, John Stuart 1859, *On Liberty*, Library of Economics and Liberty archive, viewed 16 July 2016, www.econlib.org/library/Mill/mlLbty.html

Mill, John Stuart 1879, *Utilitarianism*, Project Gutenberg EBook #11224, viewed 5 October 2016, www.gutenberg.org/files/11224/11224-h/11224-h.htm#CHAPTER_II

Parliamentary Counsel's Committee 2009, *Model Criminal Code*, Canberra, ACT, Australia, viewed 16 July 2016, www.pcc.gov.au/uniform/crime%20%28composite-2007%29-website.pdf

Payne v. Tennessee (1991) [501 U.S. 808].

Polder-Verkiel, S.E. (2012) 'Online Responsibility: Bad Samaritanism and the Influence of Internet Mediation', *Science and Engineering Ethics*, vol. 18, no. 1, pp. 117–141.

Rachels, James 1999, *The Elements of Moral Philosophy*, 4th edition, McGraw Hill Education, New York, NY, USA.

Simons, Kenneth W. 2008, 'The Crime/Tort Distinction: Legal Doctrine and Normative Principles', *Widener Law Journal*, vol. 17, pp. 719–732.

Sydney Criminal Lawyers 2016, 'What is the Law on Suicide in Australia?' *Findlaw Australia*, viewed 16 July 2016, www.findlaw.com.au/articles/5556/what-is-the-law-on-suicide-in-australia.aspx

Williams, Matthew 2000, 'Virtually Criminal: Discourse, Deviance and Anxiety Within Virtual Communities', *International Review of Law, Computers and Technology*, vol. 14, no. 1, pp. 95–104.

Yaffe, Gideon 2014, 'Criminal Attempts', *The Yale Law Journal*, vol. 124, no. 1, pp. 92–156.

2 Theorising power online

Chris Brickell

Introduction

The internet is our portal into modern life. Many of us log on first thing in the morning, look at it repeatedly throughout the day, and check in last thing at night. As a kind of portable internet, the smartphone is both a constant enabler and electronic leash that attaches cyberworlds to our bodies. Their impacts cling to us. If our social lives are lived through the internet, at least to a significant degree, it stands to reason that the pleasures and harms of modern life are intimately intertwined with it. There are reflexive processes at work here. Cyberworlds reflect our society back to us, reproducing new kinds of power relations as well as old world hierarchies. All have real-world consequences.

This chapter offers a framework to think systematically about power in relation to the internet. In particular, it focuses on 'digital sexuality', its understandings and expressions (Plummer, 2015, p. 47). How do cyberworlds enable, shape and constrain sexuality at the level of the individual and social groups both large and small? Until recently, online researchers have not tended to name power as such, framing internet dynamics in other ways instead. They have focussed on objectification, harassment, norms, safety or freedom rather than power per se (e.g. Albury, 2009; Brookey and Cannon, 2009). This is beginning to change, though, as theorists come to regard online life as a series of sites through which power circulates (e.g. Weeks, 2016). Even when researchers avoid an explicit theory of power, their empirical insights allow us to explore how power operates and is expressed in the field of online sexuality. Here I draw from existing research and offer three broad frameworks – ideal types, as sociologists would describe them – that distil some key features of power's operation. These three frameworks relate to: (1) the constitution of subjectivities and knowledges; (2) the regulation of social interactions; and (3) and the perpetuation of inequality. Power shapes what we understand about social life, our place in it and our relationships with others. It works to control the realms of the possible, both in terms of identities and social action. Power also operates in ways that form social subjects into hierarchies that are reproduced across time and space. Each of the three frameworks identifies key features within the broader framework of power relations. These perspectives often overlap, and this chapter's final section considers how the frameworks of power cross-cut and interweave in the online world.

Constituting knowledge and subjectivity

Knowledge and identities are increasingly shaped within internet settings (Crampton, 2003, p. 3). To some degree at least, we come to know what we know, and become who we are, through online experiences and interactions. When it comes to sexuality, internet researchers ask what kinds of relationships, connections and communities are encouraged, enabled and produced online.

Michel Foucault, French philosopher and historian, died in 1984, some years before the internet became a global force. Some of his writing, though, is useful in our analysis of the internet and its associated technologies. Foucault emphasised the role of knowledge in the construction of sexual subjectivities, and suggested that discourses – patterns of language and syntax that embed social assumptions – may be productive as well as proscriptive. Like electricity, power as figured by Foucault travels along the lines of language. In turn, discourses are the building blocks of social life and sexual identity; we accept and rearrange some ideas about the world and reject others as we construct our sense of who we are and how we ought to act. Discursive power informs more than it restricts; as Foucault put it, ' "[s]exuality" is far more of a positive product of power than power was ever repression of sexuality' (Foucault, 1980, p. 120). Foucault could not have foreseen our discovery and distillation of online discourses about sexuality, but his writings on knowledge construction hold true in the new context. The internet is saturated with discourse, just like the offline world.

Let us consider a specific example. In the early decades of the twentieth century, internet scholar Dennis Waskul suggests, 'coming of age is situated in a highly technological era where sexual awakenings and discoveries are profoundly mediated by new media technologies' (Waskul, 2015, p. 92). Yet the processes of knowledge acquisition do not always run smoothly. Ellen Selkie and her co-researchers examined teenagers' views on social networking sites and sexuality education, and their respondents revealed the conundrums:

> It's hard to look up questions like that [i.e. about sex] without coming across porn so it doesn't work very well.
> (Cited in Selkie *et al.*, 2011, p. 208)

> I mean if you have a question and say you go to Google and you find something that might not be correct. You really go to Google because it's fast and easy, but if there is a fast and easy way to do it [somewhere else], which there probably are in many ways, it would be a lot easier and a lot more reliable.
> (Cited in Selkie *et al.*, 2011, p. 208)

These interviewees show that the internet offers 'a vast flow of representations', to use a phrase by sociologist Ken Plummer, and they demonstrate that formal kinds of sexual knowledge are soon tangled up in other kinds of depictions (Plummer, 2015: 49). All manner of sexual discourse circulates through the internet's channels (Measor, 2004). This might raise questions of who might be believed and who might be trusted: medical professionals or pornographers? In other words, which building blocks prove useful when power constitutes knowledge? Pornography, ironically enough, is a key source of sexual knowledge for young people, even though Selkie's respondents dismissed its significance (Waskul, 2015). Instead, they felt any reliable online advice service would need to reassure them about the qualifications and experience of those providing information or offering online-assistant-type advice (Selkie *et al.*, 2011, p. 210).

Although the internet offers various forms of knowledge, some of which are presumed less reliable than others, online information can seem reassuring when the offline world appears threatening. One of the interviewees in Selkie's study put it this way:

> You go to the doc, sometimes you don't want the doctor, like, to know, you don't want nobody to know, so it's easier to do it [online] like that, sometimes.
>
> (Cited in Selkie *et al.*, 2011, p. 209)

The internet has opened up new possibilities for finding information and developing sexual selves, and anonymity plays a crucial role. A screen does not identify the person on the keypad or keyboard ('you don't want nobody to know') and offers no moral judgements that might generate shame and threaten an inquirer's sense of self. By stressing the critical importance of reliability, trust and safety, respondents in Selkie's study revealed the intertwining of possibilities and risks in online settings. Not only is sexual health considered to be a matter of risk management, but so too are the processes through which knowledge circulates and is acquired. The internet allows us to gain knowledge 'about sexualities in all their diverse forms across the world', as Plummer puts it, and that knowledge is mediated in a range of ways (Plummer, 2015, p. 49).

Public health campaigns offer further insight into the constitutive aspects of power. The new discourses and practices have deep historical roots. Incitements to self-control and self-governance moulded sexual ideals from the nineteenth century onwards, and the focus shifted from naming and shaming 'dangerous sexualities' to managing 'risk' during the late twentieth century (Ryan, 2005). Disseminating discourses of public health in an attempt to produce healthy populations, governments and allied non-governmental organisations have made use of the internet's increasingly important role in the construction of sexual knowledge. In recent years the internet has become an obvious place to build public health campaigns because those seeking sexual information – including the teenagers in Selkie's study – go there first when they search for information (Bryson, 2004; Kanuga and Rosenfeld, 2004).

Internet campaigns help build sexual knowledge in particular ways. One such example – hubba.co.nz – was developed during the 2000s by the New Zealand

Ministry of Health and targeted at teenagers. Featuring the catchy slogan 'No rubba, no hubba hubba' – referring to slang for condoms and sex respectively – it offered 'tips about sex and having safer sex'. The site offered these kinds of statements:

> If someone is telling you they love you and pressuring you at the same time, then they don't know what love is. Having sex might make you feel older but it won't make you more mature, change who you really are, or mean that someone will stay with you.
> Deciding when you're ready to have sex is probably one of the hardest decisions you'll make. Maybe that's why a lot of people act before they think, or get wasted to avoid thinking it through. There is one sure thing though – it is always your decision. No one else should make it for you.

'Hubba.co.nz' provided its teenage readers with framework for thinking about sex and risk. The first excerpt melds the desire for personal empowerment, an appeal to maturity, and an ideal of 'true love', while the second stresses sexual autonomy. This text provides a resource for subjectivity that young people adopted, modified or rejected as they pieced together their understandings of what sex is and what it means to them. At the same time, the website's authors inscribe particular ideas as truths to be taken up by its readers: love and pressure are mutually exclusive, and sexual autonomy is important. Sexual ethics take shape in online forums. The 'hubba' campaign offered an intervention into debates over chosen sex and pressured sex, reflecting the recent focus on sexual consent (Beres, 2014). Programmes like Australia's theline.org.au, online as I write this chapter in mid-2016, has some similar goals. It provides resources and links on consent and sexual violence for young people. As Carmody and Ovenden suggest, 'new approaches increasingly recognise that curricula needs to balance both the pleasurable aspects of sex with a recognition of the unintended consequences of sex including the high rates of pressured and unwanted sex experienced especially by young women' (2013, p. 794).

Social networking sites are increasingly used for public health campaigns too. On Facebook, for instance, people are invited to subscribe to named pages or groups (Gold *et al.*, 2011). 'Love Your Condom' (LYC) is a current New Zealand example of a Facebook-based safer-sex promotion campaign with regular updates on local events, links to further online resources, and tens of thousands of Facebook 'Likes'. LYC incites readers to consider risks to themselves and others, and one of its condom-promoting slogans reads: 'We Wear it to Protect Us All'. The LYC campaign presents a sexual subjectivity that implicitly defines an ethical sexuality in terms of managing for the good of oneself and one's sexual partners. 'I want to know whether I am HIV positive or not', says one of the men in a video embedded on the LYC Facebook page, 'rather than sitting around wondering and potentially putting other people at risk'. In this way, those who engage with social media are invited to participate in an 'ethical erotics', constituting themselves as both considerate partners and sexually responsible citizens on a social media forum (Cameron-Lewis and Allen, 2013). This carries some moral weight: sites like Facebook play a central role in identity creation at this point in history (Zhao *et al.*, 2008). In a ripple effect, the dialogue between sexual subjects and what they see on screen carries on to shape interactions between those subjects and their partners in everyday sexual situations.

As all these examples show, the internet constitutes knowledge and identity in several different ways. Many websites mediate and transmit a range of possibilities for sexual information, guiding their readers by privileging particular discourses over others and encouraging them to incorporate these discourses into their sexual subjectivities. Others encourage a more interactive approach to the presentation and fashioning of sexual identity, citizenship and ethics. Sexual health campaigns that make use of Facebook, for instance, provide opportunities for viewers to actively engage through the 'Like' button and comments section. These allow dialogue between sexual selves and the online apparatus through which knowledge is generated, circulated and negotiated.

Regulating social interaction

'Never before have so many people had such easy access to so much sexually explicit material', Waskul suggests. '[F]rom the comfort of one's own home and under a dense veil of anonymity, an enormous range of sex is readily available online at one's fingertips' (Waskul, 2004, p. 4). Waskul makes a valuable point – anonymity introduces new dynamics into intimate engagement, as we have already seen and will soon examine further – but this is hardly an unimpeded flow of information. Internet sexuality can be widely accessible or subject to constraint and regulation. Such regulation takes place on several different levels: individual conduct, the frameworks imposed by technology itself, the rules of institutional settings and governments' overarching purview.

John Palfrey (2010) suggests modes of institutional control of the internet have changed noticeably over the last two decades. Before 2000 many hailed the 'open internet' as a site of democratic discourse, while the following decade saw organisations and governments actively manage and even block content deemed politically or socially dangerous. More recently, the 'access contested' era, to use Palfrey's term, has seen something of a 'pushback' against the controls of earlier years. This contesting of regulation, Palfrey proposes, accompanies a growing recognition of the centrality of the internet to all aspects of everyday life. The internet is no longer seen as a separate sphere to which people travel occasionally, 'as if on vacation' (Palfrey, 2010, p. 991). Instead, in a thoroughly internet-based society, open access to online services becomes a necessity if we are to operate effectively as citizens.

Some states still impose regulatory power over online content, controlling and monitoring new communication technologies (Plummer, 2015, p. 49). Approaches have differed from country to country (Mayer-Schönberger, 2002/3; Palfrey, 2010). Some administrations attempt to regulate online spaces by targeting individuals and companies. At various times, and to varying extents, the governments of Pakistan, United Arab Emirates, Myanmar and Yemen, for instance, have required that internet service providers (ISPs) block 'pornographic websites' and politically dissident content (Deibert and Villeneuve, 2004, pp. 121–122). During the mid-1990s, some states explored the possibility of prosecuting people whose hard drives contained forbidden files. The Singaporean government, for example, held internet users and providers legally responsible for keeping the internet free of 'pornographic and politically objectionable material' (Knoll, 1995/6, p. 294). Even now, Singapore's Media Development Authority regulates the services offered by ISPs, and blog writers can be imprisoned for writing seditious posts (Ramzy, 2016). Internet controls remain especially extensive in China and Iran, where YouTube, Facebook and Twitter are blocked along with activist and pornographic websites (Palfrey, 2010).

The state is not the only agent of institutionalised regulatory power, however. 'Content blocking' occurs in a range of smaller-scale spaces, including internet cafés, schools and workplaces, in those countries where cyberworlds are not state-controlled (Deibert and Villeneuve, 2004). Many parents also install blocking software on to home computers to regulate their children's internet access. Content blocking takes several forms. Filters prevent access to websites containing specified words ('pornography', 'penis'), black-list filtering prohibits access to sites specified by systems administrators, and white-list filtering affords internet users access to stipulated sites only (Laughlin, 2002/3, pp. 272–275). Some filtering systems have been developed by companies with evangelical Christian connections, and filter content according to conservative principles (Willard, 2002). All filters 'overblock', denying access to a greater number or range of websites than was originally intended. The text-based filters in my own university, for example, misidentify gay and lesbian blogs and bookstores, breast cancer support groups, and any website dealing with sexuality, as pornographic.

The power to regulate internet access is hotly contested: many argue internet regulation threatens to curtail legitimate access to information and freedom of expression (Palfrey, 2010). Some suggest filters represent a new incarnation of 'book banning', while others advocate the use of filtering systems – especially those blocking access to pornography – in an attempt to prevent sexual harassment of workers in schools, libraries, and other places where internet services are offered (Laughlin, 2002/3). Similarly, many university internet policies assert the organisations' need to prevent users from vilifying others, and regulate internet use accordingly (Brickell, 2009). Such debates have important ramifications, for the power to regulate can have far-reaching consequences. A public library blocking system may prevent a gay or lesbian teenager, for instance, or a woman contemplating an abortion, from accessing information about local support networks.

Regulatory power has other facets too. Not only do states and institutions say 'yes' or 'no' to expressions of sexuality, but sexuality is given shape within particular constraints. Kane Race points out that new technologies contain, as well as enable, particular kinds of sexual interaction (Race, 2015). Race explains that smartphones with hook-up apps like Grindr and Tinder constitute a relatively new infrastructure of the social encounter, by which I mean to draw attention to their material specificity and also make the point that they mediate the sexual encounter in new ways; making certain activities, relations, and practices possible while obviating others.

(2015, p. 254)

The materiality of technology plays an important role here (pp. 256–257). The 'architecture' of a phone hook-up app, for instance, channels self-expression in particular ways. Images and text give off certain impressions and require degrees of technological and social skill if their creator is to attract a partner, while every participant negotiates the social limitations of physical attractiveness and sexual appeal. What might look like a realm of freedom may not, in fact, feel that way to everybody. As Foucault acknowledged, the subject constituted through power relations is never free from the constraints of context. Instead, he suggested, the subject learns to regulate him or herself with respect to the expectations of the wider society, interiorises this regulation, and becomes skilled at self-government (Danaher *et al.*, 2000; Foucault, 1991).

In the panopticon, the model prison designed by Jeremy Bentham during the eighteenth century and used by Foucault as a metaphor to illustrate surveillance techniques in modern society, inmates' backlit cells faced a louvred central guard tower that convicts could not see into (Foucault 1995, pp. 200–209). Inmates learned to check their own behaviour because they had no way of knowing whether or not the guard was watching at any given moment. The panopticon speaks clearly to the practice of internet sexuality. Backlit in their profile boxes, those watching their phones are observed by others through a search engine's louvers. Unlike Bentham's example, however, these prisoners may be willing participants. In this seductive panopticon – a 'synopticon', to use Philip Vannini's term (2004, p. 83) – distinctions between the watcher and the watched often tend to blur. This is a deeply ambiguous process in which participants project their own desires through their profiles and seek an appreciative audience. To post a profile is to create, present, project and regulate oneself simultaneously.

As these examples suggest, regulatory power takes complex twists and turns. The examples of cyberbullying and online harassment also illustrate how the power to regulate runs in more than one direction at once. Cyberbullying refers to the repeated use of communication technologies – texts, instant messages, social networking sites – to harass or socially exclude others. It may include the distribution of unsolicited and unwanted 'text or photos of a sexual nature or requesting sexual acts either online or offline' (Mishna *et al.*, 2010, p. 362). The act of cyberbullying is a form of regulation in itself, an attempt to achieve a particular outcome (ostracism, shame, stress) through attempts to subordinate the victim to the bully's will. Schools often feature in the cyberbullying literature as places where the dynamics of bullying play out: male instigators often launch homophobic attacks on male peers and perpetuate sexual harassment against female peers, creating an unsafe and hostile environment (Shariff, 2005, p. 470; see also Berson *et al.*, 2002).

We will return to questions of harassment shortly, but it is worth pointing out that remedies for cyberbullying also become tangled in their own forms of regulation. One study, for instance, found young people reluctant to report instances of bullying to their parents for fear they might respond by removing phone or internet access privileges (Mishna *et al.*, 2010, p. 371). Many felt such an outcome to be a form of re-victimisation, a misdirected response that holds responsible the objects of attack. This suggests interventions in cyberbullying raise difficult dilemmas. Shaheen Shariff writes of the need to balance freedom of expression and personal safety. On the one hand, she argues, national laws should be updated in order to properly recognise cyber aggressions. Shariff's views dovetail with those of other scholars who agree there is a case for restraining cyber-freedoms if this protects young people from harm and upholds their rights (Palfrey, 2010, p. 984; Patchin and Hinduja, 2006, p. 149; Shariff, 2005, pp. 477, 482). But there is something else here too. Shariff advocates the need to foster 'inclusive and positive school environments' and, more specifically, provide guidance to imbue young people with the qualities of 'civic-minded individuals' (p. 472). Power has come full circle: direct regulation is one strategy, but so too is the power to reconstitute subjectivity, imbue online subjects with self-governance and minimise risk in the process.

We can see that the power to regulate is both multidirectional and imbricated with other kinds of power. As these examples show, regulation is not simply the power to say no – and to enforce that declaration through coercive means if necessary – but it may involve the power to restrain and control self-expression and reconstitute subjectivity. Shariff's comment (2005, p. 476) that cyberbullying 'creates power imbalances within the school environment' brings us to the next form of power: the reproduction of social inequality.

Perpetuating inequality

As a social product and a site of social interactions, the internet is a reflexive phenomenon. It mirrors the dynamics of everyday life – sometimes intensifying or recasting them – and also reshapes offline relationships. It should come as no surprise that social inequality, a pervasive characteristic of social life in general, carries over into cyberworlds. As Shariff points out in the school setting, online representations and practices operate along several axes of social stratification, including gender, sexuality and ethnicity (see also Adam, 2002; Stokes, 2007; van Zoonen, 2002).

Pornography was the focus of early feminist writing on the internet. Some argued that pornography can be harmful to women and suggested internet pornography crosses new boundaries, opens new markets and pioneers 'new harms'. Catharine MacKinnon, for example, suggests 'electronically communicated pornography trafficks women in a yet more sophisticated form' (MacKinnon, 1995, p. 1959). MacKinnon proposed that internet pornography both replicates existing power relations and further extends the reach of exploitation. More recently, other researchers have agreed with MacKinnon's analysis. Some point to increased levels of 'violent and non-consensual sex represented in internet pornography as compared to other pornography mediums' (Powell, 2010, p. 79).

Ethnicity, gender and sexuality intersect in the world of online porn. Mireille Miller-Young documents the income disparities between black and white porn workers, noting that black actresses frequently earn fifty per cent less income than their white counterparts who carry out the same kinds of work (Miller-Young, 2010, p. 227). This takes place in a context where a slim, white femininity is maintained as the standard for all actresses to follow: 'The rule tends to be: live up to the requirements of white sexual embodiment, in other words, assimilate to white beauty standards, or risk being ghettoised in the most undervalued sectors of the business, such as the low-end genre of "ghetto porn"' (Miller-Young, 2010, p. 228). Pornography is a complex phenomenon in which inequalities of income, racial norms and representations all overlap.

Kath Albury agrees that pornographic websites reflect wider cultural currents, that representations cannot be divorced from the conditions of their making, and that some 'some sexually explicit texts eroticize misogyny' (Albury, 2009, pp. 649–650). However, Albury adds, some porn genres 'include both radical and regressive understandings of sex and gender', and others lend themselves to more transgressive readings (Albury, 2009, p. 652). What really matters, she suggests, is not so much whether a given representation is 'demeaning', but whether porn is 'produced and consumed in an ethical context', and those involved are fully aware, agreeable and fully compensated (p. 651).

Despite their differences, these feminist writers all agree the internet reflects and refracts broader patterns of social power and that internet pornography never sidesteps the material conditions of its production. Still, it may be possible to resist the dynamics of inequality by making pornography in more critically-engaged ways. Some female porn-makers offer 'woman-friendly' material to a rapidly expanding female audience, for instance (Ray, 2007). Some of Miller-Young's black female actresses have become directors, and seek to 'highlight the erotic power and beauty of the women in the images' while sustaining an ethical working environment for their co-workers (Miller-Young, 2010, p. 230). Claire Potter agrees that a 'feminist pornography' is possible: it might challenge narratives of male dominance, include performers of a range of sizes, abilities, ethnicities and gender identities, put 'the actor's pleasure and agency at the center of the story, ask for actors' consent for any sexual act, permit actors to revoke consent, and provide clean and safe working conditions' (Potter, 2016, pp. 106–107). Like Albury, Potter suggests porn does not – or need not – always reproduce sexual inequalities.

Porn sites are not the only online spaces structured by inequality and resistance. Sexual harassment and cyberstalking are other areas of concern (Adam, 2002; Barak, 2005; Powell, 2010). Unwanted sexual solicitation and persistent sexual remarks are made in chat rooms, by instant message, or by email; some harassers abuse their victims as soon as they appear online, or send pornographic pictures and spam (Patchin and Hinduja, 2006, p. 158; Philips and Morrissey, 2004, p. 67). This behaviour is highly gendered: the majority of cyberstalkers are men, the victims women (Adam, 2002, p. 134). In spite of cyberharassment's potential to perpetuate profound harms, often it is either minimised as 'harmless teasing' that (usually) women ought to tolerate or dismissed as an individual matter rather than an increasingly institutionalised feature of online life (Jane, 2016, p. 287). In fact, Anastasia Powell suggests, these activities fall along a 'continuum of sexual violence' (Powell, 2010, p. 77). 'Revenge porn' offers a similar example. This involves uploading and distributing explicit images of a previous (usually female) partner without her agreement, for the purpose of humiliating her online – and sometimes to incite offline attacks (Jane, 2016, p. 286). Powell notes that legislation rarely offers a remedy for the unauthorised distribution of images taken in one context and subsequently circulated by 'unscrupulous recipients' (2010, p. 83). As these examples show, the internet can broaden the scope of existing modes of harassment, amplify them, and give them new form.

The members of sexual minorities are also marginalised in cyberworlds, intensifying the inequalities experienced offline. In the interstices of the internet, the dominance of heterosexuality is reinforced, and blogs, music clips, online media and social networking sites all provide vehicles for heterosexism. Some researchers suggest young people who lack social support are most vulnerable to online hate material, and sexual orientation is a common target of online hate, even on such common sites as Facebook and YouTube (Oksanen *et al.*, 2014). Still, this coin has two sides. While cyberworlds can extend the scope of offline harassment, they also provide forums for resistance. Some websites provide valuable advice and resources for those seeking support with sexual harassment, for instance, while Facebook users and blog-writers organise campaigns against inequalities of gender and sexuality and encourage broader practices of community-building. Recent 'netographic' research – the term combines 'internet' and 'ethnography' – suggests online queer discussion groups provide valuable spaces for both socialising and political debate (Svensson, 2015).

Web interfaces can be deeply contradictory sites for power relations, constantly tacking backwards and forwards between re-inscribing inequalities and providing opportunities for resisting them. For instance, the young heterosexual male chat room frequenters in one study positioned themselves both inside and outside of dominant masculinities (Kendall, 2000). On the one hand they were 'nerds' who preferred technological pursuits to the physical activities traditionally associated with masculinity. On the other hand, they reiterated their identities as (heterosexual) men through frequent jokes and conversations depicting women as sexual objects (pp. 263–264). In some respects these men's online performance challenged established forms of masculine conduct, but they reinscribed gendered inequalities in other ways.

An analysis of black adolescent girls' homepages in the USA echoes these online complexities. Carla Stokes (2007) investigated how these young women negotiated several sexual scripts 'with roots in controlling images of Black female sexuality': 'freaks', 'virgins', 'down-ass chicks/bitches', 'pimpettes' and 'resisters'. Many worked with more than one script at once, both adopting the sexual expectations of the surrounding culture, especially the hypersexualised and yet passive image of Black women, and deploying alternative representations of powerful, assertive and self-determining female sexuality (Stokes, 2007, p. 179).

These kinds of examples prompt us to revisit the hope, often expressed during the internet's early years, that online initiatives might result in the erosion rather than the reinforcement of old hierarchies (Palfrey, 2010). Some commentators have suggested cyberlife allows its subjects to experiment with socially transformative understandings of gender and sexuality especially when, as in role-playing games, many interactions take place anonymously by people represented by avatars. The sky is the limit, at least in theory (Nyboe, 2004; Crampton, 2003). The final verdict, though, is mostly a pessimistic one. A 'boys' club locker room atmosphere' still pervades many online spaces, and cyberhate is mostly, if not exclusively, aimed at women (McCormick and Leonard, 2004; Jane, 2016). This is far from inexplicable. Given online subjects draw upon the norms, practices and power relations that structure offline societies, it should come as no surprise that new modes of connectivity share the stage with older forms of inequality and harassment.

Synthesising analyses of online power

The internet can be an intense place, and the level of debate is not always high. Emma A. Jane uses the term 'e-bile' to describe 'the extravagant invective, the sexualised threats of violence, and the recreational nastiness that have come to constitute a dominant tenor of Internet discourse' (Jane, 2014, pp. 531–532). A successor to previously-used terms including 'flaming', 'e-bile' delineates the hostility that circulates freely 'through the entire body of the Internet' (p. 532). Cyberworlds certainly can bring out the worst in people, a situation that reflects the anonymity of online life: to be unidentified, hiding behind an alias, is to be unaccountable. Although there is nothing new about sexual harassment or gendered (or racialised) violence, the specificities of the internet – especially online anonymity – generate novel expressions of hostility.

This chapter has suggested several ways in which power operates, considering how the 'newness' of online life has been shaped by existing modes of power, and how cyberworlds also reproduce their own modes. When e-bile silences speech, it does several things. It works to compromise selfhood, eroding the targets' confidence, self-worth and standing in online communities. E-bile is both constitutive and regulatory, shaping discourse, quietening targets' subjectivity and chilling subsequent self-expression. There is an old irony here, of course: those who shout the loudest, and proclaim their right to freedom of speech – even when it is abusive – are liable to compromise somebody else's rights. Given women and sexual minorities are the most likely to suffer the effects of e-bile, online attacks often reinforce existing social inequalities. In a further twist, the targets of online abuse may engage in 'digilantism' or the 'digital pillory' (Hess and Waller, 2014), individually or collectively shaming those who use the internet to threaten them (Vitis and Gilmour, 2016). Sometimes digilantes attack the original perpetrator 'via methods that are similar – or worse – than those being objected to in the first instance' (Jane, 2016, p. 290). Any attempt to regulate online behaviour generates its own ironies and conundrums.

Young people's search for sexual information offers another example of the ways power frameworks overlap. In some jurisdictions, governments and organisations restrict what kind of access is possible, and everywhere the architecture of the web – including the ways search engines work – imposes limits as well as generating new possibilities. Young information seekers must navigate the various kinds of regulatory power in order to obtain the information they are seeking, and negotiate the discourses they find in order to constitute themselves as sexually knowledgeable subjects. In this example, like that of e-bile, regulation continually loops back into questions of knowledge and subjectivity.

The intersections between forms of power are seemingly endless. To give one final example, Lillie suggests gay and lesbian pornographies resist and possibly even challenge heteronormative power, a challenge inherent in their expression of gay and lesbian pride in a heterosexist world. As an important resource for young people learning about their own sexuality, online gay and lesbian erotica produces 'specific sexualities, desires and modes of pleasure' (Lillie, 2004, p. 52). On the other hand, some gay male chat room users locate themselves alongside a dominant masculinity by bragging about their sexual prowess. They reproduce a key theme in one respect, even as they challenge the inevitability of heterosexuality itself (Campbell, 2004, p. 64). In settings like these, subordinate and dominant strands are caught up in a reflexive relationship.

All of these examples hint at the complexity of internet relations, and the modes of power that lie at the heart of them. Our own social and sexual entanglements reflect and refract broader social patterns, patterns that change over time and across locations and are constantly influenced by technology's relentless advance. While the internet may not displace offline identities, inequalities and varied modes of regulation, it does open up new spaces through which power and resistance – including digilantism – can circulate. In the process, cyberworlds promise to transform our lives and our societies in important ways (Zhao, 2006, p. 459). The particularities of these processes require constant attention. Does the internet allow a more fluid and transformative sexuality than we knew before? Does it impose new demands on us? Does it alter the ways we behave towards one another? Does it offer a liberation of sorts, or enforce new forms of obedience? In order to answer these kinds of questions, we need to carefully about the shifting relationships between power and sexuality.

Debates about online sexuality have a broader applicability too. Weeks suggests sexuality is a prism that refracts other kinds of social change too: 'as sexuality goes, so goes society, and as society goes, so goes sexuality' (Weeks, 2016, p. 77). Online sexual harassment tells of other forms of abuse, state regulation spans a range of concerns that both include and move beyond the sexual, and internet-based discourses build subjectivities across the spectrum of identity. As we chart the complexities of sexual power in online settings we find ourselves considering technology's impact on modern life in a whole range of ways.

References

Adam, A. (2002) 'Cyberstalking and internet pornography: gender and the gaze', *Ethics and Information Technology*, 4(2), pp. 133–142.

Albury, K. (2009) 'Reading porn reparatively', *Sexualities*, 12(5), pp. 647–653.

Barak, A. (2005) 'Sexual harassment on the internet', *Social Science Computer Review*, 23(1), pp. 77–92.

Berson, I., Berson, M. and Ferron, J. (2002) 'Emerging risks of violence in the digital age: lessons for educators from an online study of adolescent girls in the United States', *Journal of School Violence*, 1(2), pp. 51–71.

Beres, M. (2014) 'Rethinking the concept of consent for anti-sexual violence activism and education', *Feminism and Psychology*, 24(3), pp. 373–389.

Brickell, C. (2009) 'Sexuality and the dimensions of power', *Sexuality and Culture*, 13(2), pp. 57–74.

Brookey, Robert and Cannon, Kristopher (2009) 'Sex lives in second life', *Critical Studies in Media Communication*, 26(2), pp. 145–164.

Bryson, M. (2004) 'When Jill Jacks in: queer women on the net', *Feminist Media Studies*, 4, pp. 239–254.

Cameron-Lewis, V. and Allen, L. (2013) 'Teaching pleasure and danger in sexuality education', *Sexualities*, 13(2), pp. 121–132.

Campbell, J.E. (2004) *Getting it on Online: Cyberspace, Gay Male Sexuality and Embodied Identity*. New York: Harrington Park Press.

Carmody, M. and Ovenden, G. (2013) 'Putting ethical sex into practice: sexual negotiation, gender and citizenship in the lives of young women and men', *Journal of Youth Studies*, 16(6), pp. 792–807.

Crampton, J. (2003) *The Political Mapping of Cyberspace*. Chicago: University of Chicago Press.

Danaher, G., Schirato, T. and Webb, J. (2000) *Understanding Foucault*. St. Leonards, N.S.W., Australia: Allen & Unwin.

Deibert, R. and Villeneuve, N. (2004) 'Firewalls and power: an overview of global state censorship of the internet', in Klang, M. and Murray, A. (eds) *Human Rights in the Digital Age*. London: Routledge-Cavendish.

Foucault, M. (1980) *Power/Knowledge*, Colin Gordon (ed.). New York: Pantheon.

Foucault, M. (1991) 'Governmentality', in Burchell, G., Gordon, C. and Miller, P. (eds) *The Foucault Effect: Studies in Governmentality*. Chicago: University of Chicago Press, pp. 87–104.

Foucault M. (1995 [1977]) *Discipline and Punish*. New York: Vintage.

Gold, J., Pedrana, A., Sacks-Davis, R., Hellard, M., Chang, S., Howard, S., Keogh, L., Hocking, J. and Stoove, M. (2011) 'A systematic examination of the use of online social networking sites for sexual health promotion', *BMC Public Health*, 11, online at http://bmcpublichealth.biomedcentral.com/articles/10.1186/1471-2458-11-583

Hess, K. and Waller, L. (2014) 'The digital pillory: media shaming of "ordinary" people for minor crimes', *Continuum*, 28(1), pp. 101–111.

Jane, E. (2014) '"Your a ugly, whorish, slut"', *Feminist Media Studies*, 14(4), pp. 531–546.

Jane, E. (2016) 'Online misogyny and feminist digilantism', *Continuum*, 30(3), pp. 284–297.

Kanuga, M. and Rosenfeld, W. (2004) 'Adolescent sexuality and the internet: the good, the bad and the URL', *Journal of Pediatric and Adolescent Gynecology*, 17(2), pp. 117–124.

Kendall, L. (2000) 'Oh no! I'm a nerd! Hegemonic masculinity on an online forum', *Gender and Society*, 14(2), pp. 256–274.

Knoll, A. (1995/6). 'Any which way but loose: nations regulate the internet', *Tulane Journal of International and Comparative Law*, 4, pp. 275–302.

Laughlin, G. (2002/3) 'Sex, lies and library cards: the First Amendment implications of the use of software filters to control access to internet pornography in public libraries', *Drake Law Review*, 51, pp. 213–282.

Lillie, J. (2004) 'Cyberporn, sexuality, and the net apparatus', *Convergence*, 10(1), pp. 43–65.

McCormick, N. and Leonard, J. (2004) 'Gender and sexuality in the cyberspace frontier', in Waskul, D. (ed.) *Net.SeXXX: Readings on Sex, Pornography, and the Internet*. New York: Peter Lang.

MacKinnon, C. (1995) 'Vindication and resistance: a response to the Carnegie Mellon study of pornography in cyberspace', *Georgetown Law Journal*, 83(5), pp. 1959–67.

Mayer-Schönberger, V. (2002/3) 'The shape of governance: analyzing the world of internet regulation', *Virginia Journal of International Law* 43(3), pp. 605–673.

Measor, Lynda (2004) 'Young people's views of sex education: gender, information and knowledge', *Sex Education*, 4(2), pp. 153–166.

Miller-Young, M. (2010) 'Putting hypersexuality to work: black women and illicit eroticism in pornography', *Sexualities*, 13(2), pp. 219–235.

Mishna, F., Cook, C., Gadalla, T., Daciuk, J. and Solomon, S. (2010) 'Cyber bullying behaviors among middle and high school students', *American Journal of Orthopsychiatry*, 80(3), pp. 362–374.

Nyboe, L. (2004) '"You said I was not a man": performing gender and sexuality on the internet', *Convergence*, 10(2), pp. 62–80.

Oksanen, A., Hawdon, J., Holkeri, E., Näsi, M. and Räsänen, P. (2014) 'Exposure to online hate among young social media users', in Warehime, N. (ed.), *Soul of Society: A Focus on the Lives of Children and Youth*, Bingley, Emerald, pp. 253–273.

Palfrey, J. (2010) 'Four phases of internet regulation', *Social Research*, 77(3), pp. 981–996.

Patchin, J. and Hinduja, S. (2006) 'Bullies move beyond the schoolyard: a preliminary look at cyberbullying', *Youth Violence and Juvenile Justice*, 4(2), pp. 148–169.

Philips, F. and Morrissey, G. (2004) 'Cyberstalking and cyberpredators: a threat to safe sexuality on the internet', *Convergence*, 10(1), pp. 66–79.

Plummer, K. (2015) *Cosmopolitan Sexualities: Hope and the Humanist Imagination*. Cambridge: Polity.

Potter, Claire (2016) 'Not safe for work: why feminist pornography matters', *Dissent*, 63(2), pp. 104–114.

Powell, A. (2010) 'Configuring consent: emerging technologies, unauthorised sexual images and sexual assault', *Australian and New Zealand Journal of Criminology*, 43(1), pp. 76–90.

Race, K. (2015) '"Party and play": online hook-up devices and the emergence of PHP practices among gay men', *Sexualities*, 18(3), pp. 253–275.

Ramzy, A. (2016) 'Blog posts lead to jail term', *New York Times*, 24 March 2016, p. A9.

Ray, A. (2007) *Naked on the Internet: Hookups, Downloads and Cashing in on Internet Sexploration*. Emeryville, CA: Seal.

Ryan, A. (2005) 'From dangerous sexualities to risky sex: regulating sexuality in the name of public health', in Hawkes, G. and Scott, G. (eds) *Perspectives in Human Sexuality*. Melbourne: Oxford.

Selkie, E., Benson, M. and Moreno, M. (2011) 'Adolescents' views regarding uses of social networking websites and text messaging for adolescent sexual health education', *American Journal of Health Education*, 42(4), pp. 205–212.

Shariff, S. (2005) 'Cyber-dilemmas in the new millenium: school obligations to provide student safety in a virtual school environment', *McGill Journal of Education*, 40(3), pp. 467–487.

Stokes, C. (2007) 'Representin' in cyberspace: sexual scripts, self definition and hip hop culture in black adolescent girls' homepages', *Culture, Health and Sexuality*, 9(2), pp. 169–184.

Svensson, J. (2015) 'Participation as a pastime: political discussion in a queer community online', *Javnost: The Public*, 22(3), pp. 283–297.

van Zoonen, L. (2002) 'Gendering the internet: claims, controversies and cultures', *European Journal of Communication*, 17(1), pp. 5–23.

Vannini, P. (2004) '*Cosi Fan Tutti:* Foucault, Goffman, and the pornographic synopticon', in Waskul, D. (ed.) *Net.SeXXX: Readings on Sex, Pornography, and the Internet*. New York: Peter Lang.

Vitis, L. and Gilmour, F. (2016) 'Dick pics on blast: a woman's resistance to online sexual harassment using humour, art and Instagram', *Crime, Media, Culture*, online first, doi: 10.1177/1741659016652445.

Waskul, D. (2015) 'Technosexuality: the sexual pragmatists of the technological age', in Weinberg, T. and Newmahr, S. (eds), *Selves, Symbols, and Sexualities*, Thousand Oaks: Sage, pp. 89–108.

Waskul, D. (2004) 'Sex and the internet: old thrills in a new world; new thrills in an old world', in Waskul D. (ed.) *Net.SeXXX: Readings on Sex, Pornography, and the Internet*. New York: Peter Lang.

Weeks, J. (2016) *What is Sexual History?* Cambridge: Polity.

Willard, N. (2002) 'Filtering software: the religious connection', available online at www.csriu.org/onlinedocs/documents/religious2.html

Zhao, S. (2006) 'The internet and the transformation of the reality of everyday life: toward a new analytic stance in sociology', *Sociological Inquiry*, 76(4), pp. 458–474.

Zhao, S., Grasmuck, S. and Martin, J. (2008) 'Identity construction on Facebook: digital empowerment in anchored relationships', *Computers in Human Behavior*, 24(5), pp. 1816–1836.

Part II
Sexual violence, abuse, and exploitation

3 Gendered cyberhate, victim-blaming, and why the internet is more like driving a car on a road than being naked in the snow

Emma A. Jane

A (commuter) commutation test

Imagine you are driving to work on a road that is relatively new but is one you have taken many times before. You pull up at a set of lights and a man wearing a balaclava opens the driver's side door and points what looks like a gun at your head. He tells you to get out. Scared, you fumble, and he hits you across the face. Your mouth is dry, your heart pounds, and the welts on your face burn as he speeds off. You call the emergency services number but the operator who answers sounds vague.

'Maybe try a local police station?' he says and the line drops out. When you eventually flag a cab and get to a police station, you can't believe what you hear. The officer tasked with taking your statement glazes over the moment you begin giving details.

'Sorry,' he says again, giving one of his colleagues a sideways glance. 'You were driving a *what*? On, what did you call it ...' he looks down at his notepad, 'a *road*?' You break it down for him one more time but he's stopped taking notes. After you finish, you ask what will happen next. He shrugs. 'To be completely honest, probably not much,' he says. 'I don't even know if there are any laws covering this sort of thing. There's one about paths and horse-drawn carts, but it's hard to see how that might apply. Also, this "offender" you say you saw? Given you didn't get a look at his face or photo ID, it's going to be *really* hard for us to work out who he is. And you say the car's vanished, too! How on earth can we be expected to investigate something we can't even see anymore? Maybe you just imagined the gun. Or maybe it was a fake gun never intended for use.'

You point out the very real cuts and bruises on your face, and he laughs and says they don't look so bad. Certainly he's witnessed much worse at non-road crime scenes. The police officer sees your face fall and gives you a pat on the shoulder.

'Don't worry, love,' he says. 'All you need to do is take a little break from all these new-fangled "cars" and stay well away from all those high-tech "roads". In fact, maybe it's best not to leave your house at all for a while. Just to be on the safe side.'

Stunned and angry, you explain that you have to use cars and roads to do your job. You also point out that leaving your house is fairly important for, among other things, having an actual life. The officer's tone changes.

'Listen, lady,' he says. 'I know you modern girls get up to all sorts of crazy things in all sorts of crazy places, but you really do need to start taking some responsibility for what happened – if, indeed, anything really happened at all.'

The next day you talk to a journalist who writes an article you hope will help. Instead it makes everything worse. Media commentators write columns saying you're overreacting and being hysterical, that everyone *knows* the guns carjackers use are *joke* guns. Some agree with the police officer's view that you should have considered the risks involved when you first decided to drive. They question the route you were taking to work and say there are much safer roads (even though these would have quadrupled your commute time). One man publishes a photo of the type of vehicle you were driving and says you were just asking to be carjacked because it was so red and sporty. Someone else accuses you of fabricating the whole thing as part of an elaborate 'false flag' operation designed to discredit innocent male road users. Others attack you for impinging on the rights of carjackers to jack cars freely, saying it's about time the world heard *their* side of the story. The hashtag #notallcarjackers starts trending on Twitter.

Then the abuse really hits home. Your detractors call your employers and tell them you should be sacked because you don't have the requisite credentials for your job. They sign you up at psychiatric clinics. Then they discover where you live and make sure you know they know by leaving abusive notes in your mailbox. You're considering leaving your job and moving house when one of the highest ranking police officers in the country weighs in.

'People have to grow up and be realistic about the high risks involved in venturing out on a road in a car,' he tells a parliamentary inquiry into whether or not new laws are required for road safety. 'If you go out in the snow without clothes on you'll catch a cold. If you go on to the road in nothing but a sporty car, then you have to expect a carjacking or worse.'

Believe it or not

As difficult as it may be to believe, the fictional account above accurately captures many aspects of the non-fictional gendered cyberhate experience. Even the 'grow up' quote is drawn, almost word for word, from the testimony of one of the highest ranking police officers in Australia (Shane Connelly as cited in '"Grow up" and stop taking naked photos of yourself, police tell revenge porn inquiry' 2016). In this chapter, I show that – like the carjacking target – large numbers of women are being attacked via the internet and on social media platforms simply for doing their jobs or while going about their everyday lives. These attacks are often extremely brutal and would be regarded as entirely unacceptable or criminal if they occurred in offline contexts. Yet police officers, policy makers, and platform managers in many nations are failing to act. Instead women are being told – either directly or indirectly – that they are to blame for being assaulted and can solve the problem by taking 'a little break' from the internet or making significant changes to the way they engage online. Such victim-blaming is monumentally unjust in that women are being pressured to withdraw – either wholly or partially – from a domain that has become an essential part of contemporary citizenship. Further, it elides the presence and accountability of male perpetrators, and enables continued regulatory non-performance by shifting the responsibility for solving the issue from the public to the private sphere, and from institutions to individuals.

In this chapter, I use a combination of anecdotal and empirical data to demonstrate the nature, pervasiveness, and consequences of contemporary gendered cyberhate. I begin by providing an overview of empirical prevalence data to show that cyber violence against women and girls (cyber VAWG) is not rare or occurring only in the fringes of the cybersphere, but has become part of the everyday internet experience for many female internet users. I then provide details on various manifestations of gendered cyberhate, including revenge porn, doxing, sextortion, cyberstalking, and rape video blackmail. I address the ramifications of gendered cyberhate for individual women as well as for broader ideals such as digital citizenship, and equity of access and opportunity online.

As I will show, the discursive victim-blaming and perpetrator-exculpation around gendered cyberhate is both prevalent and insidious in that it tends to circulate – unquestioned – as 'common sense'. In situations like this, the deployment of a commutation test can be useful. Commutation tests have their origins in semiotics and involve thought experiments in which one element of a text or idea is replaced with another that is different but similar enough to serve as a sort of litmus test for the assumptions and double standards that may be embedded in the contextual surrounds. In European structural linguistics, such tests are conducted in a rigid and quasi-scientific manner. They have, however, been used more loosely by scholars working in cultural, media, and film studies in order to make clear that which is 'too obvious to see' by identifying the 'invisible discourses' that provide the scaffolding for dominant belief systems (McKee 2003, pp. 107, 106). This is my rationale for beginning the chapter the way I have. By sketching a typical gendered cyberhate assault but switching the online attack component for an offline variation, I hope to demonstrate that the institutional and community responses deemed reasonable and intelligible in response to gendered cyberhate seem bizarre and unjust when applied to a different but similar context. These themes will be explored at greater length when I revisit the carjacking analogy later in the chapter.

Data for this research is drawn from two, ongoing projects I am conducting into the history, manifestations, nature, prevalence, aetiology, and impact of gendered cyberhate. While these two projects formally commenced in 2011 and 2015 respectively,[1] I have been archiving and analysing examples of misogyny online since 1998. My methods are mixed and my hermeneutic is interdisciplinary. I have assembled my archives using approaches from internet historiography, and have analysed these using textual analysis. This chapter is also informed by the preliminary findings from qualitative interviews I have conducted with 52

Australian women who have experienced hostility or rape threats online.[2] Theoretically, I work across feminist and gender theory, legal theory, philosophy, literary studies, and cultural and media studies.

A limitation of this chapter is its focus on the gendered dimensions of cyberhate as opposed to those aspects of online hostility which are homophobic, transphobic, racist, culturally intolerant, and so on. While I acknowledge the political intersectionality of gender with other social identities, examining these aspects of cyberhate are beyond the parameters of my current research. Further, while this chapter does include some international statistics and case studies, its qualitative dimensions are almost entirely Anglophone. Another potential limitation is that I make a general case for increased regulation and intervention without furnishing specific details. This, however, is a deliberate move in acknowledgement not only of this book's international focus, but of the idiosyncratic nature of various jurisdictions. Expert input at the local level is what is required in this regard.

What are we seeing here?

Investigating and analysing gendered cyberhate is complicated by variations in the terms and definitions deployed by researchers working in the field. The legal scholar Danielle Keats Citron uses 'cyber harassment' to describe 'threats of violence, privacy invasions, reputation-harming lies, calls for strangers to physically harm victims, and technological attacks' (2014, p. 3). Others use terms such as 'technology violence' (Ostini and Hopkins 2015), 'technology-facilitated sexual violence' (Henry and Powell 2015), 'gendertrolling' (Mantilla 2015), and 'cyber VAWG' (United Nations 2015). In this chapter I will be using the terms 'gendered cyberhate', 'gendered e-bile', and 'cyber VAWG' interchangeably to refer to discourse and acts that are directed at women or girls; that involve abuse, threats, and/or sexually violent rhetoric; and that involve the internet, social media platforms, or communications technology such as mobile phones (although may also have offline dimensions). For the most part, I use the term 'target' rather than 'victim' in recognition of research suggesting that academic terminology around sexual assault *matters* in terms of facilitating women's empowerment and resistance (Hockett and Saucier 2015, p. 10). I do, however, use the expression 'victim-blaming' for idiomatic reasons (that is, because 'victim-blaming' has cultural and political connotations that 'target-blaming' does not).

Before moving on from nomenclature and definitions, I wish to note three terms which should be approached with caution when discussing gendered cyberhate. These are: 'cyberbullying', 'flaming', and 'trolling'. With regard to 'cyberbullying', it is true that many gendered attacks online *are* types of bullying in that they involve individuals wishing 'to inflict harm on their targets' by executing 'a series of calculated behaviors to cause them distress' (Tokunaga 2010, p. 278). That said, the vast majority of cyberbullying research refers to studies of school students (ibid.), and journalists also use this term primarily to refer to youth populations. Pace Robin M. Kowalski and Gary W. Giumetti's argument that traditional definitions of cyberbullying apply equally well to all age groups (see Chapter 9 in this book), my case is that, to avoid confusion, the term is best restricted to refer to bullying scenes in school and youth settings.

'Flaming', meanwhile, is an antiquated expression used to refer to exchanges on the internet which – while seemingly hostile – have tended to involve extremely tame language by contemporary standards. In the late 1990s, for instance, researchers classified 'you obviously don't know crap about skiing' as a flame so profane it seemed to represent 'a state beyond antagonism' (Thompsen and Foulger 1996, pp. 243, 228). Compare this with the following example of gendered cyberhate – one of countless and near-identical messages received by the feminist blogger Sady Doyle:

> *GAG GAG GLUCK* You have discovered the only vocables[3] worth hearing from Sady's cock-stuffed maw ... die tr*nny whore ... [slut walk] is a parade for people who suffer from Histrionic Personality Disorder aka Attention Whores ... I know where you live, r#tard ... why don't you do the world a favour and jump off a bridge ... Feminazi
>
> (As cited in Doyle, 2011a, emphases in original)

Such discourse clearly belongs in a different category than the low level (and non-gendered) rudeness of a message such as 'you obviously don't know crap'.

While 'trolling' is often used as a catch-all for the full spectrum of antagonistic behaviour online, the researcher Whitney Phillips argues that this term should only be deployed to refer to subcultures located in and around sites such as 4chan's /b/board (2015a, 2015b). Phillips' argument – and it is one shared by other scholars (for a literature review of this work see Jane 2015) – is that the 'highly stylized' deployment of explicitly sexist and racist language, memes,[4] and raids[5] common in subcultural trolling communities are markedly different from the violently misogynistic attacks on women that occurred, for example, during GamerGate (Phillips 2015b). ('GamerGate' is the colloquial term given to the vicious and quasi-coordinated attacks on women perpetrated by predominantly male video gamers from August 2014 onwards.) While Phillips makes many persuasive points, her approach relies heavily on the putative motivations or subcultural affiliations of online antagonists, arguably at the expense of considerations of the nature and impact of their actions. As such, my preference is to use the term 'troll' in line with early definitions; that is, to refer to people who disrupt online conversations by feigning *naïveté* or making off-topic or deliberately provocative comments. As such, while the term 'trolling' could be used to refer to very mild hostility directed at women online, for the most part it does not adequately capture the sexually explicit rhetoric, stark misogyny, or violence of contemporary gendered cyberhate.

Prevalence and manifestations

While hostile and hateful speech has always circulated on the internet, there is good evidence that the gendered dimensions, rhetorical noxiousness, directly threatening nature, and prevalence of such discourse increased over the first decade of the twenty-first century, spiked around 2010 and 2011, and has remained at very high levels since GamerGate in 2014 (Jane 2017a, pp. 16–42). Figures compiled by the UN show that 73 per cent of women and girls have been exposed to or have experienced some form of online violence; that women are 27 times more likely to be abused online than men; that 61 per cent of online harassers are male; and that women aged between 18 and 24 are at heightened risk (2015, pp. 2, 15). A Pew Research Center study shows that while men are more likely to be subjected to less severe harassment, such as name-calling and embarrassment (an 'annoyance so common that those who see or experience it say they often ignore it'), young women are particularly vulnerable to more severe kinds of cyber abuse such as being the target of physical threats, harassment over a sustained period of time, stalking, and sexual harassment (Duggan 2014). Not surprisingly, women are more likely than men to find their experience with online harassment extremely or very upsetting (ibid.). Further:

- between 60 and 70 per cent of US cyberstalking targets are female (Citron 2014, p. 13);
- internet accounts with feminine usernames incur an average of 100 sexually explicit or threatening messages a day for every four received by users with masculine names (ibid., p. 14); and
- a study of multiplayer online gamers found 70 per cent of women playing as male characters to avoid sexual harassment (ibid., p. 18).

Gendered cyberhate can be contextualised within a broader 'pandemic' of gendered violence (as per data showing that 35 per cent of women worldwide have experienced either physical and/or sexual intimate partner violence or sexual violence by a non-partner at some point in their lives (UN 2015, p. 2; UN Women 2016)). It manifests in a wide variety of practices which can be situated along various continua of violence, harm, and illegality depending on the context. With regard to law, this might range from 'annoying but legal' at one end of the continuum to 'unambiguously criminal' at the other. The bulk of cases fall somewhere in the middle, and usually have a legally liminal status. An example from the mildest end might involve a men's rights activist who clogs the Twitter feed of a high-profile feminist with messages feigning ignorance about feminist basics and/or asking 'concerned' questions about feminist issues in bad faith. A real-life case study which sits at the most extreme end is that of Jebidiah Stipe, a 28-year-old American former Marine who impersonated his former female partner on the internet site Craigslist and published a photo of her alongside text saying she wanted to play out a rape fantasy and was seeking 'a real aggressive man with no concern for women' (Black 2010; Citron 2014,

p. 5). More than 160 people responded to the ad, including a man who – after Stipe divulged his ex-partner's address – arrived at the woman's home, forced his way inside, bound and blindfolded her, and raped her at gunpoint (ibid., pp. 5–6, Black 2010). Both Stipe and the rapist were subsequently jailed for 60 years to life in prison (Neary 2010).

The following list of common manifestations of gendered e-bile is not exhaustive, nor does it describe practices which only ever involve female targets. Attacks on women frequently occur on multiple occasions and involve a multitude of assailants, channels, and tactics. My aim in sub-dividing gendered cyberhate in the following way is to provide a rough, '101' guide for newcomers to the topic, rather than to provide a comprehensive taxonomy.

Abuse, harassment, and threats

Much gendered cyberhate involves text-based harassment: via social networking sites or apps such as Twitter and Facebook; in the 'below-the-line' comment sections on news articles and blogs; on dating web sites and apps; via personal email; and/or which occurs during online gaming. Signal characteristics of this discourse include profanity, violent and sexualised rhetoric, explicit, *ad hominem* invective, and plausible threats. Aspersions are cast on women's intelligence, mental health, and sexual attractiveness. The 'ugly, fat, and slutty' trifecta is hurled with monotonous regularity. Targets are often appraised not only in terms of their 'fuckability' but also their 'rapeability'. Incitement to suicide is common, as are *en masse* attacks – known colloquially as 'dog piles'. The latter may coalesce organically, be incited by a single high profile figure, or be organised at a grassroots level by various online groups and communities (Jane 2017a, pp. 35, 60–61). Such attacks may include circulating lies about targets. During a 2007 mob attack on the tech designer Kathy Sierra, for example, people distributed false statements about her being a former sex worker and battered wife (Sandoval 2013). GamerGate, meanwhile, began when a jilted ex-partner made the baseless claim that his former girlfriend, Zoë Quinn, had slept with a journalist in order to secure a positive review of a game she had designed (Jane 2017a, pp. 29–32).

Some gendered cyberhate is expressed in the form of hostile wishful thinking – for example 'I hope you get raped with a chainsaw' (cited in Doyle 2011b). There is evidence to suggest that perpetrators are aware such sentence constructions might offer legal loopholes. For example, a Twitter user who received a police warning in 2016 for issuing direct death threats to the Australian media personality Waleed Aly and his wife (whom he called a 'hijabi scumfuk floozie'), henceforth began issuing tweets such as, 'I hope #WaleedAly ACCI-DENTLY cuts his throat while shaving' (A. Lattouf, personal communication, 27 May 2016, emphasis in original). Direct threats, however, are still common. For example, when the British Labour MP Stella Creasy spoke in support of a student feminist activist who had campaigned to have more women on British bank notes, Creasy received a tweet reading, 'YOU BETTER WATCH YOUR

BACK ... IM GONNA RAPE YOUR ASS AT 8PM AND PUT THE VIDEO ALL OVER THE INTERNET' (as cited in Jane 2014b, p. 563). Threats are also routinely made against women's online supporters, family members, friends, and pets.

Abuse and harassment can be image- as well as text-based. Photo manipulation, for example, is often used to place an image of a target into a scene involving sex and/or violence. The aforementioned attack on Sierra included doctored photos depicting her being choked by undergarments, and with nooses next to her head (Sandoval 2013). The feminist cultural critic Anita Sarkeesian, meanwhile, has received countless images of men ejaculating onto her photo (Sarkeesian 2015). One man went so far as to create an online game called 'Beat Up Anita Sarkeesian' in which players could 'punch this bitch in the face' until Sarkeesian's face became bloody and battered (as cited in Sarkeesian 2012). It has also become common practice for men to send unsolicited and unwanted photos of their genitals – aka 'dick pics'.

Doxing, swatting, Wikipedia vandalism, and Google bombing

'Doxing' refers to the publishing of personally identifying information to either explicitly or implicitly incite internet antagonists to hunt targets offline. During GamerGate, for instance, the Boston game developer, Brianna Wu, watched a mass of her personal details suddenly appear online during an attack. Within minutes someone tweeted at her saying, 'I've got a K-bar[6] and I'm coming to your house so I can shove it up your ugly feminist cunt' (as cited in Stuart 2014). During the early stages of GamerGate in 2014, other women associated with gaming, such as Sarkeesian and Quinn, also fled their homes after their addresses and other personal details were published online.

'Swatting' involves tricking police dispatchers into sending Special Weapons and Tactics (SWAT) teams to raid targets' houses. In 2015, for instance, 20 police officers arrived at the former Portland home of the digital artist and video game creator Grace Lynn after receiving a call that hostages were being held inside the house. Lynn, who found a thread on the 8chan web site planning the attack, believes she was targeted because she had previously been aligned with the GamerGate campaign but had changed her allegiances because of the movement's escalating misogyny (Parks 2015).

'Wikipedia vandalism' refers to malicious edits made to a target's Wikipedia page. For example, a 2012 mob attack against Sarkeesian included the posting of pornography on her Wikipedia page and the alteration of the text to read that she was a 'hooker' who held 'the world record for maximum amount of sexual toys in the posterior' (as cited in Greenhouse 2013). During GamerGate in 2014, Quinn's Wikipedia page was edited to read: 'Died: soon.' When this was deleted, a new entry appeared reading: 'Died: October 13, 2014' – the date of her next scheduled public appearance (as cited in Jason 2015).

'Google bombing' describes the manipulation of the Google search engine so that web users searching for a specific term are directed to content determined

Gendered cyberhate and victim-blaming 69

by the bombers. For example, during the aforementioned attacks on Sarkeesian, the first result returned by the Google search engine when her name was entered was, 'Anita Sarkeesian is a feminist video blogger and cunt' (as cited in Plunkett 2012).

Revenge pornography, rape video blackmail, and sextortion

Revenge porn involves the public circulation of sexually explicit material, usually of a former female partner, without the consent of the pictured subject. In many cases, these are photos or videos that were shared consensually during a relationship, then circulated by the former male partner – sometimes on web sites expressly designed for this purpose – after a break-up. The term has also been used more generally to refer to images obtained without consent, such as via hidden web cams. Revenge porn often occurs in the context of domestic violence scenarios in that men in possession of intimate footage of a former or current partner use these to pressure a woman into acquiescing to their demands. As with the aforementioned example involving Stipe, the posting of such material is frequently accompanied by doxing, presumably in an attempt to inflict maximum damage. While the term 'revenge porn' implies that perpetrators are motived solely or primarily by the desire for revenge, sexual and intimate images are used to coerce, threaten, harass, and abuse victims for a range of reasons. Catherine Buni and Soraya Chemaly note that, in an increasing number of nations, rapists are filming sexual assaults and using the footage to blackmail girls and women out of reporting the crimes (2014). They cite the case of a 16-year-old girl in India whose gang rape was recorded on a mobile phone and who was told the film would be uploaded onto the internet if she told her family or the police (ibid.).

Another emerging practice, 'sextortion', involves blackmailing targets – often for the purposes of extorting them to perform sexual acts online. In May 2016, for instance, the Brookings Institution published its analysis of 78 publicly available sextortion cases from 52 jurisdictions, 29 states or territories, and 4 nations, involving up to 6,500 targets (Wittes *et al.* 2016). Of the 78 specific cases under analysis, 69 involved minors (more than three quarters of them female), all the perpetrators were male, and nearly all the adult victims were female (ibid.). The original material used for blackmail was obtained via a range of techniques including hacking victims' computers and webcams, installing malware on their devices, or impersonating boyfriends (ibid.).

Cyberstalking

Cyberstalking has many parallels with offline versions of the offence. It often involves a single perpetrator and target, and may be associated with domestic violence and/or the end of an intimate relationship. Cyberstalking practices include: making multiple and unwanted attempts to contact a target via mobile phone, email, and social media; installing spyware on a target's computer; and/ or hacking into the target's email or social media account. The latter may be to gain information about the target's private life and/or to cause disruption by sending abusive or misleading messages to the target's family and friends, by cancelling professional engagements, and so on. Cyberstalkers may also place a Global Positioning System (GPS) tracker on targets' cars, or install video cameras in and around their homes, thus enabling them to track targets' movements and to confront them at unexpected locations.

Identity theft and impersonation

Identity theft and impersonation online are often associated with criminal attempts at financial gain. In the context of gendered cyberhate, however, they are more likely to be used for the purposes of stalking, reputational attack, and/or inciting abuse against a target. Caitlin Roper, an activist with the morally conservative Australian campaign group Collective Shout, has twice been impersonated on Twitter. On the first occasion, a man established an account using her name and photo, as well as a Twitter user name that was extremely similar to her genuine one (it used an additional underscore, that is, 'Caitlin__Roper', as opposed to 'Caitlin_Roper'). He then began tweeting to men – as Roper – offering to perform various sex acts and saying she loved to be raped (C. Roper, personal communication, 3 June 2015).

Ramifications

The profound suffering that can be experienced by the targets of gendered cyberhate is well documented (see Citron 2014; Mantilla 2015; Jane 2017a). The coercive force of gendered cyberhate is causing women significant emotional, social, financial, professional, and political harm. It is constraining their ability to find jobs, market themselves, network, engage politically, socialise, and partake freely in the sorts of self-expression, self-representation, creativity, interactivity, and collaborative enterprises celebrated as key benefits of the web 2.0[7] era (see Jane 2016, 2017a, 2017b). Harassment and threats at the most extreme end of the spectrum can cause women to experience debilitating fear, trauma, and life disruption. Some women have developed mental health problems or experienced breakdowns (Jane 2017a, pp. 61–64). During the height of the attack against her – a time in which she was receiving around 50 abusive and threatening messages per hour – Criado-Perez says:

> The immediate impact was that I couldn't eat or sleep. I lost half a stone in two days. I was just on an emotional edge all the time. I cried a lot. I screamed a lot. I don't know if I had a kind of breakdown. I was unable to function, unable to have normal interactions.
>
> (As cited in Day 2013)

Such accounts comport with Nicola Henry and Anastasia Powell's argument that harms in the supposedly 'virtual' world can have real bodily and psychical effects, and 'at least as much impact on a person as traditional harms occurring against the physical body' (2015, p. 765).

Despite the vicious nature and significant harms of gendered cyberhate, police, policy makers, and platform managers in many nations are failing to adequately acknowledge or address the problem. The UN observes that, in 74 per cent of Web Index[8] countries, law enforcement agencies and the courts are failing to take appropriate action in response to cyber VAWG (2015, p. 39). Further, at least one in five female internet users live in countries where harassment and abuse online is extremely unlikely to be punished (ibid.). A 2014 report by the Association for Progressive Communications (APC) identifies multiple policy failures in that, despite increases in violence against women involving information and communications technology (ICT), there has been 'very little corresponding recognition of ICT-related forms of violence against women by states, intergovernmental institutions and other actors responsible for ending violence against women' (p. 4). This empirical data comports with multiple anecdotal accounts from women who report that the standard response from police in many jurisdictions is to suggest they simply take a break from the internet (Jane 2017a, pp. 4, 88–92).

The response of platform operators is similarly problematic and inadequate. Another APC cyber VAWG report comparing the policies of Facebook, YouTube, and Twitter identifies a number of overarching issues including: a reluctance to engage directly with a problem unless it becomes a public relations issue; a lack of transparency around reporting and redress processes; a failure to engage with the perspectives of non-North American/European women; and no public commitment to human rights standards or to the promotion of rights, other than the encouragement of free speech (Nyst 2014, pp. 3–4).

The carjacking revisited

Instead of receiving support and assistance, the female targets of gendered cyberhate are frequently blamed for their online experiences. Indeed, the UN describes the victim-blaming around cyber VAWG as both widespread and destructive, calling for such practices to be 'aggressively ... addressed as a primary issue of concern' (2015, pp. 19, 30). While the most explicitly articulated examples of victim-blaming occur in media commentary, the dynamic is clearly evident in the actions (and lack of actions) of various institutions as described above. This is where we begin to see the parallels between real life practice and the thought experiment which opened this chapter.

As with the fictional carjacking scenario, online attacks often occur while women are engaged in banal – yet essential – activities in places where both passers-by and participants should be able to expect a reasonable degree of personal safety. Yet, as with the carjacking target, front-line respondents to gendered cyberhate (such as police) often possess insufficient knowledge about the domains in which the abuse is unfolding. Many are unsure what, if any, existing laws might be applicable. The difficulties involved in conducting inquiries and identifying perpetrators are used to justify inaction. Questions which should arguably be investigated by law enforcement and then tested in courts of law are returned to the victim to determine: Your perpetrator is anonymous or deleted his account? *You* find and identify him. You're unsure if the man saying he wants to rape you with a combat knife means it? *You* prove threat credibility and malicious intent. You're upset about a Facebook page where men are making rape 'jokes'? It's about time you considered *their* freedom of speech and *their* rights.

While the fictional carjacking account is based on the accounts of many non-fictional women, much of it is drawn from the experiences of Kath Read, an Australian librarian and self-described 'fat activist' whom I interviewed for my research in June 2015. Read has been targeted by a large volume of extremely vitriolic cyberhate since 2009. People have threatened to decapitate her with a chainsaw, and to smash her face in with a hammer if they see her in the street. They have signed her up for multiple appointments with personal trainers, gyms, and bariatric surgeons. They also contacted Read's employer saying she should be sacked and that she was unqualified for her job (a lie). When Read found a note in her mailbox reading, 'Hi fat bitch, I see this is where you live', she sought assistance from police. One officer told her to, 'Get offline and stop being so confident' (as cited in Jane 2017a, p. 90).

Women from other nations report similarly unhelpful responses. The US writer Amanda Hess called police after receiving death threats from a Twitter account that seemed to have been established solely for this purpose. The officer assigned to her case did not know what Twitter was (2014). Wu, who employs a full-time staffer whose sole task is to monitor and log threats against her (Sabin 2015), says she loses at least a day each week 'explaining the Internet' to police (as cited in Jason 2015). Wu has made multiple reports to Twitter, as well as to local law enforcement, the Federal Bureau of Investigation (FBI), and Homeland Security, but says she has yet to receive a satisfactory response (O'Brien 2015). The feminist writer Jessica Valenti – the *Guardian* staffer targeted for the largest number of objectionable readers' comments (Valenti 2016) – was advised by a representative of the FBI to leave her home until the threats blew over, and never to walk outside unaccompanied (as cited in Hess 2014).

Like the protagonist in the carjacking analogy, targets of gendered cyberhate who speak publicly about their experiences are often subjected to even worse abuse from online assailants. Further, media commentators castigate them for: allegedly exaggerating or fabricating their accounts of the abuse and its impacts; failing to realise that what happens online is not 'real'; failing to consider the rights and points of views of male attackers; and promoting oppressive censorship. Specifically, women have been accused: of being 'peculiarly sensitive' and 'Orwellian' (O'Neill 2011); of narcissistically imagining threats and violence where none exist (West 2015); and of 'retreating into a position of squawking victimhood' every time they receive an 'unpleasant message' (O'Doherty 2015). Even some scholars argue that much putatively misogynist discourse online is not meant to persecute women, but is instead intended: to police the purity of certain sub-cultures; to haze newcomers to such communities; and to make in-jokes about political correctness, identity politics, and attention-seeking in online environments (see Jane 2015).

Discourse about gendered cyberhate is often contradictory in that the internet is depicted both as a trivial and easy to opt-out-of diversion (on par with a video game console), *as well as* exotic and inherently extremely dangerous (on par with a potentially deadly natural environment like a remote jungle or the surrounds of an active volcano). An example of this first framing can be observed in the views of the UK actor Steven Berkoff, who says:

> There's a lot of talk about people being abused on Twitter, women being savagely insulted and degraded. I think, why get into that in the first place? If I jump into a garbage bin, I can't complain that I've got rubbish all over me.
>
> (As cited in Cavendish 2013)

An example of the second is the non-fictional version of the 'grow up' quote included at the start of this chapter. It comes from Australia's federal police assistant commissioner Shane Connelly who was addressing a 2016 government inquiry into whether new laws were required to address revenge porn. His exact words were:

> People just have to grow up in terms of what they're taking and loading on to the computer because the risk is so high.... [They say] if you go out in the snow without your clothes on you'll catch a cold – if you go on to the computer without your clothes on, you'll catch a virus.
>
> (As cited in ' "Grow up" and stop taking naked photos of yourself, police tell revenge porn inquiry' 2016)

As with the long and ongoing battle to end the victim-blaming and perpetrator-exculpation that still occurs around offline sexual assault, such framings not only blame women for being abused and attacked online, but position the problem as one that female and potential targets must solve by modifying their behaviour. Advising or coercing women to opt out of or dramatically change their online engagement is a form of digital disenfranchisement. It is at odds with the recognition by an increasing number of nations that equality of access to affordable and effective broadband is vital for nations' economic and social development (The Broadband Commission for Digital Development 2015, p. 8). Victim-blaming also has the effect – at least at the level of discourse and rhetoric – of relieving institutions and regulatory bodies of the burden of devising and enforcing interventions, as well as completely eliding the presence of harmful human agents who could conceivably be held to account for their actions. Such approaches are monumentally unjust. They inflict additional punishment on women who have already suffered, and do nothing to address what is now broadly recognised as a serious and rapidly worsening international problem (UN 2015).

Conclusion

This chapter has offered an overview of the nature and impact of gendered cyberhate, as well as highlighting the victim-blaming and perpetrator-excusing that are occurring in lieu of useful solutions. It has drawn attention to conflicting framings of the cybersphere as being both not 'real' (that is, a virtual domain where it is impossible to inflict or sustain 'real' harm), as well as inherently dangerous – a perilous place where women must expect abuse, harassment, and threats. As such, women are advised to take a multitude of 'safety' precautions including: avoiding commenting on or participating in debates about provocative political topics; taking care not to venture into unknown terrain or into conversations with unknown people; and/or refraining from posting images of themselves that male users might find too attractive (or too unattractive). Ultimately, however, it is often recommended that the safest course of action is for women to partially or completely withdraw from the cybersphere – an option framed as involving no significant reduction in life or work opportunities whatsoever. The dominance of the idea that cyber VAWG is a problem *caused* by – and therefore best *solved* by – its female targets may go part of the way to explaining the combined failure of police, policy makers, and platform operators to intervene in a timely and useful manner. It also chimes with larger, gender-related social violence problems which can be linked to the disproportionate share of political, economic, and social power still held by men (Smith 2016; UN 2015).

When inequity and oppression seem structured into the metaphorical DNA of a society – as is the case with gender – it is easy for certain 'commonsensical' views to be accepted and circulated without interrogation. A commutation test in the form of an account of a carjacking was therefore provided to encourage a critical reappraisal of dominant ideas about responsibility and blame online, as well as to reveal some of the deeply embedded assumptions and double standards underlining such views. There are obvious limits to the usefulness of using roads and cars as an analogy for the cybersphere and its multitude of umbilically attached devices. Yet while this is not a straightforward 'like for like' scenario, there are a number of significant parallels. Both road transport and the internet are new technologies (relative to human history) that have quickly become quotidian yet crucial. As with roads and cars, states will never possess the power to police the behaviour of every individual internet user. Likewise, online domains will never be 100 per cent safe nor will they ever offer absolute equality of access (not everyone will ever have the electronic equivalent of the keys to their very own Lamborghini). It is important, however, to set baseline targets and to continually strive towards achieving as much safety and equality of access as possible. This requires a combination of rules and sanctions devised and enforced by regulatory authorities, alongside reasonable levels of user compliance and commitment to good citizenship.

Given that the latter requires community education and awareness, the language used to talk about and frame social problems is important. This is why the 'being in a car on a road' parallel is helpful, while the 'being naked in the snow' analogy is not. The former acknowledges the banality yet also the necessity of a domain in which users must adhere to a set of ground rules and may be punished for transgressions, whereas the latter frames the cybersphere as an inherently perilous place whose naturally occurring and ambient hazards could never be apprehended and brought before courts of law. While changes in language alone will obviously not be sufficient to solve this large and complex problem, discursive re-framings are potentially helpful in shifting dominant social attitudes and norms. This, in turn, may assist in combatting the systemic, gender-related inequity which contributes to the ongoing and disproportionate levels of violence of all kinds perpetrated against women and girls around the world.

Notes

1 The second of these projects is being funded by the Australian government in the form of a Discovery Early Career Researcher Award (DECRA). This three-year project is called 'Cyberhate: the new digital divide?'.
2 I interviewed these women – aged between 19 to 52 – between 2015 and 2017.
3 I will not be using 'sic' after material cited from the cybersphere in recognition of the colloquialisms which are used so frequently in the domain.
4 Internet memes are images, videos, and catchphrases which are not just 'viral' (in that they are shared many times) but which are constantly being altered by users.
5 In this context a 'raid' is a coordinated attack on a site or individual.
6 My reading of 'K-bar' here is that it is a misspelling of 'ka-bar' – a combat knife.
7 The term 'web 2.0' (following from 'web 1.0') refers to changes in the design and use of the internet which facilitate user-generated content, interactivity, collaboration, and sharing.
8 The World Wide Web Foundation's Web Index covers 86 countries and measures the web's contribution to social, economic, and political progress.

References

Association for Progressive Communications 2014, 'Domestic legal remedies for technology-related violence against women: Review of related studies and literature', May, viewed 28 January 2016, www.genderit.org/sites/default/upload/domestic_legal_remedies_for_technology-related_violence_against_women_review_of_related_studies_and_literature.pdf

Black, C. 2010, 'Ex-Marine Jebidiah James stipe gets 60 years for Craigslist rape plot', CBS News, 29 June, viewed 28 September 2016, www.cbsnews.com/news/ex-marine-jebidiah-james-stipe-gets-60-years-for-craigslist-rape-plot/

Buni, C. and Chemaly, S. 2014, 'The unsafety net: how social media turned against women', The Atlantic, 9 October, viewed 27 May 2016, www.theatlantic.com/technology/archive/2014/10/the-unsafety-net-how-social-media-turned-against-women/381261/

Cavendish, D. 2013, 'Steven Berkoff: Thousands support my views on Twitter, The Telegraph, 12 August, viewed 13 May 2016, www.telegraph.co.uk/culture/theatre/edinburgh-festival/10233683/Steven-Berkoff-Thousands-support-my-views-on-Twitter.html

Citron, D.K. 2014, Hate Crimes in Cyberspace, Harvard University Press, Cambridge and London.

Day, E. 2013, 'Caroline Criado-Perez: "I don't know if I had a kind of breakdown"', *The Guardian*, 8 December, viewed 13 May 2016, www.theguardian.com/society/2013/dec/08/caroline-criado-perez-jane-austen-review-2013

Doyle, S. 2011a, 'On blogging, threats, and silence', *Tiger Beatdown*, 11 October, viewed 10 May 2016, http://tigerbeatdown.com/2011/10/11/on-blogging-threats-and-silence/

Doyle, S. 2011b, 'Why are you in such a bad mood? #MenCallMeThings responds!', *Tiger Beatdown*, 7 November, viewed 27 May 2016, http://tigerbeatdown.com/2011/11/07/why-are-you-in-such-a-bad-mood-mencallmethings-responds/

Duggan, M. 2014, 'Online harassment', *Pew Research Center*, 22 October, viewed 4 January 2016, www.pewinternet.org/2014/10/22/online-harassment/

Greenhouse, E. 2013, 'Twitter's free-speech problem', *The New Yorker*, 1 August, viewed 28 December 2015, www.newyorker.com/online/blogs/elements/2013/08/how-free-should-speech-be-on-twitter.html

'"Grow up" and stop taking naked photos of yourself, police tell revenge porn inquiry' 2016, *The Guardian*, viewed 26 February 2016, www.theguardian.com/australia-news/2016/feb/18/grow-up-and-stop-taking-naked-photos-of-yourself-says-senior-police-officer

Henry, N. and Powell, A. 2015, 'Embodied harms: Gender, shame, and technology-facilitated sexual violence', *Violence Against Women*, vol. 21, no. 6, pp. 758–779.

Hess, A. 2014, 'Why women aren't welcome on the internet', *Pacific Standard*, 6 January, viewed 17 May 2016, www.psmag.com/health-and-behavior/women-arent-welcome-internet-72170

Hockett, J.M. and Saucier, D.A. 2015, 'A systematic literature review of "rape victims" versus "rape survivors": Implications for theory, research, and practice', *Aggression and Violent Behavior*, vol. 25, pp. 1–14.

Jane, E.A. 2014a, '"Your a ugly, whorish, slut": Understanding e-bile', *Feminist Media Studies*, vol. 14, no. 4, pp. 531–546.

Jane, E.A. 2014b, '"Back to the kitchen, cunt": Speaking the unspeakable about online misogyny', *Continuum: Journal of Media & Cultural Studies*, vol. 28, no. 4, pp. 558–570.

Jane, E.A. 2015, 'Flaming? What flaming? The pitfalls and potentials of researching online hostility', *Ethics and Information Technology* vol. 17, no. 1, pp. 65–87.

Jane, E.A. 2016, 'Online misogyny and feminist digilantism', *Continuum: Journal of Media & Cultural Studies*, published online 31 March. doi: 10.1080/10304312.2016.1166560

Jane, E.A. 2017a, *Misogyny Online: A Short (And Brutish) History*. Sage, London.

Jane, E.A. 2017b (in press), 'Feminist digilante responses to a slut-shaming on Facebook', *Social Media + Society*.

Jason, Z. 2015, 'Game of fear', *Boston Magazine*, May, viewed 28 December 2015, www.bostonmagazine.com/news/article/2015/04/28/gamergate/

Mantilla, K. 2015, *Gendertrolling: How Misogyny Went Viral*. Praeger, Santa Barbara, Denver.

McKee, A. 2003, *Textual Analysis: A Beginner's Guide*. London: Sage.

Neary, B. 2010, '2nd man gets 60 years in Wyo. Internet rape case', *Ventura County Star*, 29 June, viewed 7 May 2016, www.vcstar.com/news/2nd-man-gets-60-years-in-wyo-internet-rape-case-ep-368408277-348997991.html

Nyst, C. 2014, 'End violence: Women's rights and safety online', *Association for Progressive Communications* (APC), July, viewed 28 January 2016, www.genderit.org/sites/default/upload/flow-cnyst-summary-formatted.pdf

O'Brien, S.A. 2015, '"This is the year technology hit rock bottom"', *CNN Money*, 28 October, viewed on 28 May 2016, http://money.cnn.com/2015/07/19/technology/brianna-wu-reddit-harassment/

O'Doherty, I. 2015, 'People need to toughen up and treat the Twitter trolls with deserved contempt', *Independent.ie*, 29 December, viewed 27 February 2016, www.independent.ie/opinion/columnists/ian-odoherty/people-need-to-toughen-up-and-treat-the-twitter-trolls-with-deserved-contempt-34320055.html

O'Neill, B. 2011, 'The campaign to "Stamp Out Misogyny Online" echoes Victorian efforts to protect women from coarse language', *The Telegraph*, 7 November, viewed 28 December 2015, http://blogs.telegraph.co.uk/news/brendanoneill2/100115868/the-campaign-to-stamp-out-misogyny-online-echoes-victorian-efforts-to-protect-women-from-coarse-language/

Ostini, J. and Hopkins, S. 2015, 'Online harassment is a form of violence', *The Conversation*, 8 April, viewed 11 January 2016, https://theconversation.com/online-harassment-is-a-form-of-violence-38846

Parks, C. 2015, 'Gamergate: Woman blames online harassers for hoax that sent 20 Portland cops to her former home', *The Oregonian*, 3 January, viewed 28 September 2016, www.oregonlive.com/portland/index.ssf/2015/01/gamergate_woman_says_online_ha.html

Phillips, W. 2015a, *This Is Why We Can't Have Nice Things: Mapping the Relationship Between Online Trolling and Mainstream Culture*. The MIT Press, Cambridge, London.

Phillips, W. 2015b, 'Let's call "trolling" what it really is', *The Kernel*, 10 May, viewed 9 May 2016, http://kernelmag.dailydot.com/issue-sections/staff-editorials/12898/trolling-stem-tech-sexism/

Plunkett, L. 2012, 'Awful things happen when you try to make a video about video game stereotypes', *Kotaku*, 12 June, viewed 28 December 2015, www.kotaku.com/5917623/awful-things-happenwhen-you-try-to-make-a-video-about-video-game-stereotypes

Sabin, S. 2015, 'For some tech feminists, online harassment is a constant', *CNBC*, 19 August, viewed 17 May 2016, www.cnbc.com/2015/08/19/for-some-tech-feminists-online-harassment-is-a-constant.html

Sandoval, G. 2013, 'The end of kindness: Weev and the cult of the angry young man', *The Verge*, 12 September, viewed 28 May 2016, www.theverge.com/2013/9/12/4693710/the-end-of-kindness-weev-and-the-cult-of-the-angry-young-man

Sarkeesian, A. 2012, 'Image based harassment and Visual Misogyny', *Feminist Frequency*, 1 July, viewed 28 December 2015, http://feministfrequency.com/2012/07/01/image-based-harassment-and-visual-misogyny/

Sarkeesian, A. 2015, 'Talking publicly about harassment generates more harassment', *Feminist Frequency*, 29 October, viewed 30 November 2015, http://feministfrequency.com/2015/10/29/talking-publicly-about-harassment-generates-more-harassment/#more-34166

Smith, L. 2016, 'International Women's Day 2016: Ten facts, figures and statistics about women's rights', *International Business Times*, 8 March, viewed 15 April 2016, www.ibtimes.co.uk/international-womens-day-2016-ten-facts-figures-statistics-about-womens-rights-1548083

Stuart, K. 2014, 'Brianna Wu and the human cost of Gamergate: "Every woman I know in the industry is scared"', *The Guardian*, 18 October, viewed 28 December 2015, www.theguardian.com/technology/2014/oct/17/brianna-wu-gamergate-human-cost

The Broadband Commission for Digital Development 2015, 'The state of broadband 2015', United Nations Educational, Scientific and Cultural Organization, September, viewed on 28 January 2016, www.broadbandcommission.org/documents/reports/bb-annualreport2015.pdf

Thompsen, P.A. and Foulger, D.A. 1996, 'Effects of pictographs and quoting on flaming in electronic mail', *Computers in Human Behavior* vol. 12, no. 2, pp. 225–243.

Tokunaga, R.S. 2010, 'Following you home from school: A critical review and synthesis of research on cyberbullying victimization', *Computers in Human Behavior*, vol. 26, pp. 277–287.

United Nations 2015, 'Cyber violence against women and girls: A world-wide wake-up call', UN Broadband Commission for Digital Development Working Group on Broadband and Gender, September, viewed 7 May 2016, www.unwomen.org/~/media/headquarters/attachments/sections/library/publications/2015/cyber_violence_gender%20report.pdf

UN Women 2016, 'Facts and figures: Ending violence against women', February, viewed 28 May 2016, www.unwomen.org/en/what-we-do/ending-violence-against-women/facts-and-figures

Valenti, J. 2016, 'Insults and rape threats. Writers shouldn't have to deal with this', *The Guardian*, 15 April, viewed 27 May, www.theguardian.com/commentisfree/2016/apr/14/insults-rape-threats-writers-online-harassment

West, P. 2015, 'Stop taking twitter death threats seriously', *Spiked*, 22 April, viewed 8 January 2016, www.spiked-online.com/newsite/article/stop-taking-twitter-death-threats-seriously/16895#.Vo7tgZN97Yp

Wittes, B., Poplin, C., Jurecic, Q. and Spera, C. 2016, 'Sextortion: Cybersecurity, teenagers, and remote sexual assault', *Brookings Institution*, 11 May, viewed 12 May 2016, www.brookings.edu/research/reports2/2016/05/sextortion-wittes-poplin-jurecic-spera

4 Sexting in context

Understanding gendered sexual media practices beyond inherent 'risk' and 'harm'

Amy Shields Dobson

Introduction

This chapter addresses the relatively new set of 'media practices' (Couldry, 2012) that have been described as 'sexting'. Drawing primarily on qualitative research conducted on youth sexting, the chapter aims to: (a) position sexting media practices within a gendered social, cultural, historical, and technological context; and (b) unpack the ways in which the 'risks' and 'harms' of sexting media practices, dominantly understood as inherent to digital sexual image exchange, are socially and culturally determined. Sexting is a recent phenomenon that has sparked much debate and concern about the new affordances of digitally networked devices and media platforms, and the potential for new technologies to contribute to, increase, or intensify bullying, harassment, and sexual crimes. A portmanteau first used widely in news media in the late 2000s, 'sexting' combines the words 'sex' and 'texting'. 'Sexting' potentially refers to a wide range of 'media practices' (Couldry, 2012) involving the production, exchange, and circulation of sexual texts and images via digital networks.

To conceptualise sexting primarily as a 'crime' is to assume that it principally involves non-consensual and/or illegal media practices such as the malicious or unauthorised production and/or distribution of images, or the production and/or distribution of 'pornographic' images of children. The available research, conducted mostly on sexting among teenagers and young adults in the Anglophone West, tends to indicate that this is not the case but rather that, much of the time, sexting media practices occur privately and consensually (that is, they do not come to the attention of those not intended to be involved) between peers and romantically or sexually involved partners (Drouin *et al.*, 2013; Mitchell *et al.*, 2014; Wolak and Finkelhor, 2011). As Hasinoff and Shepard (2014) note, 'Sexting is the latest incarnation of a long history of personal sexual media production, including love letters, diary entries, and Polaroid photos' (2014, p. 2935). They draw attention to the way long-standing social expectations of privacy and consent need to be remembered when it comes to sexting, suggesting that 'the privacy of any of these objects is violable, but most people would consider such a violation unreasonable and unexpected' (p. 2935).

Conceptualising sexting primarily as a crime also assumes, at least to some degree, that inherent harms and risks are involved. Discourses of 'risk' and 'harm' in relation to sexting are currently hegemonic, and are starkly gendered, constructing sexting as media practices that are 'naturally' harmful for girls and women in ways they are not for boys and men. Hegemonic discourses of risk and harm in public health campaigns, news stories, educational interventions, and some research addressing sexting serve to obscure the social construction of gendered sexual double standards, and shift focus from perpetrators to victims of harassment and abuse, as several scholars have argued (Albury and Crawford, 2012; Dobson and Ringrose, 2016; Hasinoff, 2015; Karaian, 2014; Ringrose et al., 2013; Salter et al., 2013). The term 'sexting' itself is perhaps unhelpful because it may relate to issues linked to deviance, crime, and victimhood. I suggest we conceptualise sexting more broadly as part of 'intimate and sexual media production'. However, whether or not we can let go of the term 'sexting', I suggest, it is important to reconceptualise the range of 'media practices' (Couldry, 2012) classified or potentially classified in this way as part of a broader context and 'media ecology' (van Dijck, 2013), and to unpack the constitution of digital, social, and sexual cultures within this media ecology. Flows of power and issues of equality and social justice are larger and more complex than individualised concepts of 'risk', 'harm' and 'victimhood' implied in conceptualising sexting as crime or deviance allow. This point is obscured from view without further unpacking the broader visual media context.

Sexting has now been addressed in scholarly research across a number of disciplines including legal studies, criminology, psychology, health, education, communication, and cultural studies. Perhaps in part as a result of wide interest across both cognate and less cognate disciplines, there has been a lack of consensus about precisely what media practices constitute sexting. I start by outlining the main media practices involved in sexting as it has been researched (mainly quantitatively) to date. Turning to some of the more nuanced qualitative research that has been conducted around sexting, youth, and gendered digital cultures, I go on to suggest that sexting cannot be addressed in isolation from the broader gendered visual culture and digital media ecology. In short, women and girls remain unequally vulnerable to various forms of violence in a visual cultural economy where female body images are disproportionately sexualised and fetishised. And yet, as some scholars have suggested, women, girls, young people whose gender identities, sexual desires, and practices move beyond traditional heterosexual ones, and young people marginalised along other lines such as ethnicity, class, and physical ability are among those for whom sexting media practices might potentially be most socially transformative. A substantial body of international literature has now questioned the appropriateness of current legal frameworks for dealing with cases of sexual image production and distribution involving youth (for summaries, see Crofts et al., 2013; Hasinoff, 2015) and adults (Henry and Powell, 2016; Salter and Crofts, 2015). As the literature I draw together in this chapter suggests, legal reform targeting 'sexting' alone cannot address the underlying social and cultural dynamics that contribute to the 'risks', 'harms', and experiences of victimhood in relation to sexting media practices. Rather, widespread cultural shifts are needed to ensure social justice and equality in relation to sex, desire, and sexting.

Sexting media practices

Couldry suggests that asking about 'media practices' involves asking not about unusual or idiosyncratic uses of media, but rather about 'what is possible and impossible', what people are 'likely and unlikely to do with media' (2012, pp. 33–34). He notes that 'practice is also social and relates to human needs; and it addresses the question of how people should live with media' (pp. 33–34). Couldry suggests the need for approaches that are 'interested in actions that are directly oriented to media; actions that involve media without necessarily having media as their aim or object; and actions whose possibility is conditioned by the prior existence, presence or functioning of media' (p. 35). A 'media practice' approach, in short, focuses on what people do with, and in relation to, media, rather than starting with the meaning of media texts. Sexting involves a range of media practices.

Sexting research has mainly focused on teenagers and young adults, and sexting has been broadly defined as 'youth produced sexual images' (Wolak and Finkelhor, 2011; Martellozzo *et al.*, 2016). Specific media practices that have been asked about in the mainly quantitative research conducted to date include: 'sending sexually explicit messages or photos electronically, primarily between cell phones' (Phippen, 2009); more specifically, Phippen asks about taking 'topless' or 'naked' images; creating or appearing in pictures or videos described as 'nude or nearly nude' (Mitchell *et al.*, 2011); 'sexually suggestive, nude or nearly nude' (Lenhart, 2009); 'naked or semi-naked' (Vanden Abeele *et al.*, 2014); 'sending or receiving sexually explicit texts or images via cell phones', and forwarding such messages on to third parties (Rice *et al.*, 2012; Strassberg *et al.*, 2013); and sending or receiving naked pictures via text or email (Temple *et al.*, 2013). Mitchell and colleagues (2014, p. 63) ask young people about sending or receiving sexually explicit text messages; sending nude or nearly nude photos or videos of one's self, receiving nude or nearly nude photos or videos of someone else; sending a nude or nearly nude photo or video of someone else, and 'using a social media site for sexual reasons'.

Thus, in these studies, and other quantitative ones like them, quite a wide array of media practices potentially constitute 'sexting'. Although sexting is seen as different from the production and circulation of commercial pornography or tabloid images of celebrities, for example, several of these definitions would not technically exclude such images or videos. While not always specified precisely, the emphasis in sexting research is on the production of sexual media by individuals or groups of peers, rather than media professionals or organisations, and for primarily social and/or personal, rather than commercial, circulation and consumption. In highlighting that sexting practices involve *individuals producing media* (Hasinoff, 2015), we can define these practices as not specific to youth, and as potentially engaged in by adults and children too. As we can see, some studies foreground the use of electronic and digital media in sexting practices, and mobile phones in particular, and specifically include the use of such in definitions of sexting. Further, these definitions do not necessarily exclude 'explicit' or naked images that might be quite obviously or intentionally 'non sexual' in purpose and function. As Albury *et al.* (2013, p. 9; see also Burkett, 2015, p. 846) have pointed out, there are a range of self-produced body imaging practices people engage in that can or have been defined as 'sexting' despite the claims of their producers that the meaning of such media are not intently sexual. Young people take images of various body parts on their phones that may be defined as 'sexts' by adults, for their own viewing and not intended to be shared with anyone else (2013, p. 10). Other kinds of body images produced by young people, such as 'sneaky hat' photos (Albury, 2015) where youth pose nude with a hat or cap covering their breasts or genitals, may have more aesthetic and performative conventions in common with various kinds of comedic body performance, Albury (2015) notes, than with pornographic or sexual forms of media.

Sexting in a social context

The term 'sexting' has come to shut down these kinds of possibilities because discourses of risk and harm have come to be associated with it, especially for youth and for women and girls. The qualitative research on sexting, youth, and gendered digital cultures illuminates the kind of broader cultural and social context within which sexting media practices take place. This work helps to illuminate the social conditions that shape and determine certain gendered risks and harms, rather than assuming that such risks are 'natural' or inherent to certain media practices. For example, Ringrose *et al.* (2012) suggest from their focus groups and digital ethnography with teenagers in two London high schools that sexting is a gendered phenomenon and is marked by pressure and competition in high school contexts, with such pressures and peer competition often intensified via the affordances of digital technologies. Their research serves to highlight a variety of sexual media practices engaged in by teenagers in the social context of the school, and more broadly, a postfeminist cultural and media environment where sexist and sexualised representations are common and pervasive. They note that in many school contexts, flirtatious yet harassing behaviours boys engage in towards girls that are not accepted in workplaces and other contexts – such as 'touching up', and 'daggering' girls in corridors, public discussions of girls' bodies and sexual reputations, and both on and offline displays of male possessiveness of women's bodies – are taken for granted among young people (2012, pp. 28–33). Ringrose *et al.* (2012) highlight the prevalence of smart phones at the schools in their study, and the messaging cultures young people use for both private and more public conversations across mobile networks of peers about sexuality and sexual practices. The circulation and viewing of commercial pornography via mobile phones at school was also found to be common and taken for granted by young people (2012, p. 39; see also Mulholland, 2013).

Sexting in context 83

Such behaviours can be seen as reflective of broader postfeminist media discourses about gender and sex, and popular media representations that reinforce notions of women's primary value as located in their sexuality (Ringrose *et al.*, 2013). In this context, it was not uncommon for girls to describe boys' repeatedly asking them for sexual images, for girls to feel both flattered and pressured regarding such requests (Ringrose *et al.*, 2013, p. 311), and for boys to discuss the way sexual images produced by female peers functioned as a form of social currency for them (Ringrose *et al.*, 2013; Ringrose and Harvey, 2015).

Ringrose *et al.* (2012, p. 7) suggest it is unhelpful to describe sexting in 'absolute terms – wanted vs. unwanted sexual activity, deliberate vs. accidental exposure' (2012, p. 7), as such terms fail to capture the complexities of young people's participation in digital and mediated sexual interactions. Similarly Drouin *et al.*'s (2015) research suggests that simplistic distinctions between 'consensual' and 'non-consensual' sexting practices are complicated in a social context where sexual harassment and violence against women is prevalent. They found that 12 per cent of the young men and 22 per cent of young women they surveyed in a US university said they had sexted when they did not want to. Correlations were found between sexting and physical sex coercion and intimate partner abuse of other kinds. Both men and women reported experiencing coercion from others to sext at similar rates, however, a greater proportion of women who experienced 'sexting coercion' engaged in what the authors describe as 'unwanted but consensual' sexting (2015, p. 200).

In the Australian context, Albury *et al.* (2013, p. 9) found most of the young adults in their focus groups 'did not seem to view naked or semi-naked pictures as inherently shameful or shaming for their subject (though they were considered embarrassing, particularly if viewed by parents or teachers)'. They note that participants were 'both puzzled and offended by the tendency for adults in general (and educators in particular) to bundle all naked or partially naked user-generated pictures into the category of sexting' (p. 9) rather than distinguish between various different contexts in which naked and semi-naked images might be produced and/or shared. Albury *et al.* (2013, p. 10) also note a gendered socio-cultural context that can function to over-determines girls' images in particular as sexual, noting how some girls in their study felt adults and teachers were constantly monitoring them for 'signs of sexualisation or "provocativeness"'. With Ringrose I have highlighted the construction of girls' sexting media practices as shamefully sexualised in both pedagogical 'sext education' films aimed at youth, and by young people themselves in both Australian and UK school contexts (Dobson and Ringrose, 2016). Complementary to Albury *et al.*'s (2013) suggestions about the policing of girls in a cultural context of adult-driven panic over 'sexualisation', I have discussed the way sexting is framed in terms of shame and stupidity by girls in particular in an Australian high school context where it seems girls are regularly required to distance themselves from any kind of sexual self-production in order to be perceived as 'smart', in-control, agentic subjects (Dobson, 2015, p. 84).

However, in our gender-segregated focus groups with teenagers in a school context,[1] girls, more so than boys, generally did subscribe to moralistic views of sexting practices as shaming for their subjects, and sometimes as inherently shameful (although discussions were somewhat ambivalent and contradictory on this matter – see Dobson, 2015, pp. 88–89). I note three 'Cs' that were prevalent in discussions with teenage girls about sexting: consequences, consternation, and culpability (2015, p. 86). The lines between 'consensual' image production and 'non-consensual' image production were blurred in these discussions, as were the lines between the 'consensual' and 'non-consensual' circulation or distribution of self-produced sexual images, as girls saw themselves as so heavily responsibilised to protect themselves and their reputations (see also Dobson and Ringrose, 2016). The girls with whom we spoke highlighted a social context where 'slut' was a frequently used insult from boys, both online and in the schoolyard. Girls joked about the meaninglessness of this term, and noted its puerile overuse by boys. However, they also suggested that one could only laugh off being called a slut if one knew one was 'really' not one. For them, this meant not doing 'slutty things', including taking or possessing *any potentially sexualised* photos of one's self on one's phone, even for private viewing only.

The ongoing stigmatisation of women and girls who participate in sexting as 'sluts' has also been noted by Salter (2015) and Lippman and Campbell (2014). Salter further unpacks the historically gendered divide between 'public' and 'private' spheres which he suggests continues to shape socio-cultural discourses about nudity and sexting media practices for young men and women. Young Australian women in Salter's gender-segregated focus groups described experiences of pressure from boyfriends who asked for images of them to use sexually 'instead of pornography', and also spoke of the frequency with which 'dick pics' are received from young men, while both young men and women downplayed the significance and social impact of public male nudity. He suggests that 'digital images of bodies circulate online in a manner that reinforces gender inequalities, as the public feminine body is narrowly conflated with pornography in contrast to the range of meanings that can append to the public masculine body' (2015, p. 2).

Qualitative research on gender and social media also provides examples of the broader digital and visual cultures within which sexting media practices take place. In research investigating young people's online self-presentation we can often see the workings of traditional gender binaries so prevalent in advertising and other forms of commercial media in the ways young women and men represent themselves through social media and digital technologies, and also in the ways young women and men consume and/or circulate images of women via digital technologies (De Ridder and Van Bauwel, 2013; Dobson, 2014a, 2015; Grisso and Weiss, 2005; Livingstone, 2008; Magnuson and Dundes, 2008; Manago *et al.*, 2008; Ringrose, 2010; Ringrose and Eriksson Barajas, 2011; Sveningsson Elm, 2007, 2009; van Doorn, 2009). However, as some scholars have noted, aspects of traditional gender traits and heteronormativity are complicated on social media via young people's performative constructions of newer gendered identities based around notions of sexual freedom, humour, playfulness, and queer or gender-bending performativity that sometimes accompanies this (Albury, 2015; Dobson, 2014b; van Doorn, 2009). The research into gendered self-presentation on social network sites helps illuminate to some extent the kind of cultural and visual feedback loops that exist between self-produced social media representations and more traditional forms of commercial media such as television, magazines, advertising, and music videos. The kind of popular constructs of sex and gender that circulate digitally via self-produced media representations and more traditional commercial media representations cannot be easily separated, but rather, influence and interact with each other.

Gendered visual representations and cultures

Practices of producing, sharing, and circulating sexual self-images and images of peers needs to be contextualised within this convergent sexed and gendered digital visual media culture, and explored further in terms of their relationship with the sharing and circulation of other kinds of sexed and gendered images – for example, commercial pornography (Vanden Abeele et al., 2014). Sexual images and videos that are self-produced are one kind of representation within a strongly gendered digital visual environment. Images of male and female bodies are produced with a wide range of different intentions, and function in a range of different ways, across a wide range of media forms and genres. However, certain significations or meanings of visual images of male and female bodies are common, or at least over-determined by gender. Sexual self-images may be shared with romantic interests or circulated digitally with flirtatious intents to provoke sexual desire or attraction. So, too, may commercial pornographic media, or other kinds of commercial sexualised representations such as advertising images of celebrities and models, gifs, music videos, and so on. Sexual self-images may be shared or circulated digitally with the intention to intimidate the receiver(s), to assert one's power or authority, or to provoke discomfort in others. So, too, may the sharing or circulation of a range of other digital sexed and gendered representations function this way, or be intended to function in this way. Images received featuring peers within one's immediate social network, school, workplace, or neighbourhood may be circulated further in the network for similar reasons to those outlined above, or out of a desire to participate in scandal, gossip, or 'drama' (Marwick and boyd, 2011; Ringrose et al., 2012), to 'be a part of it' (Dobson, 2015). Again, other kinds of digital, commercially produced, sexed and gendered images may be circulated within peer groups and social networks for similar reasons. Related media practices that do not specifically involve images but may often encompass similar ranges of intentions and functions to those mentioned so far include text messages or social media posts stating feelings of attraction or desire, texts or posts requesting sexual acts or images (Ringrose et al., 2012), texts or posts about one's sexual conquests or intentions, and claims about the sexual experiences, practices, or intentions of others (Dobson, 2015). Such textual media practices may involve the circulation of 'self-produced' media content or content reposted from other media sources. Again, textual sexual media practices may be enacted with a range of intentions, but certain meanings and impacts are strongly determined by gender.

Certainly, some sexed and gendered media practices (remembering Couldry, things people do *with* and *in relation to* media) that specifically involve self-produced rather than commercial media content are likely to have very specific intentions and result in impacts specific to the practice of self-production. For example, the intentions and impacts of asking someone for a self-produced explicit image are likely to be quite different to the intentions and impacts of asking someone for a commercially produced explicit image. Circulating sexual images of peers is likely to have very different impacts to those of circulating sexual images of celebrities. My point here is not to advocate a dismissal of the specific qualities and impacts of media practices involving self-production at some level, but rather to suggest that it is also important to think through the possible commonalities and overlaps in *meaning* of various forms of sexed and gendered media representations, that in turn help determine the way sexual media practices take common shapes, forms, and functions.

The sexual objectification of women's bodies in visual culture has a long history, and representations of female bodies are overdetermined as sexual in comparison to representations of male bodies across a range of visual and cultural forms. Art historian Rosemary Betterton has summarised the feminist perspective that a common gender ideology underlies many different forms of representation. She writes:

> In the struggle to change the place ascribed to women in culture and language, the women's movement has challenged the distinction between High Art and mass culture and the compartmentalisation between disciplines. Arguing that cultural forms as diverse as Page Three pin-up and the female nude in Renaissance painting articulate similar ideologies of female sexuality, feminist criticism undermines old cultural categories and makes a radical critique of all forms of representation.
>
> (Betterton, 1987, p. 2)

Betterton suggests that it is important to grasp the specific differences in 'the power and productiveness' of images made for women, and we might add to this in the context of 'demotic' (Turner, 2010) and digital media cultures, self-produced representations made *by* women. However, she suggests, 'it is equally important to see where different kinds of representation draw upon and state the same relationships of sexual power and subordination between men and women' (Betterton, 1987, p. 2). The long history of women's sexual objectification within visual culture informs the current social context in which images of female bodies that feature or focus on the body itself, that reveal flesh, that show still or 'passive' bodies posed for a camera (Goffman, 1979; Mulvey, 1989), and more recently also depictions of female bodies in action or vigorous motion (see Dobson, 2015, pp. 157–158) can be 'dominantly' (Hall *et al.*, 1997) read as sexualised more easily than images featuring male bodies in similar poses. The gendered visual cultural history means that self-produced images of women's bodies may often be read *a priori* in terms of sexuality, provoking or being intended to provoke sexual desire, and can easily be fetishised and function as a kind of valuable social currency. Images of male bodies, on the other hand, can also be read dominantly as intended to provoke sexual desire, but I would suggest that readings of male bodies images in this social and historical context are generally based more on the specific semiotic composition of representations and are less overdetermined as sexual than are women's. Images of male bodies are also read as intended to provoke laughter/humour, and to signal strength and power. They are not as straightforwardly fetishised or valued as a form of social currency, and sometimes the practice of bodily display for men functions dominantly to signal homosexuality, weakness, and other devalued, feminised traits (Bordo, 2000; Edgar and McPhee, 1974; Goffman, 1979; Hatton and Trautner, 2011). Self-produced images of male and female bodies may continue to signify a similar range of gendered connotations and denotations as do commercially produced sexed and gendered media images, and thus may function in similar ways, as some findings in relation to gender and sexting suggest (Albury 2015; Dobson, 2015; Ringrose and Harvey, 2015; Salter, 2015).[2]

In sum, self-produced sexual images need to be understood as a part of, and fundamentally related to, a broader gendered visual culture with a long history. At the same time, it is important to acknowledge that the social impacts of being seen to produce or participate in the creation of images of one's own body for private and/or personal use, circulation, or consumption can be quite different to the social impacts of being seen to produce sexual or body images for more public, commercial, or artistic purposes (Dobson, 2015). As Hasinoff (2015) points out, commercial media production is legitimated in mainstream discourse (although this is still dependent on gender as well as age), while the production of 'selfies' and sexts is often viewed as illegitimate, deviant, or abnormal behaviour. In self-produced sexual media, the visual cultural history that overdetermines the meaning of images of female bodies as sexual objects combines with long-standing gendered double standards around sexual desire and sexual practices, often resulting in the harsher social judgement of girls' and women's media practices involving self-produced sexual or body images (Dobson and Ringrose, 2016; Hasinoff, 2015; Karaian, 2014; Lippman and Campbell, 2014; Ringrose et al., 2013; Salter, 2015).

Socially transformative sexual media practices?

And yet there may be many benefits for girls and women in particular, as well as for youths who may be marginalised along other lines of social inequality, including by their sexual and gendered identities and/or desires in participating in various sexting media practices.

In regards to girls and women, I have outlined elsewhere the way in which feminist performers and artists have long used their own explicit bodies in critique of sexist cultural norms and double standards around sex and gender, and suggested the possibility that girls and young women are capable of enacting similar forms of social critique and political resistance via sexual self-produced digital representations (Dobson, 2011), possibly to politically and personally fruitful ends. Further, Hasinoff has suggested that, for girls and young women in particular, sexting media practices may provide opportunities for the expression of sexual desire and help girls and young women develop confidence in expressing what they want and do not want (2015, p. 118). Developing the ability to communicate confidently about sex is seen as a vital aspect of sexual violence prevention (Burkett and Hamilton, 2012; Carmody, 2009; Tolman, 2002). In focus groups with young men and women aged 18–25 conducted by Burkett (2015), several young women described finding sexual image and text exchange fun and exciting with unknown romantic interests in online dating and mobile app contexts, as long as both partners understood that exchanges were 'just fun' and not necessarily a precursor to physical sex (p. 851). Young women in Burkett's study also described the pleasures involved in sending sexual images to partners in intimate relationships in order to spark desire, although, as Burkett notes, such exchanges 'can constitute another form of "work"' to be performed unequally by women in efforts to boost intimacy and sex lives (p. 855). Burkett also describes how some women felt pressured into sexting in the context of intimate relationships in order to please their partners, echoing dynamics described in other research on heterosexual relationships (p. 858). Sexting media practices currently hold particularly weighty socially and culturally determined impacts for girls and women, as I have discussed throughout, and may also hold particular importance for female subjects in processes of social change.

Young people who identify as LGBTQI and/or engage in practices beyond conventional heterosexual ones are another group for whom sexual media practices hold particularly weighty social impacts, as well as important potential benefits. Hasinoff (2015) has documented several cases in the US that demonstrate the criminalisation of lesbian and gay youth sexual relationships through sexting-related offences, as well as the lack of media attention such cases typically receive in comparison with the media hype surrounding youth sexting incidences involving middle class white girls. Rubin and McClelland have outlined the ways in which participation in social media produces 'uneven consequences for people already labouring under the weight of Otherness in their everyday lives' (2015, p. 522). They note that many queer youth remain in 'the virtual closet' online, 'passing' on their profiles as straight for fear of cyberbullying (p. 513); research into bullying and cyberbullying suggests these are problems faced unequally by LGBTQI identified youth (Meyer, 2009; Rivers and Duncan, 2013).

Pascoe (2011) suggests that while dangers for teens online are framed in terms of sexual attention seeking or sexting practices putting them in danger of unwanted sexual attention, the real danger is the replication online of existing social inequalities, whereby youth marginalised offline by gender, sexuality, class, ethnicity, and ability are also marginalised in the ways they can use social and mobile media. Digital networking and online social interaction is a vital way for youth of diverse genders and sexualities, for example, to meet and connect with peers and romantic interests outside of their immediate geographic areas, Pascoe notes (2011, p. 9). This kind of networking may include sexting media practices, and may also be valuable for youth marginalised along lines of class, ethnicity, or physical ability. Same-sex attracted young men and women in Albury and Byron's (2014) focus groups discussed sexual image and text exchange via social media and dating apps as media practices that are not without risks, but still often considered routine or mundane parts of participating in dating and sexual digital cultures. Youth in their study clearly articulated their own sets of 'rules' about risk, context, and ethics in the management of participating in such media practices (2014, p. 143). In line with the suggestions of other scholars, same-sex attracted young people articulated the primary risks not in terms of unknown sexual partners, but the potential for unwanted 'outing' or homophobic bullying to result from engagement in digital sexual cultures (p. 143).

Conclusion

This chapter has highlighted the diverse range of media practices which can be seen to constitute sexting, suggesting that the usefulness of the term itself is questionable for understanding the diversity and complexity of flows of power within this range of media practices. I have unpacked the gendered and context-specific nature of the commonly articulated 'risks', 'harms', and 'consequences' associated with sexting, drawing on qualitative research on sexting, youth, and digital cultures. I have also attempted to position sexting media practices within a broader visual cultural landscape and historical trajectory of sexed and gendered media images and discourses. When we place sexting in this broader context, it is clear that legal reforms targeting 'sexting' alone, as it is typically defined, could not address the underlying social and cultural dynamics that contribute to risks, harms, and experiences of victimhood in relation to sexting media practices. Nor could legal reform aimed at sexting media practices alone open the kind of material-discursive space necessary for these media practices to function in more socially transformative ways for all subjects – regardless of sex, gender identity, sexuality, class, ethnicity or ability. Inequalities are at stake in who currently benefits from being able to participate in sexting media practices with less 'risk', and more fun, pleasure, and creative or political potential. Hence, as I have suggested elsewhere, it is vital that future research and interventions seek to address sexting and other kinds of intimate and sexual media production more explicitly from a 'social justice perspective' – that is, with the goal of better understanding and addressing axes of social inequality regarding participation and distribution of benefits in sexual media practices. Wider efforts would involve the availability of sex education to all young people that addresses pleasure, gender and sexual diversity, and ethics and consent, as advocated by Carmody (2009), Albury *et al.* (2013), Hasinoff (2015), and Ringrose *et al.* (2012). Elsewhere I have outlined the kind of shifts needed in 'sext education' specifically, in moving from 'abstinence' to 'harm minimisation' approaches (Dobson and Ringrose, 2016). Wider efforts would also vitally include social reform and activism in relation to sexism, racism, and homophobia in media and visual culture more broadly (Gill, 2012). Reform and activist work that targets homophobia and advocates for LGBTQI rights more broadly is also implicated in shifting the dynamics of 'risk' and 'harm' in relation to sexting media practices. Those involved in youth cyber safety education, for example, need to be aware of the potential added imperatives of participating in sexting media practices for marginalised youth (Pascoe, 2011), rather than condemning such practices outright. These are some of the possible wider social and cultural shifts needed to shift the current dynamics of 'risk', 'harm' and 'victimhood' in relation to sexting media practices, and improve social justice and equality in relation to sex, desire, and digital media practices and cultures.

Notes

1 For details of this research see Dobson, 2015, pp. 17–18.
2 For further background on the debates and historical trajectory I am referring to here regarding gender, media, and visual culture see key texts by Goffman (1979), Mulvey (1989), Gill (2007) and Thornham (2007).

References

Albury, K. (2015). Selfies, sexts and sneaky hats: young people's understandings of gendered Practices of self-representation. *International Journal of Communication, 9*(12), 1734–1745.

Albury, K., and Byron, P. (2014). Queering sexting and sexualisation. *Media International Australia, 153*(November), 138–147.

Albury, K., and Crawford, K. (2012). Sexting, consent and young people's ethics: beyond Megan's Story. *Continuum: Journal of Media & Cultural Studies, 3*(26), 1–11.

Albury, K., Crawford, K., Byron, P., and Mathews, B. (2013). *Young People and Sexting in Australia: Ethics, Representation and the Law*. ARC Centre for Creative Industries and Innovation/ Journalism and Media Research Centre, University of New South Wales, Australia. Available online at http://jmrc.arts.unsw.edu.au/media/File/Young_People_And_Sexting_Final.pdf

Betterton, R. (ed.). (1987). *Looking On: Images of Femininity in the Visual Arts and Media*. London; New York: Pandora.

Bordo, S. (2000). *The Male Body: A New Look at Men in Public and in Private*. New York: Farrar, Straus, and Giroux.

Burkett, M. (2015). Sex(t) talk: a qualitative analysis of young adults' negotiations of the pleasures and perils of sexting. *Sexuality & Culture, 19*(4), 835–863.

Burkett, M., and Hamilton, K. (2012). Postfeminist sexual agency: young women's negotiations of sexual consent. *Sexualities, 15*(7), 815–833. doi: 10.1177/1363460712454076

Carmody, M. (2009). *Sex and Ethics: Young People and Ethical Sex*. South Yarra: Palgrave-Macmillan.

Conley, T. D., and Ramsey, L. R. (2011). Killing us softly? Investigating portrayals of women and men in contemporary magazine advertisements. *Psychology of Women Quarterly, 35*(3), 469–478. doi: 10.1177/0361684311413383

Couldry, N. (2012). *Media, Society, World: Social Theory and Digital Media Practice*. Cambridge, UK: Polity.

Crofts, T., and Lee, M. (2013). 'Sexting', children and child pornography. *Sydney Law Review, 35*(1), 85–106.

Crofts, T., Lee, M., McGovern, A., and Milivojevic, S. (2015). *Sexting and Young People.* New York: Palgrave Macmillan.

De Ridder, S., and Van Bauwel, S. (2013). Commenting on pictures: teens negotiating gender and sexualities on social networking sites. *Sexualities, 16*(5–6), 565–586.

Dobson, A. S. (2015). *Postfeminist Digital Cultures: Femininity, Social Media, and Self-Representation.* New York: Palgrave Macmillan.

Dobson, A. S. (2014a). Performative shamelessness on young women's social network sites: shielding the self and resisting gender melancholia. *Feminism & Psychology, 24*(1), 97–114. doi: 10.1177/0959353513510651

Dobson, A. S. (2014b). Laddishness online: the possible significations and significance of 'performative shamelessness' for young women in the post-feminist context. *Cultural Studies, 28*(1), 142–164. doi: 10.1080/09502386.2013.778893

Dobson, A. S., and Ringrose, J. (2016). Sex education: pedagogies of sex, gender and shame in the schoolyards of *Tagged* and *Exposed. Sex Education, 16*(1), 8–21. doi: 10.1080/14681811.2015.1050486

Drouin, M., Ross, J., and Tobin, E. (2015). Sexting: a new, digital vehicle for intimate partner aggression? *Computers in Human Behavior, 50*(0), 197–204.

Edgar, P., and McPhee, H. (1974). *Media She/Media He.* Melbourne: Heinemann.

Gill, R. (2007). *Gender and the Media.* Cambridge; Malden: Polity Press.

Gill, R. (2012). Media, empowerment and the 'sexualization of culture' debates. *Sex Roles, 66*(11), 736–745.

Goffman, E. (1979). *Gender Advertisements.* New York: Harper & Row.

Grisso, A. D., and Weiss, D. (2005). What are gURLS talking about? Adolescent girls' construction of sexual identity on gURL.com. In S. R. Mazzarella (ed.), *Girl Wide Web: Girls, the Internet, and the Negotiation of Identity* (pp. 31–49). New York: Peter Lang.

Hall, S., Evans, J., and Nixon, S. (1997). *Representation* (2nd edition). London: SAGE.

Hasinoff, A. A. (2015). *Sexting Panic: Rethinking Criminalization, Privacy, and Consent.* Urbana: University of Illinois Press.

Hasinoff, A. A., and Shepherd, T. (2014). Sexting in context: privacy norms and expectations. *International Journal of Communication, 8,* 2932–2955.

Hatton, E., and Trautner, M. (2011). Equal opportunity objectification? The sexualization of men and women on the cover of *Rolling Stone. Sexuality & Culture, 15*(3), 256–278. doi: 10.1007/s12119-011-9093-2

Henry, N., and Powell, A. (2016 efirst). Sexual violence in the digital age: the scope and limits of criminal law. *Social & Legal Studies.* doi: 10.1177/0964663915624273

Karaian, L. (2014). Policing 'sexting': responsibilization, respectability and sexual subjectivity in child protection/crime prevention responses to teenagers' digital sexual expression. *Theoretical Criminology, 18*(3), 282–299. doi: 10.1177/1362480613504331

Lenhart, A. (2009). *Teens and Sexting: Hhow and Why Minor Teens Are Sending Sexually Suggestive Nude or Nearly Nude Images Via Text Messaging.* Washington: Pew.

Lippman, J. R., and Campbell, S. W. (2014). Damned if you do, damned if you don't ... If you're a girl: relational and normative contexts of adolescent sexting in the United States. *Journal of Children and Media, 8*(4), 371–386. doi: 10.1080/17482798. 2014.923009

Livingstone, S. (2008). Taking risky opportunities in youthful content creation: teenagers' use of social networking sites for intimacy, privacy and self-expression. *New Media and Society, 10*(3), 393–411. doi: 10.1177/1461444808089415

Magnuson, M. J., and Dundes, L. (2008). Gender differences in 'social portraits' reflected in MySpace profiles. *CyberPsychology & Behavior, 11*(2), 239–241.

Manago, A. M., Graham, M. B., Greenfield, P. M., and Salimkhan, G. (2008). Self-presentation and gender on MySpace. *Journal of Applied Developmental Psychology, 29*(6), 446–458.

Marwick, A., and boyd, d. (2011). The drama! Teen conflict, gossip, and bullying in networked publics. Paper presented at the A Decade in Internet Time: Symposium on the Dynamics of the Internet and Society, Oxford.

Martellozzo, E., Horvath, M., Adler, J., Davidson, Leyva, R., and Monaghan, A. (2016) *A Quantitative and Qualitative Examination of the Impact of Legal Pornography on the Values, Attitudes, Beliefs and Behaviours of Children and Young People.* London: NSPCC & OCC.

Meyer, E. (2009). *Gender, Bullying, and Harassment: Strategies to End Sexism and Homophobia in Schools.* New York: Teachers College Press.

Mitchell, A., Kent, P., Heywood, W., Blackman, P., and Pitts, M. (2014). *National Survey of Australian Secondary Students and Sexual Heath 2013.* La Trobe University Melbourne: Australian Research Centre in Sex, Health and Society.

Mitchell, K. J., Finkelhor, D., Jones, L. M., and Wolak, J. (2012). Prevalence and characteristics of youth sexting: a national study. *Pediatrics, 129*(1), 13–20.

Mulholland, M. (2013). *Young People and Pornography: Negotiating Pornification.* New York: Palgrave Macmillan.

Mulvey, L. (1989). *Visual and Other Pleasures.* Houndmills, Basingstoke, Hampshire: Palgrave.

Pascoe, C. J. (2011). Resource and risk: youth sexuality and new media use. *Sexuality Research and Social Policy, 8*(5), 5–17.

Phippen, A. (2009). *Sharing Personal Images and Videos Among Young People.* Exeter: South West Grid for Learning.

Rice, E., Rhoades, H., Winetrobe, H., Sanchez, M., Montoya, J., Plant, A., and Kordic, T. (2012). Sexually explicit cell phone messaging associated with sexual risk among adolescents. *Pediatrics.* doi: 10.1542/peds.2012-0021

Ringrose, J. (2010). Sluts, whores, fat slags and playboy bunnies: teen girls' negotiations of 'sexy' on social networking sites and at school. In C. Jackson, C. Paechter, and E. Renold (eds), *Girls and Education* (pp. 170–182). Maidenhead, Berkshire: Open University Press.

Ringrose, J., and Eriksson Barajas, K. (2011). Gendered risks and opportunities? Exploring teen girls' digitized sexual identities in postfeminist media contexts. *International Journal of Media & Cultural Politics, 7*(2), 121–138.

Ringrose, J., and Harvey, L. (2015). Boobs, back-off, six packs and bits: mediated body parts, gendered reward, and sexual shame in teens' sexting images. *Continuum, 29*(2), 205–217. doi: 10.1080/10304312.2015.1022952

Ringrose, J., Gill, R., Livingstone, S., and Harvey, L. (2012). A qualitative study of children, young people and 'sexting': a report prepared for the NSPCC. London: NSPCC.

Ringrose, J., Harvey, L., Gill, R., and Livingstone, S. (2013). Teen girls, sexual double standards and 'sexting': gendered value in digital image exchange. *Feminist Theory, 14*(3), 305–323. doi: 10.1177/1464700113499853

Rivers, I., and Duncan, N. (eds) (2013). *Bullying: Experiences and Discourses of Sexuality and Gender.* Oxon, UK: Routledge.

Rubin, J. D., and McClelland, S. I. (2015). 'Even though it's a small checkbox, it's a big deal': stresses and strains of managing sexual identity(s) on Facebook. *Culture, Health & Sexuality, 17*(4), 512–526. doi: 10.1080/13691058.2014.994229

Salter, M. (2015). Privates in the online public: sex(ting) and reputation on social media. *New Media & Society*. doi: 10.1177/1461444815604133

Salter, M., and Crofts, T. (2015). Responding to revenge porn: challenging online legal impunity. In L. Comella and S. Tarrant (eds), *New Views on Pornography: Sexuality, Politics and the Law*. Westport: Praeger.

Salter, M., Crofts, T., and Lee, M. (2013). Beyond criminalisation and responsibilisation: sexting, gender and young people. *Current Issues in Criminal Justice, 24*(3), 301–316.

Strassberg, D., McKinnon, R., Sustaíta, M., and Rullo, J. (2013). Sexting by high school students: an exploratory and descriptive study. *Archives of Sexual Behavior, 42*(1), 15–21. doi: 10.1007/s10508-012-9969-8

Sveningsson Elm, M. (2009). 'Teenagers get undressed on the internet': young people's exposure of bodies in a Swedish Internet community. *Nordicom Review, 30*(2), 87–103.

Temple, J., Paul, J., van den Berg, P., Le, V. D., McElhany, A., and Temple, B. (2012). Teen sexting and its association with sexual behaviors. *Archives of Pediatric and Adolescent Medicine, 166*(9), 828–833.

Thornham, S. (2007). *Women, Feminism and Media*. Edinburgh: Edinburgh University Press.

Tolman, D. L. (2002). *Dilemmas of Desire: Teenage Girls Talk About Sexuality*. Cambridge, MA; Harvard University Press.

Turner, G. (2010). *Ordinary People and the Media: The Demotic Turn*. London: Sage.

Vanden Abeele, M., Campbell, S. W., Eggermont, S., and Roe, K. (2014). Sexting, mobile porn use, and peer group dynamics: boys' and girls' self-perceived popularity, need for popularity, and perceived peer pressure. *Media Psychology, 17*(1), 6–33. doi: 10.1080/15213269.2013.801725

Van Doorn, N. (2009). The ties that bind: the networked performance of gender, sexuality and friendship on MySpace. *New Media and Society, 11*(8), 1–22.

Van Dijck, J. (2013). *The Culture of Connectivity: A Critical History of Social Media*. Oxford: Oxford University Press.

Wolak, J., and Finkelhor, D. (2011). *Sexting: A Typology*. Crimes Against Children Research Center.

5 Victims of sex trafficking and online sexual exploitation

Kristine Hickle

Introduction

Sex trafficking is a pervasive and complex problem throughout the world (Cianciarulo, 2008). It is a highly profitable, low risk, and ever-changing criminal enterprise that has been given increased attention since 2000, when the United States (US) enacted the Victims of Trafficking and Violence Protection act (TVPA) and the United Nations (UN) adopted the Protocol to Prevent, Suppress, and Punish Trafficking in Persons, Especially Women and Children (2000). These legal frameworks provided a common language to identify what had previously been an undefined and not well-regulated phenomenon (Gallagher, 2015). Countries throughout the world have used this common language to begin the process of developing policies and practices to combat human trafficking in its varied forms. Despite these efforts, much remains unknown about the prevalence of human trafficking, including sex trafficking, a crime that is: often hidden; made more complex by the rapid growth of digital technologies that facilitate sex trafficking online (Latonero, 2012); and considered by some to be 'placeless yet everywhere' (Mendel & Sharapov, 2014, p. 14).

In the last decade, researchers have begun to explore the role of the Internet in facilitating sex trafficking among vulnerable children and adults in the US and throughout the world, including the barriers to identifying and protecting victims and prosecuting perpetrators. Drawing primarily upon research conducted in the US, this chapter will summarize current research on Internet-facilitated sex trafficking, demonstrating the ways in which cyberspace provides a new environment for traffickers to recruit, blackmail, exchange, and advertise victims to potential sex buyers who are also complicit in the victimization of both children and adults (Janson et al., 2013; Monto & Milrod, 2013). It will also explore some of the controversies surrounding sex trafficking, particularly in relation to its prevalence and the role that technology plays both in creating new opportunities to exploit people and facilitating exploitation that would likely happen whether or not emerging technologies played a part. I will discuss the impact of anti-trafficking campaigns, recent legislative and policy initiatives, and current research focused on situating sex trafficking as a problem embedded in particular cultural and social contexts.

An introduction to sex trafficking victimization

Sex trafficking is one form of human trafficking that can be understood in terms of supply and demand (Kotrla, 2010). Demand is present when a prospective trafficker is motivated by the possibility of making money and a buyer/consumer is willing to purchase sexual services from a trafficked person. A 'supply' of victims may include children, young people, and adults of any race, age, gender, sexual orientation, and socioeconomic background; however, known victims in the United States and throughout the world are most often women and girls (Kotrla, 2010). In 2015, the Department of Justice opened 1,034 human trafficking investigations and eventually initiated 257 federal prosecutions (248 for sex trafficking cases); this represents an increase from the prior year (U.S. Department of State, 2016), but remains significantly lower that early estimates by Richard Estes and Neil Weiner (2000) and others who believed that potentially hundreds of thousands of children (their research did not include adults) were at risk for sex trafficking. Indeed, the few efforts to estimate the prevalence of sex trafficking in the US have been widely criticized for being methodologically flawed (Gerassi, 2015), and currently no reliable estimates are available. This is primarily because of the covert nature of sex trafficking and because no uniform system of identifying victims exists (Gerassi, 2015).

Risk factors associated with becoming vulnerable to sex trafficking include physical, sexual and emotional abuse in childhood (Dalla, 2000; Reid, 2014b; Roe-Sepowitz, 2012; Simons & Whitbeck, 1991). Additional risk factors include parental drug and alcohol use (Kramer & Berg, 2003), domestic violence (Dalla, 2003), involvement in child protection/child welfare systems (Nixon et al., 2002), substance misuse (Reid, 2014b), running away from home (McClanahan et al., 1999) and homelessness (Hudson & Nandy, 2012).

Sex trafficking and sexual exploitation in its varied forms occurs in the context of relationships between people who are vulnerable and people in positions of power willing to use this power to profit financially, socially, and/or politically from exploiting others. Traffickers use myriad tactics to gain – and keep – control of victims. For example, research on internally/domestically trafficked children and young people in both the USA and UK confirm the use of grooming techniques as a means to build trusting relationships in order to control victims (Brayley et al., 2011; Reid, 2014a). Grooming techniques include befriending and helping or protecting a young person who is in a difficult or dangerous situation. Grooming often includes flattering and romancing, and posing as a boyfriend or romantic partner. In addition, traffickers may attempt to normalize sex through exposure to pornography, sexual activity, or may use other trafficked young people to help deceive/convince new recruits to engage in sexual activity. Grooming behaviours also involve intentionally isolating victims from positive social support, disorienting them through constantly changing locations, and offering drugs and alcohol (Brayley et al., 2011; Reid, 2014a). Once traffickers have gained some control, a variety of techniques are then used to maintain control. Joan Reid (2014a) describes these as 'enmeshment' tactics, including shame (i.e. telling a victim that once they've sold sex, they cannot do anything else) and blackmail. Commonly referred to as 'sextortion', traffickers may blackmail victims by threatening to share photos or videos of them (Wittes et al., 2016). Traffickers may force victims to be complicit in crimes (including trafficking other people), and they may aim to get victims pregnant in order to secure the connection they have. Traffickers maintain control by prolonging isolation and maintaining financial control over victims.

Negative consequences of sex trafficking victimization

Survivors of sex trafficking face a number of barriers to leaving or escaping trafficking situations and healing from the traumatic victimization they have endured. As a result of experiencing violent and coercive relationships, substance misuse, and financial instability, victims may feel that they have lost control over their lives and experience a range of mental and physical health issues. In a study of 204 women trafficked in seven European countries, Mazeda Hossain and colleagues (2010) found that a majority reported mental health problems including posttraumatic stress disorder (77 per cent), depression (54.9 per cent) and anxiety (48 per cent). Physical health issues include untreated injuries and sexually transmitted infections (Lederer & Wetzel, 2014). For survivors who were given drugs by their traffickers as a means to control them, or those who utilized substances as a means of coping with psychological distress and violence (Young et al., 2000), addiction can be another primary barrier to healing and regaining control of their own lives. Survivors may have difficulty leaving behind negative social networks, and when they do, may experience isolation (Davis, 2000). Trusting people and forming new relationships, or re-engaging with loved ones (e.g. children and family) can be very difficult without formal support services to help facilitate the formation of healthy relationships (Hedin & Månsson, 2004). After having moved frequently whilst being trafficked, survivors may find establishing new routines difficult as well. This can be particularly true for trafficked children and young people who may have been out of school for long periods of time and are either behind in their studies or in need of extra support as a result of having learning disabilities (Klatt et al., 2014). In order address these many complex experiences, practitioners and researchers are continually seeking out new and innovative ways of providing help both during and after trafficking victimization (e.g. Gibbs et al., 2014; Schwarz & Britton, 2015).

A changing landscape

Sex trafficking has only been a focus of research, policy, and practice since it became part of international legislation in 2000 (e.g. the Palermo Protocol and the Trafficking Victims Protection Act). However, this pernicious form of violent victimization is not new: people have long used grooming and controlling behaviours to sexually exploit and maintain power over others. What has changed is the role of emerging technologies in relation to how, when, and where sex trafficking flourishes in society. As Mitali Thakor and danah boyd (2014) point out, technology is 'reconfiguring many of the networks that underpin many aspects of human trafficking' (p. 280) by changing how information is exchanged and re-defining what is and is not visible. In a large scale study on the underground commercial sex economy in eight major US cities, Meredith Dank and colleagues (2014) found:

> [The] widespread availability and rapid expansion of the Internet has redefined spatial and social limitations of the sex market by introducing new markets of recruitment and advertisement ... offenders report new marking opportunities for pimps [traffickers] to connect with both recruits and clientele, including online classifieds, social media, and networking websites.
>
> (p. 3)

Traffickers can utilize social media and other forms of online communication to search for, make contact with potential victims (Katrla, 2010), and use online communication to befriend and convey romantic intentions. They can easily create online advertisements for employment or other money-generating opportunities that appear legitimate in order to deceive victims into working for them. They can expose victims to pornography online and blackmail them by threating to share pornographic films/photographs of victims through websites, including social media, and mobile text and picture messaging. They can engage in cyberstalking (Southworth et al., 2007) to monitor victims' physical location and Internet activity. They can also restrict victims' access to technology as a means of isolation from positive social support and help-seeking (Bouché, 2015). In a study of 35 cases involving child sex trafficking in the USA, Melissa Wells and colleagues (2012) found the Internet played a central role in facilitating trafficking in almost all (91 per cent) cases. Often communication with victims occurred online (via e-mail, chat rooms, text messages) and in a majority of the cases, online sex ad websites were used to advertise victims as escorts. The internet also facilitated child pornography production, wherein child victims were bribed or promised payment for participation. In each of these examples, the role of technology is clear – it was the means through which a child was victimized. What remains less clear is whether or not that victimization would have taken place in some other way, had the technology not been available to perpetrators in the first place. I will address competing perspectives on this issue later in the chapter, but will now move on to discussing how technology has shaped the environments in which sex trafficking occurs.

Working 'without place'

Technology has blurred the lines between what was previously considered two distinctly separate environments: indoor and outdoor sex work. Before the Internet, research clearly differentiated between outdoor and indoor sex work. Outdoor work (e.g. street-based prostitution) was seen as less protected, more dangerous, (Raphael & Shapiro, 2004), and often the option most available to women experiencing poverty and/or drug addiction. These women were often considered less agentic, at greater risk of being trafficked, and had less control over their work environment overall. Indoor work was – and still is – seen as the safer option for individuals with greater agency and autonomy to participate in sex work (Dewey, 2012; Jones, 2015). Indoor sex workers can screen customers, communicate with them without revealing a location, and profit from forms of sex work, such as web cam work, that do not include direct contact with customers at all (Jones, 2015).

In many ways, technology has provided increased opportunities for individuals who may have otherwise been involved in outdoor, street-based sex work to move indoors, to safer and more controlled working environments. However, for many trafficking victims the possibility of working indoors has not necessarily made them safer. The expansion of digital technologies, particularly the wide spread use of mobile phones and the proliferation of social networking sites, has provided new opportunities for exploitation (Latonero, 2012), and for individuals vulnerable to being trafficked, indoor internet-facilitated sex work does not necessarily come with the benefits previously associated with indoor work. In a study investigating the role of sex trafficking victimization upon entry into sex work, Hickle and Roe-Sepowitz (2016) found that women who were initially trafficked into the sex industry were significantly more likely than non-sex trafficked women to indicate that they participated in *both* outdoor and indoor sex work (including internet-facilitated work). Sex trafficked women were more likely to report a greater variety of sex work experiences overall, and one possible explanation for this is that trafficked individuals are often pressured to meet a 'quota' and bring in a certain amount of money each day; thus they feel pressured to earn money by any means possible (Hickle & Roe-Sepowitz, 2016). Dank et al. (2014) found a similar connection between indoor and outdoor work among sex trafficking victims in their study. In nearly all of the eight cities they conducted research in, clear trends were evident among trafficked adults and young people working both outdoors in street-based prostitution and indoors, in what was considered 'higher end' work (i.e. charging higher prices) via online escort service advertisements.

For these victims, technology may be facilitating new ways to be victimized that are increasingly anonymous, invisible, and are not rooted in a specific location – they are 'without place'. In Dank et al.'s (2014) study nearly half (49 per cent) of their respondents (including traffickers, customers, and victims) reported using the Internet to participate in commercial sex exchanges, and law enforcement in several cities noted the way in which the Internet has dramatically changed the way they identify victims. Police in Miami, Florida reported that, even five years ago, most trafficked children and young people would be found out working on the street; now they more often advertised online. In Dallas, Texas police identified the Internet as their biggest challenge, as it made previously visible street-walking victims invisible online. It also provides a way for traffickers to advertise victims covertly, using language in advertisements that clearly communicate sex services to customers but are vague enough to avoid detection from law enforcement. Dank et al. (2014) also noted that traffickers who place victims both on the street and online continue to travel across the country in known routes or 'circuits'. If pressure from law enforcement appears to increase, traffickers may move victims elsewhere. Traffickers may also decide to work 'remotely', placing online ads in other locations ahead of time.

Most of these examples indicate how sex trafficking takes place in open markets, visible via publicly accessible web platforms (Martin et al., 2014), particularly those providing opportunities to post online sex ads for little to no cost. In a number of recent cases involving sex trafficking victims under the age of 18, a range of other media platforms were also utilized to advertise and facilitate communication between traffickers, victims, and sex buyers. These include mainstream social media sites such as Facebook, mobile-based social networking applications (e.g. Snapchat, WhatsApp), and gaming systems that have social networking capability, such as Xbox Live (Latonero, 2012). In a recent study on the use of technology among former child sex trafficking victims in the US, Vanessa Bouché (2015) found that while most victims still initially meet traffickers in person, younger victims were significantly more likely to have met them online, and to have formed a relationship relatively quickly; many (48 per cent) reported trusting their traffickers within a month of meeting, even if most or all communication had occurred online. Younger victims in her study presented with additional complex circumstances; they reported greater autonomy in their work, communicating more directly with sex buyers in a range of ways (e.g. text messaging, via escort websites, and email), and were more likely to report that they did not want help getting out of their trafficking situation. They also reported that while technology played a role in their trafficking situation, it did not play a role in eventually helping them get out. These young people represent a very hard-to-reach subset of victims who may feel less trapped by their circumstances because they do have some autonomy in their work, but they are still vulnerable in that they are required to hand over most or all of their earnings to a trafficker/trafficking network. While being trafficked, they remain isolated from people outside trafficking networks 'who might support them in getting out and help them to recognize the controlling nature of their relationships with their traffickers.

Technology: source and solution?

The possibility that vulnerable children can be contacted, recruited and trafficked via communication that happens entirely online may be alarming to both parents and professionals responsible for protecting children particularly as we become aware that ever-evolving social networking sites and online spaces used by the general public are simultaneously being used by traffickers. As a result, anti-trafficking organizations, law enforcement, and policy makers have begun to explore ways of using technology to reach out to victims and pursue perpetrators. This may include monitoring online sex ad websites, working undercover by posing as customers to contact individuals believed to be vulnerable to trafficking. While this does represent one way in which law enforcement is now using technology to identify both victims and perpetrators, critics of this approach argue that police are only interacting with victims who are visible in the open market, often in areas of sex work that generate less income (e.g. street-based work, free/publicly available websites), and are controlled by traffickers/pimps who are the least technologically savvy (Latonero, 2012). This can mean that efforts to train law enforcement officers in methods that best disrupt sex trafficking networks and help victims are not adequately sufficient for policing a crime that is taking shape in increasingly technologically sophisticated ways. Pimps/traffickers are now more aware of police presence on these sites, and they are beginning to find alternative ways of advertising sexual services and communicating with customers. Traffickers are also increasingly using inexpensive pre-paid disposable mobile phones, which do not require a contract, a credit check, or any form of personal identification to maintain anonymity whilst engaging in criminal activity (Latonero, 2012).

Throughout the US, anti-trafficking campaigns have been influential in shaping recent legislation aimed at penalizing traffickers and 'rescuing' victims. Beginning in 2010, anti-trafficking advocates pressured Craigslist to remove the 'adult services' section of their website (Thakor & boyd, 2013). In 2015, backpage.com, a classified advertising website that generated substantial income from the adult services section, was forced to change its payment policy for adult entertainment ads after several major credit card companies refused to allow their cards to be used to pay for ads. Shortly thereafter, myredbook.com, a popular sex ad venue in California and throughout the West coast, was shut down by law enforcement after confirming 50 young people under age 18 were posted on the site. The site's owner was recently sentenced to prison (Rocha, 2015). In addition, policy makers throughout the US have been successfully passing legislation intended to penalize traffickers and protect victims. One such law, passed in 2012 in California, provided harsher penalties and fines for convicted traffickers; the law also required traffickers to provide law enforcement with online identities and other information about Internet activity (Musto & boyd, 2014). It is this aspect of the law that has become particularly contested, and I will now explore some of the controversies central to combatting trafficking online.

Human trafficking (particularly sex trafficking) is increasingly understood as a technological problem that must be addressed by:

1. better understanding how information flows between traffickers, victims, and sex buyers;
2. disrupting and destabilizing trafficking networks; and
3. finding new ways to harness technology as a means to help victims.

Each of these tasks is complicated by competing ideologies about sex work, freedom of information, and the definition of risk (particularly among children and young people). Underlying political agendas and an ever-changing technological landscape add to this complexity. One recent trend evident in the growing transnational anti-trafficking industry involves the promotion of collaborations between state actors and non-governmental organizations; in the US, these often include faith-based organizations that can garner financial support for their causes and for-profit technology companies that can provide the technology needed by law enforcement to monitor and collect evidence in building a case against a trafficker/trafficking networks. The case of California's 2012, 'Californians Against Sexual Exploitation Act' is an example of one such collaboration. Framed by its supporters as a necessary way to strengthen responses to human trafficking, the law does not specify how providing law enforcement with increased access to suspected traffickers' online activity may also impact, and infringe upon, the rights of potential victims who may also be subject to surveillance and monitoring. Musto and boyd (2014) argue that this kind of legislation, enabling increased network surveillance and blurring the lines between government responsibility and private technology expertise should trouble us, and cause us to consider how these new laws provide too much access to individuals that may or may not be victims of a crime. They point out that, in an effort to combat trafficking, there has not been a similar degree of attention to how technologies and innovative tools are being leveraged to observe and keep tabs on individuals seen as at risk of trafficking, including sex trade involved youth and adults. This is a curious and troubling omission, particularly since law enforcement may look to both groups to gather evidence and may employ different surveillance strategies as a means of gaining access to the digital and mobile phone evidentiary material of the individuals suspected of exploiting them and purchasing their services (p. 10).

This aspect of victims' experiences has not yet been explored well in research or practice, as so much of the attention given towards the role of technology in sex trafficking has been aimed at identifying the problems caused by technology and the impact on traffickers and sex buyers rather than victims.

It is important to note that this concern over the role of technology is not unique to sex trafficking; in recent decades, discussions about the risks and consequences of expanding digital technologies, particularly among children and young people, have become commonplace. Concerns about how young people navigate social and digital media, how they understand their online interactions (and how they may differ from adults' understanding or interpretation), and how people are understood as either victims or perpetrators are key issues associated with understanding children and young people's online worlds (Berriman & Thomson, 2015). These issues translate well into how we might think about the role of technology in sex trafficking; as we consider how to protect and intervene in sex trafficking victims' lives, we need to understand more about how they navigate social media, how they interpret their own online interactions, who they perceive to be perpetrators (or victims), and how our core assumptions about their experiences (and our role in monitoring these experiences) may differ from their own.

Technology, vulnerability, and place

In addition to concerns about online privacy and means used to monitor criminal activity, researchers and practitioners have also begun to consider the ways in which current discourses about sex trafficking: (1) misrepresent the problem by upholding ideal victim stereotypes; and (2) minimize the role that structural violence plays in creating a global environment where trafficking flourishes. These are two central features of a particular political ideology that prioritizes punitive measures of control (Bernstein, 2010). Before we can begin to consider the technological implications of this problem, we must consider social and cultural contexts of the problem (Thakor & boyd, 2013) and the way in which it has evolved as an outcome of both globalization and neoliberalism (O'Connel Davidson, 2010).

In a neoliberal political climate, the private sector (e.g. faith-based and for-profit technology organizations) can play an increasingly important and powerful role in interpreting what constitutes trafficking behaviour, the nature of a 'true' victim, and who is best able to intervene and help victims (Musto & boyd, 2014). It also frames sex trafficking as a problem that can and should be dealt with via micro-level and intermediate level anti-trafficking strategies that allow 'policymakers to remain ignorant of other aspects of the trafficking-technology interface' (Mendel & Sharapov, 2014, p. 3). Such strategies might encourage the general public to feel confident that human trafficking is being addressed by the government. That is, they encourage the view that this is a crime happening largely outside of their direct experience or control, rather than one in which broader systemic issues such as growing income inequality, poverty, war and political instability contribute. In a study of perceptions about human trafficking in three European countries, Jonathan Mendel and Kiril Sharapov (2014) found that most people do not think about human trafficking as a problem that directly affects them – rather, it happens elsewhere (in other countries), to other people (the foreign/migrant 'other') and in other online spaces such as the deep web (i.e. content that is not searchable via typical search engines) and the dark web (part of the deep web including encrypted content that can only be accessed via secure and anonymous web browsers).

In many ways, anti-trafficking advocacy and awareness campaigns are debunking these common myths about sex trafficking, including ideas about who trafficking affects and where it occurs. However, in other more subtle ways, this work has sustained neoliberal ideology thorough framing the problem as a relatively straightforward crime committed by malicious individuals and organized crime groups against individual 'ideal' victims who are worthy of help. Currently, much of the current anti-trafficking work undertaken in the US and throughout the world is predicated on an understanding of sex trafficking that perpetuates this ideal victim stereotype, that is, as presenting only those victims as being perceived to be 'innocent', unwilling, and without agency (Hoyle at al., 2011). Media stories of sex trafficking in the US often highlight cases that represent the ideal victim as middle class, white, female, and 'tricked' by traffickers (Thakor & boyd, 2013). Other ideal victims include foreign nationals who were kidnapped or forced to emigrate against their will, thus excluding those men, women, and children who may have chosen to come willingly but then found themselves in exploitative working conditions. This ideal victim stereotype is heavily raced and classed, and perpetuates assumptions that individualized aspects of this crime are the problem, namely a perpetrator, a buyer, and a victim for whom access to technology is both the source and solution. This stereotype also perpetuates the notion that trafficking victims are always stripped of any sense of agency or autonomy in their experiences, when this does not accurately represent the lived experiences of many sex trafficking victims (Hickle & Roe-Sepowitz, 2016).

Structural and systemic inequalities also play an important role in shaping the wider context sex trafficking occurs within; poverty and a lack of opportunities for education, employment, and stable housing place women at risk for being exploited (Martin, et al., 2010). Increased fears regarding unwanted migration shape trafficking policies (Jahnsen & Skilbrei, 2015) and affect the ways in which international trafficking victims are identified and protected. Children and young people experiencing abuse and neglect, particularly those running from home and going missing for periods of time, are still most vulnerable to being trafficked, and often services provided for these young people are among the least protected and most vulnerable in times of austerity. Like many victims of trafficking, they may form a relationship with an individual trafficker, or trafficking network, as they believe it to be the best option available to them; thus, they exercise some degree of autonomy in entering this relationship or agreeing to engage in sex work but do so in very constrained and desperate circumstances. This example demonstrates what Long (2004) refers to as a 'continuum of limited autonomy', wherein victims may experience some degree of agency and the ability to make their own decisions whilst not being entirely free.

While not unique to internet-facilitated sex trafficking, the framework of a 'continuum of limited autonomy' remains relevant in the changing technological landscape through which sex trafficking is taking place. For example, it is useful in considering the hard-to-reach young people in Bouché's (2015) study who have some autonomy in their work, retain access to the internet (i.e. the world outside their trafficking network), and do not perceive themselves to be trafficked at all. It is also helpful in considering the experiences of trafficking victims who may have willingly been smuggled across international borders but are then trapped by ever-increasing debts to their traffickers or deceived by traffickers who promise one form of work by deliver another. Each of these examples illuminates the complexity surrounding sex trafficking victimization as both a global phenomenon and widely perpetuated human rights abuse, as well as a very individualized experience that is shaped by exploitative relationships between the powerful and vulnerable.

Conclusions and future directions

Sex trafficking is a crime that will continue to be changed and shaped both in cyberspace and in the very tangible social and cultural contexts in which traffickers, victims, and sex buyers live. In order to address the problem holistically, researchers, policy makers and practitioners need to seek out responses that reflect the complexity of the problem. Micro-level interventions, including well trained law enforcement and available victim support and legal aide, need to be sufficiently funded in order to meet the increasing numbers of identified trafficking victims. Jennifer Martin and Ramona Alaggia (2013) also suggest that social workers and other helping professionals must conceptualize cyberspace as part of a child or young person's ecological system and thus incorporate the possibility of internet-facilitated abuse into their investigations and assessments. Intermediate level interventions, including national police sting operations and policies aimed at supporting police and prosecution need to be thoughtfully constructed, informed by research, and balanced by careful understanding of the implications for victims' right to privacy (Latonero, 2012). Finally, macro level issues must be more widely understood; particularly in relation to structural violence that creates environments where potential victims remain vulnerable, stigmatized, and hidden (Mendel & Sharapov, 2014).

Considering the relatively recent focus in research and practice on human trafficking, much still remains unknown regarding how to address this problem over time. Very little is known about the ways that technology can be harnessed to reach out to victims and directly provide help or information about the help that is available (e.g. a national trafficking hotline). Recently, anti-trafficking organizations have begun to explore ways to reach out via emailing, Facebook messaging, and text messaging to potential (or known) victims. While this represents one innovative and promising response, any efforts to do this must be tempered by a careful consideration of the risks a victim may incur in the process (e.g. repercussions if a trafficker who is monitoring online activity discovers this contact). Emerging research does indicate that this is an important strategy, and one that can be employed alongside other efforts including: (1) widespread training and education programmes for teachers, social workers, police, health professionals, taxi drivers, and hotel staff who may interact with trafficking victims on a regular basis; and (2) advertised information about available help via billboards, print ads, and online ads (Bouché, 2015). These strategies are crucial in providing victim-centred services that create space for individuals to reach out, trust, and disclose the abuse they have suffered whilst being provided with resources to meet the needs that their traffickers may have been meeting for them (e.g. food and shelter). Finally, these strategies should be implemented alongside concerted efforts to advocate for national and international policies that prevent vulnerabilities associated with trafficking in the first place.

References

Bernstein, E. (2007). The sexual politics of the 'new abolitionism'. *differences*, *18*(3), 128–151.

Bernstein, E. (2010). Militarized humanitarianism meets carceral feminism: The politics of sex, rights, and freedom in contemporary antitrafficking campaigns. *Signs, 36*, 45–71.

Berriman, L., & Thomson, R. (2015). Spectacles of intimacy? Mapping the moral landscape of teenage social media. *Journal of Youth Studies, 18*(5), 583–597. doi: 10.1080/13676261.2014.992323

Bouché, V. (2015). *A report on the use of technology to recruit, groom, and sell domestic minor sex trafficking victims.* Thorn: Digital Defenders of Children, available online at www.wearethorn.org/wp-content/uploads/2015/02/Survivor_Survey_r5.pdf

Brayley, H., & Cockbain, E. (2014). British children can be trafficked too: Towards an inclusive definition of internal child sex trafficking. *Child Abuse Review, 23*, 171–184.

Brayley, H., Cockbain, E., & Laycock, G. (2011). The value of crime scripting: Deconstructing internal child sex trafficking. *Policing, 5*, 132–143. doi: 10.1093/police/par024

Cianciarulo, M. S. (2008). What is choice? Examining sex trafficking legislation through the lenses of rape law and prostitution. *University of St. Thomas Law Journal, 6*(1), 54–76.

Dalla, R. L. (2000). Exposing the 'pretty woman' myth: A qualitative examination of the lives of female streetwalking prostitutes. *Journal of Sex Research, 37*(4), 344–353. doi: 10.1080=00224490009552057

Dalla, R. L. (2003). When the bough breaks ... : Examining intergenerational parent-child relational patterns among street level sex workers and their parents and children. *Applied Developmental Science, 7*(4), 216–228.

Dank, M., Khan, B., Downey, P. M., Kotonias, C., Mayer, D., Owens, C., ... Yu, L. (2014). Estimating the size and structure of the underground commercial sex economy in eight major US cities. Urban Institute Website, available online at www.urban.org/UploadedPDF/413047-Underground-Commercial-Sex-Economy.pdf

Davis, N. J. (2000). From victims to survivors: Working with recovering street prostitutes. In R. Weitzer (ed.), *Sex for sale* (pp. 139–155). New York: Routledge.

Dewey, S. (2012). The feminized labor of sex work: Two decades of feminist historical and ethnographic research. *Labor, 9*(2), 113–132.

Estes, R. J., & Weiner, N. A. (2001). *The commercial sexual exploitation of children in the U.S., Canada and Mexico.* Philadelphia: University of Pennsylvania.

Gallagher, A. (2015). Two cheers for the trafficking protocol. *Anti-Trafficking Review, 4*, 14–32, available online at www.antitraffickingreview.org

Gerassi, L. (2015). From exploitation to industry: Definitions, risks, and consequences of domestic sexual exploitation and sex work among women and girls. *Journal of Human Behavior in the Social Environment, 25*(6), 591–605.

Gibbs, D. A., Walters, J. L. H., Lutnick, A., Miller, S., & Kluckman, M. (2014). Services to domestic minor victims of sex trafficking: Opportunities for engagement and support. *Children and youth services review, 54*, 1–7.

Hedin, U. C., & Månsson, S. A. (2004). The importance of supportive relationships among women leaving prostitution. *Journal of Trauma Practice, 2*(3–4), 223–237.

Hickle, K., & Roe-Sepowitz, D. (2016). 'Curiosity and a pimp': Exploring sex trafficking victimization in experiences of entering sex trade industry work among participants in a prostitution diversion program. *Women & Criminal Justice*, 1–17.

Hossain, M., Zimmerman, C., Abas, M., Light, M., & Watts, C. (2010). The relationship of trauma to mental disorders among trafficked and sexually exploited girls and women. *American Journal of Public Health, 100*(12), 2442–2449.

Hoyle, C., Bosworth, M., & Dempsey, M. (2011). Labelling the victims of sex trafficking: Exploring the borderland between rhetoric and reality. *Social & Legal Studies, 20*(3), 313–329. doi: 10.1177/0964663911405394

Hudson, A., & Nandy, K. (2012). Comparisons of substance abuse, high risk sexual behavior and depressive symptoms among homeless youth with and without a history of foster care placement. *Contemporary Nursing, 42*, 178–186.

Jahnsen, S. Ø., & Skilbrei, M. L. (2015). From Palermo to the streets of Oslo: Pros and cons of the trafficking framework. *Anti-Trafficking Review, 4*, 156–160.

Janson, L., Durchlag, R., Mann, H., Marro, R., & Matvey, A. (2013). *"Our great hobby": An analysis of online networks for buyers of sex in Illinois.* A Report by Chicago Alliance Against Sexual Exploitation. Available online at http://icasa.org/hyperonix/docs/misc/caase%20report%20online%20buyers%20of%20sex%20in%20illinois.pdf

Jones, A. (2015). For black models scroll down: webcam modeling and the racialization of erotic labor. *Sexuality & Culture, 19*(4), 776–799.

Klatt, T., Cavner, D., & Egan, V. (2014). Rationalising predictors of child sexual exploitation and sex-trading. *Child Abuse & Neglect, 38*(2), 252–260. doi: 10.1016/j.chiabu.2013.08.019

Kotrla, K. (2010). Domestic minor sex trafficking in the United States. *Social Work, 55*, 181–187. doi: 10.1093/sw/55.2.18

Kramer, L. A., & Berg, E. C. (2003). A survival analysis of timing of entry into prostitution: The differential impact of race, educational level, and childhood=adolescent risk factors. *Sociological Inquiry, 37*, 511–528.

Latonero, M. (2012). Technology and human trafficking: The rise of mobile and the diffusion of technology-facilitated trafficking. Available online at SSRN 2177556.

Lederer, L., & Wetzel, C. (2014). The health consequences of sex trafficking and their implications for identifying victims in healthcare facilities. *Annals of Health Law, 23*, 61–91.

Long, L. D. (2004). Anthropological perspectives on the trafficking of women for sexual exploitation. *International Migration, 42*(1), 5–31.

Macy, R. J., & Graham, L. M. (2012). Identifying domestic and international sex-trafficking victims during human service provision. *Trauma, Violence, & Abuse, 13*(2), 59–76. doi: 10.1177/1524838012440340

Martin, J., & Alaggia, R. (2013). Sexual abuse images in cyberspace: Expanding the ecology of the child. *Journal of child sexual abuse, 22*(4), 398–415.

Martin, L., & Pierce, A. (2014). Mapping the market for sex with trafficked minors in Minneapolis: Structures, functions, and patterns: Full Report: Preliminary findings. University of Minnesota.

Martin, L., Hearst, M. O., & Widome, R. (2010). Meaningful differences: Comparison of adult women who first trade sex as a juvenile versus as an adult. *Violence Against Women, 16*, 1252–1269.

McClanahan, S. F., McClelland, G. M., Abram, K. M., & Teplin, L. A. (1999). Pathways into prostitution among female jail detainees and their implications for mental health services. *Psychiatric Services, 50*, 1606–1613.

Mendel, J., & Sharapov, K. (2014). *Human trafficking and online networks.* Policy Briefing, Center for Policy Studies, Central European University. Available online at http://cps.ceu.edu/sites/default/files/field_attachment/news/node-41082/cps-policy-brief-upkat-human-trafficking-and-online-networks-2014

Monto, M., & Milrod, C. (2013). Ordinary or peculiar men? Comparing the customers of prostitutes with a nationally representative sample of men. *Journal of Offender Therapy and Comparative Criminology.* doi: 11.1177/0306624X1340487

Musto, J. L., & boyd, d. (2014). The trafficking-technology nexus. *Social Politics: International Studies in Gender, State & Society*, jxu018.

Nixon, K., Tutty, L., Downe, P., Gorkoff, K., & Ursel, J. (2002). The everyday occurrence: Violence in the lives of girls exploited through prostitution. *Violence Against Women, 8*, 1016–1043.

O'Connel Davidson, J. (2010). New slavery, old binaries: Human trafficking and the borders of "freedom". *Global Networks, 10*(2), 244–261.

Raphael, J., & Shapiro, D. L. (2004). Violence in indoor and outdoor prostitution venues. *Violence Against Women, 10*(2), 126–139. doi: 10.1177/1077801203260529.

Reid, J. (2014a). Entrapment and enmeshment schemes used by sex traffickers. *Sex Abuse: A Journal of Research and Treatment*, 1–12. doi: 10.1177/1079063214544334

Reid, J. (2014b). Risk and resiliency factors influencing onset and adolescence-limited commercial sexual exploitation of disadvantaged girls. *Criminal Behavior and Mental Health, 24*, 332–44.

Rocha, V. (2015). 'Operator of prostitution website myRedBook sentenced to federal prison', *Los Angeles Times*, 22 May. Available online at www.latimes.com/local/lanow/la-me-ln-prostitution-website-federal-prison-20150522-story.html

Roe-Sepowitz, D. (2012). Juvenile entry into prostitution: The role of emotional abuse. *Violence Against Women, 18*, 562–579.

Roe-Sepowitz, D., Gallagher, J., & Hickle, K. (2014). *Exploring sex trafficking and prostitution demand during the Super Bowl 2014*. Office of Sex Trafficking Intervention Research, Arizona State University.

Roe-Sepowitz, D., Hickle, K., Gallagher, J., Smith, J, & Hedberg, E. (2013) Invisible offenders. a study estimating online sex customers. Available online at https://copp.asu.edu/college-news/research-docs/invisible-offenders-a-study-estimating-online-sex-customers-executive-summary/view

Schwarz, C., & Britton, H. E. (2015). Queering the support for trafficked persons: LGBTQ communities and human trafficking in the heartland. *Social Inclusion, 3*(1).

Simons, R. L., & Whitbeck, L. B. (1991). Sexual abuse as a precursor to prostitution and victimization among adolescent and adult homeless women. *Journal of Family Issues, 12*(3), 361–379.

Southworth, C., Finn, J., Dawson, S., Fraser, C., & Tucker, S. (2007). Intimate partner violence, technology, and stalking. *Violence Against Women, 13*(8), 842–856.

Thakor, M., & boyd, d. (2013). Networked trafficking: Reflections on technology and the anti-trafficking movement. *Dialectical Anthropology, 37*(2), 277–290.

Wells, M., Mitchell, K. J., & Kai, J. (2012). Exploring the role of the internet in juvenile prostitution cases coming to the attention of law enforcement. *Journal of Child Sexual Abuse, 21*, 327–342. doi: 10.1080/10538712.2012.669823

Wittes, B., Poplin, C., Jurecic, Q., & Spera, C. (2016). *Sextortion: Cybersecurity, teenagers, and remote sexual assault*, Centre for Technology Innovation at Brookings. Available online at www.brookings.edu/wp-content/uploads/2016/05/sextortion1-1.pdf

U.S. Department of State. (2000). Victims of Trafficking and Violence Protection Act of 2000. Available online at www.state.gov/j/tip/laws/61124.htm

U.S. Department of State. (2016). Trafficking in Persons Report. Available online at www.state.gov/documents/organization/258876.pdf

UN Protocol to Prevent, Suppress, and Punish Trafficking in Persons, Especially Women and Children, available online at www.unodc.org/unodc/en/treaties/CTOC/index.html

Young, A. M., Boyd, C., & Hubbell, A. (2000). Prostitution, drug use, and coping with psychological distress. *Journal of Drug Issues, 30*(4), 789–800.

6 Online sexual grooming
Children as victims of online abuse

Elena Martellozzo

Introduction

Children do not exist in isolation. When they are born, they belong to a family and as they grow older they become part of a wider community, with its own culture and beliefs (Belsky, 1980). In today's digital age, children are not only exposed to the immediate community that visibly surrounds them, but also to that less visible and less tangible world of cyberspace. As a result, they are exposed to a new level of vulnerability that did not exist before. It can be argued that the emergence of communication technologies in our everyday lives may be considered a contributing factor to the increase in ways in which children may be sexually victimised. Children may be victimised online in a number of ways: they may become the subjects of indecent images; they may be groomed for sexual abuse which takes place offline or they may be groomed online and the abuse may be carried out via the use of webcams, for example.

Over the past decade, the greatest public, policy and media concern for children's safety on the internet has been that of children being sexually abused by someone they met online. However, there are many other online risks that children and young people can encounter when online. Potential risks can include: exposure to adult and age inappropriate content; contact, which includes sexual exploitation and the production of indecent images of children; and conduct, where harassment and sexting are potential outcomes (Phippen, 2009; Ahern & Mechling, 2013; Webster et al., 2014). This chapter gives focus to the problem of online contact, in particular the phenomenon of online sexual grooming, which often features other forms of risk such as indecent images, sexting, harassment and bullying also identified in this book.

Effects of communication technologies on online behaviour

It is not possible to determine who is more likely to become a victim of online abuse and why, without exploring the online environment and its unique characteristics that influence people's online behaviour. Possibly one of the most distinct characteristics is that of anonymity, although, it might be worth noting that it is becoming more difficult to use mainstream internet fora anonymously because of, for example, Facebook's "real name" policies. When communicating via social networks, email, instant messaging, etc., the physical boundaries that exist in the real world are completely removed. In this way people can be more open to the increase of self-disclosure, as they do not have to deal with face-to-face reactions or unpleasant arguments.

Elisabeth Staksrud and her colleagues (Staksrud et al., 2013) found that the use of social networking sites (SNS) encourages the sharing of personal information, which may be mundane or more intimate information. Online anonymity allows people to feel disinhibited, to do and say things in a cyber context that they would never consider in the real world. Sadly, the possibility of online anonymity is appealing not only for abusers who wish to groom children and hide their true identity (Martellozzo, 2015), but also to young people who are often perceived as naturally curious, inexperienced, thrill seeking (Atkinson & Newton, 2010) and impulsive (Romer, 2010). John Suler (2004:324) argues that the online "disinhibition effect", fuelled by anonymity, may reveal, "the true needs, emotions, and self attributes that dwell beneath surface personality presentations".

According to Suler, several online factors may cause disinhibition. The first he describes as dissociative anonymity, which enables people to dissociate their actions from their real world identity, making them feel more open and less vulnerable. Therefore, individuals are able to alter their identities, became aggressive or more sexualised, for example. Invisibility is also a distinctive feature of the online world, although interrelated with anonymity. Suler (2004) explains: "There are some important differences. In the text communication of e-mail, chat, instant messaging, and blogs, people may know a great deal about each other's identities and lives. However, they still cannot see or hear each other" (ibid., 2004:322). In other words, it refers to individuals not being physically seen or heard which, in turn may disinhibit them, and motivate them to visit sites and behave in ways they would not do in the physical world. Suler argues that even if the online identity is visible, the opportunity to be physically invisible amplifies disinhibition in the sense that allows people to say what they wish to say openly without being concerned with the consequences, such as embarrassing themselves or being rejected. Furthermore, communication online is not synchronised, that is, people do not interact with each other in real-time or at regular intervals. Suler calls this characteristic of online communications "asynchronicity" and he explains that because communication is not happening in real time, the person communicating does not have to deal with the immediate reaction of the people they are communicating with, further adding to the disinhibition effect (Suler, 2004:323). The last factor given by Suler is minimisation of status and authority online, where the absence of cues in dress, body language, and environmental settings reduce the effect of people's authority (Suler, 2004). In real world terms, authority figures such as teachers, police officers or even parents can express their status and power through a uniform, facial expressions and in the symbols of their environmental settings such as a police car or station, a classroom, or the home etc. The absence of these cues in the milieu environment of cyberspace may reduce the impact of their authority, which in turns allows people, particularly young people, to speak out and misbehave more. Suler argues that as cyberspace grows and continues to create open new environments "many of its inhabitants see themselves as innovative, independent-minded explorers and pioneers. This atmosphere and this philosophy contribute to the minimising of authority" (Suler, 2004:324). Sexual grooming takes place in this anonymous and disinhibited environment, where limited possibilities for regulation and control exist.

Defining online sexual grooming

Online grooming is a *modus operandi* that is commonly associated with sexual abuse and it can involve both children and adults. However, it is a method that perpetrators can use to prepare a person to commit a number of different other crimes: from cyberbullying to terrorism.

John McCarthy and Nathan Gaunt (2005) define the phenomenon of online sexual grooming "as a type of online behaviour designed to 'seduce' or lure children into sexual behaviour or conversations with or without children's knowledge" (ibid., 2005), with the intent of arranging to meet the child in the "real world" to sexually abuse them. Prior to arranging the meeting, the abuser would attempt to form a virtual "friendship" with the children, with the intention of physically meeting them and carrying out the abuse. However, sexual grooming may also be carried out in order to prepare a child for another person to abuse (Whittle et al., 2013). Therefore, a more condign definition is the one provided by Craven et al. (2006), which states that online grooming is:

> a process by which a person prepares a child, significant adults and the environment for the abuse of this child. Specific goals include gaining access to the child, gaining the child's compliance and maintaining the child's secrecy to avoid disclosure. This process serves to strengthen the offender's abusive pattern, as it may be used as a means of justifying or denying their actions.
>
> (Ibid., 2006:297)

A particular problem that occurs when we attempt to define the grooming process is that it is often not possible to establish when it starts or stops (Gillespie, 2004:10–11). In his latest pioneering work, Michael Seto[1] (2013) explains that there are three main variables that contribute to the commission of sexual abuse against children. These are: an antisocial trait in the offender; a sexual interest in children; and situational factors such as access to children. He argues that the presence of antisocial behaviour and opportunity factors can be the distinguishing factors that may trigger contact abuse. His 'Motivation-Facilitation Model of Sexual Offending against Children', is supported by the findings from the most recent meta-analysis on internet sex offenders, which recognises that the main predictors of recidivistic contact sex offending amongst offenders who use indecent images of children are being antisocial, having access to children and the lack of barriers to acting on one's deviant impulses (Babchishin, Hanson & VanZuylen, 2014).

Grooming is a crucial part of the so-called 'cycle of abuse' (Wolf, 1985; Finkelhor, 1986; Eldridge, 1998; Sullivan and Beech, 2004) and it does not only take place online, although this is a recent and major concern. The grooming process consists of sex offenders socialising and grooming children over prolonged periods of time to gain their trust and prepare them for sexual abuse and to ensure that abuse is not discovered or disclosed (Webster et al., 2014). Recent studies on sex offenders' grooming behaviour support the idea that the Internet does not create new stages in the cycle of abuse, but allows the cycle of abuse to be accelerated (Martellozzo, 2012, 2015; Webster et al., 2012).

Classifying online offenders

Up until very recently, the figure of the online offender, or even the concept of a child being sexually groomed and abused via the internet, was difficult to fathom. A clear understanding of the online offender is necessary to inform our understanding of how online sexual grooming occurs and the vulnerability of children and young people when online. Research in the area of sexual abuse against children has repeatedly shown that sex offenders cannot be easily 'picked out' of a crowd (Grubin, 1998; Stanko, 1990). There is no consistent model or typology into which they can be accurately placed for the purpose of identification and isolation – and public denunciation. This contention can also be applied to online forms of child sexual abuse. Notwithstanding this caveat, a number of empirical studies have been carried out to ascertain, through the development of typologies and classifications of internet grooming offenders, what characterises these individuals and how they groom children online.

Table 6.1 summarises some of the key and most recent existing typologies of internet child sex offenders.

Independent of these classifications, online groomers seem to form two distinct groups: those whose offences relate to fantasy and meeting sexual needs online, and those whose primary intention is to meet young people offline to carry out the abuse (Briggs et al., 2011). Online, individuals have the opportunity to explore the dark side of their sexuality by assuming desired identities and by disclosing as much or as little about themselves as they wish to others (Cooper, McLoughlin & Campbell, 2000). Moreover, by hiding behind their fictitious avatar, they may explore any opportunities cyberspace may offer, including possibilities to sexually abuse children (Websteret al., 2014; Martellozzo, 2012).

Between 2004 and 2008, I carried out an empirical study seeking to understand and explain the problem of online child sexual abuse and the way in which investigative tactics and operational procedures were employed by the London Metropolitan Police High Technological Crime Unit (HTCU) and Paedophile Unit. During this study, I observed one of the first Metropolitan Police undercover operations carried out in London, where a fictitious girl's profile was set

Table 6.1 Classification of online sex offenders

Sullivan and Beech (2004)	**Type 1** Collects images as part of a larger part of sexual offending, possibly including contact offending.	**Type 2** Collects images to feed a developing sexual interest in children which may escalate and cross-over to contact offending.	**Type 3** Accesses images out of curiosity which is unlikely to lead to contact sexual offending in most cases.
Beech et al. (2008)	**Periodically prurient** Accesses impulsively, or out of a general curiosity.	**Fantasy only** Accesses/trades images to fuel a sexual interest in children; no known history of contact sexual offending.	**Direct victimisation** Uses online technology as part of a larger pattern of sex offending, including child abuse material and the grooming of children online in order to facilitate contact sexual offending.	**Commercial exploitation** Criminally minded individual who produces or trades images to make money.
Elliot and Ashfield (2011)	**Solo type 1** Solo offenders who abuse adolescent children (the euphemistic 'teacher/lover' group[2]).	**Solo type 2** Solo offenders who abuse pre-pubescent children.	**Psychiatrically disordered** Have a variety of victim types. These individuals' behaviours may be attributed to a psychiatric disorder.	**Financial SOs** Motivated by commercial profit; provides victims for child molesters in return for money.	**Male associated** (a) male-coerced (those who participate under the explicit threat of emotional abuse or physical violence) (b) active male-accompanied (those who play an interested or active role) (c) passive male-accompanied (those who provide opportunities for abuse or do not act to prevent abuse, but do not take an active role).

Gottschalk (2011)	**Distorted attachment** Wants a relationship with young people.	**Adaptable online groomer** Wants to satisfy his/her own needs and sees the victim as mature and capable.	**Hyper-sexualised** Possesses child abuse material and has significant online contact with other paedophiles.
Martellozzo (2012)	**Hyper-confident groomers** May create a decent (fully clothed photo) or indecent (naked or semi-naked photo) profile. Friendships normally develop after the profile is added to the child's list of friends.	**Hyper-cautious groomers** Are so concerned about being caught that they are not willing to furnish details about themselves until confident they are speaking to a "real" person.	
Webster et al. (2012)	**Intimacy-seeking** Do not have previous convictions for sexual offending or engage in networking with other sex offenders and are unlikely to have child abuse material. They are likely to engage in an intimate relationship with the younger person and believe the contact to be consensual.	**Adaptable style** Tend to have previous convictions for sexual offending against children and view young people as mature and capable. Not avid networkers or collectors of indecent images. They adapt their approach according to the young person being engaged and their reactions.	**Hyper-sexualised** Tend to have significant collections of indecent images and network extensively with other online sex offenders. They use deception and contact with young people is likely to progress rapidly and be of a sexual nature. Progression to contact offences with the young person is less likely with this type than the other types.

up by undercover officers to attract online groomers resulting in the girl's profile being viewed by more than 1,300 individuals in the short space of time of one month (Martellozzo, 2012). Of these, more than 450 individuals with adult male profiles initiated contact with the 'fictitious' child, and 80 became virtual 'friends', communicated regularly with the girl in a sexual manner. Young (2001:300) defines such individuals as 'fantasy users', and distinguishes those who utilise online chat rooms and instant messaging services for the express purpose of role-playing in online fantasy sex chat.

Quayle et al. (2014), in an exploratory qualitative study with 14 men convicted of online sexual grooming, also found that all of the men interviewed admitted that meeting a young person online enables sexual fantasies, which lead to sexual pleasure. Within this group of respondents, five men arranged to meet their victim offline for sexual purposes. Similarly, in my study (Martellozzo, 2012) of 23 suspects, nine turned up to meet the undercover officer posing as a young girl, a further five had arranged to meet 'her' but did not turn up or cancelled at the last minute. Unfortunately, it was not possible to establish what made some of the subjects turn up to meet the 'girl' and others to cancel. However, fear of apprehension alone may have prevented some subjects from turning up to a pre-arranged meeting.

The law

Sexual grooming using information and communication technology has been criminalised in England and Wales since 2013, Scotland since 2005 and in some European Union (EU) countries for a number of years: Ireland, Norway and France (2007), the Netherlands and Spain (2010) and Austria and Italy (2012) (IRC, 2012). In the United Kingdom, Section 15 of the Sexual Offences Act (SOA) 2003 makes 'meeting a child following sexual grooming' a serious offence. This applies to internet-enabled technologies (smart phones, mobile phones, game consoles and tablets) and the 'real world' where a person arranges to meet a child who is under 18, having communicated with them on at least one previous occasion (in person, via the internet or via other technologies), with the intention of performing sexual activity on the child (Davidson & Martellozzo, 2008).

The grooming legislation in the UK has recently been updated. Section 67 of the Serious Crime Act 2015 creates a new offence of sexual communication with a child, which helps ensure that young people are fully protected by the law and allow the authorities to intervene earlier to prevent more serious offending against children. The new offence criminalises a person aged 18 years or over who communicates with a child under 16 (who the adult does not reasonably believe to be 16 or over), if the communication is sexual or if it is intended to elicit from the child a communication which is sexual. 'Sexual Grooming' has also been added to the Crimes Amendment Act 2005 in New Zealand. Under Australian law, grooming occurs when a person uses an internet or telephone device to send an indecent communication to a young person under the age of 16. The legislation in the UK differs in that the sexual grooming offence applies both to the internet and the 'real world' whereas legislation in other countries addresses only electronic grooming via the internet and mobile phones. While the term 'grooming' has not been defined in international law the term 'solicitation' is defined in international law, for example in the European Commission Directive. In some jurisdictions such as Canada and the US, the term 'luring' is used instead and it is applied to minors who are younger than 16 years of age.

Children as victims of online sexual abuse: exploring the risk factors

The vast majority of children and young people's online experiences and interactions are positive and, for most, their internet and technology use delivers significant benefits in terms of social, educational and creative engagements. The use of technologies has become such an integral part of their daily existence, that the distinction between their online and offline activities is now redundant. The online and offline worlds have converged in such a way that one feeds into the other, each influencing and shaping the other (Fogela & Nehmadb, 2009). So, for example, a young person may meet someone on holiday abroad and this new relationship, despite the geographical distance, and possibly the time zone difference, can continue online and become a significant friendship. Similarly, friendships may start in the online environment and develop into deep and meaningful experiences for those involved, even if a physical meeting never occurs.

Adolescents, and many adults, have embraced the openness, anonymity and the freedom of expression that the internet offers. Some are more likely to engage in risky behaviours, putting themselves in danger and becoming more open to the attention of those who wish to abuse them. There is little research evidence to ascertain with confidence the characteristics of exactly who is more likely to become a victim of online abuse. Nevertheless, from what we know, it is possible to state that gender is one of the key factors (Whittle et al. 2013). Although there are inconsistent research findings on whether boys use the internet more than girls in developed nations, we have found that they are more likely to reveal personal information to strangers online (Davidson & Martellozzo, 2016), whereas girls are more at risk of becoming victims of online abuse (Baumgartner et al., 2010; Wolak et al., 2008). However, this is not to say that boys are safer than girls. On the contrary, it may be possible that boys simply appear to be less at risk than girls because, if they are victimised, they may have problems reporting abuse to the authorities because of sex-role stereotyping and the heavily negative stigma it carries (Davidson & Martellozzo, 2008).

In relation to offline abuse, Finkelhor (1984) states that "boys will be less likely to report abuse as long as it is considered unmanly to ask for help or suffer a hurt and as long as being the victim of a sexual assault is threat to masculinity" (ibid., 1984:233).

In other words, boys may not report abuse because of the emasculating experience of being abused and being seen as victims. What needs to be acknowledged is that boys find it difficult to comprehend that they are also at risk of becoming victims of online sexual abuse (Davidson & Martellozzo, 2004). In their research on behalf of the Child Exploitation and Online Protection Centre (CEOP) exploring internet abuse amongst young people in England, Julia Davidson and Elena Martellozzo (2012) found that this problem also repeatedly emerges in the sphere of online abuse. Some of the children that took part in the CEOP research believe that girls are more at risk than boys and therefore boys behave with greater disinhibition when online.

Furthermore, same sex-attracted boys in particular may feel confused and insecure about their sexuality, which can be easily picked up by callous online sex offenders (Whittle et al., 2013), who are overwhelmingly male (Wolak et al., 2008; Martellozzo, 2012). Clearly this is a gender stereotype that needs to be taken into account when looking at issues of vulnerability.

Age is another important key risk factor that deserves attention for the understanding of online victimisation. In the child sexual abuse literature, some studies suggest that abuse is most prevalent before puberty (Children's Bureau and Department of Health and Human Services, 2010) while others suggest that adolescent children are mostly at risk (Bebbington et al., 2011). Quayle (2010) argues that pre-pubescent youth are more at risk of victimisation through sexual computer mediated crimes than children under the age of nine. One possible explanation for this heightened risk in older children may be due to the much higher level of online communication and variety of access platforms for older children (Ólafsson et al., 2013), together with the fact that they are simply more knowledgeable regarding technology and favourable to exploration, including sexual exploration.

Undoubtedly, social networking sites and more recently the rise of messaging apps like 'WhatsApp' and image sharing apps, like Snapchat and Instagram, have captured the interest of many adolescents and young adults, and are a ubiquitous influence in how they both develop and socialise with others (Tiffany A. Pempek et al., 2009). Recent British research conducted by the Office of Communications (OFCOM, 2016), examining the nature of access and use of the internet among a national sample of children aged five to 15, showed that the vast majority of children use the internet, with over 88 per cent having access to the internet at home. Furthermore, the average 16- to 24-year-old now spends just under 9 hours a day with online media and communications, compared to an adult person, who spends 25 hours in an entire week on it, up from 9 hours in 2005 (OFCOM, 2016). This is quickly becoming a reality also for children from the developing world where internet penetration and use of mobile technology has increased exponentially. For example, the International Communications Union (ITU, 2011) shows that one in three children in the Arab States are online, and 20.7 per cent in Africa, are online, with that number rising annually. Furthermore, recent research conducted in the Kingdom of Bahrain (Davidson & Martellozzo, 2016), also shows that the majority of adolescents and young adults utilise social networking sites and that the number of memberships increases with age. Julia Davidson and Elena Martellozzo found that among those children and young people (aged 10 to 18) surveyed, the use of such sites is nearly universal. It is evident that there has been an increase in the amount of time young people are spending online, with nearly one-quarter of those surveyed responding that they spend more than four hours online in any given day. The mean time spent was 2.58 with a standard deviation of 1.75, in other words two-thirds of the sample of school youth spent between 0.83 and 4.33 hours per week online. Furthermore, the survey data suggested that doing homework/research online (65.2 per cent) was one of the most common online activities. One young person stated that the internet was a useful tool 'for looking up things I do not know' (male, age 13), demonstrating a keen interest in auto-didactic and information gathering. Many were using instant messaging (45.6 per cent) to 'communicate with my friends' (female, age 14) and 'spending time' with friends (51.1 per cent), and they were communicating with their friends through 'social media apps, like Snapchat and Instagram' (female, age 14).

Another explanation as to why older children are more vulnerable to online grooming is related to common intrapersonal features such as low self-esteem, emotional disturbances and psychological disorders (Webster et al., 2012). Sonia Livingstone and her colleagues found that across Europe, young people with mental health issues are more likely to become victims of online dangers and to be more affected by the negative experience (Livingstone et al., 2011). Furthermore, a possible lower level of supervision and control provided by caregivers to the older groups in comparison to that offered to children 11 years old and below (Davidson & Martellozzo, 2016), may also increase the risk of becoming an online victim of abuse. It may be the case that increased supervision can lower the risks that young people are willing to take, through increasing the fear of being caught. However, it is becoming more difficult to supervise children and young people, given the recent, sudden boom in the availability of internet-enabled devices that can be carried around, outside the controlled home environment (Vincent, 2015). This online mobility can certainly be interpreted as a positive opportunity for children, in the sense that they know can create their own personal connection to the internet without the pressure of being supervised by adults (ibid., 2015:1). However, Eric Rice (2012) and his colleagues (Rice et al., 2012) found that American adolescents with daily access to the internet through a mobile phone are more likely to report being solicited for online sex, being sexually active and having sex with partners that they met online. Nonetheless, high levels of access alone are not a necessary, or a sufficient cause, of online victimization. Other factors, presented later in this chapter, may underpin it.

Furthermore, as shown in my research previously discussed, the fictitious accounts of young girls created by undercover police officers to attract online groomers were not designed with any stereotypical vulnerable child in mind (Martellozzo, 2012). The details of the children's life and possible vulnerabilities could only be captured during the interaction between the 'child' and the suspect. As Whittle et al. (2013) argue, this could mean that any child could be vulnerable to seduction by any adult online, by simply being accessible to potential online predators. However, "it is likely that only the vulnerable responds while the resilient remains unaffected" (Whittle et al., 2013:142). Finding potential child victims may not happen as quickly, as not all children are at risk of online abuse, as argued by Sonia Livingstone: "the identification of online risk does not imply that harm will follow, nor that all users are equally effected; rather, it is a probabilistic judgment regarding an outcome that depends on the particular and contingent interaction between user and environment" (Livingstone et al., 2011:3).

Online risks in some cases may lead to harm but in others, they may facilitate resilience (Livingstone et al., 2011:13). However, it appears to be the case that offline vulnerability extends its consequences online, as risk migrates from traditional to new sites. Therefore, children who are 'vulnerable' and risk-taking offline are more likely to be susceptible to online abuse. Quayle et al.'s (2014) sample of respondents claimed that they were only interested in young people who showed an interest in them. Furthermore, these men claimed they were seeking for young people, whose profiles were revealing certain information, including images. The researchers argued:

> Such information was used to both fuel fantasy, facilitate contact with young people and to accrue a body of information that enabled this skillful manipulation of technological platforms in the absence of historical expertise. This use of technology allowed for the compartmentalization of offending behaviour away from every-day activities and enabled the majority of these men to live apparently 'normal' lives while at the same time engaging in high rates of illegal sexual behaviour.
>
> (Quayle et al., 2014:374)

Explaining the under-reporting of child sexual abuse (CSA)

What makes it difficult to determine the extent of child sexual abuse, whether it takes place online or offline, is that official criminal statistics describing the incidence of sexual offences are unreliable indicators of the true prevalence of this illegal behaviour in society. Research conducted by the National Society for the Prevention of Cruelty to Children (Bunting, 2005) provides concerning evidence that one in four males and one in three females will experience sexual abuse before they reach the age of eighteen and only one in eight children who are sexually abused are identified by professionals (OCC, 2015). Translated in different terms, in the UK this would account for over 20 per cent of the population. Similarly, research conducted in the United States show that one in 10 children will become victims of sexual abuse by the age of 18 and that of those who are sexually abused, 20 per cent are abused before the age of eight (www.d2l.org). Whatever the accurate figure is, it is a serious problem and far greater than recorded crime statistics would suggest.

One of the main obstacles impeding the development of a coherent and reliable overview of the nature and extent of child sexual abuse across different countries and jurisdictions is this lack of reporting. Very few children disclose sexual abuse and even fewer disclose their abuse when the actual abuse has occurred via new technologies (Allnock, 2010). The silent nature of the victims of abuse has been well documented in recent times and has been considered closely by charities specialising in child protection and the prevention of cruelty to children (see, for example, the National Society for the Prevention of Cruelty to Children, the internet Watch Foundation, the Lucy Faithful Foundation in the UK; the Australian Childhood Foundation in Australia; Prometeo in Italy etc.). The reasons for this silence and therefore for the significant level of underreporting are complex and varied. Cawson et al. (2000:83), in a study on child maltreatment in the UK found that three-quarters (72 per cent) of sexually abused children did not tell anyone about the abuse at the time. Twenty seven per cent told someone later. Around a third (31 per cent) still had not told anyone about their experience(s) by early adulthood.

Jean La Fontaine (1990) suggested that this large percentage of unreported cases is a symptom of an uncomfortable silence around the topic. It is important that the matter of silence is understood, as it relates to the issues such as a lack of understanding of sexual matters, combined with feelings of guilt, embarrassment, and/or shame. What may help the formulation of a constructive answer to why children fail to report sexual abuse is the analysis and evaluation of the seduction, or grooming process, which commences long before any physical contact (Cawson et al., 2000), assuming anything physical happens at all (Martellozzo, 2015). The grooming process usually begins with the identification of the appropriate child victim and it continues, often for a long time, through careful and meticulous research about the interests, passions and weaknesses of the child (Lanning, 2005:56).

Elena Martellozzo (2012) showed that the process of grooming may never leave the comfortable environment of cyberspace, where the offender can remain anonymous. According to Quayle et al. (2014), this high level of anonymity benefits sex offenders greatly: it allows offenders to manipulate their identity; to avoid detection by selecting sites that do not require registration; to enable the control of privacy and to move freely from one platform to another. The online abuse may involve different forms of criminal online sexual behaviour such as encouraging children to hold sexual conversations, exposing themselves online via webcams, perhaps leading to pressure to engage in, and talk about sexual behaviour. An abuser may be looking for young people to engage in this sort of behaviour in locations that are used predominantly by young people such as teen chatrooms or social networking sites. Preferential sex offenders know how to select a child for potential sexual abuse: they are usually very good at obtaining cooperation and gaining control of the child through well-planned seduction that employs adult authority, attention and gifts (Finkelhor, 1986; Finkelhor, 1994) and possibly bribery.

Thus, given the complex strategies that sex offenders employ to reach their aims, it is understandable that many victims fail to realise the ultimate goal of their perpetrators. In the online word, despite the lack of physical contact between the abuser and the child, children may be traumatised and harmed by online abuse and may find it difficult to talk about. As this teen age girl, groomed on the internet, states:

> I couldn't wait to get back from school, switch on my computer and get chatting with him. I can't believe he'd hurt other girls. I felt I could trust him with my life.
>
> (Lucy Faithfull Foundation, 2016:4)

Even when they do realise that attention, affection and gifts were only offered as means toward exploitation, they may find it difficult to report the abuse. Difficulties may arise due to a strong bond created with the offender over time, or through feelings of guilt and a sense of compulsion to inform the offender of their decision first, thus placing themselves at risk of being persuaded to remain silent (Lanning, 2005). Indeed, the offender may continue to manipulate the child even after disclosure has been made and an investigation has begun – for example, by making the child feel guilty or disloyal (ibid.). Some prevalent reasons why children do not disclose their sexual abuse are explained below.

The non-violent nature of CSA

La Fontaine (1990) has indicated that, contrary to public opinion, the vast majority of child sexual abuse CSA is of a non-physically violent nature. This is not an understatement of the extreme emotional and psychological violence involved in sexual abuse. Usually, CSA begins with relatively inappropriate touching by a familiar adult whom the child trusts. In this manner, the child does not become distressed and is unaware of the implications of what is happening. This behaviour gradually continues and becomes more and more sexual in nature, so the child becomes accustomed to what is happening. This is what Gallagher (2000) defines as 'entrapment', i.e. the process in which "perpetrators draw children into abusive situations and make it difficult for them to disclose" (Gallagher, 2000:810). He argues that this method consists of a number of techniques, but "chief among these is the involvement of children in increasingly intimate physical contact, and the provision of a variety of inducements, whether these are material, illicit or emotional in nature" (Gallagher, 2000:810). Because of this gradual nature of abuse, some children cannot define such behaviour as wrong until a later stage.

Berliner and Conte (1990) also stated that most children did not understand initially that they were being abused. Many victims later realise that they have engaged willingly in the previous behaviour and feel that it is too late to stop it (Lanning, 2005). However, these assertions cannot be used to explain intra-familial sexual abuse when this is carried out with the use of extreme physical violence. They can, however, be used to explain online grooming. As discussed previously in this chapter, research suggests that grooming online can be faster, or can take place over a long period of time (Martellozzo, 2012; Webster et al., 2013) but it is always anonymous. As a result, children tend to trust an online 'friend' more than they would trust someone that they have just met face-to-face. Therefore, sex offenders who wish to groom children for the purpose of abusing them are able stay anonymous and access any personal information of the child, particularly if the child has not placed particular emphasis on ensuring that his/her online digital privacy and security are robust.

As stated by this 13-year-old boy who met his chat room friend online:

> She was great. I felt I could talk to her about anything. It felt like she was my best friend. When I met her, 'she' turned out to be 'he' and was much older than me. He frightened and hurt me.

Sex offenders who groom children online are not restricted by space, time or access and they are not antagonised by those responsible for protecting their children, as they would be in the real world.

Use of threats and coercion

Threats are by far the most common way to induce compliance with sexual abuse (Featherstone & Evans, 2004). However, the most common form of threats used is to ask the child what would happen if the abuse were to be disclosed. The abuser typically insinuates that the child would be taken away from their home, the family would be broken up, and the abuser would go to jail (this is particularly convincing in intra-familial abuse cases where the abuser is someone close to the child). Supporting this argument is the claim of Louise, a 14-year-old girl, who, after months of abuse, called the UK's ChildLine and confessed:

> My stepfather makes me have sex with him. I want to stop, but I don't want to tell the police. I think they'll think it's my fault and will break up the family.
>
> (NSPCC, 2007)

This threat to remove the child from his or her family environment remains a very potent deterrent. Furthermore, the evidence (e.g. Featherstone & Evans, 2004) suggests that when children do disclose, it tends to be to family members, as they often are reluctant to approach authority figures and statutory services.

When Eddie, a 15-year-old boy, called ChildLine, he explained:

> I told a teacher what had been happening and she got social services to come talk to me, but I wouldn't say who had done it. It would break my Mum's heart.
>
> (Featherstone & Evans, 2004)

Children's ignorance and innocence

Children's ignorance and innocence are major sources of their own weakness. Children and young people often struggle with making decisions and are impulsive and risk taking. As Charlotte Walsh (2011) explains, this is to do with the frontal lobe, responsible for executive functioning and decision-making processes, that has not completed developing until the beginning of our third decade of life. Therefore, children and young people are likely to act in an impulsive manner, both offline, but more so when online (Livingstone & O'Brien, 2014), given the anonymous and disinhibited nature of the internet.

When the abuse starts and finishes in the real world or it moves from the online sphere to offline physical contact (Quayle & Ribisl, 2013), victim accounts indicate that children believe that the abuse is their fault and it is them who ought to be despised and punished (NSPCC, 2007). Sex offenders often use this to their advantage (Miller, 1997).

Arguably, the innocence and ignorance of children has been compounded by the lack of sex education in schools and families. One issue in this regard has been the role of religion. For example, in the 1990s, in Catholic countries like Ireland or some parts of Italy, schools were run predominantly by the Church. Therefore, children grew up with little or no formal sex education. Thus, if children received such an education, it usually came within the context of Catholic dogma, with little or no mention of the sexual act. Parents, who had experienced the same education as their children and had listened to regular sermons in church on the possible evils of extra-marital sexual activity, had difficulty teaching their children about sex. Therefore, those children who were abused may have had little or no knowledge of what was happening to them, or, if they did, may have understood it in a Catholic, guilt-ridden manner. This produced additional difficulties for those who were abused at that time. In the past, the lack of knowledge and education may have been a key contributory factor for the perpetration of child sexual abuse. Today sex education is covered in Personal Social and Health Education (PSHE) lessons under the National Curriculum in the UK and awareness is more present, however appropriate and inappropriate sexual behaviour is still not properly addressed (Martellozzo et al., 2017).

The child's 'love' for the abuser

Elaine Sharland (Sharland et al., 1996) suggests that children 'love' their abuser as parent, sibling, or friend. The type of love a child has must be differentiated from the so-called love that an abuser has for a child. Children love their abusers in the purest sense – they respect their abuser, do not want them to get into trouble, and thus do not want to lose them as friend. This can lead to a terrible dilemma for the child, even when they are fully aware that they are being abused. The following are two observations noted by social workers after interviewing children about their abuser:

> The child doesn't want him (the abuser) to go to prison. He fears he'll be hurt there.
>
> Throughout, the child was confused. He knew the man had been wrong but he felt affection for him. It was very hard to reassure him.
>
> (Sharland et al., 1996:139)

Silence is recognised mainly from the subjective experience of others who have come forward and verbalised their own experiences. Nevertheless, experts can never quantify the silence that lies at the heart of the community. Professionals and the media often discuss abuse in terms of 'unrecognised' or 'underestimated' reports. This in turn creates the notion of an invisible risk, something that is unquantifiable and unknown. As a consequence:

> the debate on child abuse has seen the clash of opinion about dimensions of the problem. Many specialists adopt the tip of the iceberg approach. They claim that the incidence of abuse is far greater that society is prepared to accept. Consequently, many of those involved in the sphere of child protection are convinced that what is invisible is more relevant that the so-called facts.
>
> (Furedi, 1997:40)

As a result of this process, there is a 'disproportionality' (Goode and Ben-Yehuda, 1994) surrounding reports of child sexual abuse.

Conclusions

The internet offers wonderful opportunities for learning, communicating and socialising. However, its complex architecture can present many challenges, particularly to the most vulnerable and ill-informed children. As this chapter argued, the reasons why children and young people become victims of online abuse are numerous. Although research in this area is still in its infancy, it is possible to claim that young people, particularly female teenagers, are those that are mostly at risk. Other vulnerabilities presented here are: intrapersonal features such as low self-esteem, emotional disturbances and psychological disorders; high levels of internet access; risk taking behaviours; poor parental involvement; and lack of reporting. As explained earlier, the reasons why children do not report sexual abuse can be complex and varied in both the real and the cyber world. One of the reasons why online abuse tends not to be reported is because most children do not realise they have been abused and do not understand what constitutes virtual abuse (Berelowitz et al., 2012). Should online grooming at some point become physical abuse in the real world, then those reasons for not disclosing abuse to responsible parents or authorities already discussed equally apply here. There are certain important spatial and temporal dynamics to the online grooming of children such as 'the paradox of online intimacy', in which spatially distant strangers effectively abuse vulnerable children within the intimate surroundings of the child's home and often without meeting them face-to-face.

Furthermore, there are recent concerns around the overlapping phenomenon of online child sexual extortion, sextortion and peer-perpetrated abuse. There is increasing recognition that children who abuse others using technology may not always be aware of the illegal nature of the behaviour (e.g. a boy who sends a girl a picture of his penis as a way of asking her out) and are not receiving formal educational intervention for example through PSHE classes which could help them to recognise the abusive/illegal nature of sending sexual images to others. This raises some interesting challenges to the traditional notion of the 'child as victim' and defines new ways in which children have become vulnerable to perpetration – blurring the boundary between victim and perpetrator in the online context.

In the past few years, many efforts have been made to ensure that awareness messages about online abuse and the consequences of online risk taking behaviour have reached out to children and young people (a good example is the police 'Think Before you Send' campaign in England www.westyorkshire.police.uk/sexting). And although education and awareness is improving, it is clear that more needs to be done in ensuring that children are fully aware of such online harms and are enabled to respond appropriately and safely. There is an additional need to ensure that children are taught to become responsible digital citizens, aware of ethical online behaviour and their online rights from a young age.

Notes

1 Much of Michael Seto's early research has focused on the psychological characteristics of sex offenders and their risk for reoffending. His latest research has focused on sex offending in cyberspace, specifically around the link between the use of indecent images of children and contact offending. Furthermore, he and his colleagues have found that the same kinds of risk factors are valid for online offenders as they are for conventional contact offenders, including age, criminal history, substance use, and sexual attraction to children.
2 Typically abused adolescents who may have perceived the abuse as a love affair.

References

Ahern, N. I., & Mechling, B. (2013). Sexting, serious problems for youth. *Journal of Psychosocial Nursing, 51* (7), 23–30.

Allnock, D. (2010). *Children and young people disclosing sexual abuse: an introduction to the research.* London: NSPCC.

Atkinson, C., & Newton, D. (2010). Online behaviours of adolescents: Victims, perpetrators and Web 2.0. *Journal of Sexual Aggression: An international, interdisciplinary forum for research, theory and practice* (16), 107–120.

Babchishin, K. M. (2004). Online child pornography offenders are different: A meta analysis of the characteristics of online and offline offenders against children. *Archives of Sexual Behaviour, 44* (1), 45–66.

Babchishin, K. M., Hanson, R. K., & Van Zuylen, H. (2004). Online child pornography offenders are different: A meta analysis of the characteristics of online and offline offenders against children. *Archives of Sexual Behaviour,* doi: 10.1007/s 10508-014-0270

Baumgartner, S. E., Valkenburg, P. M., & Peter, J. (2010). Unwanted online sexual solicitation and risky sexual online behaviour across the lifespan. *Journal of Applied Developmental Psychology, 31,* 275–290.

Bebbington, P. E., Jonas, S., Brugha, T., Meltzer, H., Jenkins, R., Cooper, C., King, M., & McManus, S. (2011). Child sexual abuse reported by an English national sample:

Characteristics and demography. *Social Psychiatry Psychiatric Epidemiology, 46* (3), 255–262.
Beech, A. R. (2008). The internet and child sexual offending: A criminological review. *Aggression and Violent Behavior, 13*, 216–228.
Belsky, J. (1980). Child maltreatment: An ecological integration. *American Psychologist* (35), 320–335.
Berelowitz, S., Firmin, C., Edwards, G., & Gulyurtlu, S. (2012). *Inquiry into Child Sexual Exploitation In Gangs and Groups. I Thought I Was the Only One. The Only One in the World.* The Office of the Children's Commissioner, London: OCC. Available online at www.childrenscommissioner.gov.uk/publications/"i-thought-i-was-only-one-only-one-world"-interim-report
Berliner, L., & Conte, J. (1990). The process of victimisation: The victims' perspective. *Child Abuse and Neglect, 14* (1), 29–45 .
Briggs, P., Simon, W. T., & Simonsen, S. (2011). An exploratory study of internet-initiated sexual offenses and the chat room sex offender: Has the internet enabled a new typology of sex offender? *Sexual Abuse: A Journal of Research and Treatment, 23*, 72–91, doi: 10.117/1079063210384275
Briggs, P. S. (2011). An exploratory study of internet initiated sexual offences an the chat room sex offender: as the internet enabled new typology of sex offender? *Sexual Abuse: A Journal of Research and Treatment, 23* (1), 72–91.
Bunting, L. (2005). *Females Who Sexually Offend Against Children: Responses of the Child Protection and Criminal Justice Systems.* NSPCC, Policy Practice Research Series, London.
Calder, M. (2004). *Child Sexual Abuse and the Internet: Tackling New Frontier.* Dorset: Russell House Publishing.
Cawson, P., Wattam, C., Brooker, S., & Kelly, G. (2000). *Child Maltreatment in the United Kingdom: A Study of the Prevalence of Child Abuse and Neglect.* London: NSPCC.
Children's Bureau and Department of Health and Human Services. (2010). *Child Maltreatment 2010.* Available online at www.acf.hhs.gov.programs/cb/puns/com10/cm10.pdf
Cooper, A., McLoughlin, I., & Campbell, K. (2000). Sexuality in cyberspace: Update for the 21st century. *Cyber Psychology and Behaviour, 3* (4), 521–536.
Craven, S., Brown, S., & Gilchrist, E. (2006). Sexual grooming of children: Review of literature and theoretical considerations. *Journal of Sexual Aggression: An international, interdisciplinary forum for research, theory and practice, 12* (3), 287–299.
Davidson, J., & Martellozzo, E. (2008). Protecting children in cyberspace. In G. Letherby, P. Birch, M. Cain, & K. Williams, *Sex Crime.* Cullompton: Willan Publishers.
Davidson, J., & Martellozzo, E. (2012). Exploring young people's use of social networking sites and digital media in the internet safety context: A comparison of the UK and Bahrain. *Information, Communication and Society, 1* (21).
Davidson, J., & Martellozzo, E. (2016). *Kingdom of Bahrain: National Internet Safety Review.* TRA. Manama: TRA.
Eldridge, H. (1998). *Therapist's Guide to Maintaining Change.* London: Sage.
Elliott, I. A. (2011). The use of online technology in the modus operandi of female sex offenders, *Journal of Sexual Aggression: An International, Interdisciplinary Forum for Research, Theory and Practice, 17* (1), 92–104.
Featherstone, B. A., & Evans, H. (2004). *Children Experiencing Maltreatment: Who Do They Turn To?* London: NSPCC.
Finkelhor, D. (1986). *A Sourcebook on Child Sexual Abuse.* Beverly Hills: Sage.

Finkelhor, D. (1984). *Child Sexual Abuse; New Theory and Research*. New York: Free Press.

Finkelhor, D. G. H. (1994). Sexual abuse in a national survey of adult men and women: Prevalence, characteristics, and risk factors. *Child Abuse and Neglect, 14* (1), 19–28.

Fogela, J., & Nehmadb, E. (2009). Internet social network communities: Risk taking, trust, and privacy concerns. *Computers in Human Behavior, 25* (1), 153–160.

Furedi, F. (1997). *Culture of Fear. Risk Taking and the Morality of Low Expectation*. London: Cassell.

Gallagher, B. (2000). The extent and nature of known cases of institutional child sexual abuse. *British Journal of Social Work, 30*, 795–817.

Gillespie, A. (2004). Internet grooming: The new law. *Childright, 204*.

Gillespie, A. (2008). Tackling grooming. *The Police Journal, 81*, 196–208.

Goode, E., & Ben-Yehuda, N. (1994). *Moral Panics. The Social Construction of Deviance*. Oxford: Blackwell.

Gottschalk, P. (2011). A dark side of computing and information sciences: Characteristics of online groomers. *Journal of Emerging Trends in Computing and Information Sciences, 2* (9), 447–455.

Grubin, D. (1998). *Sex Offending against Children: Understanding the Risk* (Vol. 99). Police Research Series. Available online at www.d2l.org/atf/cf/%7B64AF78C4-5EB8-45AA-BC28-F7EE2B581919%7D/Statistics_1_Magnitude.pdf

Innocenti Research Centre (IRC) (2012). *Child Safety Online: Global Challenges and Strategies. Technical Report*. Florence: Innocenti Publications.

ITU (2011). *The Role of ICT in Advancing Growth in LDCs. Trends, Challenges and Opportunities*. Geneva: ITU.

La Fontaine, J. S. (1990). *Child Sexual Abuse*. Cambridge: Polity Press, in association with Basil Blackwell.

Lanning, K. (2005). Complaint child victims: Confronting an uncomfortable reality. Viewing child pornography on the internet. Understanding the offence, managing the Offender, helping the victims. In Quayle, E., & Taylor, M., *Viewing Child Pornography on the Internet*. Lyme Regis: Russell House Publishing.

Livingstone, S., & O'Neill, B. (2014). Annual research review: Harms experienced by child users of online and mobile technologies: The nature, prevalence and management of sexual and aggressive risks in the digital age. *Journal of Child Psychology and Psychiatry, 55* (6), 635–654.

Livingstone, S., Haddon, L., Görzig, A., & Ólafsson, K. (2011). Risks and safety on the internet. Perspective from European children. Full findings and Policy implications from EU kids online survey of 9–16 years olds and their parents in 25 countries. Available online at www.eukidsonline.net

Lucy Faithfull Foundation (2016). *The Internet and Children ... What's the Problem?*

Martellozzo, E. (2012). *Online Child Sexual Abuse: Grooming, Policing and Child Protection in a Multi-Media World*. London: Routledge.

Martellozzo, E. (2015). Policing online child sexual abuse: The British experience. *European Journal of Policing Studies, 3* (1), 32–52.

Martellozzo, E., Monaghan, A., Adler, J., Davidson, J., Leyva, R., & Horvath, M. (2017). *"I Wasn't Sure it Was Normal to Watch it..." A Quantitative and Qualitative Examination of The Impact of Legal Pornography on the Values, Attitudes, Beliefs and Behaviours of Children and Young People*. London: NSPCC and OCC.

McCarthy, J., & Gaunt, N. (2005). But I was only looking.... Paper presented at the 'Responding effectively to on-line child pornography offenders' conference, Oxford University.

Miller, K. (1997). Detection and reporting of child sexual abuse (specifically paedophilia): A law enforcement perspective. *Paedophilia: Policy and Prevention*, *12*, 32–38.
NSPCC (2007). www.nspcc.org.uk/helpandadvice/whatchildabuse/sexualabuse/sexual abuse_wda36370.html
OCC (2015). www.childrenscommissioner.gov.uk/news/only-1-8-children-who-are-sexually-abused-are-identified-professionals
OFCOM (2014). *Children and Parents: Media Use and Attitudes Report*. OFCOM, London.
OFCOM (2016). *The Communications Market Report: United Kingdom 2016.* Available online at http://stakeholders.ofcom.org.uk/market-data-research/market-data/communications-market-reports/cmr16/uk/
Ólafsson, K., Livingstone, S., & Haddon, L. (2013). Children's use of online technologies in Europe: A review of the European evidence base. *Findings from the UK Children Go Online Project*. London, UK: LSE Research Online.
Pempek, T. A., Yermolayeva, Y. A., & Calvert, S. L. (2009). College students' social networking experiences on Facebook. *Journal of Applied Developmental Psychology*, *30* (3), 227–238.
Phillips, S. P. (1992). Sexual harassment of female doctors by patients. *The New England Journal of Medicine*, *329* (26), 1936–1939.
Phippen, A. (2009). *Sharing Personal Images and Videos Among Young People*. Available online at www.swgfl.org
Quayle, E. (2010). Child Pornography. In Y. Jewkes, & Y. Majid, *Handbook of Internet Crime* (pp. 343–368). Collumpton: Willan Publishing.
Quayle, E., & Ribisl, K. M. (2013). *Understanding and Preventing Online Sexual Exploitation of Children*. New York: Routledge.
Quayle, E., Allegro, S., Hutton, L., Sheath, M., & Loof, L. (2014). Rapid skill acquisition and online sexual grooming of children. *Computers in Human Behavior*, *39*, 368–375.
Rice, R., Winetrobe, H., Holloway, I. W., Montoya, J., Plant, A., & Kordic, T. (2012). Cell phone internet access, online sexual solicitation, partner seeking, and sexual risk behaviour among adolescents. *Archives of Sexual Behaviour*, *1* (9).
Romer, D. (2010). Adolescent risk taking, impulsivity, and brain development: Implications for preventions. *Developmental Psychology*, *52* (3), 263–276.
Seto, M. (2013). *Internet Sex Offenders.* Washington, DC: American Psychological Association.
Seto, M., & Hanson, R. (2011). Introduction to special issue on Internet-facilitated sexual offending. *Sexual Abuse: A Journal of Research and Treatment*, *23*, 3–6.
Sharland, E., Seal, H., Croucher, M., Aldgate, J., & Jones, D. (1996). *Professional Intervention in Child Sexual Abuse*. London: HMSO.
Staksrud, E., Ólafsson, K., & Livingstone, S. (2013). Does the use of social networking sites increase children's risk of harm? *Computers in Human Behavior*, *29* (1), 40–50.
Stanko, E. (1990). *Everyday Violence*. London: Unwin Hyman.
Suler, J. (2004). The online disinhibition effect. *Cyber Psychology and Behavior*, *7*, 321–326.
Sullivan, J. & Beech, A. (2004). *Are Collectors of Child Abuse Images a Risk to Children?* London: The John Grieve Centre for Policing and Community Safety.
Vincent, J. (2015). *Mobile Opportunities. Exploring Positive Mobile Media Opportunities for European Children*. London: Polis, LSE.
Walsh, C. (2011). Youth justice and neuroscience: A dual-use dilemma. *British Journal of Criminology*, *51* (1), 21–39.

Webster, S., Davidson, J., & Bifulco, A. (2014). *Online Offending Behaviour and Child Victimisation: New Findings and Policy*. London: Palgrave Macmillan.

Webster, S., Davidson, J., Bifulco, A., Gottschalk, P., Caretti, V., Pham, T., Grove-Hills, J., Turley, C., Tompkins, C., Ciulla, S., Milazzo, V., Schimmenti, A., & Craparo, G. (2012). *Final Report: European Online Grooming Project*. London: European Commission Safer Internet Plus Programme.

Whittle, H., Hamilton-Giachristsis, C., Beech, A., & Collings, G. (2013). A review of young people's vunerabilities to online grooming. *Aggression and Violent Behavior, 18*, 135–146.

Wolak, J., Finkelhor, D., & Mitchell, K. J. (2004). Internet-initiated sex crimes against minors: Implications for prevention based on findings from a national study. *Journal of Adolescent Health, 35* (5), 411–420.

Wolak, J., Ybarra, M., & Finkelhor, D. (2007). Current research knowledge about adolescent victimisation via the internet. *Adolescent Medicine: State of the Art Reviews, 18* (2), 325–341.

Wolak, J., Finkelhor, D., Mitchell, K. J., & Ybarra, M. L. (2008). Online 'predators' and their victims: Myths, realities and implications for prevention and treatment. *American Psychologist, 63*, 111–128.

Wolf, S. (1985). A multi factor model of deviant sexuality. *Victimology: An Internal Journal, 10*, 359–374.

Young, K. S. (2001). *Tangled in the Web: Understanding Cybersex from Fantasy to Addiction*. Bloomington: Authorhouse.

Part III
Race and culture

7 Online racial hate speech

Jamie Cleland

Introduction

Since the turn of the twenty-first century, message boards and social media sites such as Twitter and Facebook have provided unprecedented opportunities for people around the world to engage in synchronous (i.e. real-time) and asynchronous (i.e. outside of real-time) debates and conversations.[1] This has become an important feature of social interaction for millions of international internet users who engage with disparate and often unknown others, and who use the cybersphere as an important social space for identity construction and personal networking.

The proliferation of anonymity and pseudonymity online has, however, been accompanied by an increase in sexist, homophobic and racist hate speech (see Awan 2014; Banks 2010; Cleland 2014, 2015; Cleland and Cashmore 2014, 2016; Rivers 2011). As James Banks argues, the internet 'has become the "new frontier" for spreading hate, as millions can be reached through an inexpensive and unencumbered social network that has enabled previously diverse and fragmented groups to connect, engendering a collective identity and sense of community' (2010, p. 234).

From a research perspective, this has created opportunities for scholars to examine the extent of racism within new channels of communication. Relevant to the focus of this chapter is Chris Allen's (2014) contention that racial hate speech and Islamophobia are not just present on social network sites such as Facebook and Twitter, but also on blogs and platforms such as message boards. Racist discourse online often takes two particular forms, in that it tends to be: (1) directed *at* ethnically different Others (using the term 'Other' here to describe the viewing or treating of a person or group as distinct or opposite from oneself on the grounds of race); or (2) it is *about* ethnically different Others.[2] This comports with Teun van Dijk's definition of racist discourse as 'a form of discriminatory social practice that manifests itself in text, talk and communication. Together with other (non-verbal) discriminatory practices, racist discourse contributes to the reproduction of racism as a form of ethnic or "racial" domination' (2004, p. 351).

With regards to mapping everyday expressions of racism, message boards provide researchers with an opportunity to observe, record, and analyse discussions taking place online in an unobtrusive way (Clavio 2008). By way of illustration, this chapter draws on data collected as part of two research projects focused on message boards. The intention across both projects was not to influence the behaviour of these online communities in a positive or negative way, but to simply observe the discourse taking place. Two methodological approaches were deployed. The first project thematically analysed more than 500 comments made on two prominent football message boards from November 2011 to February 2012. These comments were made in response to an opening post I made asking users their thoughts on the extent of racism in English football (Cleland 2014). My analysis of the data generated during this project showed that while the message boards did contain evidence of Islamophobia, hostility, resistance towards the Muslim 'Other', and framings positing the superiority of 'whiteness', the majority of racist comments were openly challenged and contested by other users across both message boards.

The second project was a four-week, non-participant observation of an English Defence League (EDL) message board from 20 September 2013 to 19 October 2013. The reason for non-participant observation in this instance was that far-right groups such as the EDL are 'renowned for refusing to grant outsiders [i.e. academics and journalists] access' (Carter 2005, p. 66). Some research has been conducted on the ideology and attitude of EDL supporters (see, for example, Allen 2010, 2011; Busher 2013, 2016; Copsey 2010; Garland and Treadwell 2010; Goodwin 2013; Jackson and Feldman 2011; Kassimeris and Jackson 2015; Pupcenoks and McCabe 2013; Treadwell and Garland 2011). That said, I concur with Alex Oaten when he states that, 'at present there seems to be little interest in a detailed examination of the language that the EDL as a movement uses and how a collective identity is constructed' (2014, p. 336). Thus, my decision to observe this board without announcing my presence was in line with Robert Kozinets' argument that '"covert studies" of online communities are sometimes desirable' (2010, p. 74). During the research period for this second project, the EDL leader, Tommy Robinson, and its deputy leader, Kevin Carroll, resigned,[3] and much discourse on the message board moved onto the topic of whether the League would survive these leadership losses. Given that my primary intention with this second project was to examine the comments and reaction by EDL sympathisers towards Muslims and Islam, I have chosen not to focus on the leadership narrative in this chapter.

After thematically analysing a total of 1,960 comments across the general discussion message board in this second project, I found evidence of the centralisation of Muslims and Islam in narratives that were often focused on the broader issues of Islamophobia, racial ordering, war, and the collective presentation of non-Muslims as victims. Unlike the discourse analysed in the first project, however, racist discourse on the EDL board was rarely contested or challenged. Rather, the discourse under analysis highlighted the way social and cultural division are central to the prejudice against, and scapegoating and stereotyping of towards Islam and Muslims.

The police and online hate speech

Given the volume of overt and covert racist messages being communicated across the internet, it has been rare for police forces in the United Kingdom (UK) to investigate unless a hate crime is reported. In many ways, it could be argued that online racism is not seen as a public priority given the budget restraints under which the police are working. Moves to tackle online hate speech were, however, made in 2013 when the Crown Prosecution Service and the Association of Chief Police Officers in England and Wales announced plans to prosecute individuals engaging in racist and homophobic communication (BBC News 2013). The implementation of this policy on Twitter and Facebook remains problematic, however, because these platforms are hosted in the United States. When British police have tried to investigate the personal details of an individual who may be hiding behind the use of a pseudonym, they often fail to be granted a subpoena to take matters further. These sorts of problems were recognised, to a degree, in February 2015 when Twitter's then chief executive, Dick Costolo, sent an internal memo to staff admitting that the platform 'sucks at dealing with abuse and trolls' (Hern 2015). As suggested by Banks (2010), Internet Service Providers can reduce the level of online hate by deleting content or cancelling the service if Terms of Service (TOS) agreements are broken. Despite the prohibition of discriminatory communication across many of these online platforms, however, Banks reports that 'many TOS agreements are extremely narrow in focus' (2010, p. 237).

Referring to the Crown Prosecution Service, Imran Awan states that for a prosecution to take place there must be 'a credible threat of violence; communications which specifically target an individual or group of people; communications which amount to a breach of a court order; or communications which may be considered grossly offensive, indecent, obscene or false' (2014, pp. 138–139). Those prosecuted are often charged in relation to criminal behaviour related to communications that are 'racially motivated' or 'religiously motivated'. However, the continued presence of online hate speech suggests such measures do not constitute an effective deterrent. In many ways, social media platforms and message boards are reliant on users to self-police and report discriminatory hate speech. Here we can see an upside to anonymity online, in that facelessness allows users to challenge and criticise comments that are posted on message boards and other social media platforms without having to fear for their safety. Irrespective of the potential punishment, however, some individuals will continue to communicate racist thoughts online, and the data presented later in this chapter should remind the relevant authorities of the challenges faced.

Conceptualising online racist discourse

Jamie Cleland and Ellis Cashmore (2016) use the conceptual framework of Pierre Bourdieu to explain some of the reasons behind the continued evidence of deep-rooted racial inequality apparent online. Pierre Bourdieu's (1984) concept 'habitus' captures the way that internalised dispositions consisting of tastes, rules, habits, perceptions and expressions are unconsciously ingrained in individuals, and are reflected in everyday thought processes and practices. As Christine Mennesson has argued, 'the more longlasting, the stronger, and the more concerned by emotional relations a socialization process is, the stronger the constructed dispositions will be' (2010, p. 6). Bourdieu explains the way social conditions such as social group, family and the community in which a person engages can inform personal taste and practice, and reflect the volume and varying kinds of capital (for example, economic, social and cultural) each individual possesses.

This conceptual framework has also been applied to debates about race, in particular 'the structural and cultural conditions associated with an actor's location within the racialised social system' (Perry 2012, p. 90). Advancing this further, Samuel Perry refers to a 'racial habitus' which is 'a matrix of tastes, perceptions, and cognitive frameworks that are often unconscious (particularly for whites), and that regulate the racial practices of actors such that they tend to reproduce the very racial distinctions and inequalities that produced them' (2012, p. 90). On matters of racial inequality, Eduardo Bonilla-Silva (2003) posits the existence of a 'white habitus' that regulates the practice and condition of 'whiteness' with regards to taste, perception, feelings and views. This is shown to reinforce and promote solidarity amongst whites while negatively stereotyping non-whites. Mary McDonald (2009, p. 9) defines whiteness as 'institutionalized discourses and exclusionary practices seeking social, cultural, economic and psychic advantage for those bodies racially marked as white'. McDonald contends that this was a feature of British society until the 1950s when mass immigration led to increasing social tension. The latter was inflamed by the infamous 'Rivers of Blood' speech by Conservative MP, Enoch Powell, who, in 1968, claimed black immigrants were a threat to jobs, housing, and social cohesion. It was at this time that the far-right became a feature of British society, including the National Front in the late 1960s, and continuing with the British National Party from the 1980s, the EDL since 2009, and more, recently, Britain First, since 2011.

Given the history of whiteness in Britain, I concur with Jeffery Sallaz when he states that 'individuals who came of age in one racial formation will tend to generate practices that simultaneously preserve entrenched racial schemata' (2010, p. 296). Thus, racism remains embedded in everyday practice for some individuals and the internet offers a platform for these views to be broadcast. Progress in communication technologies means racism is not static and old racial schemata are now able to be anonymously broadcast in new social settings. As suggested by Sallaz, the 'dispositions of the habitus should prove durable and may even improvise new practices that transpose old racial schemata into new settings' (2010, p. 294). Evidence of the latter – drawn from the two research projects outlined above – forms the basis of the remainder of this chapter. The cited examples will be presented as they appeared on each message board, including grammatical mistakes, misspelled words, and profanity.

Non-Muslims as victims

The origins of the EDL can be traced to a homecoming parade by the British Army's Royal Anglian Regiment on 10 March 2009 which was disrupted by a demonstration by a faction of the Islamist movement, Ahlus Sunnah wal Jamaah. In response, the United People of Luton organised a counter demonstration titled 'Respect Our Troops'. This subsequently led to the formation of the EDL, led by Tommy Robinson (a pseudonym for his real name, Stephen Yaxley-Lennon), along with Robinson's cousin, Kevin Carroll, as the deputy leader. The EDL portrays itself as a streets-based (i.e. streets or roads are used as the location for protest) human rights movement that protects non-Muslims from the challenge of Islamic extremism and Sharia law. Given that protests are often staged in areas heavily populated by Muslims, violent confrontations often take place with counter protestors and/or the police. Initial support for the EDL came from white working class men associated with football communities, as well as former members of the British National Party (BNP) and anti-jihad groups such as the United British Alliance (Copsey 2010). Looking deeper into its following, Jamie Bartlett and Mark Littler (2011) analysed EDL supporters on Facebook to determine that 81 per cent were male, 28 per cent were over 30 years of age, 15 per cent had a professional qualification, and 30 per cent were educated at university or college standard. When probed about why they supported the EDL, the most consistently mentioned responses related to immigration (42 per cent), 'radical Islam' (31 per cent), lack of jobs (26 per cent), and terrorism (19 per cent).

These findings comport with my own research conclusions. Across both of my projects, there was evidence of a collective presentation of non-Muslims as blameless 'victims'. Naturally, this was more prominent on the EDL message board given the origins behind the movement, with numerous comments such as this below stressing the need to combat what was perceived as Islamic extremism:

> Never in our history as a movement have we reached a point when we need more than at any other time in our countries history to unite as one and make a stand against the evil that is Radical Islam...Our country faces a threat that we have not seen before, a threat from within by an enemy who not only wants our country for their own but to subjugate and kill all who do not bow before the evil cult called Islam and abide by their law of Sharia. There is a real and imminent danger and we must make our stand before time runs out and we are left as a minority in our own country subject to the laws and whims of an evil dictatorship called Islam.

In both projects, discourse referring to Muslims tended to centre on racialisation (differentiating or categorising according to race), in which a homogenous host culture was framed as needing to defend itself from the perceived threat of a Muslim Other. For EDL contributors such as the one cited above, the movement is seen as a 'symptom'. The message board can therefore be seen as an additional platform to engage in discriminatory and prejudicial discourse against Muslims and Islam outside of the street-based demonstrations. Indeed, there was evidence of a fairly widespread Islamophobia, defined by the Runnymede Trust as 'an outlook or world-view involving an unfounded dread and dislike of Muslims which results in practices of exclusion and discrimination' (1997, p. 1). While Islamophobia was present before 9/11, the terrorist attacks on that day have led to marked increases in cultural racism in national discourse in the UK. Consider the following discussion from the EDL message board in response to a video placed on YouTube by a Muslim preacher:

> EDL contributor 3: I think it would be a grave mistake to dismiss this muppet as just another Muslim rabble rouser and hate preacher, directing his hatred towards 'kaffirs'. There is one statement he made, in his otherwise ramblings of hate, and that is he claimed that in a few years we English will be the minority and the Muslims will be the majority. He is well aware of the current demographic of comparative birth rates – e.g. about 1.7 children for European couples against 4 or 5 children for Muslims, other Asians and Africans. It is expected, given these figures, that we English will become the ethnic minority in our land by roughly 2050/2060. And, that is not far away.... By the time the Muslims outnumber us they will have far more young, fit men on the streets to wage jihad and they will be facing a broadly older population. So, it's no wonder this Muslim git is so arrogant and confident in successfully creating England into an Islamic state.
>
> EDL contributor 7: Why are we posting videos made by horrible little muzzie shits like this? We already know their attitude to our country; we know the frightening demographics that say in so many years' time the muslims will be the majority! Of course we should be discussing muslim leaders and their utterings but we do not need to give oxygen to some little wannabee muzzie mafia shithead.
>
> EDL contributor 12: The biggest danger to our way of life Britain has ever faced. People need to wake up and wake up now before it's too late for us to do anything about it, I don't want to say to my kids, sorry your wearing rags now, I should have tried harder, but I didn't just sat around and waited for someone else to do it for me, that's not a nice thing to think about is it people, we have to do it now, not the next day, or next week, the longer we leave it the better it gets for the muzzies, our children look up to us, I'm not going to let mine down, are you?

According to the 2011 Census for England and Wales, there are 2.7 million British Muslims (up from 1.5 million in 2001) which represents just 4.8 per cent of the population (Office for National Statistics 2011). Yet the reference to 'our land' by EDL contributor 3 and 'in so many years' time the Muslims will be the majority' by EDL contributor 7 illustrate a sense of collective identity in terms of their continued commitment to the ideology of the EDL. This reflects the 'imagined community' recognised by Benedict Anderson (1983) as there are markers of difference that place non-Muslims as victims. Islam, Muslims and the British government are, meanwhile, blamed for a perceived social decline in the UK:

> EDL contributor 5: They are quite safe because 'the powers that be' are only clamping down on their own native citizens.... It angers me that innocent poor citizens are lumbered with this fucking Muslim infestation and that the governments think that we're all too stupid to know what's going on.

> EDL contributor 6: I tell you what angers me the most with these Muslims.... Not even what they do. They do it because they know that they can. If authorities clamped down ... they wouldn't know what had hit them. This is not only in Britain, but in the whole western world! Why is this? Are the authorities unable to clamp down? You must be having a laugh! They can clamp down on the EDL and discredit UKIP and other patriotic groups whenever they want ... so it isn't that!

> EDL contributor 8: The politicians of all governments are guilty and culpable for allowing the gradual Islamification of our country.... It is the politicians who embarked on an agenda that will result in the cultural genocide of the English and our race replacement in our own land by alien cultures and creeds.

> EDL contributor 18: Their political and ideological agenda will become plain for all to see and in much larger areas of the country. Thus giving us time to organise effective opposition. They may even cause the ruling elites sufficient cause to change the rules of engagement when it comes to dealing with Muslims, if only for their own survival.

> EDL contributor 34: For many decades, our rulers have acted as if we still live in a country that was peaceful and largely contented as it was in the pre-war and immediate post war period of the fifties and sixties and that nothing has really changed. Well, thanks to them, it has changed and not for the better. Our old laws and tolerances can no longer apply because we have millions of new 'British' who do not believe in them. Not only that, they want to change them to suit the culture and creed that they imported into our country.

As suggested by Joel Busher (2013), there is a collective victimisation presented across message board discussions such as this where some contributors perceive an institutionalised (i.e. national government) bias against non-Muslims. The perceived threat to traditional British culture and identity outlined by EDL contributors 22 and 34 illustrate the existence of a racial habitus (of the sort identified by Bonilla-Silva 2003) through a deep dislike of Muslims on cultural grounds. The changes post 9/11 have been discussed by Tariq Modood (2007) who notes that traditional biological differences have now been replaced by culturally focused markers, such as religion or beliefs, that are now used for discriminatory purposes. For example, Awan (2014) examined 500 tweets from 100 different Twitter users regarding online abuse directed towards Muslims and found a deeply embedded anti-Muslim narrative. For Sharla Alegria (2014), racial stereotyping through language used to highlight cultural difference reinforces the notion of racialisation and resistance to the Other and subsequently encourages an 'us' and 'them' discourse, or what Raymond Taras refers to as 'stigmatizing strangers through essentialist framing' (2013, p. 422). As suggested by George Kassimeris and Leonie Jackson (2015), culturally racist discourse is much more than individual prejudice as it defines who belongs in a superior in-group and an out-group that threatens this position and privilege.

Identity

Referring to the British Social Attitudes Survey in 2010, Allen reports that 45 per cent of Britons felt that 'religious diversity was having a negative impact on society' (2011, p. 292). Illustrating how Muslim immigration remains low, data released by the Home Office (2014) shows that out of those nationalities granted permission to permanently reside in the UK (a total number of 129,749 residents), 20.4 per cent were Indian and 10 per cent Pakistani. The heightened focus on immigration is partly driven by the media. Allen (2011) argues that the print media often portray a homogenous image of Islam, while Amir Saeed and Dan Kilvington make the case that stories about Muslims are 'commonly written and spoken about in a tone which suggests anxiety over the erosion of the perceived "indigenous" national culture' (2011, p. 602). In their analysis of the tabloid newspaper *The Sun's* coverage of England at the 2010 football World Cup in South Africa, John Vincent and John Hill conclude that it reflects 'a historic yearning for a bygone authentic era when England was White, masculine, and working-class' (2011, p. 200). Nostalgia surrounding whiteness was a feature of the football project where a number of fans reflected on the successful 1966 World Cup won by England and compared it to a recent England squad that had been selected as part of an international fixture (cited in Cleland 2014, p. 426):

> Huddersfield Town fan 79: Racism is part of life. Denying it is pointless. England recently had 9 players on the pitch of non-English heritage recently. That pretty much answers the question. Do you see any blacks in Spain or Italy's national team? Did we have any in '66? No, and we won the damn thing.

> Huddersfield Town fan 81: You are not allowed to mention the England football team, it could offend our ethnic cousins … well actually it wouldn't

but it might offend the PC brigade … what a load of bollocks. ENGLAND: LOVE IT OR LEAVE IT.

Huddersfield Town fan 82: We are told that our ethnic friends are as English as you and me. Yeah right. If a dog is born in a stable it doesn't make it a horse …

Huddersfield Town fan 85: That is a terrible analogy. My friend at work has Pakistani parents. He was born in Sheffield and supports Wednesday and England, but supports Pakistan at cricket. He is English. You obviously don't think he is. He will probably marry someone in this country and have children. Will his children be English? Will their children be English?

Huddersfield Town fan 89: I wouldn't class him as English if he doesn't support England as it seems he doesn't think of himself as English.

Huddersfield Town fan 91: Your parents determine what you are surely. Two Africans having a child in England makes an AFRICAN born in England. It does not make them English.

Although some of these comments were challenged, they comport with the findings of Modood (2007) who suggests that communities seeking to be culturally different are forgotten about in the pursuit of showcasing a homogenous host culture which is viewed as superior through a discourse that elevates whiteness and national identity. Of course, given its ideology, debates about Islam and Muslims on the EDL message board were more prominent than on the football message boards. However, there was also a clear emphasis on a homogenous culture where Islamophobia existed to elevate whiteness and national identity on the football message boards (cited in Cleland 2014, p. 423):

Huddersfield Town fan 33: I live in an almost white area and would not want to move to an area where white people are a minority. Not because I dislike anyone who isn't white; it is because I would feel slightly uncomfortable as I am used to a white community and the culture that involves (it is also because most non-white areas are shitholes).

Huddersfield Town fan 35: Non-white areas are shitholes. Don't get me wrong, there are some council estates that are as rough as hell with some knobheads living on them, but you show me a town or city where the crime infested shitholes are and then tell me what communities live there … Chapeltown, Leeds; Handsworth, Birmingham; St Pauls, Bristol.

Huddersfield Town fan 40: Personally I would not want to live in many parts of West Yorkshire where I was born due to it not being like England anymore – or the England I grew up in.

> Huddersfield Town fan 42: Racism will always be present unless we live in a society which is educated and without prejudice (which will never happen). People have an automatic distrust of change and of people who are different from them and distrust leads to discrimination. People also have natural instincts to protect what is theirs, including communities and cultures. If they feel that their community is threatened with change from outside cultures then this tends to lead to conflict.

Deep concern surrounding national identity and religion leads to hostility, scapegoating and stereotyping about the perception of Muslims and may be the reason discourse such as 'non-white areas are shitholes' by Huddersfield Town fan 33 and 'crime infested shitholes' by Huddersfield Town fan 35 was uncontested on this particular thread.[4] These themes also comport with Allen's case that, rather than focusing on biological differences, racist discourse may focus on 'other markers of difference' such as specific areas within cities (2011, p. 291). My own research certainly showed that Tower Hamlets – an area in London recognised nationally as one of the worst for social deprivation and above average levels of ethnic residents – was widely referred to in discussions. Reference to particular areas having a predominantly Muslim population provided evidence of a hierarchical ordering of racialised identities through comments written *about* the Muslim Other (van Dijk 2004).

In fact, the boundaries of acceptability, particularly on the EDL message board, were almost non-existent and this allowed contributors to be openly racist and discriminatory through the racializing of Muslim culture where Muslims were seen as the distinct opposite to British values and identity (Meer 2008; Weedon 2011). Explaining the exclusion of less powerful groups by more established ones, Norbert Elias and John Scotson (1994) refer to the notion of 'established-outsider relations' and this had relevance to both some football supporters as well as EDL members who distinguished themselves in relation to the Other (cited in Cleland 2014, p. 421):

> Huddersfield Town fan 16: Let us not forget that parts of the Queens Road area of Halifax and parts of Dewsbury are no-go areas for whites after dark. White people are often attacked up there.... I am sorry but a large percentage of the younger Pakistanis are arseholes. If that makes me a racist then so be it.

> Huddersfield Town fan 17: How could they tell what colour someone is if it is dark?

> Huddersfield Town fan 26: You drive through many large areas of somewhere like Bradford, then the 'minority' are white people. Are there support organisations specifically named 'white person's ...' in those areas? Do you think there would be uproar from the left if there was? I do.

Huddersfield Town fan 27: It is very hard to determine whether you are on the wind up at times. I remember your 'I just don't like all Muslims' statement a while back, ring fencing every person of that religious persuasion in the 'I don't like pile' ... each to their own of course, but it says a lot about a person who makes sweeping generalisations about people they do not know. I think seeing colour, race and religion and making an assessment on whether I like them or not before I have even interacted, spoken to, listened to or shook their hand is akin to childish school yard syndrome.

Huddersfield Town fan 16: As for my 'I just don't like all Muslims' statement you think I said, this was years ago.... I don't like the Muslim religion, though as an atheist myself I am not struck on any religion, but the Muslim brand I find totally dislikeable. On a personal level I do not dislike every Muslim, but as I acknowledged all those years ago Muslims are not people I can have much time for due to their religion (I should emphasise here it has nothing to do with race – i.e. skin colour).

Based on examples such as those above, it was clear some contributors were happy to communicate racist thoughts irrespective of the reaction that followed. Whilst some contributors such as Huddersfield Town fan 16 were happy to acknowledge his/her thoughts as racist, others might argue such comments constitute a form of 'casual racism', where outbursts are an unintended aspect of social ignorance. On racial hate speech, Carwyn Jones and Scott Fleming (2007) refer to it as either 'ethically excusable' (unwittingly racist through ignorance) or 'ethically inexcusable' (deliberately racist and evil). In an American study, Joe Feagin (2010) found that whites often speak in a way that reinforces racial inequality without the speakers recognising the moral implications of their words and actions.

Across the message boards were examples of fans trying to categorise racial difference and separate themselves from the Muslim Other. In line with the argument made by Jones and Fleming (2007), there was an attempt to categorise racial difference, but, unlike the EDL message board, the football message boards did provide evidence of racist discourse being challenged and criticised on a frequent basis (cited in Cleland 2014, p. 425):

Huddersfield Town fan 57: What pisses me off is the last 2–3 governments opening the floodgates for every fucker to come into my country and take all the frigging jobs and bleed the system dry ... the country is on its knees due to the fact we are overrun with foreigners ... I say they should all **** off and leave us be.... I am not a racist but in my opinion we should look after our own.

Huddersfield Town fan 60: That post for me sums up what is going wrong in society. When somebody fails, blame somebody else. Thank god we do not all share your liberal, progressive views.

142 J. Cleland

Huddersfield Town fan 61: It is an opinion I endorse wholeheartedly, along with dozens of my friends, thousands of voters and most probably millions of Britons.

Huddersfield Town fan 64: I don't think you have any life experience of hate or abuse. Everything you are angry about is media related.

Huddersfield Town fan 69: Towns and cities have steadily filled up with foreigners (of all colours) and to many people it does not feel like their own country any more.

Huddersfield Town fan 74: It is these kinds of archaic viewpoints that prevent any decent political debate in regards to immigration. The 'come here and take our jobs' rubbish is complete nonsense. The vast majority came over here to do the jobs that us proud Englanders didn't want to do. The parasites that sit in 4-bedroomed council houses with 6 kids and live off social benefits for the rest of their lives, correct me if I am wrong, will be white 'nationalists'. The country is on its knees because of greedy financial companies (again run by white men) ... but that's obviously far too complicated to comprehend so let's just blame it on the darkies.

War and territoriality

In his analysis of the public statements released by the EDL, Oaten argues that a sense of collective identity allows non-Muslims to be portrayed as the 'true' victims 'against those who are understood as perpetrators' (2014, p. 347). On some occasions, the debates that existed on the EDL message board resulted in war-like discussions about the way to eradicate Islam:

EDL contributor 3: The way things are going civil war seems an inevitable part of me can't help hoping sooner rather than later while we still have the advantage it won't be long before we're outnumbered.

EDL contributor 7: Can you imagine, if it came to a civil war ... and the police were fighting on the side of Muslims? Too easy to imagine at the moment.

EDL contributor 13: The only way to cure the illness of Islam is through ethnic cleansing such as under the government of Dzhokhar Dudayev in Chechnya.

EDL contributor 17: Anger is good, anger gets things done. If Britain and indeed Europe ever gets angry enough we can stop thus muslamic plague once and for all!

EDL contributor 29: I cannot see the UK using chemical or biological agents against Islamists in rebel strong hold areas such as Tower Hamlets and Sparkbrook in Birmingham. The only way to deal with such cancer is to cut it out in a systematic process before it spreads.

References to 'ethnic cleansing' by EDL contributor 13, 'muslamic plague' by EDL contributor 17, and 'using chemical or biological agents against Islamists' as 'the only way to deal with such cancer' by EDL contributor 29, illustrates how hate speech is used to replicate going to war against a perceived 'enemy'. Furthermore, across the EDL message board were military symbols, where members had a 'rank' depending on the number of comments they made and how many of them were 'liked' by other members (as with Facebook, comments can be 'liked' by other users). This hierarchical ordering positioned established members – the self-named 'Old Guard' – higher in 'rank' to new members. The war-like acronym of NS (No Surrender) was also used as a symbol of defiance across the EDL message board with reference to rising immigration and how this would increase the threat of Islamic extremism:

EDL contributor 5: This forum is so important to us, it brings us all together, united in our cause, the defeat of Radical Islamists in our country. Stay strong, stand firm. NS!

EDL contributor 11: They come here steal everything they want, shops, jobs, clothes, houses, our children, our communities, and they want to call England f.cking Pakistan, over my dead body they will, I say the next march, Walsall, their f.cking town no our town we just let you rats look after it until we take it back you stinking rat bastards, they hate black men do they, well they've stole their accents and their music, they hate anything not muzzie, we need to wake up and band together, then who will be the racist, us the EDL or them, you decide my friends you decide ... NS.

EDL contributor 32: All muzzies are the same all over, child molesting f.cking animals, all child molesters need to be hanged by law, in public as a warning, and it's in your streets as we speak on any corner they are their looking at our children and thinking the same, it has to stop if the 'so called' police don't do anything, parents will take it upon themselves to do it for them, and as a father and grandfather, I will do it for them no matter what happens to me, it's not my future, it's theirs, when do we stand up for them then tomorrow, next week, next month, no I say f.cking now before it's too late, it makes me think what my kids would say to me if I did let them down, it's too sad to even think about it so I won't let it happen, f.ck all muzzie bastards. NS, f.cking ever.

Across threads like this, Muslims were frequently portrayed as cultural outsiders in an in-group and out-group of racist discourse construction, where Western culture was viewed as tolerant and progressive, whereas Muslim culture was portrayed as threatening, intolerant and backward (Kassimeris and Jackson

2015). Reference to particular locations and a deep hatred towards Muslims in the example above demonstrate the way territoriality and belonging are culturally ingrained in some individuals and communities. This supports the findings of Keith Kintrea, Jon Bannister, Jon Pickering, Maggie Reid and Naofumi Suzuki (2008) in their analysis of deprived areas in the UK where ethnic distinctions are prominent.

Conclusion

Scholars across a variety of disciplinary areas have argued that racism remains embedded in British culture (Awan 2014; Cleland and Cashmore 2014, 2016; Gillborn 2008; Modood 2007; Skey 2011). As this chapter has illustrated, technological advances in communication, particularly since the growth of social media in the twenty-first century, have provided a platform for the expression of racist thoughts and beliefs. As suggested by Taras (2012), the internet has created opportunities where those individuals and religions seen as 'different' can become ideological, political, and religious 'targets' for dominant groups who attack individuals' faith and ethnicity as a result of the perception that they pose a threat. This religious intolerance allows for the presentation of a white racial frame that now uses the internet to elevate whiteness and reinforce traditional notions of national identity as well as to present non-Muslims as victims.

When analysing online communities, researchers have to be aware of a number of considerations. The first thing to consider is the potential for some of the contributors to 'perform' in a way that does not accurately reflect their offline behaviour. This not only involves new users to message boards who are looking to boost their online capital among virtual communities, but also to more established contributors who might attempt to 'pull rank' via their comments. Secondly, complete anonymity between contributors could not be assumed as there was evidence across both research projects that people knew each other, if only in terms of their online identity (such as via the pseudonym they used). This could therefore also influence the discussions taking place, where senior contributors might be regarded as having the power to influence the direction of the discussion. In the football project, outspoken views were often challenged, but the lack of this on the EDL message board suggests such conversations were moderated by sympathisers more concerned with the preservation of traditional ethnocultural dominance.

Notes

1 According to www.statista.com, the number of monthly active users for the second quarter of 2016 on Facebook was 1.71 billion, and for Twitter it was 313 million.
2 For a wider debate on the racial Other, see Mary Bucholtz (1999) and Harry van den Berg, Margaret Wetherell and Hanneke Houtkoop-Steenstra (2003).
3 These resignations occurred on 8 October 2013.
4 When an opening comment receives responses by other users a 'thread' then develops that details the virtual conversation taking place.

References

Alegria, S. (2014) 'Constructing racial difference through group talk: An analysis of white focus groups' discussion of racial profiling', *Ethnic and Racial Studies*, 37, 2: 241–260.

Allen, C. (2010) *Islamophobia*. London: Ashgate.

Allen, C. (2011) 'Opposing Islamification or promoting Islamophobia? Understanding the English Defence League', *Patterns of Prejudice*, 45, 4: 279–294.

Allen, C. (2014) 'Findings from a pilot study on opposing Dudley Mosque using Facebook groups as both site and method for research', Sage Open. Available online at http://sgo.sagepub.com/content/4/1/2158244014522074.fulltext.pdfþhtml

Anderson, B. (1983) *Imagined Communities: Reflections on the Origin and Spread of Nationalism*. London: Verso.

Awan, I. (2014) 'Islamophobia and Twitter: A typology of online hate against Muslims on social media', *Policy & Internet*, 6, 2: 133–150.

Banks, J. (2010) 'Regulating hate speech online', *International Review of Law, Computers & Technology*, 24, 3: 233–239.

Bartlett, J. and Littler, M. (2011) *Inside the EDL: Populist Politics in a Digital Age*. London: Demos.

British Social Attitudes (2010) *The 26th Report*. London: Sage.

BBC News (2013) 'Online football abuse targeted by police'. 23 August. Available online at www.bbc.co.uk/news/uk-23796712

Bonilla-Silva, E. (2003) *Racism without Racists: Color-Blind Racism and the Persistence of Racial Inequality in the United States*. Lanham: Rowman and Littlefield.

Bourdieu, P. (1984) *Distinction: A Social Critique of the Judgement of Taste*. London: Routledge and Kegan Paul.

Bucholtz, M. (1999) 'You da man: Narrating the racial other in the production of white masculinity', *Journal of Sociolinguistics*, 3, 4: 443–460.

Busher, J. (2013) 'Grassroots activism in the English Defence League: Discourse and public (dis)order'. In Taylor, M., Currie, P.M. and Holbrook, D. (eds) *Extreme Right Wing Political Violence and Terrorism* (pp. 65–84). London: Bloomsbury.

Busher, J. (2016) *The Making of Anti-Muslim Protest: Grassroots Activism in the English Defence League*. London: Routledge.

Carter, E. (2005) *The Extreme Right in Western Europe: Success Or Failure?* Manchester: Manchester University Press.

Clavio, G. (2008) 'Demographics and usage profiles of users of college sport message boards', *International Journal of Sport Communication*, 1, 4: 434–443.

Cleland, J. (2014) 'Racism, football fans and online message boards: How social media has added a new dimension to racist discourse in British football', *Journal of Sport and Social Issues*, 38, 5: 415–431.

Cleland, J. (2015) 'Discussing homosexuality on association football fan message boards: A changing cultural context', *International Review for the Sociology of Sport*, 50, 2: 125–140.

Cleland, J. and Cashmore, E. (2014) 'Fans, racism and British football in the 21st century: The existence of a colour-blind ideology', *Journal of Ethnic and Migration Studies*, 40, 4: 638–654.

Cleland, J. and Cashmore, E. (2016) 'Football fans' views of racism in British football', *International Review for the Sociology of Sport*, 51, 1: 27–43.

Copsey, N. (2010) *The English Defence League: Challenging our Country and our Values of Social Inclusion, Fairness and Equality*. London: Faith Matters.

Elias, N. and Scotson, J. (1994) *The Established and the Outsiders* (2nd edition). London: Sage.

Feagin, J. (2010) *The White Racial Frame: Centuries of Framing and Counter-Framing.* New York: Routledge.

Garland, J. and Treadwell, J. (2010) '"No surrender to the Taliban!" Football hooliganism, Islamophobia and the rise of the English Defence League', Papers from the British Criminology Conference, 10: 19–35.

Gillborn, D. (2008) *Racism and Education: Coincidence or Conspiracy?* New York: Routledge.

Goodwin, M. (2013) *The Roots of Extremism: The EDL and the Counter-Jihad Challenge.* London: Chatham House.

Hern, A. (2015) 'Twitter CEO: We suck at dealing with trolls and abuse'. 5 February, *Guardian*. Available online at www.theguardian.com/technology/2015/feb/05/twitter-ceo-we-suck-dealing-with-trolls-abuse

Home Office (2014) 'Immigration statistics October 2013 to December 2013'. Available online at www.gov.uk/government/statistics/immigration-statistics-october-to-december-2013

Jackson, P. and Feldman, M. (2011) *The EDL: Britain's 'New Far Right' Social Movement.* Northampton: The University of Northampton.

Jones, C. and Fleming, S. (2007) '"I'd rather wear a turban than a rose": A case study of the ethics of chanting', *Race, Ethnicity, and Education*, 10, 4: 401–414.

Kassimeris, G. and Jackson, L. (2015) 'The ideology and discourse of the English Defence League: "Not racist, not violent, just no longer silent"'. *The British Journal of Politics & International Relations*, 17, 1: 171–188.

Kintrea, K., Bannister, J., Pickering, J., Reid, M. and Suzuki, N. (2008) 'Young people and territoriality in British cities (project report)', York, UK: Joseph Rowntree Foundation.

Kozinets, R. (2010) *Netnography: Doing Ethnographic Research Online.* London: Sage.

McDonald, M. (2009) 'Dialogues on whiteness, leisure, and (anti)racism', *Journal of Leisure Research*, 41, 1: 5–21.

Meer, N. (2008) 'The politics of voluntary and involuntary identities: Are Muslims in Britain an ethnic, racial, or religious minority?' *Patterns of Prejudice*, 42, 1: 61–81.

Mennesson, C. (2010) 'Gender regimes and habitus: An avenue for analysing gender building in sports contexts', *Sociology of Sport Journal*, 29, 4: 4–21.

Modood, T. (2007) *Multiculturalism.* Cambridge: Polity.

Oaten, A. (2014) 'The cult of the victim: An analysis of the collective identity of the English Defence League', *Patterns of Prejudice*, 48, 4: 331–349.

Office for National Statistics (2011) 'Religion in England and Wales 2011.' Available online at www.ons.gov.uk/ons/rel/census/2011-census/key-statistics-for-local-authorities-in-england-and-wales/rpt-religion.html

Perry, S. (2012) 'Racial habitus, moral conflict, and white moral hegemony within interracial evangelical organizations', *Qualitative Sociology*, 35, 1: 89–108.

Pupcenoks, J. and McCabe, R. (2013) 'The rise of the fringe: Right wing populists, Islamists and politics in the UK', *Journal of Muslim Minority Affairs*, 33, 2: 171–184.

Rivers, I. (2011) *Homophobic Bullying: Research and Theoretical Perspectives.* New York: Oxford University Press.

Runnymede Trust (1997) *Islamophobia: A Challenge for Us All.* London: Runnymede Trust.

Saeed, A. and Kilvington, D. (2011) 'British-Asians and racism within contemporary English football', *Soccer & Society*, 12, 5: 600–610.

Sallaz, J. (2010) 'Talking race, marketing culture: The racial habitus in and out of apartheid', *Social Problems*, 57, 2: 294–314.
Skey, M. (2011) *National Belonging and Everyday Life: The Significance of Nationhood in an Uncertain World*. Basingstoke: Palgrave Macmillan.
Taras, R. (2013) '"Islamophobia never stands still": Race, religion, and culture', *Ethnic and Racial Studies*, 36, 3: 417–433.
Treadwell, J. and Garland, J. (2011) 'Masculinity, marginalization and violence: A case study of the English Defence League', *British Journal of Criminology*, 51, 4: 621–634.
van den Berg, H., Wetherell, M. and Houtkoop-Steenstra, H. (2003) *Analyzing Race Talk: Multidisciplinary Perspectives on the Research Interview*. Cambridge: Cambridge University Press.
van Dijk, T. (2004). 'Racist discourse'. In Cashmore, E. (ed.) *Encyclopaedia of Race and Ethnic Studies* (pp. 351–355). London: Routledge.
Vincent, J. and Hill, J. (2011) 'Flying the flag for the En-ger-land: The Sun's (re)construction of English identity during the 2010 World Cup', *Journal of Sport & Tourism*, 16, 3: 187–209.
Weedon, C. (2011) 'Identity, difference and social cohesion in contemporary Britain', *Journal of Intercultural Studies*, 32, 3: 209–227.

8 Malign images, malevolent networks

Social media, extremist violence, and public anxieties

Ramaswami Harindranath

Introduction

The reverberations from acts of terror and the accentuated sense of public insecurity that invariably attends such acts affect different sections of the population in diverse ways. This was recently exemplified in a relatively minor news item in *The Guardian* (Thursday, 24 March, 2016).[1] Carrying the headline 'Man charged after tweet "confronting Muslim woman" on Brussels attacks', it reported an incident in which a white man had stopped a 'Muslim woman' on the streets of London and challenged her to 'explain Brussels', a reference to a terrorist act that had occurred in Brussels in the days before this incident. Men and women of 'Muslim appearance' are – like any other group – potential innocent victims of horrific extremist mass violence that kills indiscriminately and rarely distinguishes between religions or ethnicities. They are, however, also victims of the backlash that often follows such acts and also of state policies to counter terrorist violence. The incident mentioned above encapsulates the regrettable new 'burden of representation' whereby communities and individuals perceived to be Muslims living in Western multicultural, multiethnic societies are seen to bear some responsibility towards, or at the very least be tainted by, terrorist acts carried out by Islamic extremists anywhere in the West, in particular mass killings and suicide attacks by young men and women who reside in and are citizens of Western countries.

The racial violence that followed the 9/11 attacks (see Ahmad, 2002; Mankekar, 2015) can be seen as indicative of a deep suspicion of and antipathy towards Muslim (and 'Muslim-looking') men and women in Europe and the United States. As Ahmad notes, 'Among the enormous violence done by the United States since the tragedies suffered on September 11 has been an unrelenting, multivalent assault on the bodies, psyches, and rights of Arab, Muslim, and South Asian immigrants' (2002, p. 101). This has included '[r]estrictions on immigration of young men from Muslim countries, racial profiling and detention of "Muslim-looking" individuals, and an epidemic of hate violence' (p. 101). Massumi's (2005) declaration that 'insecurity … is the new normal' (p. 1) takes on a different import for Muslim communities living in contemporary Western societies. This essay examines the relatively recent concerns regarding the use of the Internet and social media for alleged recruitment and propaganda purposes by Islamic extremists, and the ways in which this has contributed to increasing public anxieties, especially in Europe, the US and Australia. It also looks at the challenges faced by state authorities attempting to fashion counter-terrorist measures and forming counter-radicalisation narratives. As Kundnani (2012) points out,

> Since 2004, the term 'radicalisation' has become central to terrorism studies and counter-terrorism policy-making. As US and European governments have focused on stemming 'home-grown' Islamist political violence, the concept of radicalisation has become the master signifier of the late 'war on terror' and provided a new lens through which to view Muslim minorities.
> (p. 3)

Kundnani's observation highlights the ways in which the nature of terrorist attacks and their targets have changed since September 11, 2001. Significant among these are amendments to conceptions of terrorism and the necessary shifts in strategies to predict and prevent acts of terror, and the modifications in counter-radicalisation policies that have accompanied concerns about the extremists' use of media technologies to disseminate videos of attacks and to radicalise Muslim youth in the West. The last 15 years have witnessed changing attitudes and responses to terrorist attacks. If 9/11 was conceived as an epoch-defining event of global proportions, the response to which was predicated on an attempt to neutralise the perceived source of 'evil' *external* to the US and Europe, the more recent, relatively smaller terrorist attacks seem to have engendered approaches that attempt to take into account more complex conjunctures. And through all these shifts and turns in terrorist strategies as well as counter-terrorist policies, the one constant has been the media image – from satellite news channels to digital multimedia platforms. Media images have been centrally implicated in attempts to destabilise everyday security. Their dissemination on social media is seen as a major factor in radicalisation, and they have also contributed to the stereotyping of the non-white Other in the West thereby threatening the cohesion of multicultural communities and resulting in the increase in anti-immigrant racism.

In his commentary on conceptual frameworks that underpin Marxist historical political economy, Callinicos (2005) distinguishes between two analytics – *epoch*, 'a specific phase of capitalist development' as characterised by Frederic Jameson's approach, and *conjuncture*, 'a determinate historical moment', favoured by Perry Anderson (p. 355). This, Callinicos finds, is indicative of 'two different analytical registers', one concerned with outlining 'the broad features of a distinct phase of capitalist development, the other seeking ... to locate a more specific historical constellation' (p. 360). This chapter is an attempt to outline the present conjuncture of online radicalisation and the consequences of the efforts to counter that, within the context of present concerns regarding the rise of terrorist violence.

The time at which I write this – early spring 2016 (or autumn 2016 in Australia) – the key features that comprise the present conjuncture include suicide bombings at an airport and a metro station in Brussels and another in a crowded public park in Lahore, the responses to these horrific incidents from analysts, and the way in which these attacks have been used to bolster political discourse of the right. Allied to these are clear indications of the strong anti-immigrant sentiment in the United States and also in Europe, which has witnessed a great influx of asylum seekers, mostly Muslim, fleeing conflict in Syria, Iraq and Afghanistan. The broader context for these developments, in turn, includes attempts by state authorities and counter-terrorism experts to comprehend and negate the perceived influence of the prevalence of grisly images and extremist propaganda videos on social media. Significant too, are security policies that demand a rapid increase in surveillance – specifically, of individuals and communities seen to be potential threats – which undermine the right to privacy. And, finally, the present political context also involves the rise in anti-Muslim rhetoric and racist attacks on minorities in the West. Given this set of conjunctures, an account of the role of social media in radicalisation, public anxiety and racialised politics seems an expedient intervention.

Images and insecurity

It has been said often enough, in both academic and journalistic analyses, that the attacks on 9/11 inaugurated a new epoch, a novel configuration of international politics. This claim has, in general, been widely accepted. The attacks on the Twin Towers have been variously construed as a declaration of war against the United States, as the horrific manifestation of the rise of Islam and the clash of civilisations, as the appalling opening announcement of the attempt to create a global Caliphate or a jihad, as a grisly statement of the hatred of Western liberal democracy and 'way of life', or as a response to Western attacks on Iraq and parts of the Middle East, among others. Whatever the interpretation, an undeniable consequence of 9/11 was the shattering of the hitherto sense of collective security, as civilians became victims of terrorists' attacks on 'soft' targets. As Habermas has observed, unlike earlier terrorist incidents that had specific political objectives, 9/11 initiated a kind of senseless violence whose sole objective seemed to be to create fear and insecurity. As he argues in Borradori (2003), 9/11 was 'the first world historic event' that was unlike 'indiscriminate guerrilla warfare', such as that of Palestinian or Sri Lankan suicide militants, of 'paramilitary guerrilla warfare', such as national liberation movements, global terrorism was even less politically legitimate, as it did not seem be accompanied by any demands, nor did it express any goal (Borradori, 2003, 56). For Habermas, the uniqueness of the event rests on the communicative modality that characterised it, chiefly in the form of a global circulation of unedited television images that created a 'universal eyewitness' of a global audience (Borradori, 2003, p. 49). He diagnoses global fundamentalist violence as a 'communicative pathology' (Borradori, 2003, p. 20), a state of affairs that constitute 'a paradoxical and tragic implication: in spite of not expressing realistic political objectives, global terrorism succeeds in the supremely political goal of de-legitimizing the authority of the state' (Borradori, 2003, p. 56) offers a perspicacious insight. Of even greater concern, for Habermas, is how this could lead to a spiral of mistrust between communities, breaking down communication and disavowing the possibility of any exchange of perspectives (Borradori, 2003, p. 21), thereby undermining the emergence of a truly democratic, multi-ethnic public-sphere.

Habermas's reading of 9/11 as 'the first historic world event' marks it as presaging an epochal shift in which the attacks launched a novel configuration of the world and of global politics. The declaration of the 'war on terror' provided the 'clash of civilizations' thesis a different flavour and significance, and proclaimed a moral purpose (Ivie, 2005), whereby most of the political and media discourse following 9/11 re-affirmed older West versus the Rest distinctions, or identified the attacks as heralding a new struggle between European and Islamic values that re-enacted ideological, inter-religious and military struggles from the distant past. Commenting on the symbolic consequences of acts of terror, Zizek (2002) observes that our preliminary response to 9/11 can only be understood 'only against the background of the border which today separates the digitalised First World from the Third World "desert of the Real". It is the awareness that we live in an insulated artificial universe which generates the notion that some ominous agent is threatening us all the time with total destruction. In this paranoiac perspective, the terrorists are turned into an irrational abstract agency.... Every explanation which evokes social circumstances is dismissed as covert justification of terror' (p. 16).

While the 'paranoiac perspective' still persists among a proportion of the political elite and with sections of the population subscribing to anxieties about the Islamist takeover of Western forms of life and to beliefs of a nihilistic form of extremist Islam intent on global destruction, Zizek's observation on the perceived distinction between the digitalised First World and the 'desert of the Real' is no longer valid. Not only has the digitised First World moved to the 'desert', it is also talking back, through macabre images and videos, to the First World. As a consequence, both the understandings of global terror as well as the measures to counter these have shifted. Butler's (2004) assessment of the use of the term 'terrorism' in official speech or state discourse as being constituted by outmoded distinctions between the civilised and the barbarian echoes Zizek's sentiments and concerns. On the other hand, her reading of the official pronouncements that followed 9/11 as media performances, 'a form of speech that establishes a domain of official utterance distinct from legal discourse' (2004, p. 80) raises a set of relevant issues, including the discursive performativity that underpins and justifies counter-terror policies, in which the performatives of state discourse offer a preamble to the enactment of measures to counter radicalisation. This calls for a re-examination of who – in terms of both individuals and communities – are the victims of violent extremism and of state policies. Crucial to these arguments, and deeply implicated in both the enactments of terror as well as political pronouncements that have followed them, is the role of the image, in other words, the media. These have moved from concerns over satellite news broadcasting following 9/11 to the more recent apprehensions over the sophisticated use of social media and the Internet by extremists located abroad to radicalise youth living at 'home' in Europe, North America and Australia. Borderless global technologies challenge both the technical expertise and the democratic ideals in multi-ethnic societies.

Among the flurry of academic and popular publications on contemporary forms of terrorism and the media that quickly followed 9/11 were a few that focussed on terror as spectacle, locating the singularity of the event in the battle over control of images, and linking the subsequent increase in the culture of insecurity to the global circulation of the iconic media images of the event and its aftermath. What has become fairly commonplace by now – the understanding that, beyond the harm caused to the victims of extremist violence, the 'street theatre' enacted by acts of terror seeks an audience of mass publics through the media – was noted by several scholars reflecting on the meaning and significance of 9/11 (see, for example, Nacos, 2002). In its polemic against leftist interpretations of the Gulf War as 'blood for oil', the San Francisco based collective of activist-scholars, Retort (2005), identified as one of the main reason for that conflict as the struggle for control of global images. Building on Guy Debord's thesis on the 'politics of spectacle', the ideological management of appearances, Retort diagnosed post-9/11 American politics as an attempt to restore hegemony over the image, which had been undermined by the event: 'outright defeat in the war of appearance is something that no present-day hegemon can tolerate' (p. 14). Similarly, Giroux (2006) underscored the singularity of 9/11 in the sphere of the spectacular: those attacks, he argued,

> were designed to be visible, designed to be spectacular. They not only bear an eerie similarity to violence-saturated Hollywood disaster films, but are similarly suited to – and intended for – endless instant replay on the nightly news, bringing an end to democratic freedoms with democracy's blessings.
> (p. 47)

Buck-Morss (2013) echoed this argument recently, declaring that the 9/11 attacks initiated an entirely new understanding of global terror by staging mass violence as a global spectacle. We shall return to the point regarding the threat to democratic freedoms later in this essay. For now, however, the links Giroux makes between images of the 9/11 attacks endlessly replayed on the news and those from Hollywood disaster films are worth noting, as they illustrate Sontag's (2003) argument about what she regards the paradoxical nature of contemporary representations in the image-rich societies in which most of us live, in particular, that mediated imagery informs the vocabulary available to us to not only describe, but also *experience* spectacular incidents such as 9/11. This, in turn recalls Appadurai's (1996) conception of global mediascapes as providing visual, narrative and plot-driven 'scripts' that influence modern cultures' imagining of themselves and others in the global environment.

Following this argument, it is possible to see how one of the main fallouts from the post 9/11 struggle over the 'war of appearance' (Retort, p. 14) has been the precarity of life for minorities of colour in the First World, whose true allegiances have come under suspicion, perceived as they are as torn between the nation and something akin to a form of 'global Islam'. Significant here is Altheide's (2006) observation that terrorism 'plays well with audiences accustomed to the discourse of fear as well as political leadership oriented to social policy geared to protecting those audiences from crime.' (p. 127). As the notion of both the crime and the criminal – in this case, religious extremist – has shifted from that of an external aggressor to the 'home grown' terrorist, who constitutes the victims of such crimes and their aftermath too, needs to be reassessed. Intrinsic in this is the argument of how the apprehension of the Muslim Other, including the perception of the 'veiled threat' (Aly and Walker, 2007), has contributed to an 'affective contagion' (Thrift, 2008, p. 235) or a 'transmission of affect' (Brennan, 2004), the performative dimensions of which can be seen as responses to media representations of terrorism and the widely disseminated images of horrific violence. As Thrift (2008) argues, 'the proliferation of mass media tends to both multiply and keep this kind of affective platform in the public mind in a way which promotes anxiety and can sometimes even be likened to obsession or compulsion' (p. 242). Crucial to note here, is 'the rise of more and more affective techniques, premised on making appeals to the heart, passion, emotional imagination' (p. 243).

A lot has changed since 9/11, including, crucially, the extremists' utilisation of social media and the consequent changes in the modality of communication. Such developments have given rise to a new set of concerns regarding a clutch of issues, including how the affordances of social media and the Internet have resulted in new forms of terrorist activity and extremist propaganda, and new kinds of overtures to potential recruits to the extremists' cause. As a consequence, there have been urgent calls for new ways to counter such activities in multicultural, multi-ethnic societies.

The struggle over control of images continues, however, with the arrival of new media technologies. The site of this struggle has shifted from satellite and cable television news – as in the case of the reporting of 9/11, which were more amenable to policy changes and government regulations – to the much less controllable, constantly shifting and rapidly developing technologies of social media. Ironically, the very affordances that were exploited to such spectacular effect as in the unfortunately brief Arab Spring, that gave rise to popular grassroots movements for democratic change, are the very ones that are now being utilised by extremist groups for horrific ends. As Jason Burke has argued in a recent report,

> the use and broadcast of graphic and violent images has reached an unprecedented level. Much of this is due to the emergence of the Islamic State (Isis).... But much is also the result of the capabilities of the new technology that Isis has been able to exploit.[2]

Tracking the history of the exploitation of the media in democracies since the mid-nineteenth century, Burke underlines the significance and dual impact of the dissemination of gruesome images of terrorist violence on social media:

> New technologies have not only made it possible to produce propaganda with astonishing ease – they have also made it far easier to disseminate these films and images. Isis videos include the execution of western aid workers and journalists, Syrian government soldiers, alleged spies and suspected homosexuals, a Jordanian pilot, Christian migrant workers, and others. Some have been decapitated, others shot, blown up, hurled from tall buildings or burnt alive.... Though it accounts for only a fraction of the overall propaganda output of Isis, this material has had a disproportionate impact, just as planned. Many of the clips serve a dual purpose, inspiring one group of people while disgusting and frightening the other.[3]

The display of such expertise in the manipulation and use of the latest media technologies came as a shock to many of those involved in counter-terrorism:

> Such surprise appears rooted in the expectation that a supposedly 'medieval' organisation would use 'medieval' means. The group's use of social media marks it out from predecessors such as al-Qaida. So, too, do the high production values and visual image derived from video games and Hollywood blockbusters. But terrorists have always exploited the latest technologies, whether dynamite or digital communications. And the group's exploitation of cutting-edge contemporary media falls squarely within the long tradition of terrorist organisations rapidly adapting to change.[4]

The global availability and the constant updating of these images and videos have raised major concerns among counter-terrorism authorities across the world. Particularly significant among these concerns has been the unease about the potential radicalisation of young men and women from Muslim communities in the West. Recent terrorist attacks in Boston, Paris, Brussels and Sydney have been associated with radicalised youth.

Radicalisation and counter-radicalisation

In his provocative essay entitled 'What do pictures *really* want?', written as a thought-piece and as an attempt to go beyond the rhetorical and interpretive traditions of analysis of meaning and power in the disciplines of art history and in visual culture, W.J.T. Mitchell (1996), outlines his intention to reorient the focus of the analysis of the 'scopic regimes' of pictures as agents of specific ideologies:

> I shift the question from what pictures *do* to what they *want*, from power to desire, from the model of the dominant power to be opposed to the model of the subaltern to be interrogated or (better) to be invited to speak.
> (p. 74; emphasis in original)

Despite the risk of being accused of totemism or fetishism that such 'dubious personification of inanimate objects' (p. 70) potentially involves, Mitchell argues that his 'subaltern model' offers the possibility of analysing 'the dialectics of power and desire in our relation to pictures' (p. 75). For our present purposes, what is particularly instructive in Mitchell's intervention is his analysis of the famous 'Uncle Sam' poster used by the US Army. While acknowledging that his attempt to shift the analytical focus not only includes interpretation of a picture, but also that 'all it accomplishes is a subtle dislocation of the target of interpretation' (p. 81), Mitchell suggests an Althusserean reading of the Uncle Sam poster as 'hailing' the viewer, its 'immediate desire' being to transfix the viewer, and then to 'send him' to 'the nearest recruitment station'. A deep analysis of what this picture wants, he argues, would 'take us deep into the political unconscious of a nation' as a 'disembodied abstraction, an Enlightenment polity of laws and not men, principles and not blood relationships, and actually embodied as a place where old white men send young men of all races to fight wars' (p. 76).

This is not the place for a deep analysis of the images that make up the extremist recruitment videos currently circulating in social media. Nevertheless, extending Mitchell's provocation, asking what these images 'want', could potentially be a productive exercise. For one of the abiding questions that have puzzled academic researchers, security experts and policy makers is what exactly is the basis on which radicalisation and recruitment happens? What, in this instance, is the 'disembodied abstraction' that young men and women are being called upon to willingly kill and die for? The explanations that have thus far been presented – ranging from virgins in heaven to the creation of a Caliphate – are more often than not indicative of a profound lack of understanding of the roles of the local socio-cultural contexts and of the politics at both the local and global levels in the process of radicalisation.

The affordances of the new media ecology, including global portals such as YouTube and Twitter and other multimedia platforms, user-generated content, on-line social networking, and the inexpensiveness and portability of new recording and editing hardware and software have allowed the uploading and wide dissemination of violent extremist content. It is important to consider that

> these global portals are known and attractive to young people in particular, and that multi-media content, especially moving images, is thought to be more convincing than text in terms of its ability to influence. Couple this with the internet's crowd-sourcing properties, and the violent jihadi online milieu is born.
>
> (Conway, 2012, p. 4)

The 'jihadisphere', Conway (2012) argues, was facilitated by 'the advent of Web 2.0 that offered violent radicals the means to transform their largely broadcast internet presences into meaningful interactive radical milieu' (p. 1). Both Burke and Conway make similar observations on the ways in which developments in digital technologies have shifted the links between terrorist acts and the media:

for instance, while until the advent of Web 2.0 extremist propaganda techniques were based on major terrorist incidents followed by the distribution of videos to major news organisations by jihadists such as Bin Laden, the newer technologies have allowed access to a global online network. A consequence of this is seen as relatively smaller terrorist attacks, carried out by 'lone-wolf' extremists or small groups, the meticulously planned, epoch-changing grant terror of 9/11 being replaced by acts of terror carried out by local cells in Europe. Believing that this online jihadi milieu is in many ways a facilitator of acts of extremist violence in the 'real world', counter-terrorism experts have expressed concern about the difficulties of countering digital platforms carrying violent jihadi videos and images, 'especially because portals such as YouTube and Twitter generally cannot be shut down the same way as, for example, jihadi online forums' (Conway, 2012, p. 4). This, in turn, has intensified alarm and anxieties about how such online material has contributed to the increase in attacks by small groups or individuals, as in the Boston Marathon bombing in 2013 by the Tsamaev brothers.

This recent increase in 'home grown' and 'lone wolf' extremist attacks in various locations in Europe has promoted an array of academic studies on the notion and process of radicalisation, and investigations and policy recommendations on how to counter this process of violent radicalisation. However, as Schmid (2012) has noted, beyond recognising it as a potential cause for violent acts of terror, there doesn't seem to be a consensus among scholars or policy makers on what constitutes radicalisation: 'Rik Coolsaet, a Belgian expert ... recently described the very notion of radicalisation as "ill-defined, complex and controversial".... Along similar lines, an Australian team of authors concluded that, "about the only thing that radicalisation experts agree on is that radicalisation is a process. Beyond that there is considerably variation as to make existing research incomparable"' (p. 1). Other scholars such as Kundnani (2012) and Sedgwick (2010) too have commented on this lack of agreement between researchers.

While part of the problem stems from the evolution of the meaning of the terms 'radical' and 'radicalisation' – from that suggesting a largely positive force mounting a political and social challenge to the status quo, to one that prefigures and possibly contributes to violent acts of terror, the main reason for the incommensurability of definitions of the term, according to Schmid, arises from a lack of engagement with the *context* within which radicalisation could be said to occur. As researchers such as Schmid (2012) and Kundnani (2012) have argued, exclusive focus on the individual perceived to be vulnerable to overtures from radicalised others misses important aspects of the process: 'causes for radicalisation that can lead to terrorism ought to be sought not just on the micro-level but also on the meso- and macro-levels', in which correspond, respectively, to 'the individual level' (*micro*), the 'wider radical milieu – the supportive and even complicit social surround' (*meso*) and 'the role of government and society at home and abroad, the radicalisation of public opinion and party politics, tense majority-minority relationships' (*macro*) (Schmid, 2013, p. 4).

While arguments concerning perceived links between online jihadi content and radicalisation at the micro level echo assumptions regarding the effects of violent content on television and cinema on 'vulnerable' individuals that were successfully challenged by empirical research in the 1990s that showed no such direct influence of watching violence on behaviour, the meso- and macro-levels of jihadi milieus deserve closer examination. The macro-level, in particular – the role of the state and the potential fracturing of relations and increase in suspicion between the majority and minority communities in Western democracies – demands scrutiny in terms of both the consequences of counter-terrorism and counter-radicalisation for democracies and for the perception among Muslim and non-Muslim minorities of being victims of their appearance and their religious beliefs.

As argued elsewhere (Harindranath, 2011, 2014), Butler's (1995, 2004, 2010) notion of performativity, considered together with Derrida's argument of terrorism and counter-terrorism as 'auto-immune disorder (in Borradori, 2003), helps us understand better the discursive, performative aspects of counter-terrorism and counter-radicalisation discourse, the role of political and official speech in the formulation of policies, and the damaging consequences of such measures. First, and most pertinent for our immediate purposes, is Butler's argument that performative speech acts of the 'illocutionary' variety, through a process of iteration and repetition, create that which constitute those acts: illocutionary performatives 'characterise speech acts characterise acts that bring about certain realities', such as the pronouncements of a judge (Butler, 2010, p. 147). More broadly, for her the notion of 'performativity' underlines the process through which, through recitation and repetition, discourses come to constitute cultural and historical understandings and practices. Given this, '[h]ow might we account for the injurious word within such a framework, the word that not only names a social subject, but constructs that subject in the naming, and constructs that subject through a violating interpellation' she asks (Butler, 1995, p. 203).

In the present context, one of the consequences of the power dynamics that characterise official and much of popular discourse on terrorism and counter-terrorism, as displayed in the media, has been the demonization of Islam and the rise in anti-Muslim sentiments. The resulting climate of fear and the racialisation of politics have together contributed to the potential undermining of multiculturalism, civil society, and the sense of belonging among ethnic and religious minorities. Similarly, Derrida's analysis of 9/11 and the counter-terrorism policies that it gave rise to (in Borradori, 2003) as indicators of 'auto-immune disorder' points to the threats posed by both terrorist acts and counter-terror policies to the body politic through the suspension of several rights – allegedly temporary – that are fundamental to democracy and its legal institutions. The racial politics of affect that followed 9/11 and which has metastasised into anti-immigrant, anti-Muslim attitudes, has led to not only surveillance in communities perceived to be threats, but also more stringent measures such as incarceration without charge. The 'vicious circle of repression' is one of the three 'moments' that Derrida identifies in the auto-immune disorder that was precipitated by 9/11, including defences against another terrorist incident which could itself 'work to regenerate, in the short or long term, the cause of the evil they claim to eradicate' (in Borradori, 2003, p. 100).

Counter-radicalisation, 'atmosfear', and affect

In an impassioned critique of rhetorical constructions of terrorism, Ivie (2003) warns against the simple and simplistic recourse to the rhetoric of good versus evil that prevailed immediately after the 9/11 attacks: 'to speak of evil ... or of vanquishing evil enemies, is to step into a circle of reciprocal violence which supplants diplomacy and democracy with the method of terror' (p. 184). Ivie wrote this at a time when this rhetoric was invoked with reference to a threat from *outside* the United States and Europe, and embodied by Saddam Hussein. As we saw earlier, the focus and the rhetoric has shifted since then, in particular as a consequence of the London bombings in 2005, which prompted a change of focus to the 'enemy within', in the form of Muslim extremists living in Europe, United States or Australia. With the increase in awareness of the sophistication and reach of extremist propaganda in the 'jihadisphere', attention is now being paid to processes of radicalisation and attempts to counter these. Among counter-terrorism experts, the online presence of extremists has raised concerns about individuals and groups living in the West being radicalised through social media. In their social network analysis of a real YouTube data set, Bermingham *et al.* (2009) decry 'the dearth of empirical academic research' addressing online radicalisation, and by way of underlining the links between the Internet, social media and radicalisation, they present a preliminary analysis of both textual and interactive components of YouTube videos on the basis of their working conception of online radicalisation as 'a process whereby individuals, through their online interactions and exposure to various types of Internet content, come to view violence as a legitimate method of solving social and political conflicts' (p. 1). Despite its potential to contribute to a systematic analysis of relevant social media content however, this conception of radicalisation reproduces the problems associated with focussing exclusively on the micro-individual level of analysis (Schmid, 2013).

As Schmid (2013) reminds us, '"radicalisation" is not just a socio-psychological scientific concept but also a political construct' (p. 19) and, as such, the various definitions offered by state and legal authorities attest to a performative discourse with consequences that transgress or undermine the intended ones, no matter how sensitively worded these definitions are. For instance, the Australian government website 'Living Safe Together: Building Community Resilience to Violent Extremism' contains a 'Radicalisation awareness information kit', which offers the following notion of the process of radicalisation that attempts to provide a clear distinction between radicalisation per se, and violent extremism without making any over link with Islam or Muslims:

> Radicalisation happens when a person's thinking and behaviour become significantly different from how most of the members of their society and community view social issues and participate politically. Only small numbers of people radicalise and they can be from a diverse range of ethnic, national, political and religious groups.

> As a person radicalises they may begin to seek to change significantly the nature of society and government. However, if someone decides that using fear, terror or violence is justified to achieve ideological, political or social change – this is violent extremism.[5]

Notwithstanding such careful phrasing, the macro-level context is comprised of performative discourses, including racialised, anti-Muslim, anti-immigrant rhetoric that has, for instance, reiterated calls for the Muslim communities living in the West to clearly and continually articulate their allegiances to the nation and to the national culture and 'ways of life'. If anything, this illustrates the contradictions inherent in counter-terrorism and counter-radicalisation discourse caught between the perceived need to focus their energies on Muslim youth while at the same time recognising the significance of working with the Muslim community. Anxieties regarding social media images contributing to possible radicalisation of young men and women, while justifiable, also raise serious questions about how these discourses affect the Muslim minorities in the West.

The 'atmosfear' of terror, argue Aly and Balnaves (2005), manifests differently among the Muslim minorities in Australia. These include

> the fear of backlash from some sectors of the wider community; the fear of subversion of Islamic identity in meeting the requirements of politically defined 'moderate' Islam; the fear of being identified as a potential terrorist or 'person of interest' and the fear of potentially losing the rights bestowed on all other citizens.
>
> (p. 1)

Again, it is important to note that the media are centrally implicated in this 'atmosfear':

> This fear or fears are grounded in the political and the media responses to terrorism that perpetuates a popular belief that Muslims, as a culturally and religiously incompatible 'other', pose a threat to the Australian collective identity and, ostensibly, to Australia's security.
>
> (p. 1)

Derrida (in Borradori, 2003) reads the televised images of the September 11 attacks, together with the label '9/11' itself, as indicative of the trauma suffered by the 'technoeconomic power of the media', and acknowledges the importance of global television news for the event:

> what would 'September 11' have been without television?... Maximum media coverage was in the *common* interest of the perpetrators of 'September 11', the terrorist, and those who, in the name of victims, wanted to declare 'war on terrorism'.
>
> (p. 108; emphasis in original)

Claiming that the event was incomprehensible through the utilisation of existing frameworks and concepts, he calls for their revision, arguing that philosophy in the time of terrorism requires a fundamental reappraisal of theories and debates with which philosophy had hitherto been preoccupied. It is possible to argue that, given the state of affairs regarding social media images and radicalisation/counter-radicalisation, a similar reassessment of extant notions and concepts appears urgent. In other words, the current conjuncture requires us to critically reconsider accepted ideas and to problematize and examine existing understandings of what the performative dimensions of discourse on both terrorism and counter-terrorism cause to bring into being culturally, politically and socially.

For instance, in order to grasp the complex configurations that underlie the prevalent 'atmosfear' among Muslim minorities, the notion of 'affect' seems appropriate. Reference was made earlier to Thrift's concept of 'affective contagion' and Brennan's idea of 'transmission of affect', both of which suggest an engagement with affect as a social issue, rather than a personal, subjective one. However, as Wetherell (2015) has pointed out, despite the conceptual richness of Thrift's formulation of affect, he reduces people to their 'body parts' that

> are assailed by events, by smells, the social relations of organizing spaces, material objects and global economic forces.... People en masse are best seen, in Thrift's view, as like schools of fish or flocks of starlings, incomprehensibly wheeling, pulsing, moving, reacting, as body speaks directly to body.
>
> (p. 149)

The spreading of affect, in this formulation, is subjectless. Arguing that '[c]ontext, past and current practice, and complex acts of *meaning-making* and *representation* are involved in the spreading of affect, no matter how random or viral it appears' (p. 154; emphasis in original), Wetherell makes a case for Ahmed's conception of affect and the 'cultural politics of emotion' (Ahmed, 2004a, 2004b).

Two aspects of Ahmed's conceptualisation of affect are particularly relevant to our present concerns. The first of these is her argument that,

> Affect does not reside in an object or sign, but is an affect of the circulation between objects and signs (= the accumulation of affective value over time). Some signs, that is, increase in affective value as an effect of the movement between signs: the more they circulate, the more affective they become, and the more they appear to 'contain' affect.
>
> (2004a, p. 120)

This recalls Butler's insistence that performativity both includes iteration and repetition, and that discourse 'precedes and makes possible the subject who speaks' (2010, p. 148). The second aspect of Ahmed's theorisation is 'stickiness' – 'sticky associations' are those through which emotions 'move sideways'

(p. 120), and connections are made between words, objects, and emotions, such as in the case of asylum seekers: 'words like *flood* and *swamped* are used, which create associations between asylum and the loss of control, as well as dirt and sewage, and hence work by mobilizing fear' (p. 122; emphasis in original). More significantly, 'the word *terrorist* sticks to some bodies as it reopens past histories of naming, just as it slides into other words in the accounts of the wars in Afghanistan (such as *fundamentalism, Islam, Arab, repressive, primitive*)' (p. 131; emphasis in original). The amassing of affective value is more often than not dependent on a history that is evoked either deliberately or through unconscious associations. As such, the discourse on radicalisation immediately evokes notions of Islam, of Islamism, of Islamic extremism and of the Muslim Other, regardless of whether or not it makes an explicit reference to Islam. Given this, the state of 'atmosfear' becomes explicable. As Titley (2014), commenting on the fecundity of Ahmed's notion of 'stickiness', observes,

> Stickiness ... implies not only moment of discursive concentration and circulation in networks of exchange, but also historically generated repertoires, vocabularies, indices and symbolic relations that, to extend the metaphor, have varying degrees of adhesiveness according to the context of production and reception.
>
> (p. 47)

As noted earlier, our present conjuncture with regard to radicalisation and social media images comes weighted with the history of the images of the September 11 attacks and the subsequent racist violence against individuals who 'looked Muslim'. And this is relevant, in the way it evokes fear and hatred, for both the wider community as well as for some racial minorities, who are, as mentioned earlier, victims twice over – as potential victims of random and indiscriminate terrorist attacks by radicalised young men and women, and victims of racial hatred and racialised politics arising from the perception of them as potential radicals or terrorists.

Concluding remarks

Derrida argued (in Borradori, 2003) that the epochal September 11 attacks demanded a re-examination of 'the most deep-seated conceptual presuppositions in philosophical discourse', since 'the concepts with which this "event" has most often been described, named, categorized, are the products of a "dogmatic slumber"' (p. 100). Contemporary anxieties regarding social media images, radicalisation, 'home-grown' terror and the ways in which attempts to counter them have, in turn, raised levels of insecurity among minorities of colour. Ironically, this could potentially contribute to further marginalisation and increase the risk of radicalisation. These developments demand a similar re-assessment of received concepts, of prevailing views on victimhood and the racial Other as a possible threat, and finally, of assumptions that underpin counter-radicalisation measures. The present conjuncture requires a more careful consideration of its various aspects, including the production and use of social media imagery, and the development of grounded theories based on a sustained engagement with these aspects. As De Leo and Mehan (2012) argue, 'Post 9/11, it no longer seems responsible for theorist to engage in *a*political analysis; to dwell on the concept at the expense of the empirical; to ignore the social while reveling in the ideal' (p. 18; emphasis in original).

Notes

1 www.theguardian.com/uk-news/2016/mar/25/man-charged-tweet-confront-muslim-woman-brussels-attacks
2 www.theguardian.com/world/2016/feb/25/how-changing-media-changing-terrorism
3 Ibid.
4 Ibid.
5 www.livingsafetogether.gov.au/informationadvice/Pages/what-is-radicalisation/what-is-radicalisation.aspx

References

Ahmad, M. (2002) 'Homeland insecurities: racial violence the day after September 11', *Social Text*, 20(3).
Ahmed, S. (2004a) 'Affective economies', *Social Text* 79, 22(2).
Ahmed, S. (2004b) *The Cultural Politics of Emotion*. New York: Routledge.
Altheide, D. (2006) *Terrorism and the Politics of Fear*. Lanham, MD: Rowman and Littlefield.
Aly, A. and M. Balnaves (2005) 'The atmosfear of terror: affective modulation and the war on terror', *M/C Journal*, 8(6).
Aly, A. and D. Walker (2007) 'Veiled threats: recurrent cultural anxieties in Australia', *Journal of Muslim Minority Affairs*, 27(2).
Appadurai, A. (1996) *Modernity at Large: Cultural Dimensions of Globalization*. Minneapolis: University of Minnesota Press.
Bermingham, A, M. Conway, L. McInerney, N. O'Hare, and A. Smeaton (2009) 'Combining social network analysis and sentiment analysis to explore the potential for online radicalisation', in ASONAM 2009, International Conference on Advances in Social Networks Analysis and Mining, available online at: http://ieeexplore.ieee.org/xpls/abs_all.jsp?arnumber=5231878&tag=1
Borradori, G. (ed.) (2003) *Philosophy in the Time of Terror: Dialogues with Jurgen Habermas and Jacques Derrida*. Chicago: University of Chicago Press.
Brennan, T. (2004) *The Transmission of Affect*. Ithaca, NJ: Cornell University Press.
Buck-Morss, S. (2003) *Thinking Past Terror: Islamism and Critical Theory on the Left*. London: Verso.
Butler, J. (1995) 'Burning acts, injurious speech', in A. Parker and E. Sedgwick (eds) *Performativity and Performance*. New York: Routledge.
Butler, J. (2004) *Precarious Lives: the Powers of Mourning and Violence*. London: Verso.
Butler, J. (2010) 'Performative agency', *Journal of Cultural Economy*, 3(2).
Callinicos, A. (2005) 'Epoch and conjuncture in Marxist political economy', *International Politics*, 42.

Conway M. (2012) 'From al-Zarqawi to al-Awlaki: the emergence and development of an online radical milieu', *CTX: Combating Terrorism Exchange*, 2(4).

Di Leo, J. and U. Mehan (2012) 'Theory ground zero: terror, theory and the humanities after 9/11', in J. Di Leo and U. Mehan (eds) *Terror, Theory and the Humanities*, Open Humanities Press.

Giroux, H. (2006) *Beyond the Spectacle of Terrorism: Global Uncertainty and the Challenge of the New Media*. Boulder, CO: Paradigm Publishers.

Harindranath, R. (2011) 'Performing terror, anti-terror and public affect: towards an analytical framework', *Continuum*, 25(2).

Harindranath, R. (2014) 'Counterterrorism as contested terrain: performative contradictions and "autoimmune disorder"', in D. Pisoiu (ed.) *Arguing Counter-terrorism*. London: Routledge.

Ivie, R. (2003) 'Evil enemy versus agonistic other: rhetorical constructions of terrorism', *Review of Education, Pedagogy and Cultural Studies*, 25(3).

Ivie, R. (2005) 'Savagery in democracy's empire', *Third World Quarterly*, 26(1).

Jameson, F. (2002) 'The dialectics of disaster', *South Atlantic Quarterly*, 101(2).

Kundnani, A. (2012) 'Radicalisation: the journey of a concept', *Race & Class*, 54(2).

Mankekar, P. (2015) *Unsettling India: Affect, Temporality, Transnationality*. Durham: Duke University Press.

Massumi, B. (2005) 'Fear (The Spectrum Said)', *Positions: East Asia Cultures Critique*, 13(1).

Mitchell, W.J.T. (1996) 'What do pictures *really* want?' *October 77*.

Nacos, B. (2002) *Mass-Mediated Terrorism: the Role of the Media in Terrorism and Counter-terrorism*. London: Rowman and Littlefield.

Omotoyinbo, F.R. (2014) 'Online radicalisation: the net or the netizen?', *Social Technologies*, 4(1).

Retort (I. Boal, T.J. Clark, J. Matthews and M. Watts) (2005) *Afflicted Powers: Capital and Spectacle in a New Age of War*. London: Verso.

Schmid, A. (2013), 'Radicalisation, de-radicalisation, counter-radicalisation: a conceptual discussion and literature review', ICCT Research Paper, International Centre for Counter-Terrorism, The Hague, available online at www.icct.nl/publications/icct-papers/radicalisation-de-radicalisation-counter-radicalisation-a-conceptual-discussion-and-literature-review

Sedgwick, M. (2010), 'The concept of radicalisation as a source of confusion', *Terrorism and Political Violence*, 22(4).

Sontag, S. (2003) *Where the Stress Falls*. London: Vintage.

Thrift, N. (2008) *Non-representational Theory: Space/Politics/Affect*. London: Routledge.

Titley, G. (2014) 'No apologies for cross-posting: European trans-media space and the digital circuitries of racism', *Crossings: Journal of Migration & Culture*, 5(1).

Wetherell, M. (2015) 'Trends in the turn to affect: a social psychological critique', *Body & Society*, 21(2).

Zizek, S. (2002) *Welcome to the Desert of the Real!* London: Verso.

Part IV
Social violence

9 Bullying in the digital age

Robin M. Kowalski and Gary W. Giumetti

Introduction

It is difficult to imagine where we would be today without technology. Ask any parent whose children keep themselves occupied on iPads or mobile phones. Think of the feeling when you realize you have left your mobile phone at home and will be without it for the day. Imagine the panic when the wireless in your home temporarily stops working. While technology serves us well throughout our day, it is also fraught with many perils as well. Many young people today experience FoMO (fear of missing out) as they spend countless hours perusing the seemingly perfectly profiled lives of their friends and acquaintances on social media (Alt, 2015; Przybylski, Murayama, DeHaan & Gladwell, 2013). Victims of online or offline identity theft are often affected for years when someone absconds with their social security number, birthdate, name, and address. And, of relevance to the present chapter, victims of cyberbullying imagine a very different world without technology. They imagine a world where they wouldn't feel anxious, depressed, and, in some instances, suicidal in part because of the barrage of online and textual bullying that they have experienced.

Cyberbullying defined

Defining cyberbullying has proven to be one of many challenges facing researchers in the area (Kowalski et al., 2014; Kowalski et al., 2012; Smith, 2015). One reason for this may be that cyberbullying is studied by researchers from an array of different disciplines. Because we are psychologists, our approach in this chapter will have a decidedly psychological track to it. However, the literature cited comes not only from psychology, but also sociology and medicine. Some researchers define cyberbullying broadly as simply bullying that occurs through the use of technology. Others are more specific in defining cyberbullying in terms of the specific venue by which it might be perpetrated (e.g., e-mail, chat rooms, web pages, social media). Still others focus on the specific form that cyberbullying takes. Nancy Willard (2007), for example, has outlined a taxonomy of cyberbullying behaviors that includes flaming, harassment, outing and trickery, exclusion, impersonation, cyber-stalking, and sexting.[1]

Many derive their definition of cyberbullying from Dan Olweus' (1993) definition of traditional bullying, whereby bullying in whatever form is defined as an aggressive act that is intended to cause harm or distress, that is typically repeated over time, and that occurs among individuals whose relationship is characterized by a power imbalance. With cyberbullying, some features of this definition require conceptual tweaking when compared to traditional bullying (Kowalski et al., 2014). For example, while cyberbullying acts can be repetitive in the traditional sense, repetition in cyberbullying may also take the form of a single message being sent to or viewed by hundreds or perhaps thousands of individuals. In addition, the power differential that characterizes relationships in traditional bullying is often framed as differences in physical stature or social status. With cyberbullying, on the other hand, power differentials can be created by variations in technological expertise or even by the anonymity that surrounds many instances of cyberbullying. A perpetrator knowing the identity of the target but the victim not knowing the perpetrator's identity accords power to the instigator (Smith, 2015). In keeping with the Olweus tradition, cyberbullying will be defined in this paper as "an aggressive, intentional act carried out by a group or individual, using electronic forms of contact, repeatedly and over time against a victim who cannot easily defend him or herself" (Smith et al., 2008, p. 376). Although most of the extant literature on cyberbullying has focused on victimization and perpetration among young people, as will be discussed later in this chapter, cyberbullying is not limited to a particular age demographic. The definition provided here is a useful one to use regardless of the age of the individuals involved.

Framing cyberbullying using terms typically reserved for traditional bullying suggests that cyberbullying may be just an extension of traditional bullying. However, while cyberbullying does share particular features in common with traditional bullying (i.e., act of aggression, repeated over time, imbalance of power in the relationship), there are critical ways in which the two types of bullying differ from one another. First, perceived anonymity is a key component of many instances of cyberbullying. In one study with over 3,700 sixth, seventh, and eighth grade students, just under 50 percent of the cyberbullying victims did not know the identity of the perpetrator (Kowalski & Limber, 2007). Similarly, Elizabeth Englander (2012) found that 72 percent of third grade cyberbullying victims did not know the identity of the perpetrator. Not only does this give power to the perpetrator as mentioned previously, but it also opens up the pool of individuals who might perpetrate cyberbullying. Research on deindividuation demonstrates that people will say and do things anonymously that they would never say and do in face-to-face interactions (Suler, 2004). Second, most traditional bullying occurs at school during the school day (Nansel et al., 2001). With cyberbullying, however, the accessibility of victims to perpetrators is 24/7. Even though targets may not view the objectionable content or may turn off the incoming messages feature on their cellular phone, the cyberbullying is still being perpetrated against them. Third, many adults can recall instances of traditional bullying victimization when they were younger, leading parents to be able to relate to experiences that their victimized children may have. The technological digital divide creates a different situation with cyberbullying. Because many adults are digital immigrants and youth are digital natives, not all parents had experience with cyberbullying when they were in school (Prensky, 2001). Thus, many young people perceive that their parents will not understand if they report their victimization experiences to them. Reporting victimization is an issue with both traditional bullying and cyberbullying, albeit for different reasons. Key among the many reasons for not telling, victims of traditional bullying are reluctant to disclose their victimization out of fears that the perpetrator will retaliate. Cyberbullying victims, on the other hand, fear that the adults to whom they disclose their victimization will remove the technology by which they are being targeted (Kowalski et al., 2012).

Cyberbullying prevalence

Recently, researchers have debated whether incidents of cyberbullying are increasing, decreasing, or remaining relatively stable. Robert Slonje and Peter Smith (2008), for example, suggest that, with more and varied types of technology, prevalence rates of cyberbullying are on the rise. Others, such as Dan Olweus (2012, 2013), counter that cyberbullying rates are not only not increasing but that only 10 percent of instances of cyberbullying occur independently of traditional bullying. Indeed, perceptions that the frequency of cyberbullying victimization and perpetration are increasing may be an artifact of increased awareness of the behavior.

Additionally, just as defining cyberbullying has been a muddy issue, so, too, has the issue of generating clear prevalence rates. Different ways of conceptualizing cyberbullying lead to differences in how cyberbullying is measured which, in turn, affect reported prevalence rates of cyberbullying (Smith, 2015). Not surprisingly, then, reported frequencies of cyberbullying depend on the particular study being read. Prevalence rates are affected by demographic characteristics of the sample (e.g., age, race, sex), time parameter used to determine when the cyberbullying occurred (e.g., previous two months, previous six months, past year, lifetime), the general ("Have you ever been cyberbullied?") versus specific (e.g., "Have you been cyberbullied via instant messaging?") wording used to measure cyberbullying, the criterion used to determine that cyberbullying occurred (happened at least once versus occurred two to three times or more), whether a definition of cyberbullying is provided (Frisen et al., 2013; Kowalski et al., 2014; Smith, 2015), and the country of origin of the cyberbullying behavior (Kowalski et al., 2014).

Examined across studies, overall prevalence rates for cyberbullying typically range between 10 percent and 40 percent (Kowalski et al., 2014; Lenhart, 2010; O'Brennan et al., 2009). Justin Patchin and Sameer Hinduja (2012), for example, describe in their review of 35 peer-reviewed studies that, overall, 24 percent of students reported being victims of cyberbullying compared to 17 percent who reported perpetrating cyberbullying. Robin Kowalski and Susan Limber (2007), in an examination of over 3,700 U.S. middle school children's experiences with cyberbullying, reported that 18 percent had been cyberbullied at least once in the previous two months, whereas 11 percent had cyberbullied others in the same time frame.

As noted above, these prevalence rates are affected by demographic characteristics of the individuals sampled. Just as there are age-related variations in the experience of traditional bullying so, too, are there age-related changes in the reported incidents of cyberbullying (Tokunaga, 2010). Adolescence seems to be a particularly vulnerable time for cyberbullying victimization and perpetration relative to other age demographics (Wang et al., 2009; see, however, Turner et al., 2011; Walrave & Heiman, 2011). Even among adolescents, however, there are variations in the frequency of cyberbullying. As students move through school from sixth to eighth grade, they experience an increased likelihood of becoming involved in cyberbullying as victim and/or perpetrator (Hinduja & Patchin, 2008; Kowalski et al., 2014; Williams & Guerra, 2007). Two points deserve note here, however. First, increasing numbers of elementary school students (Englander, 2012) as well as college students and older adults are experiencing cyberbullying (Hoff & Mitchell, 2009; Kowalski et al., 2016). Second, prevalence rates for a given age demographic are affected by the modality used to perpetrate cyberbullying. Thus, whereas sixth through twelfth grade students may be more likely to experience cyberbullying through social networking, elementary school students perpetrate and are victims of cyberbullying most commonly through online gaming (Englander, 2012).

In addition to age, gender is another demographic variable that, depending on the study read, influences prevalence rates of cyberbullying victimization and perpetration. Reports of the relationship between gender and cyberbullying are very mixed. On one hand are studies that find no sex differences in cyberbullying victimization and perpetration (Hinduja & Patchin, 2008; Slonje & Smith, 2008; Williams & Guerra, 2007). On the other hand are studies finding that females are significantly more likely than males to be victims and perpetrators of cyberbullying (e.g., Hoff & Mitchell, 2009; Kowalski & Limber, 2007; Tokunaga, 2010). Still other research has found that males are more likely than females to perpetrate cyberbullying, but females are more likely to be targets of cyberbullying (Sourander et al., 2010). Additional research states that there are not sex differences in overall cyberbullying victimization or perpetration, but sex differences can be found when specific venues are examined (see, e.g., Hinduja & Patchin, 2008). In a meta-analysis of cyberbullying where gender was treated as a moderator, gender moderated the cybervictimization-depression relationship (Kowalski et al., 2014). The larger the percentage of females in the sample, the stronger the cybervictimization-depression relationship, suggesting that cybervictimization may be particularly harmful for females. Additionally, in a meta-analysis by Christopher Barlett and Sarah Coyne (2014), the authors found that, overall, males were more likely to perpetrate cyberbullying than females, but the size of this effect was very small. However, Barlett and Coyne also found that age was a significant moderator of this gender difference, with females being more likely to perpetrate cyberbullying at younger ages, and males being more likely to perpetrate cyberbullying at older ages.

One additional demographic variable to be examined in relation to prevalence rates of cyberbullying victimization and perpetration has received the least attention: race. Hinduja and Patchin (2008) and Michelle Ybarra and colleagues (2007) both examined racial differences in cyberbullying involvement. In neither study were any significant differences as a function of race observed. Jing Wang et al. (2009) observed significant differences by race with cyber perpetration but not cyber victimization. African American respondents reported the highest degree of cyberbullying perpetration (10.9 percent) followed by Hispanics (9.6 percent), others (7.3 percent), and Caucasians (6.7 percent). Other races (12.7 percent) showed the highest rates of victimization followed by African Americans (9.8 percent), Hispanics (9.8 percent), and Caucasians (9.0 percent). In contrast, Heather Turner et al. (2011) observed a higher rate of cyberbullying victimization (defined in the study as Internet harassment) among whites (3.1 percent), compared to African Americans (1.9 percent), and Hispanics (1.3 percent). Similar to Wang et al. (2009), other races reported the highest rates of victimization (4.2 percent) (see also Kessel Schneider et al., 2012). Clearly, as with gender, there is variability in the reports of cyberbullying prevalence by racial group across studies. Unlike with traditional bullying where race is a visible feature and where the identity of both the target and perpetrator are known, cyberbullying occurs in the virtual world, where the actual identity and demographic characteristics of both the victim and perpetrator *may* remain anonymous. Thus, race *may* play a less important role in cyberbullying than in traditional bullying situations (Kowalski et al., 2012). We emphasize the word "may" because some researchers (e.g., Nakamura & Chow-White, 2002) have suggested that race also creates a digital divide affecting access to and interaction on the Internet, which, subsequently, affects involvement in cyberbullying as both victim and perpetrator.

Importantly, prevalence rates of cyberbullying are affected by the country in which the data are collected. Meta-analytic results by Robin Kowalski and her colleagues (2014) found that cyber victimization rates were marginally lower in European/Australian samples than in North American samples. However, no differences were found between the groups in prevalence rates of cyberbullying perpetration.

Cyberbullying antecedents and consequences

A number of factors have been identified as potentially leading to cyberbullying, including a host of individual differences or "person factors" along with many features of the environment or "situational factors" (Kowalski et al., 2014). Personality is among the "person factors" that has received the most attention. Several traits have been identified as possible antecedents to cyberbullying behavior. On the victimization side, researchers have examined hyperactivity, social anxiety, and social intelligence as possible precursors to experiencing cyberbullying victimization (Kowalski et al., 2014). For example, recent work has identified an association between cyberbullying victimization and social anxiety (Álvarez-Garcia et al., 2015). Further evidence for a possible causal linkage between social anxiety and cyberbullying victimization was found in a longitudinal study of adolescents in Belgium (Pabian & Vandebosch, 2016). These authors found that individuals with high levels of social anxiety were more likely to report high levels of victimization in both traditional bullying and cyberbullying over time.

Another person factor that has been identified as a possible protective factor against cyberbullying victimization is social intelligence. For example, in a study of 10- to 12-year-old students from Spain, social intelligence was a significant predictor of cyberbullying victimization, with individuals having higher social intelligence being less likely to report cyber victimization (Navarro et al., 2012).

On the cyberbullying perpetration side, researchers have also identified a number of personality antecedents, including anger, moral disengagement, and empathy. For example, in their meta-analysis, Kowalski et al. (2014) found that there was a significant positive relationship overall between anger and cyberbullying perpetration. That is, individuals who were more prone to irritability, hostility, or rage were more likely to report perpetrating cyberbullying. Research has also consistently found a positive relationship between moral disengagement (or telling oneself that moral principles of right and wrong do not apply to one's own behavior) and cyberbullying perpetration (Bussey et al., 2015; Kowalski et al., 2014).

A few variables have also been identified as playing a preventative role with regard to cyberbullying perpetration, including empathy. In a recent study of British adolescents between 16 and 18 years old, Gayle Brewer and Jade Kerslake (2015) found that there was a negative association between empathy (or the ability to understand the emotions of others) and cyberbullying perpetration, such that individuals with high levels of empathy were less likely to engage in cyberbullying others.

Regarding situational antecedents of cyberbullying behavior, a number of factors have been identified as possibly leading to cyberbullying, including lack of parental monitoring, distant school climate, and provocation. Generally speaking, higher levels of monitoring of children's online behavior by parents are associated with lower levels of both cyberbullying victimization and perpetration (Kowalski et al., 2014). The same pattern of relationships exists for school climate as well, with schools that are perceived as trusting, fair and pleasant being associated with lower rates of cyberbullying behavior (Simon & Olsen, 2014; Williams & Guerra, 2007). Finally, regarding provocation, one study found that adolescents who were provoked were more likely to respond to the provocation with certain forms of cyberbullying behavior, including posting mean messages or photos (Law et al., 2012). Much other research has found a large association between reports of experiencing cyberbullying victimization and cyberbullying perpetration, with an average correlation of 0.5 (Kowalski et al., 2014).

Beyond antecedents of cyberbullying, researchers have also identified a host of possible outcomes of cyberbullying for both victims and perpetrators. These include depression, low self-esteem, anxiety, loneliness, drug and alcohol use, poor academic achievement, somatic symptoms, stress, reduced life satisfaction, and suicidal ideation (e.g., Didden et al., 2009; Hinduja & Patchin, 2010; Kowalski & Limber, 2013; Kowalski et al., 2014; Vazsonyi et al., 2012), among many possible others. Unfortunately, much of the previous research on cyberbullying has been cross-sectional in nature, with reports of cyberbullying and outcomes being measured at the same time. This type of study design makes it difficult to infer a causal relationship between cyberbullying and these outcome variables.

However, there have been a number of recent longitudinal studies that help to provide support for possible causal relationships. For example, one study examined the links between cyberbullying victimization and outcomes among a sample of adolescents from Spain across two time points (Gámez-Guadix et al., 2013). The authors found that cyberbullying victimization at the first time point was linked with depressive symptoms at the second time point, suggesting a possible causal linkage between these two variables. Another recent longitudinal study found that, among a sample of Australian adolescents, students who experienced both cyberbullying victimization and traditional bullying victimization were more likely to be absent from school than students who were only traditionally bullied (Cross, Lester et al., 2015). Other longitudinal data suggest that experiencing cyberbullying victimization is associated with increased externalizing problems and loneliness (Schultze-Krumbholz et al., 2012), increased likelihood of engaging in problem behaviors (which include stealing, fighting, breaking things, smoking cigarettes and drinking alcohol; Lester et al., 2012), and increased anxiety (Rose & Tynes, 2015). Additional research is needed that examines these and other possible outcomes of cyberbullying behavior.

Contributions of cyberbullying compared to traditional bullying

As noted above, the definitions for traditional bullying and cyberbullying share several features in common. Additionally, many researchers have also found that the experience of traditional bullying and cyberbullying overlap to a large extent, with up to 88 percent of victims/perpetrators of cyberbullying also reporting involvement in traditional bullying victimization/perpetration (Olweus, 2013). Thus, in order to understand the complete picture when it comes to cyberbullying, one must take into consideration the unique effects of both cyberbullying and traditional bullying. To do so, researchers need to measure both cyberbullying and traditional bullying in their studies, and then conduct the appropriate analysis (e.g., sequential regression or relative weights analysis) to determine the unique effects of each form of bullying. Sequential regression is a type of multiple regression analysis where a researcher adds one set of predictors in the first model of the regression analysis and then another set of predictors is added in a second model. The researcher then examines the change in amount of variance accounted for from the addition of the second set of predictors by examining the change in R^2 between the two models (Tabachnick & Fidell, 2013). Relative weights analysis is another type of statistical analysis that involves determining the relative contribution of an individual variable to the prediction of an outcome (Tonidandel & LeBreton, 2011). Relative weights analysis is especially helpful when the predictor variables being examined are highly correlated with one another, as would be expected with traditional bullying and cyberbullying.

A number of researchers have begun to examine the unique effects of cyberbullying over and above traditional bullying (e.g., Cross et al., 2015; Dempsey et al., 2009; Fredstrom et al., 2011; Giumetti & Kowalski, 2015; Machmutow et al., 2012; Menesini et al., 2012; Perren et al., 2010; Perren & Gutzwiller-Helfenfinger, 2012; Sakellariou et al., 2012), and the results suggest that cyberbullying does indeed have a unique impact on psychological and physical health behaviors while controlling for the effect of traditional bullying. For example, Dempsey et al. (2009) studied middle school students from the United States and found that cyberbullying victimization was uniquely related to social anxiety while controlling for traditional forms of bullying victimization.

Another study that examined the unique effects of cyberbullying over traditional bullying was conducted by Perren et al. (2010). The sample for this study contained adolescents from Switzerland and Australia, and the authors measured cyberbullying victimization and perpetration, traditional bullying victimization and perpetration, and depressive symptoms. The findings indicated that cyberbullying victimization had a significant relationship with depressive symptoms even after controlling for the effects of traditional bullying. Taken together, these findings suggest that cyberbullying is a unique phenomenon that warrants further research investigation. These results also suggest that researchers should plan to measure bullying in these multiple forms to get the best understanding of how the different forms of bullying are impacting individuals.

Privacy concerns and cyberbullying

As technology use has spread and users become more technology savvy, awareness of privacy concerns has increased. According to Patchin and Hinduja (2010), in 2006, fewer than 40 percent of youth enlisted privacy settings on their social media profiles. Three years later, 85 percent restricted access to their social networking profiles. A Pew Research Report in 2013 showed that only 60 percent of teen Facebook users restricted access to their profiles (Madden et al., 2013). Yet, the same report found that 64 percent of teen Twitter users keep their accounts public. Where privacy issues often fall short for many adolescents and young children is a failure to appreciate the extent to which their privacy may, indeed, be compromised online; for example, the lack of understanding that what they post online remains online even if they later choose to remove it, which many do (Madden et al., 2013). For example, an adolescent who posts a questionable picture that they later remove has no guarantee that the picture has not been downloaded by someone else only to reappear at a later date. In addition, many adolescents falsify their age to establish profiles on social media sites, such as Facebook. Congress established the Children's Online Privacy Protection Act (COPPA), which prohibited websites from obtaining information from minors under the age of 13 without parental consent (O'Keeffe & Clarke-Pearson, 2011). However, all too often adolescents skirt this age restriction by falsifying their age (O'Keeffe & Clarke-Pearson, 2011). The American Academy of Pediatrics has upheld the age restriction guideline as developmentally minors do not have the foresight to anticipate the consequences of particular online behaviors, such as contacting strangers, posting inappropriate messages or images, or cyberbullying.

In a desire to protect private information, some people engage in lurking. Lurking has been defined as "a strategic attempt by users [social media users] to maintain the privacy of their personal information while still connected in online communities [social media platforms] to passively participate in conversations" (Osatuyi, 2015, p. 324). While some evaluate lurkers negatively, arguing that they are not active contributors to the online communities that they visit, others suggest that lurking is not as passive an activity as it appears and that, indeed, "lurkers may be the hidden asset in online communities" (Edelmann, 2013, p. 647). To our knowledge, no research has examined the relationship between lurking and cyberbullying perpetration and victimization. While the desire of lurkers to protect their privacy may protect them from becoming targets of cyberbullying, the information that they acquire from observing others online could be used to perpetrate cyberbullying. According to Edelmann (2013, p. 645), "lurking is a popular activity among online users, made possible by technology that provides users access without having to be visible or publicly participate, and leaves no traces."

Legal issues surrounding cyberbullying

Since the mass shooting of 13 high school students by classmates Eric Harris and Dylan Klebold at Columbine High School in Colorado in 1999, not only has there been a great increase in research attention devoted to the topic of bullying and cyberbullying, but the legal system has also devoted attention to the topic. Looking at the legal system within the United States, first, all 50 states plus the District of Columbia have in place laws geared toward bullying prevention (Hinduja & Patchin, 2014; Kowalski et al., 2012). With the exception of Montana, these laws require schools to have policies in place regarding bullying prevention. All but two of these states (Alaska and Wisconsin) include some type of legislation related to cyberbullying or electronic harassment. However, the wording is variable across states, and confusion exists surrounding the extent to which rights to freedom of speech and a reasonable expectation of privacy can be expected online (Kowalski et al., 2012). In some instances, the law states specifically that the bullying incident must occur on school grounds. For example,

Pennsylvania law defines bullying as "an intentional electronic, written, verbal, or physical act, or series of acts ... which occurs in a school setting." The law defines school setting as "in the school, on school grounds, in school vehicles, at a designated bus stop or at any activity sponsored, supervised, or sanctioned by the school" (24 P.S. § 13–1303. 1-A, 2010; Kowalski et al., 2012, p. 197).

Other state laws include bullying acts that occur off of school grounds, as long as they involve the use of school equipment. Georgia law, for example, defines bullying as

> an act which occurs on school property, on school vehicles, at designated bus stops, or at school related functions or activities, or by the use of data or software that is accessed through a computer, computer system, computer network, or other electronic technology of a local school system.
> (O.C.G.A. § 20–2-751.4, 2010; Kowalski et al., 2012, p. 197)

Still other states are even more explicit about policies related to off-campus bullying. Arkansas law, for example, states that cyberbullying

> applies to an electronic act whether or not the electronic act originated on school property or with school equipment, if the electronic act is directed specifically at students or school personnel and maliciously intended for the purpose of disrupting school, and has a high likelihood of succeeding in that purpose.
> (A.C.A. Tit. 6, Subtit. 2, Ch. 18, Subch.5 Note (2010))

Similarly, with Assembly Bill No. 256, California modified its existing law to state that

> electronic act means the creation and transmission originated in or off the school site.... Causing a reasonable pupil to experience substantial interference with his or her ability to participate in or benefit from the services, activities, or privileges provided by a school.

Currently, modification of this bill is being considered to change "creation and transmission" to "creation or transmission" (Assembly Bill 881, 2015).

As these laws suggest, schools are clearly a major player in legislative issues related to cyberbullying. More specifically, three issues arise for schools related to discipline in cyberbullying situations: (a) when may school personnel be held liable (under federal and state laws) for failing to address cyberbullying; (b) under what circumstances can school personnel address cyberbullying without fear of violating students' First Amendment rights to freedom of speech and expression; and (c) under what circumstances can school personnel monitor or search student Internet records without fear of violating students' constitutional protections against searches and seizures (Kowalski et al., 2012)?

School personnel may be held liable for failing to intervene in bullying situations if those personnel are found to have acted negligently or if they violate federal or state laws (e.g., laws related to racial, gender, or disability harassment). Laws regarding whether school personnel can be found negligent in protecting students from cyberbullying are muddy. Clearly, school personnel have a legal duty to protect students. This duty is clearly outlined in the Children's Internet Protection Act (CIPA, 2007), a federal law that, among other things, requires schools to adopt a policy "addressing the safety and security of students when using e-mail, chat rooms, and other forms of direct electronic communications" (Kowalski et al., 2012, p. 205). School personnel should also be able to foresee the misuse of cyber technology to cause harm, given the proliferation of information about cyberbullying available to both the lay public and school teachers and administrators. What remains vague, however, is the standard of reasonable care that school personnel can be expected to provide, defined by most as "what a reasonably prudent person would do in a similar circumstance" (Willard, 2006, p. 70). Among the things that a reasonably prudent school teacher, staff, or administrator might do would be to develop clear rules prohibiting the use of district technology to perpetrate bullying, education of all students and school personnel about cyberbullying, and the provision of appropriate means for students to report incidents of cyberbullying.

This becomes particularly relevant when the behavior has been directed against a member of a protected class. In the landmark *Davis v. Monroe County Board of Education* case in 1999,

> the U.S. Supreme Court ruled that, under Title IX, schools and school districts (but not individual school personnel) may be liable for student-on-student sexual harassment when it can be shown that the school or district acted with "deliberate indifference" toward harassment that was "so severe, pervasive, and objectively offensive" (p. 650) that it denies victims equal access to education.
>
> (Kowalski et al., 2012, p. 200)

More specifically, the Supreme Court established four conditions by which a school could be held liable: (a) the behavior must be based on the target's membership in a protected category; (b) the behavior must be severe; (c) the school must be aware of the harassment; and (d) the school must be indifferent to the harassment (Cornell & Limber, 2015). Although cyberbullying was not specifically mentioned in the ruling, the standards in the *Davis v. Monroe County Board of Education* case would certainly be applied. In addition, these standards have been reinforced in a series of Dear Colleague letters issued by the U.S. Department of Education Office for Civil Rights to school officials. The most recent "Dear Colleague" letter stated

> If a school's investigation reveals that bullying based on disability created a hostile environment – i.e., the conduct was sufficiently serious to interfere

with or limit a student's ability to participate in or benefit from the services, activities, or opportunities offered by a school – the school must take prompt and effective steps reasonably calculated to end the bullying, eliminate the hostile environment, prevent it from recurring, and, as appropriate, remedy its effects. Therefore, OCR would find a disability-based harassment violation under Section 504 and Title II when: (1) a student is bullied based on a disability; (2) the bullying is sufficiently serious to create a hostile environment; (3) school officials know or should know about the bullying; and (4) the school does not respond appropriately.

(U.S. Department of Education, Office for Civil Rights, 2014)

Of course, these standards would only apply to individuals in protected classes, leaving open those individuals who do not fall into a protected class (Cornell & Limber, 2015). Although most incidents of cyberbullying do not rise to the level of requiring legal action (Hinduja & Patchin, 2015), the lack of federal legislation specifically devoted to cyberbullying and that entitles all individuals to the right to an education free from bullying is noteworthy.

Determining when school personnel can limit students' speech must be examined in terms of on-campus speech and off-campus speech. School personnel can limit students' on-campus speech if it constitutes a threat, if it is lewd, vulgar, or profane, if it is (or appears to be) sponsored by the school, or if it otherwise materially disrupts the school or invades the rights of others. A landmark case that weighs on schools' decisions to intervene in situations involving student speech was decided in 1969: *Tinker v. Des Moines Independent School District*. The case involved several high school students who wore black armbands to school to protest the Vietnam War. The court ruled that, although students retain the right to free speech while at school, schools represent a special setting in which school officials could prohibit student speech if that speech "would substantially interfere with the work of the school or impinge upon the rights of other students" (*Tinker v. Des Moines Independent School District*, p. 506). However, in this situation, the court reserved the right of the students to protest because the protest was not ruled to have created a substantial disruption in the school day. Importantly, the incident in the *Tinker* case involved behavior that occurred on school grounds.

A case in which the U.S. Supreme Court ruled on behalf of the school and stated that schools have a duty to teach "students the boundaries of socially appropriate behavior" was the *Bethel School District v. Fraser* (1986). Matthew Fraser used a series of sexually explicit comments during his school assembly speech endorsing a classmate running for school office. Fraser was suspended for three days. His parents sued and the District Court of Washington stated that Fraser's right to free speech had been violated. On appeal by the school to the Supreme Court, however, the decision was reversed.

Even more problematic from a legal perspective is the extent to which schools have the right to prohibit student speech that occurs off of school grounds. In *J. S. v. Bethlehem Area School District* (2000), the court upheld the expulsion of students who had created a website containing negative comments about and direct threats toward some teachers and administrators at the school. The court ruled that, even though the behavior occurred off of school grounds, it still caused a substantial disruption in the school, including negative emotions experienced by the teacher against whom threats had been levied. In keeping with the *Tinker* case, school personnel may limit students' off-campus speech if the speech has caused or could cause a substantial disruption in school or if the speech interferes with the right of other students to feel secure.

Alternatively, a more recent case in Florida (*Evans v. Bayers*; Case No. 08-61952-Civ-Garber) reached a different outcome. Katherine Evans used her home computer to create a Facebook group deriding her English teacher. After being suspended for three days and being removed from her AP classes on the grounds of "'Bullying/Cyberbullying/Harassment towards a staff member' and "Disruptive behavior'," Katherine and her parents sued Principal Peter Bayer on the grounds that Katherine's rights to freedom of expression had been violated. U.S. Magistrate Garber upheld Katherine's argument stating that "It was an opinion of a student about a teacher, that was published off-campus, did not cause any disruption on-campus, and was not lewd, vulgar, threatening, or advocating illegal or dangerous behavior" (Case No. 08-61952-Civ-Garber).

Just as parents may monitor their child's online behavior, so, too, schools may wish to monitor the online activities of the students. However, the fourth amendment protects students against unreasonable searches and seizures. State and federal law state that school officials may search a student's electronic communications if there is reasonable suspicion of a violation of a law or policy, and the search is conducted in a manner that is not overly intrusive. In the case of *Klump v. Nazareth Area School District* (2006), a teacher confiscated a student's cell phone that was visible in class because it violated the school policy prohibiting the display or use of cell phones during class time. A school administrator then searched the student's text messages and phone directory. The student filed suit, claiming the search was unreasonable. The court ruled that the district had reasonable suspicion that the school policy regarding the display of cell phones had been violated, but that it did not have reasonable suspicion that a law or policy had been violated warranting the search of the phone.

As schools and legal authorities have struggled to address where cyberbullying fits within the legal system, sixteen states with bullying laws that specifically reference cyberbullying or electronic harassment criminalize cyberbullying. North Carolina, for example (§14–458.1), criminalizes cyberbullying as a misdemeanor offense. Several other states have cyberbullying criminal legislation in the proposal stage.

While the legislation covered in this chapter has focused on the American legal system, similar issues confront legislators in other countries. In the United Kingdom, for example, under the School Standards and Framework Act of 1998, all forms of bullying are to be prevented in schools. Importantly, while this would be taken to include cyberbullying, it does not expressly state that.

In general, the laws are having a difficult time keeping up with the technology. Many cases involving cyberbullying have to rely on existing laws that were created before the Internet and that, therefore, don't quite fit the crime (Levenson, 2011). For example, the Protection from Harassment Act in the United Kingdom has been used to prosecute individuals who send obscene or offensive communications via e-mail ("Anti cyberbullying," 2014). In addition, across countries, there is often a delicate balance between the right to freedom of expression and threats to safety and security. Finally, the laws in some countries, such as the United Kingdom, are designed to protect victims who are targeted by perpetrators within the United Kingdom. Questions remain regarding what type of legal action can be taken when the perpetrator originates outside the United Kingdom ("Anti cyberbullying," 2014).

Cyberbullying prevention and intervention

Given the seriousness of many of the potential negative outcomes for cyberbullying victims, prevention and intervention efforts are important for addressing these negative outcomes and also decreasing the likelihood of others engaging in cyberbullying in the future. Scholars in the traditional bullying and cyberbullying literature have noted the success of utilizing the socio-ecological framework when designing and implementing prevention and intervention efforts (Cross, Barnes et al., 2015; Espelage, 2014). The idea behind using this model is that bullying occurs in a larger social context, and so we need to involve stakeholders at the multiple levels of this social context, including students, peers, family, schools, and community (Kowalski et al., in press).

Whereas previous research indicates that the majority of bullying and cyberbullying intervention programs conducted between 2000 and 2013 did not lead to improvements in the long term (Cantone et al., 2015), several recent studies have reported on the success of prevention/intervention programs. For example, the ConRed Program focused on implementing a proactive action plan for dealing with the risks of using the Internet and social networks, improving skills for safe use of the Internet, providing a safe space and facilities for using the Internet, and encouraging participation from students, teachers, and families (Ortega-Ruiz et al., 2012). The ConRed program was implemented using a quasi-experimental design with 893 secondary school students in Spain, where roughly half of the group received the intervention and half did not. The authors found that the ConRed program was effective for reducing cyberbullying and increasing the perception of safety at school. Success for similar school-level programs was also found by Cross, Shaw et al. (2015) for the Cyber Friendly Schools Program in Australia and Wölfer et al. (2014) for the Media Heroes Program in Germany.

Other interventions have attempted to target both cyberbullying and traditional bullying at the same time, based on the notion that the two forms of bullying co-occur together. For example, a study by Gradinger et al. (2015) examined the effectiveness of the ViSC program among a sample of Austrian secondary students. This program was aimed at reducing aggressive behavior and bullying and improving social skills in school by training teachers how to recognize and deal with bullying and how to implement preventive measures. To evaluate the program's success, Gradinger et al. examined differences in rates of cyberbullying and cyber victimization across time between an intervention group and a control group. Results indicated that the program was successful for reducing both perpetration and victimization from cyberbullying. This suggests that teachers can play an important role in reducing this deleterious behavior.

Whereas training of teachers and students is important for the success of any cyberbullying intervention program, parents also play a pivotal role in the process. There is a wealth of resources available to parents to help them understand and take appropriate action to reduce cyberbullying and its effects. To that end, Walker (2012) provides a "toolbox" of prevention-related resources that can be utilized by parents and other stakeholders. These include books, and other printed material (such as quick reference guides for parents available online at www.cyberbullyhelp.com), family use agreements, filters and other technology-based safety features, DVDs and videos, and conversation starters.

The most effective prevention and intervention programs adopt a system-wide approach to attend to the person and situation factors alluded to earlier that precede instances of cyberbullying.

> Effective efforts to prevent and address bullying require attention to individual factors that may contribute to the likelihood of bullying, such as characteristics, assets and challenges of individual children and youth, as well as factors within the individual's social ecology, including the child's family, school, peer group, and community.
>
> (Limber et al., in press)

School climate factors (i.e., situational factors), such as promoting empathy and digital citizenship, are also critical (Kowalski & Morgan, in press). With more education and effective prevention and intervention efforts, not only will the prevalence rates of cyberbullying and other types of bullying likely decrease, but clarity may be added to some of the legal muddiness that currently engulfs many of these issues and situations.

Note

1 Willard (2007) uses the term "flaming" to refer to an online fight. While not everyone shares the opinion that flaming is actually cyberbullying due to the equal power status between the individuals involved, others suggest that it still be included in discussions of cyberbullying due to is repetitive and aggressive nature. Similar discussions have been had about "sexting" and the degree to which sexting reflects cyberbullying behavior. These discussions are typically resolved by examining the intent behind the behavior.

References

Alt, D. (2015). College students' academic motivation, media engagement and fear of missing out. *Computers in Human Behavior*, *49*, 111–119. doi: 10.1016/j.chb.2015.02.057

Álvarez-García, D., Pérez, J. N., González, A. D., & Pérez, C. R. (2015). Risk factors associated with cybervictimization in adolescence. *International Journal of Clinical and Health Psychology*, *15*(3), 226–235. doi: 10.1016/j.ijchp.2015.03.002

Anti cyberbullying laws in UK. (2014, October 19). Retrieved from http://nobullying.com/anti-cyber-bullying-legislative-matters-in-the-uk/

Bartlett, C., & Coyne, S. M. (2014). A meta-analysis of sex differences in cyber-bullying behavior: The moderating role of age. *Aggressive Behavior*, *40*(5), 474–488. doi: 10.1002/ab.21555

Bethel School District v. Fraser, 478 U.S. 675 (1986).

Brewer, G., & Kerslake, J. (2015). Cyberbullying, self-esteem, empathy and loneliness. *Computers in Human Behavior*, *48*, 255–260. doi: 10.1016/j.chb.2015.01.073

Bussey, K., Fitzpatrick, S., & Raman, A. (2015). The role of moral disengagement and self-efficacy in cyberbullying. *Journal of School Violence*, *14*(1), 30–46. doi: 10.1080/15388220.2014.954045

Cantone, E., Piras, A. P., Vellante, M., Preti, A., Daníelsdóttir, S., D'Aloja1, E., ... Bhugra, D. (2015). Interventions on bullying and cyberbullying in schools: A systematic review. *Clinical Practice & Epidemiology in Mental Health*, *11 (Supp. 1:M4)*, 58–76. Retrieved from http://benthamopen.com/contents/pdf/CPEMH/CPEMH-11-58.pdf

Children's Internet Protection Act, 20 U.S.C. § 9134(f). (2007).

Cornell, D., & Limber, S. P. (2015). Law and policy on the concept of bullying at school. *American Psychologist*, *70*(4), 333–343. doi: 10.1037/a0038558

Cross, D., Lester, L., & Barnes, A. (2015). A longitudinal study of the social and emotional predictors and consequences of cyber and traditional bullying victimisation. *International Journal of Public Health*, *60*(2), 207–217. doi: 10.1007/s00038-015-0655-1

Cross, D., Barnes, A., Papageorgiou, A., Hadwen, K., Hearn, L., & Lester, L. (2015). A social–ecological framework for understanding and reducing cyberbullying behaviours. *Aggression and Violent Behavior*, *23*, 109–117. doi: 10.1016/j.avb.2015.05.016

Cross, D., Shaw, T., Hadwen, K., Cardoso, P., Slee, P., Roberts, C., & ... Barnes, A. (2015). Longitudinal impact of the cyber friendly schools program on adolescents' cyberbullying behavior. *Aggressive Behavior*, I, 166–180. doi: 10.1002/ab.21609

Davis v. Monroe County Bd. of Educ., 526 U.S. 629 (1999).

Dempsey, A. G., Sulkowski, M. L., Nichols, R., & Storch, E. A. (2009). Differences between peer victimization in cyber and physical settings and associated psychosocial adjustment in early adolescence. *Psychology in the Schools*, *46*, 962–972. doi: 10.1002/pits.20437

Didden, R., Scholte, R. H. J., Korzilius, H., de Moor, J. M. H., Vermeulen, A., O'Reilly, M., ... Lancioni, G. E. (2009). Cyberbullying among students with intellectual and developmental disability in special education settings. *Developmental Neurorehabilitation*, *12*, 146–151. doi: 10.1080/17518420902971356

Edelmann, N. (2013). Reviewing the definitions of "lurkers" and some implications for online research. *Cyberpsychology, Behavior, and Social Networking*, *16*, 645–649. doi: 10.1089/cyber.2012.0362

Englander, E. (2012, November 12). Cyberbullying among 11,700 elementary school students. Paper presented at the annual meeting of the International Bullying Prevention Association, Kansas City, MO.

Espelage, D.L. (2014). Ecological theory: Preventing youth bullying, aggression, and victimization. *Theory into Practice*, *53*(4), 257–264. doi: 10.1080/00405841.2014.947216

Evans v. Bayer, No. 08–61952-CIV-GARBER (S.D. Fla. February 12, 2010).

Fredstrom, B. K., Adams, R. E., & Gilman, R. (2011). Electronic and school-based victimization: Unique contexts for adjustment difficulties during adolescence. *Journal of Youth & Adolescence, 40*(4), 405–415. doi: 10.1007/s10964-010-9569-7

Frisen, A., Berne, S., Schultze-Krumbholz, A., Scheithauer, H., Naruskov, K., Luik, P., Katzer, C., Erentaite, R., & Zukauskiene, R. (2013). Measurement issues: A systematic review of cyberbullying instruments. In P. K. Smith & G. Steffgen (eds), *Cyberbullying through the new media: Findings from an international network* (pp. 37–62). Hove: Psychology Press.

Gámez-Guadix, M., Orue, I., Smith, P. K., & Calvete, E. (2013). Longitudinal and reciprocal relations of cyberbullying with depression, substance use, and problematic Internet use among adolescents. *Journal of Adolescent Health, 53*(4), 446–452. doi: 10.1016/j.jadohealth.2013.03.030

Giumetti, G. W., & Kowalski, R. M. (2015). Cyberbullying matters: Examining the incremental impact of cyberbullying on outcomes over and above traditional bullying. In S. Yubero, E. Larranaga, & R. Navarro (eds), *Cyberbullying across the globe: Gender, family, and mental health*. New York: Springer. doi: 10.1007/978-3-319-25552-1_6

Gradinger, P., Yanagida, T., Strohmeier, D., & Spiel, C. (2015). Prevention of cyberbullying and cyber victimization: Evaluation of the ViSC Social Competence Program. *Journal of School Violence, 14*(1), 87–110. doi: 10.1080/15388220.2014.963231

Hinduja, S., & Patchin, J. W. (2008). Cyberbullying: An exploratory analysis of factors related to offending and victimization. *Deviant Behavior, 29*, 129–156. doi: 10.1080/01639620701457816

Hinduja, S., & Patchin, J. W. (2010). Bullying, cyberbullying, and suicide. *Archives of Suicide Research, 14*(3), 206–221. doi: 10.1080/13811118.2010.494133

Hinduja, S., & Patchin, J. W. (2014). *Bullying beyond the schoolyard*. Thousand Oaks, CA: Sage.

Hinduja, S., & Patchin, J. W. (2015). Cyberbullying legislation and case law: Implications for school policy and practice. Retrieved from http://cyberbullying.org/cyberbullying-legal-issues.pdf

Hoff, D. L., & Mitchell, S. N. (2009). Cyberbullying: Causes, effects, and remedies. *Journal of Educational Administration, 47*, 652–665. doi: 10.1108/09578230910981107

J.S. v. Bethlehem Area School District, 757 A.2d 412 (Pa. 2002).

Kessel Schneider, S., O'Donnell, L., Stueve, A., & Coulter, R. W. S. (2012). Cyberbullying, school bullying, and psychological distress: A regional census of high school students. *American Journal of Public Health, 102*(1), 171–177.

Klump v. Nazareth Area School District 425 F. Supp. 2d 622 (E.D. Pa. 2006).

Kowalski, R. M., & Limber, S. P. (2007). Electronic bullying among middle school students. *Journal of Adolescent Health, 41*(6, Suppl.), S22–S30. doi: 10.1016/j.jadohealth.2007.08.017

Kowalski, R. M., & Limber, S. P. (2013). Psychological, physical, and academic correlates of cyberbullying and traditional bullying. *Journal of Adolescent Health, 53*, S13–S20.

Kowalski, R. M., & Morgan, M. (in press). Cyberbullying in schools. In P. Sturmey (ed.), *The Wiley handbook of violence and aggression (Vol. 3)*. Hoboken, NJ: Wiley.

Kowalski, R. M., Giumetti, G. W., & Limber, S. P. (in press). Bullying and cyberbullying among rural youth. In J. P. Jameson & K. Michael (eds), *Handbook of rural school mental health*. New York: Springer.

Kowalski, R. M., Limber, S. E., & Agatston, P. W. (2012). *Cyberbullying: Bullying in the digital age* (2nd ed.). Malden, MA: Wiley-Blackwell.

Kowalski, R. M., Giumetti, G. W., Schroeder, A. N., & Lattanner, M. R. (2014). Bullying in the digital age: A critical review and meta-analysis of cyberbullying research among youth. *Psychological Bulletin, 140*(4), 1073–1137. doi: 10.1037/a0035618

Kowalski, R. M., Morgan, C., Drake-Lavelle, K., & Allison, B. (2016). Cyberbullying among college students with disabilities. *Computers in Human Behavior, 57*, 416–427. doi.org/10.1016/j.chb.2015.12.044.

Law, D. M., Shapka, J. D., Domene, J. F., & Gagné, M. H. (2012). Are cyberbullies really bullies? An investigation of reactive and proactive online aggression. *Computers in Human Behavior, 28*, 664–672. doi: 10.1016/j.chb.2011.11.013

Lenhart, A. (2010, May 6). Cyberbullying: What the research is telling us. Retrieved from www.pewinternet.org/Presentations/2010/May/Cyberbullying-2010.aspx

Lester, L., Cross, D., & Shaw, T. (2012). Problem behaviours, traditional bullying and cyberbullying among adolescents: Longitudinal analyses. *Emotional & Behavioural Difficulties, 17*(3–4), 435–447. doi: 10.1080/13632752.2012.704313

Levenson, L. (2011, May 24). What isn't known about suicides. Retrieved from www.nytimes.com/roomfordebate/2010/09/30/cyberbullying-and-a-students-suicide/what-isnt-know-about-suicides

Limber, S., Kowalski, R. M., Agatston, P., & Huynh, H. (in press). Bullying and children with disabilities. In B. Spodek & O. Saracho (eds), *Research on bullying in early childhood education*. New York: Information Age Publishing.

Machmutow, K., Perren, S., Sticca, F., & Alsaker, F. D. (2012). Peer victimisation and depressive symptoms: Can specific coping strategies buffer the negative impact of cybervictimisation? *Emotional & Behavioural Difficulties, 17*, 403–420. doi: 10.1080/13632752.2012.704310

Madden, M., Lenhart, A., Cortesi, S., Gasser, U., Duggan, M., Smith, A., & Beaton, M. (2013, May 21). Teens, social media, and privacy. Retrieved from www.pewinternet.org/2013/05/21/teens-social-media-and-privacy/

Menesini, E., Calussi, P., & Nocentini, A. (2012). Cyberbullying and traditional bullying: Unique, additive, and synergistic effects on psychological health symptoms. In Q. Li, D. Cross, & P. K. Smith (eds), *Cyberbullying in the global playground: Research on international perspectives* (pp. 245–262). Malden, MA: Blackwell.

Nakamura, L., & Chow-White, P. (2011). *Race after the Internet*. New York: Routledge.

Nansel, T., Overpeck, M., Pilla, R., Ruan, W., Simons-Morton, B., & Scheidt, P. (2001). Bullying behaviors among US youth: Prevalence and association with psychosocial adjustment. *Journal of the American Medical Association, 285*, 2094–2100. doi: 10.1001/jama.285.16.2094

Navarro, R., Yubero, S., Larrañaga, E., & Martínez, V. (2012). Children's cyberbullying victimization: Associations with social anxiety and social competence in a Spanish sample. *Child Indicators Research, 5*, 281–295. doi: 10.1007/s12187-011-9132-4

O'Brennan, L. M., Bradshaw, C. P., & Sawyer, A. L. (2009). Examining developmental differences in the social-emotional problems among frequent bullies, victims, and bully/victims. *Psychology in Schools, 46*, 100–115. doi: 10.1002/pits.20357

O'Keeffe, G. S., & Clarke-Pearson, K. (2011). The impact of social media on children, adolescents, and families. *Pediatrics, 127*(4), 800–804. doi: 10.1542/peds.2011-0054

Olweus, D. (1993). *Bullying at school: What we know and what we can do*. New York: Blackwell.

Olweus, D. (2012). Cyberbullying: An overrated phenomenon? *European Journal of Developmental Psychology*, *9*, 520–538.

Olweus, D. (2013). School bullying: Development and some important challenges. *Annual Review of Clinical Psychology*, *9*, 1–14. doi: 10.1146/annurev-clinpsy-050212-185516

Ortega-Ruiz, R., Del Rey, R., & Casas, J. A. (2012). Knowing, building and living together on internet and social networks: The ConRed Cyberbullying Prevention Program. *Journal of Conflict and Violence*, *6*, 302–312. Retrieved from http://ijcv.org/index.php/ijcv/article/view/250/pdf_67

Osatuyi, B. (2015). Is lurking an anxiety-masking strategy on social media sites? The effects of lurking and computer anxiety on explaining information privacy concern on social media platforms. *Computers in Human Behavior*, *49*, 324–332. doi: 10.1016/j.chb.2015.02.062

Pabian, S., & Vandebosch, H. (2016). An investigation of short-term longitudinal associations between social anxiety and victimization and perpetration of traditional bullying and cyberbullying. *Journal of Youth and Adolescence*, *45*, 328. doi: 10.1007/s10964-015-0259-3

Patchin, J., & Hinduja, S. (2010). Cyberbullying and self-esteem. *Journal of School Health*, *80*(12), 614–621. doi: 10.1111/j.1746-1561.2010.00548.x

Patchin, J. W., & Hinduja, S. (2012). *Preventing and responding to cyberbullying: Expert perspectives.* Thousand Oaks, CA: Routledge.

Perren, S., & Gutzwiller-Helfenfinger, E. (2012). Cyberbullying and traditional bullying in adolescence: Differential roles of moral disengagement, moral emotions, and moral values. *European Journal of Developmental Psychology*, *9*, 195–209. doi: 10.1080/17405629.2011.643168

Perren, S., Dooley, J., Shaw, T., & Cross, D. (2010). Bullying in school and cyberspace: Associations with depressive symptoms in Swiss and Australian adolescents. *Child and Adolescent Psychiatry and Mental Health*, *4*, 28. doi: 10.1186/1753-2000-4-28

Prensky, M. (2001). Digital natives, digital immigrants, Part 1. *On the Horizon*, *9*, 1–6.

Przybylski, A. K., Murayama, K., DeHaan, C. R., & Gladwell, V. (2013). Motivational, emotional, and behavioral correlates of fear of missing out. *Computers in Human Behavior*, *29*(4), 1841–1848. doi: 10.1016/j.chb.2013.02.014

Rose, C. A., & Tynes, B. M. (2015). Longitudinal associations between cybervictimization and mental health among U.S. adolescents. *Journal of Adolescent Health*, *57*(3), 305–312. doi: 10.1016/j.jadohealth.2015.05.002

Sakellariou, T., Carroll, A., & Houghton, S. (2012). Rates of cyber victimization and bullying among male Australian primary and high school students. *School Psychology International*, *33*, 533–549. doi: 10.1177/0143034311430374

School Standards and Framework Act (1998). Retrieved from www.legislation.gov.uk/ukpga/1998/31/pdfs/ukpga_19980031_en.pdf

Schultze-Krumbholz, A., Jäkel, A., Schultze, M., & Scheithauer, H. (2012). Emotional and behavioural problems in the context of cyberbullying: A longitudinal study among German adolescents. *Emotional & Behavioural Difficulties*, *17*(3–4), 329–345. doi: 10.1080/13632752.2012.704317

Simon, P. & Olson, R. (2014). *Building capacity to reduce bullying*. Washington, DC: Institute of Medicine, and National Research Council. Retrieved from www.iom.edu/Reports/2014/Building-Capacity-to-Reduce-Bullying.aspx

Slonje, R., & Smith P. K. (2008). Cyberbullying: Another main type of bullying? *Scandinavian Journal of Psychology*, *49*, 147–154. doi: 10.1111/j.1467-9450.2007.00611.x

Smith, P. K. (2015). The nature of cyberbullying and what we can do about it. *Journal of Research in Special Education Needs*, *15*, 176–184.

Smith, P. K., Mahdavi, J., Carvalho, M., Fisher, S., Russell, S., & Tippett, N. (2008). Cyberbullying: Its nature and impact in secondary school pupils. *Journal of Child Psychology and Psychiatry*, *49*(4), 376–385. doi: 10.1111/j.1469-7610.2007.01846.x

Sourander, A., Klomek, A. B., Ikonen, M., Lindroos, J., Luntamo, T., Koskelainen, M., Ristkari, T., & Henenius, H. (2010). Psychosocial risk factors associated with cyberbullying among adolescents. *Archives of General Psychiatry*, *67*, 720–728. doi: 10.1001/archgenpsychiatry.2010.79

Suler, J. (2004). The online disinhibition effect. *Cyberpsychology & Behavior, 7*, 321–326.

Tabachnick, B. G., & Fidell, L. S. (2013). *Using multivariate statistics* (6th edition). Boston, MA: Pearson.

Tinker v. Des Moines Independent Community School District, 383 U.S. 503 (1969).

Tokunaga, R. S. (2010). Following you home from school: A critical review and synthesis of research on cyber bullying victimization. *Computers in Human Behavior, 26*, 277–287. doi: 10.1016/j.chb.2009.11.014

Tonidandel, S., & LeBreton, J. M. (2011). Relative importance analysis: A useful supplement to regression analysis. *Journal of Business and Psychology*, *26*(1), 1–9. doi: 10.1007/s10869-010-9204-3

Turner, H.A., Finkelhor, D., Hamby, S. L., Shattuck, A. & Ormrod, R. K. (2011). Specifying the type and location of peer victimization in a national sample of children and youth. *Journal of Youth & Adolescence, 40*, 1052–1067.

U.S. Department of Education, Office for Civil Rights. (2014). Dear colleague letter: Responding To bullying of students with disabilities. Retrieved from www2.ed.gov/about/offices/list/ocr/letters/colleague-bullying-201410.pdf

Vazsonyi, A. T., Machackova, H., Sevcikova, A., Smahel, D., & Cerna, A. (2012). Cyberbullying in context: Direct and indirect effects by low self-control across 25 European countries. *European Journal of Developmental Psychology*, *9*(2), 210–227. doi: 10.1080/17405629.2011.644919

Walker, J. (2012). A 'toolbox' of cyberbullying prevention initiatives and activities. In J. W. Patchin, & S. Hinduja (eds), *Cyberbullying prevention and response: Expert perspectives* (pp. 128–148). New York, NY: Routledge/Taylor & Francis Group.

Walrave, M., & Heirman, W. (2011). Cyberbullying: Predicting victimisation and perpetration. *Children & Society*, *25*, 59–72. doi: 10.1111/j.1099-0860.2009.00260.x

Wang, J., Iannotti, R. J., & Nansel, T. R. (2009). School bullying among adolescents in the United States: Physical, verbal, relational, and cyber. *Journal of Adolescent Health*, *45*, 368–375. doi: 10.1016/j.jadohealth.2009.03.021

Willard, N. E. (2006). *Cyberbullying and cyberthreats: Responding to the challenge of online social aggression, threats, and distress*. Champaign, IL, US: Research Press.

Willard, N. E. (2007). *An educator's guide to cyberbullying*. Center for Safe and Responsible Internet Use. Retrieved from www.cyberbullying.org/docs/cpct.educators.pdf

Williams, K. R., & Guerra, N. G. (2007). Prevalence and predictors of internet bullying. *Journal of Adolescent Health, 41*, 14–21. doi: 10.1016/j.jadohealth.2007.08.018

Wölfer, R., Schultze-Krumbholz, A., Zagorscak, P., Jäkel, A., Göbel, K., & Scheithauer, H. (2014). Prevention 2.0: Targeting cyberbullying @ school. *Prevention Science*, *15*(6), 879–887. doi: 10.1007/s11121-013-0438-y

Ybarra, M. L., Diener-West, M., & Leaf, P. J. (2007). Examining the overlap in internet harassment and school bullying: implications for school intervention. *Journal of Adolescent Health, 41*, 42–50. doi: 10.1016/j.jadohealth.2007.09.004

10 Internet suicide and communities of affirmation*

Ronald Niezen

Internet identity

The permissiveness of the Internet is one of its more widely noted distinctive features, with unfiltered, unedited, loosely controlled communications revealing both the promise and perils of anonymous human conduct. This communicative license is clearest in forums, discussion boards in online communities, and social media platforms like Facebook and Twitter constructed around ideas and practices that may not be accepted in wider society. Here we can readily find obsessions that coalesce into group identities, supported by the unique capacity of the Web to create multiuser spaces that invite and facilitate the formation of close-knit communities (Manovich, 2001, p. 258). One feature evident in some of these communities is what could be seen as a rejection of professional intervention aimed at, for example, drug addiction, anorexia, self-harm, and obsession with suicide. While these habits and states might be seen as problematic by outsiders, participants often regard them as a definitive core quality, as something essential to their identity. For some Internet users, their online community can readily become a vehicle by which they reject unwanted judgment and intervention in their lives, all the while making use of the Web's powerful capacity for posting enabling information.

These qualities of Internet communication have made suicide forums in particular a focus of both professional and popular concern. A thematic focal point of suicide in instant interactive mass communication was already available to the computer savvy a few years before the advent of the Internet. Starting in 1990, the pre-Internet Usenet platform hosted the first non-moderated suicide news-group, alt.suicide.holiday (a.s.h.).[1] Beginning as a threaded discussion of the possible connections between suicide and holiday seasons, the group soon moved on to the expression of a wide range of opinions, from "pro-life" to (more commonly) "pro-choice," the construction of a "methods file," and the formation of a community of regular participants who identified themselves as "ashers," following the a.s.h. acronym. Several suicides committed by regular alt.suicide. holiday participants provoked media attention and controversy, including that of a 20-year-old Norwegian man who in February 2000 used the news-group to find a suicide partner, a 17-year-old Austrian girl, to jump with him from Norway's

1,900 foot Pulpit Rock. Then in 2003 there was the self-inflicted death of 19-year-old Suzie Gonzales, who, carefully following information made available through the news-group, posed as a jeweler to obtain a lethal dose of potassium cyanide and then self-administered a carefully measured dose of the poison in a Tallahassee hotel. She had also arranged for her death to be announced to police, family, and friends via a time-delayed e-mail message. The meticulousness of her suicide prompted media coverage critical of the newsgroup's methods file and "pro-choice" advocacy. An article in the San Francisco Chronicle (Scherees, 2003, p. 1), for example, expressed the view that Gonzales's newsgroup encouraged suicide in the context of "hopeless rants about life's miseries, advertisements for suicide partners, and requests for feedback on self-murder plans."

Since the advent of the Usenet community, the enormously expanded use of the Internet has made the subject of suicide more easily accessible than ever before, as any Internet search of any aspect of the topic will clearly demonstrate. At the time of writing, for example, a Google search using the keywords "suicide methods" produced 40,800,000 results; and online discussion groups are simply too numerous – and often too hidden – to even begin to quantify.[2] Suicide forums tend to be rigorous, rational, and instrumentally effective when it comes to exchanging information on the techniques of self-inflicted death, including nicotine poisoning, helium asphyxiation, carbon monoxide poisoning, the effects of (and underground sources for) phenobarbital, and mental coaching techniques for overcoming instinctive inhibitions against falling.[3]

Moreover, discussion groups that profess to be "open" often incline toward the negation of life and affirmation of the positive value of self-inflicted death. This immediately introduces a basic question concerning the potential consequences of online identity based on self-destruction for the actual manifestation of self-destructive behavior. The seemingly limitless potential of the Internet to carry more information to more people raises the spectre that some, possibly many, forums might encourage vulnerable individuals to act on inclinations toward self-destruction. As the prominent suicides associated with alt.suicide.holiday suggest, there could well be an aggravated "cohort effect" that occurs when depressed or otherwise desperate individuals, who may once have been socially isolated, find others in online communities that share suicide-oriented information and motivation. Does the Internet influence suicide through provocation and encouragement to act? Or is there a preventive effect that accompanies new venues for communication and belonging? Alternatively, might there be an "and/or" quality to this last question, in which consequences differ according to the life conditions and inclinations of individuals and perhaps entire societies?

This chapter examines the literature and online discourse to explore the possibility that the Internet facilitates a normalization of suicide, and if so whether and under what circumstances it might encourage or provoke, and/or discourage and hedge against acts of self-destruction. In addressing this question, I also consider in a more general way some of the new and emerging conditions for the formation of online communities and identities. These two objectives are closely related: one cannot properly understand the particular nature of Internet suicide without considering the wider context of online identity formation in which it is situated.

Routes of exposure and the cohort effect

If we accept the notion that ideas and images of suicide can be sources of inspiration for suicide-related behavior, then certainly the ready access to online information on effective strategies for self-inflicted death would be expected to have an influence on acts of suicide. We would expect that in an online community where the formation of group identity develops around the heroic value of suicide, particularly those in which a self-inflicted death is openly discussed as a "success," there would be a greater willingness to act on inclinations toward self-destruction, possibly – and paradoxically – in pursuit of group acceptance and inclusion. We know that some of the Internet sites where participants share information on methods and express acceptance of suicide as a moral good or even a civil right do at times encourage individuals or groups of individuals toward acts of suicide. It is less clear whether this marks the beginning of a trend that has yet to fully manifest itself. Can we find in online communities new and emerging ways by which ideas are connected to acts of suicide?

A growing number of researchers are arguing that the "routes of exposure," the channels by which ideas associated with suicide become normalized and more readily acted upon, should be seen as a significant part of suicidal behavior (Gould et al., 1989; Kral, 1994, 1998; Gould et al., 2003; Niederkrotenthaler et al. 2010; Niezen 2015). The main thrust of this line of inquiry is that the decision of individuals to commit suicide is "a culturally situated concept that becomes part of an individual's repertoire of choices" (Kral & Dyck, 1995, p. 201).

The fundamental link between communication of ideas and suicide calls into question the widely prevalent and durable Durkheimian emphasis on social integration and moral regulation as the only significant variables by which a society's suicide rates can be understood. For Durkheim in his 1897 book *Le Suicide*, the act of suicide was a litmus test for the problem of social cohesion; it revealed the regularities and laws through which societies are formed by indicating the consequences of extremes in cohesion and regulation, each predictably reflected, he argued, in high rates of suicide. Durkheim was famously dismissive of efforts to go beyond the social forces of cohesion and regulation in his approach to suicide; and his views remained unchallenged by any plausible alternative through most of the twentieth century (Joiner, 2005, pp. 33–35). His dismissiveness included resistance to the observation that communication was undeniably involved in the choice of method, and hence of lethality, which in turn would have clear consequences for rates of suicide. His solution to the problem of regularities in the method of suicide was simply to emphasize an "affinity" between the method chosen and the social cause, reverting to the overarching influence of basic conditions of social integration and regulation to explain both suicide rates and the "scenography," the mood and motive of the act of suicide (which he considered to be epiphenomenal); he was never tempted to do a thoroughgoing analysis of the connection between suicide rates and methods (Gane, 2005).

A communication-based approach to the study of suicide, by contrast, points to the reach of ideas shared with others as having an independent influence on individuals who are already predisposed toward suicide. It begins with acts and processes of communication and interactive or collaborative identity formation and moves on to consider how ideas and networks of interaction can influence patterns of suicide. The direct or indirect communication of values that make suicide noteworthy, acceptable, or even heroic, is every bit as important in understanding lethality as is the precipitating crisis, the background of depression, failure, burdensomeness, and isolation that may have contributed to an individual's decision to take his or her own life (Kral, 1994, p. 245).

The influence of ideas on lethality can be seen clearly in the phenomena associated with "imitation" or "emulation." An imitative effect in suicide became widely accepted by suicide researchers in the 1980s with a compelling body of correlations established between suicides publicized in media and increased frequencies of suicides in the regions covered by the publicity (e.g., Phillips, 1982; Schmidtke & Häfner, 1988). Though there continues to be debate and ongoing research surrounding the causes of these imitative suicides, the correlation itself was sufficiently consistent to have widely influenced journalistic standards in media coverage of suicides.

Concentrated episodes of self-destruction have also been found to occur within relatively closed communities such as school campuses, prisons, barracks, or aboriginal villages. These are forms of imitative suicide that in their very nature embody a contradiction that has been inherent in the sociological study of suicide from its beginnings in France in the late nineteenth century. A defining quality of these "clusters" is a paradox in which those who take their own lives are driven by a profound sense of social isolation and loneliness, yet act to end their suffering in ways closely resembling the suicidal acts of others, often in the same social milieu, demonstrating "a linkage between individuals, a true group or collective behavior beyond the society's norms" (Coleman, 1987, p. 3). I first encountered the influence of a cohort effect on self-destructive behavior in 1999 during my work as an ethnographer in the northern Canadian aboriginal community of Cross Lake (Niezen, 2009). The intense concentration of self-destructive behavior in this reservation village, it seemed to me, could not be understood without taking into consideration the powerful influence that an age group or cohort was having in normalizing the idea of suicide, and in providing examples of suicidal acts for others to witness – and even to follow. This made it possible to develop the connection between routes of exposure and the lethality of self-destruction by pointing to a situation in which suicidal individuals were finding a sense of belonging with other suicidal people, in some instances acting on their decision to die in communication – and in a broad sense even in community – with others.

This conclusion applies directly to efforts to understand the potential impacts of digital media on suicidal behavior. Shifting the focus from perturbation to communication in accounting for collective patterns of self-destruction, while raising the possibility of the formation of suicidal cohorts or communities, would give the new phenomena of Internet forums dedicated to suicide a privileged place as a possible cause of acts of self-destruction.

Some of the strongest evidence that this influence is in fact occurring can be found in studies of youth suicide in Japan. Before the late 1990s, Japan had a fairly high, but not extraordinary suicide rate (around 18 or 19 per 100,000) (Takahashi et al., 1998). The annual national frequency increased dramatically in 1998 (rising suddenly to 26.0) against a backdrop of economic recession and increased unemployment, and has remained around this level to the present (24.2 in 2005 and 24.6 in 2009). As a prelude to seeking an explanation for this increase in frequency, Naito (2007, p. 587) adds two cultural factors to the discussion: (a) the culturally iconic approach to suicide as an honourable way to respond to defeat; and (b) the reluctance of the Japanese to seek professional help for mental illness, often choosing instead to suffer in isolation. Her study also examines a trend in Japanese suicide that is genuinely unprecedented: youth suicide is sharply on the rise, as indicated by the statistics for 2003, in which, of the more than 30,000 victims, 613 were under 20 years of age, an increase of 111 over the previous year (Naito, 2007, p. 584). Youth suicide in Japan has also changed qualitatively. The most basic transformation is one from solitary suicide ideation and acts of suicide to the expression of negative feelings with like-minded people over the Internet, while occasionally finding companions with whom to die (Naito, 2007, p. 591). Ozawa-de Silva (2008, 2010) adds to the reason for concern over this recent trend with her convincing analysis of the distinctiveness of the connections between social suffering and suicide in Japan, including an element of cultural continuity in the decision to die through online suicide pacts: "The decision of the Group ... becomes something that [suicidal individuals] can follow – are indeed obligated, according to cultural prescriptions, to follow; social obligation is thereby reconciled to individual choice" (Ozawa-de Silva, 2008, p. 546).

At the same time, Naito (2007) argues that traditional suicide pacts are fundamentally different from what she terms "Net suicide" in that the pacts occur among groups of friends who know one another personally, whereas Net suicides occur among strangers who make arrangements online for ending their lives together at a predetermined location. In 2004, a year in which 32,325 suicides were recorded in Japan, some 60 people (the figure may be inexact because of forensic uncertainties) ended their lives through such online arrangements. While Naito is justified in pointing to the recent influence of online relationships on youth suicides as a "worrying trend," the low figures associated with Net suicide relative to the total number of suicides suggest that the news media – ever drawn to unusual and sensational deaths – have had an effect in exaggerating the significance of this phenomenon. It remains to be seen whether concerns about Net suicide as an emerging trend, including concerns about its possible spread from Japan and South Korea to other parts of the world, are warranted.

Meanwhile, the findings from Japan suggest a problem that is somewhat less grim: Given conditions of high Internet use and growing frequencies of youth suicide in Japan, why are the figures specifically for Net suicide so low? There is a syllogistic way to broaden this question: Given the literature that offers convincing evidence that communication of suicide can have lethal effects, and given the burgeoning amount of information and discourse on suicide available on the Net, why do we not find many more instances than we do of Internet communication having a demonstrable influence on acts of self-destruction? Why is the evidence not more compelling? A prevalent (though usually implicit) explanation for this observation, to which I now turn, is the affirmative, ameliorative qualities of online therapies which are seen by some researchers to act preventively against suicide – not just by addressing the despair of individuals but equally by acting against the dark influence of Internet-based suicide advocacy.

A Manichean dualism

There is a Manichean quality – a struggle of death against life, cultivated despair against rediscovered purpose, pathology versus well-being – in some general accounts of Internet suicide forums. Since no one is able to accurately measure the impact of the Internet on suicide rates (at least not beyond the indirect observation that frequencies have not significantly altered on a global scale in parallel with increasing Internet use) analyses usually resort to description of the various countervailing pressures that impel those who are at risk of suicide in one direction or another. Articles on the impact of the Internet on suicide typically contrast forums that provide information on methods of suicide and that advocate and celebrate acts of suicide with forums that provide support, counter-information, and online counseling using methods of intervention recognized by professional consensus. Several studies conducted among Japanese adolescents, for example, make a connection between suicide ideation and histories of searching the Internet for suicide-related topics. The authors then recommend as a preventive action the creation of anti-suicide websites, which would ideally lead adolescents considering suicide or self-injury to sources of help (Katsumata et al., 2008, p. 746), or developing "search engine optimization strategies" that would improve the mechanisms for blocking sites that provide descriptions of suicide methods (Sueki, 2013: 352). Some clinicians point out that in addition to its widely recognized negative effects, the Internet has potential uses in suicide intervention, including ready recognition of the at-risk individual and follow-up efforts to prevent suicide and support survivors, with chat rooms and email exchange taking the place of telephone outreach and/or help lines (Haas et al., 2008; Tam et al., 2007). The British-based charity organization The Samaritans, for example, receives about 50,000 emails from suicidal patients and their relatives each year (Alao et al., 2006, p. 490). Some therapists argue there are advantages to therapy via email communication, which would tend to attract those same computer users who are finding (and losing themselves in) less life-affirming identity attachments on the Internet. Alao et al. speculate that:

The use of written communication may be acceptable to individuals who have lack of trust, those who fear being labeled, and some patients with paranoid ideations or delusions. Computer mediated counseling may thus protect anonymity, decrease self-awareness [and] avoid stereotypes.

(2006, p. 490)

A common argument in the emerging Internet suicide literature thus posits that forums offering innovative online intervention programs are at least to some degree offsetting the effects of suicide advocacy forums. So there is indeed an increase in the ready communication of the idea of suicide with the advent of the Internet, but manifested in a contest of ideas, a battle of life affirmation versus life negation, which in general counterbalance one another in their actual consequences for acts of suicide.

This dualism is somewhat complicated by the finding that not all efforts to intervene through online therapy are equally effective. A study of 52 English language suicide prevention websites gathered through an Australian Google search, for example, found that feedback to website administrators on intervention techniques based on professional consensus did not generally lead to notable improvement in suicide intervention techniques (Jorm et al., 2010). The authors of this study speculate that there may be common structural failures of communication between technicians receiving feedback and administrators who are more qualified to revise website content. This could well be true, but it is equally likely that suicide sites are among the most recent venues for charlatanism, for marketing methods (or books about methods) that have no grounding in professional therapeutic research or practise.

Notwithstanding the limitations of current research, studies of Internet suicide justifiably emphasize the usefulness of support groups and other forms of online intervention. This can involve creating a counter-narrative to the online promotion of suicide through the construction of rival alternatives. If there are sites promoting the idea of suicide and even encouraging their participants toward acts of self-destruction, while remaining adamantly closed to counter-persuasion, then the best way to proceed therapeutically is to establish sites that offer counseling and support while promoting positive, life-affirming values.

It is easy to agree that overall there is significant value and equally significant unrealized potential in sites dedicated to online therapy. But the Manichean dualism in Internet suicide research that sets the influence of effective online therapy against suicide advocacy is based on an unrealistic understanding of the actual values, discourse, and consequences for behavior of a great many suicide-oriented sites. Besides the unevenness of the quality of online therapy, the dualism is further complicated by the possibility of a paradoxical ameliorative effect produced by the acceptance of suicide – even suicide advocacy – in the context of a supportive online community. There will always be those situations in online communities in which pressures toward conformity and singleness of purpose in suicide advocacy can influence vulnerable individuals toward taking their own lives. But this still leaves us with the common experience, evident in the narratives of current and former participants, of finding solace and renewed attachment to life through immersion in online communities dedicated to open discussion of self-inflicted death, including, paradoxically, the methods by which it might be acted on.

Many suicide forums are based, explicitly or implicitly, on a premise of acceptance of a quality of personality – dissatisfaction with life, alienation from others, and persistent thoughts and/or behavior toward self-inflicted death – that is rejected by those around them. Taking part in a preferred site or in a network of related forums, participants discover that they are not alone, but have a great deal in common with a community of online peers. In this affirmative quality many suicide forums share similarities with a wider range of sites based on a variety of socially rejected inclinations, obsessions, and life choices. I have chosen to refer to these forums as *communities of affirmation* to emphasize the potentially life-changing realization by marginalized individuals that their socially isolating obsessions are in fact shared with others, that through access to the Internet they have a way to belong, to be human in a distinct way in society with others.

Communities of affirmation

Among the proliferation of Web-based communities are those that attempt to normalize or promote life choices widely seen as pathological.[4] Extreme opinions can be formed by separating a group from the rest of society while sharply curtailing a group's access to information, leaving opinion to converge narrowly within enclaves of loyalty or shared delusion (Sunstein, 2009). In keeping with this observation, Internet identities are facilitated in part by effective enclosure and resistance to information seen to be at variance with core values. To begin with, the simple act of constructing a personal profile, while varying widely in procedure from one platform/forum to another, generally allows Web users to include what they accept and exclude what they reject, a process of selectivity that, according to Sunstein, encourages radicalization of opinion, "as like-minded people sort themselves into virtual communities that seem comfortable and comforting" (2006, p. 97).

The communities that form through the Web's encouragement of creativity and choice include those based on seemingly innocent descents into fantasy, like sites whose participants see themselves as vampires, while drawing distinctions between "blood-drinkers," "energy vampires," and "Vampyre lifestylers," all of whom are welcome to participate; or sites whose participants refer to themselves as "Otherkin," whose inner essence is considered to be other than human, something like a totem, whether it be an animal or (more commonly) something or someone with special powers like an elf or a dragon.[5] Such online imaginings in support of identity affirmations and role playing do not have to be quite so picturesque, but can include the simple indulgence in alternative ways of being human. Without his Internet community, for example, Stanley, a self-avowed "infantalist" featured by National Geographic, would not likely find others whose lifestyle choice centered on coming home from work and changing into "baby mode," passively having his every need attended to by a partner while dressing and behaving as an infant (National Geographic Features Adult Babies, n.d.).

Then there are those more disturbing sites based on various forms of self-harm and self-destruction such as self-mutilation (Adler & Adler, 2008), bulimia, anorexia (sometimes referred to as "pro-ana"), and morbid obesity facilitated by "feeders" (with pro-obesity sites blending seamlessly with fetishism and pornography). Here we see a close similarity to sites based on the positive value of suicide, except that on these sites the form of self-destruction chosen as the focal point of collective identity is not oriented toward the final, irrevocable end of life.

Other Internet communities are based on rare pathologies, including a form of body integrity identity disorder (or BDD), sometimes also called "amputee disorder," in which sufferers are obsessed with the amputation of a healthy limb (Braam et al., 2006; First, 2005; Ryan, 2009); as well as communities formed around other manifestations of BDD, or "body dysmorphic disorder," in which otherwise healthy individuals base their "authentic selves" on the desire to be paralyzed, blind, or deaf (Ryan, 2009). Perhaps the most disturbing of these communities is that which is dedicated to promoting the spread of HIV/AIDS, with the obsessed individuals who seek infection referred to as "bug chasers" (Gauthier & Forsyth, 1999; Loveless 2015). Participants in such forums are, as one dismayed bioethicist notes, defending their right to wear and live by their labels, producing a new force in the social production of madness and greatly complicating the task of therapy (Charland, 2004, p. 336).

The community of affirmation that seems to have gone the furthest toward consolidating its members' identities through online interaction is based on the self-diagnosis of Asperger's syndrome, a developmental disorder, which participants in "Aspie" sites situate on a continuum with the professionally recognized diagnosis of autism. This community manifests itself through several interconnected sites, including one, "Aspies for Freedom," that, as the title suggests, claims a legal identity, with the following "welcome" statement posted on the opening page:

> We know that autism is not a disease, and we oppose any attempts to "cure" someone of an autism spectrum condition, or any attempts to make them "normal" against their will. We are part of building the autism culture. We aim to strengthen autism rights, oppose all forms of discrimination against aspies and auties, and work to bring the community together both online and offline.
>
> (Welcome to AFF, n.d.)

The "Aspie" community has also established a dating service on a website titled "Aspie Affection," which makes the claim to its visitors that it provides "the best way to make friends and find a date who's like you," making possible an "exciting journey towards finding your Aspie soulmate" (Welcome to Aspie Affection, n.d.). These two sites alone make complete the construction of a collective identity based on legal claims of difference and a boundary of kinship through preferred marriage, two of the core ingredients common to many legally recognized "real-life" communities.

While not every community of affirmation goes as far as the "Aspies" in constructing a boundary of inclusion and exclusion, they do have in common the establishment of regimes for patrolling the content of their sites, primarily in an effort to protect their contributing members from abuse or "trolling" (about which more will be said immediately below) from unwelcome, uncommitted participants. This means that communities of affirmation provide a closed space for the exchange of ideas and formation of solidarity that is quite distinct from other forms of recognition and acceptance (or negation) that might be found elsewhere on the Net. Web browsers might encounter a range of reactions from an anonymous public if they were to reveal their self-defining obsessions in an open forum: from rejection, ridicule, and "cyber-bullying" to recognition, understanding, and support. But open forums differ in significant ways from carefully monitored bulletin boards, discussion groups, and chat rooms of sites that announce themselves as having minimum standards of acceptance of particular ideas and/or identities as a condition of participation. The prevalence of closed forums is being increasingly facilitated by technological improvements, such as Facebook's "fix" of a glitch in profile restrictions in 2007 in response to information made public by a technology blogger (Debatin et al., 2009). We can expect that with privacy in Facebook being technically supported and growing in usage, networks based on controversial criteria of belonging will become increasingly common.

While it would be reasonable to expect recognition, acceptance, and affirmation to be progressively more involved forms of engagement, reflecting an almost natural range of public opinion in an online interaction or community, there is usually in fact a divide constructed in sites hosted by communities of affirmation that separates the committed from those who would reject them – or worse, who would ridicule and goad them from the Internet's cover of anonymity. Trolling, a form of Internet behavior that involves posting inflammatory or off-topic messages in online communities with a view to provoking emotional responses, is relevant for our understanding of Net-based provocations of suicide. More broadly, trolling has had a formative influence on the dynamics of online discourse and on the forms, particularly the degrees of enclosure, of online communities. The widely known injunction "do not feed the trolls" is often taken further than the mere avoidance of any kind of response to provocation, through the cultivation of core communities of regular participants who shelter themselves from mockery with rules of participation enforced by administrators and (because exposure to trolling is almost inevitable) who protect themselves from its emotional effects with heightened collective expressions of support.

A review of the introductory pages of such sites makes it clear that the central objective behind their insistence on enclosure is to protect their core constituencies – those whose marginal identities correspond with the central criteria of inclusion and participation in the site. The sites make it clear that they will not permit negative comments, rejection, and bullying from the non-committed. The self-injury site, "SIFriends," for example, posts on its welcome page a mission statement that aptly expresses the combined goals of protection from hostile intruders and support for members:

> [Our mission is] [t]o Provide [sic] a worldwide online community to help people male and female, young and old whose lives are personally effected [sic] by SI (self injury/self harm). To offer a friendly place where people with a similar condition can get together and openly discuss the issues, struggles, joys and challenges that they meet and contend with daily in their lives. To give people who self harm a community where they will not be ashamed, afraid, judged, insulted or viewed as strange or different because of who they are and the behaviours they exhibit. To offer a forum where there is support, hope, compassion, empathy and comfort for those individuals around the world who intentionally injure themselves whether their condition has been professionally diagnosed or not. To provide an atmosphere that is clean and friendly for people of any gender, nationality, race and age group that lives [sic] a life of injuring themselves. This is SIFriends. Welcome.
>
> (SIFriends Mission Statement, n.d.)[6]

In efforts to prevent, to the extent possible, shame, fear, judgment, insults, and misperceptions and foster a climate of support, hope, compassion, and empathy, communities of affirmation usually establish their own rules of interaction, which prohibit the kind of negative discourse associated with trolling. But with protective enclosure established (to the extent that it is possible) in determining access to a community's discussion groups and chat rooms, there can then be a more literal closure to competing ideas (broadly or narrowly defined) by forum moderators. The ideological boundaries of the communities of the outcast are often vigorously defended in ways that go beyond anti-trolling defenses. Part of the effectiveness of the Internet in creating space for communities of affirmation derives from a certain imperviousness to unwelcome information. Website administrators are able to create their own ontological niche protected from – and at times actively defending itself against – competing opinions. For example, any effort to argue that suicide is and should be preventable, that the depressions resulting in suicidal thought and action are often temporary, or that the act of suicide is calamitous for surviving relatives – can be effectively off limits on prochoice sites. Suicide-affirming discourse is similarly resisted, with opposite argumentation, in sites dedicated to prevention. Dissenting ideas can lead participants to be "banned" from the forum and, when forum managers are in communication with one another, from networks of connected forums. (Of course, those who are banned from Web forums sometimes reappear with another address and online profile, but they are frequently re-exposed by their distinct styles of expression.) The new generation of Internet filters – the "filter bubble"

– that use algorithms to predict and personalize Web searches, further transform the way we encounter ideas and information in the direction of enclosure and confirmation in community with like-minded others (Pariser, 2011). This is an especially important mechanism for those who form communities around pathology or life choices that are widely disparaged.

The result is that the Internet operates in ways that are entirely consistent with the central paradox of globalizing modernity: untrammelled, global forms of expression encourage and facilitate the erection of boundaries and the enclosure of communities. This can be seen most clearly in the effort of some communities of affirmation to create a "culture" through identification of core beliefs and recruitment of adherents. This strategically oriented aspect of online community formation is illustrated in the statement of purpose posted by the vampire website, "Sanguinarius," in which its core members are called upon to "increase communication and understanding among and concerning blood-drinkers, psi/energy vampires, and Vampyre lifestylers; as well as to work toward unification into a cohesive culture" and, further, "[t]o develop outreach and a system of support for those estranged from the vampiric community" (Statement of Purpose, n.d.). The idea of a deep, permanent inner essence as the foundation and core criterion of inclusion in group identity is again expressed most explicitly by those who refer to themselves as Aspies, but who see the essence of who they are in autism:

> Being autistic is something that influences every single element of who a person is – from the interests we have, the ethical systems we use, the way we view the world, and the way we live our lives. As such, autism is a part of who we are. To "cure" someone of autism would be to take away the person they are, and replace them with someone else.
> (Welcome to AFF, n.d.)

Through these various means – establishing rules of etiquette, enforcing these rules by patrolling their site's content and denying access to violators, and emphasizing the permanent and essential qualities of their core identity – communities of affirmation create a sharp break between criticism/rejection and acceptance/recognition from those who participate in bulletin boards and chat rooms. The plethora and relative anonymity of websites means that rival opinion has little effect on the values, ideas, and information preferred by administrators. A century ago, when three or four newspapers appeared visibly and tangibly on street corners as the sole legitimate sources of information and opinion, comparison was explicit and exchange between them expected. Web administrators, by contrast, are able to dismiss calls for answerability without risking their credibility (while possibly even adding to it).

The extreme ideologies of many Internet sites begin quite simply with the technology's remarkable capacity for small-scale censorship, which in turn enables enclosure into communities that validate the ideas and identities of those who would otherwise be forced into privacy or social exclusion. These communities protect their members from the Kantian injunction that freedom of speech carries with it a corresponding obligation to listen to those who might disagree. Communities of affirmation have at their disposal a technology of communication that allows them to avoid answerability for their opinions, identity choices, and life commitments (see Bell, 2007). Such sites make themselves havens of affirmation by articulating a core ideology, often based on the positive "rebellious" aspects of marginality and delusion, and then setting about to excoriate anything that might pose a threat to its integrity.

Persistence, provocation, and links to behavior

The most important distinctions we can draw between various kinds of online communities should begin with the extent to which they cultivate durable commitments from their members and, following from this, the extent to which they provoke or pressure their members to act in conformity with common values. Situating suicide forums within this range of influence may give us some idea of the extent to which toxic forms of behaviour are actively encouraged online and what kind of community, with what forms of protective enclosure, makes such forms of conformity possible.

Even in the absence of comparative research on the durability of commitments to online groups, we can speculate that there is a spectrum in the degree of their permanence of membership. At one end of the spectrum there could be a temporary "new hat" quality to identity choices based on fantasy. Participants do profess enthusiasm for and commitment to their online community, but we can speculate that long-term membership would tend to be unstable as participants are able to come and go anonymously and without consequence. This likely would follow from several general qualities of Internet sociability: the tendency to cultivate friendships based on narrowly defined realms of experience that are open and expressive, while facilitating change of commitment without consequence. The way the effects of finding a community of affirmation are described by participants sometimes sounds like a "born again" religious experience; but there is no corresponding language of apostasy when people leave their groups.

But on the other end of the spectrum the pathologies that bring people together seem to provide a sense of community that would otherwise be absent from participants' lives, while the pathologies themselves would tend to remain. Where affirmation is based on an ineradicable infirmity or intractable obsession there will be less of a tendency toward "forum shopping." Online identities will tend to be stable (recall the "Aspies" and their dating site) even though individuals may surf widely and participate in multiple chat rooms.

Perhaps the most troubling aspect of the ready communication of ideas about suicide – which follows from the effective resistance to competing values, and the facility with which identity formation takes place around it – is the possibility that this enclosure and isolation based on self-destruction might well have an influence on the behavior of those who find a sense of belonging in these sites. This has significant implications for the work of those who emphasize the communication of ideas in the social dynamics of suicide, which could ultimately lead to acts of suicide. To what extent (and in what way) might acceptance of the label "suicidal" as a reference point for online identity lead to conformist behavior associated with it? Here the similarity between other communities of affirmation based on mental illness diagnoses and those based on suicide may differ. Active participation in pro-anorexia or pro-obesity sites, and many others based on medical terminology, presupposes that identities are firmly connected to the central diagnostic category, whereas suicide forums call for less biologically inscribed identity and appear more commonly to have porous boundaries, even while providing members with a sense of belonging and acceptance.

The exceptions to this situation of flux are important in that they point to two of the very different (and in the literature undifferentiated) possible ways that Internet discourse might further incline vulnerable individuals toward acts of suicide. Sites that do not create a defended corporate identity may not be protecting vulnerable individuals from provocation; and some of the most dangerous sites may therefore be those that do not have adequate protective barriers and support for participants. Under circumstances in which suicide forums are unmoderated and there is no barrier or compassionate response to trolling, anonymous provocations can deepen an individual's already acute sense of worthlessness and social isolation and convince them all the more to act on their felt need to die. Alt.suicide.holiday was such a non-moderated forum; and a side effect of its openness (which its members valued highly) was the manifestation of a high volume of trolling (which its members did not). It is, of course, not normally possible to determine what part, if any, the provocations of trolls might have had in the suicides that are traceable to particular forums, but common sense (not to mention professional therapeutic experience) would dictate that an incitement toward self-inflicted death through anonymous online discourse might incline the recipient/victim more than ever before toward feeling poignantly rejected and alone and willing to take his or her own life. Considering suicide forums as potential spaces for communities of affirmation raises another possible source for lethal communication: those forums in which enclosure is taken as far as possible in the direction of conformity built around the positive value of death. In extreme (highly publicized) cases this can create space for those who, driven by "the thrill of the chase," try to provoke vulnerable individuals to end their lives. In May 2011, for example, William Melchert-Dinkel of Minnesota was sentenced to 360 days in prison for his part in the suicides of an English man and a Canadian woman. The evidence presented by the prosecution revealed that he had communicated with up to 20 people in suicide chat rooms, in which he occasionally posed as a female nurse (he had a nursing background) and in other instances entered into suicide pacts, which he never intended to fulfill (Pilkington, 2011). Such criminality can only find a foothold in communities that are already inclined toward the formation of cohorts through closed, carefully patrolled discussion forums. The provocation to act can become acute in communities that enclose themselves within a narrow range of consensually accepted ideas, including discussion of former members' suicides as markers of personal achievement. It is true, and a true source of concern, that the Internet has a unique potential to facilitate this kind of cohort effect.

Such provocations to act, however, appear to be uncommon and certainly do not complete the inventory of those suicide-oriented websites – or their effects on participants – that reject professional intervention. Contrary to the oft-assumed direct correspondence between suicide advocacy forums and the increased occurrence of suicide, such forums can act paradoxically as hedges against self- destructive behavior. Statements given by participants indicate that those who are seeking an end to personal suffering, often resulting from or manifested in social isolation, find community with others experiencing similar feelings, seeking a similar solution in the end of life. Much the same preventive phenomenon can occur in social media sites like Facebook, in which constructive support and empathy can be mobilized in response to an expression of crisis, such as posting a suicide note (Ruder et al., 2011). Part of the appeal of Internet forums derives from the euphoria of unexpectedly finding a network-based community that understands and even approves of ideas and feelings that are marginal and socially rejected, and which would almost never be affirmed in one's face-to-face relationships and interactions. The testimony of a former administrator of a suicide advocacy site provides an example:

> [By exploring the Web I was able] to finally find a way through life, to get help, to find friends that I wouldn't otherwise have. I got to know people then who seemed to understand me. All of a sudden I felt as though I belonged to something and that I was approved of. Yeah, and then I thought, wait, this is helping me. And I went through a kind of euphoric phase, where I thought that this forum was really doing me good.
>
> (Prass, 2002, p. 50)[7]

Even though this particular testimony comes from an individual who had survived the Internet-mediated efforts of a pharmacist (later criminally convicted) to supply her with phenobarbital and convince her to kill herself, this kind of experience is not necessarily (or usually) to be found in the context of dangerous provocations to act. It can occur through forums that are more inclusive in their discussions, even in those that are accepting of suicide as a legitimate act.

A sense of belonging in an online community, however shallow and contingent it might be, finds expression in shared ideals and an ease with which self-revelation can take place and feelings can be expressed. This is supported by Adler and Adler's (2008, p. 34) finding in a study of self-injury websites, to the effect that a transition has recently taken place in which those who were once "'loners,' bereft of the subcultural support, knowledge, and interaction with others who live on the margins" are now more readily forming "cyber subcultures that transform face-to-face (FTF) loner deviants into cyber 'colleagues'" encountered through the anonymous intimacy of cyberspace.

This quality of communities of affirmation directly replicates a common experience of participants in group therapy: the realization by patients that they are not alone with their struggle, but are part of a group for the very reason that others are just like them (Bieling et al., 2006, p. 27). Yalom and Leszcz (2005) refer to this as "universality," meaning that patients often come to a profound realization early in their therapy that their social isolation and sense of uniqueness are unfounded, that others – potentially many others besides those in the group – share their feelings. While we might be led to question the appropriateness of the term universality for some of the bizarre obsessions revealed and facilitated online, their basic point is incontrovertible. In the early stages of group therapy, the disconfirmation of a sense of loneliness through validation from other clients can be a life-changing event: "After hearing other members disclose concerns similar to their own, clients report feeling more in touch with the world and describe the process as a 'welcome to the human race' experience" (Yalom & Leszcz, 2005, p. 6). This finding from group psychotherapy complicates the dualism that separates online therapy from pro-suicide sites. Those arguing for the benefits of sites based on professional intervention may be overlooking a paradox in which open, anonymous discussion of suicide in so-called pro-suicide sites may act as a hedge against acts of suicide. The mere recognition, and hence validation, of pain in an online community can in itself be a model of group therapy in which anonymity encourages openness and intimacy.

Conclusion

The Internet does indeed facilitate a normalization of suicide, but at the same time many of the communities that form on the Internet also promote a normalization and validation of the obsessions and loneliness that lead people in the direction of self-destruction. This means that the stark dichotomy between "open" and therapeutic sites is misleading; and there is room to reconsider the ideas of imitation, contagion, and the cohort effect with regard to the consequences of Web-based communities. Interaction that is honest and affect-laden occurs more readily online than in "real world" settings, with particularly heightened effects, positive or negative, for lonely, isolated individuals. At the same time, the Internet is a venue for sources of identity that are simultaneously life-changing and shallow, to which members escape more often through a wider search for meaning than through self-destruction for the approval of a community of strangers.

Exploring the broad category of communities of affirmation gives us insight into the unique potential for the Internet to support the creation of groups that explicitly offer acceptance, even celebration, of otherwise socially isolating pathologies. There are two aspects of these communities that complicate the dualism that separates suicide advocacy from therapy (even while I present them in the form of an alternative dualism). First, the sources of harm, the provocations toward self-inflicted death, may not be straightforwardly attributable to the ideas and information exchanged on "open" sites. Also to be considered are the full implications of provocations that come from outside, above all the effect of trolling in aggravating tendencies toward enclosure and restricted ranges of opinion, in some (often highly publicized) cases leading to the heightened social pressures behind suicide pacts and clusters.

At the same time, communities of affirmation, including those oriented toward suicide, replicate one of the common experiences of group therapy, in which patients discover early on that "there is no human deed or thought that lies fully outside the experience of other people" (Yalom & Leszcz, 2005, p. 6) and that as individuals they are not uniquely flawed or unusually overwhelmed by their experience. By including "open" suicide sites in the category of communities of affirmation it becomes easier to see their potential to act against suicidal behavior, even while unreservedly discussing the value of suicide and exchanging information on the means toward it. Finding community in a suicide forum can be ameliorative in the absence of therapeutic intent.

Notes

* An earlier version of this article appeared in *Transcultural Psychiatry* (50: 303–322, 2013) under the title, "Internet Suicide: Communities of Affirmation and the Lethality of Communication." The author wishes to thank the reviewers of this article and the editors of the current volume for their very helpful suggestions.

1 An archive of posts from the ash.holiday.suicide forum from the years 1993 to mid-2002 can be found at http://ashspace.org
2 A similar search by Tam et al. in their 2007 article "The Internet and Suicide" produced 1,740,000 hits, which by comparison with the current result of over 46 million, indicates that the amount of information on suicide methods on the Web has increased exponentially in recent years.
3 This observation comes from exploration of numerous suicide-oriented websites, including that of http://ashspace.org
4 The discussions that follow on communities of affirmation are not guided by the usual norms of research ethics because everything that is posted and readily accessible online is in the public domain and hence openly available to researchers – including discourse that, while anonymous, is manifestly not intended for a public audience. In the interest of protecting potentially vulnerable individuals, I will therefore only cite online material that is clearly intended for a mass readership.
5 The Otherkin Alliance website has been dismantled and re-established, currently to be found at www.gaiaonline.com/guilds-home/otherkin-alliance/g.242905/
6 The website www.sifriends.org/index.asp, where the "SIFriends Mission Statement" was once posted, is no longer online.
7 Endlich einen Web ins Leben zu finden, Hilfe zu bekommen, Freunde zu finden, die ich sonst nicht hatte. Ich hatte dann Leute kennengelernt, die mich anscheinend verstanden. Auf einmal fühlte ich mich so zugehörig zu irgendwas, wo's mir halt gut ging. Ja und dann dachte ich halt, das hilft mir. Und ich hatte so 'ne euphorische Phase, wo ich dachte, dass diese Foren mir so richtig gut tan (my translation).

References

Adler, P., & Adler, P. (2008). The cyber worlds of self-injurers: Deviant communities, relationships, and selves. *Symbolic Interaction*, *31*(1): 33–56.

Alao, A., Soderberg, M., Pohl, E., & Alao, A. (2006). Cybersuicide: Review of the role of the Internet on suicide. *CyberPsychology and Behavior*, *9*(4): 489–493.

Bell, V. (2007). Online information, extreme communities and Internet therapy: Is the Internet good for our mental health? *Journal of Mental Health*, *16*(4): 445–457.

Bieling, P., McCabe, R., & Antony, M. (2006). *Cognitive behavioral therapy in groups*. New York, NY: Guilford.

Braam, A., Visser, S., Cath, D., & Hoogendijk, W. J. G. (2006). Investigation of the syndrome of apotemnophilia and course of a cognitive-behavioural therapy. *Psychopathology*, *39*: 32–37.

Charland, L. (2004). A madness for identity: Psychiatric labels, consumer autonomy, and the perils of the Internet. *Philosophy, Psychiatry, and Psychology*, *11*(4): 335–349.

Coleman, L. (1987). *Suicide clusters*. Boston, MA: Faber and Faber.

Debatin, B., Lovejoy, J. Horn, A-K., & Hughes, B. (2009). Facebook and online privacy: Attitudes, behaviors, and unintended consequences. *Journal of Computer-Mediated Communication*, *15*(1): 83–108.

First, M. (2005). Desire for amputation of a limb: Paraphilia, psychosis, or a new type of identity disorder. *Psychological Medicine*, *35*: 919–928.

Gane, M. (2005). Durkheim's scenography of suicide. *Economy and Society*, *34*(2): 223–240.

Gauthier, D., & Forsyth, C. (1999). Bareback sex, bug chasers, and the gift of death. *Deviant Behavior*, *20*(1): 85–100.

Gould, M., Jamieson, P., & Romer, D. (2003). Media contagion and suicide among the young. *American Behavioral Scientist*, *46*(9): 1269–1284.

Gould, M., Wallenstein, S., & Davidson, L. (1989). Suicide clusters: A critical review. *Suicide and Life-Threatening Behavior*, *19*(1): 17–29.

Haas, A., Koestner, B., Rosenberg, J., Moore, D., Garlow, S., Sedway, J., ... Nemeroff, C. (2008). An interactive web-based method of outreach to college students at risk for suicide. *Journal of American College Health*, *57*(1): 15–22.

Joiner, T. (2005). *Why people die by suicide*. Cambridge, MA: Harvard University Press.

Jorm, A., Fischer, J.-A., & Oh, E. (2010). Effect of feedback on the quality of suicide prevention websites: Randomized controlled trial. *British Journal of Psychiatry*, *19*: 73–74.

Katsumata, Y., Matsumoto, T., Kitani, M., & Takeshima, T. (2008). Electronic media use and suicidal ideation in Japanese youth. *Psychiatry and Clinical Neurosciences*, *62*: 744–746.

Kral, M. (1994). Suicide as social logic. *Suicide and Life-Threatening Behavior*, *24*(3): 245–255.

Kral, M. (1998). Suicide and the internalization of culture: Three questions. *Transcultural Psychiatry*, *35*(2): 221–233.

Kral, M., & Dyck, R. (1995). Public option, private choice: Impact of culture on suicide. In B. Mishara (ed.), *The impact of suicide* (pp. 200–214). New York, NY: Springer.

Loveless, T. (2015). Bug chasers: Gay men and the intentional pursuit of HIV – A narrative analysis. AETC National Coordinating Resource Center. Retrieved from https://aidsetc.org/blog/bug-chasers-gay-men-and-intentional-pursuit-hiv- narrative-analysis (accessed 21 September 2016).

Manovich, L. (2001). *The language of new media*. Cambridge, MA: The MIT Press.

Naito, A. (2007). Internet suicide in Japan: Implications for child and adolescent mental health, *Clinical Child Psychology and Psychiatry*, *12*(4): 583–597.

National Geographic features adult babies. (n.d.). Retrieved from www.sfgate.com/cgi-bin/blogs/sfmoms/detail?entry_id1/488255

Niederkrotenthaler, T., Voracek, M., Herberth, A., Till, B., Strauss, M., Etzersdorfer, E., Eisenwort, B., & Sonneck, G. (2010). Role of media reports in completed and prevented suicide: Werther v. Papageno effects. *The British Journal of Psychiatry, 197*: 234–243.

Niezen, R. (2009). Suicide as a way of belonging: Causes and consequences of cluster suicides in aboriginal communities. In L. J. Kirmayer, & G. G. Valaskakis (eds), *Healing traditions: The mental health of Aboriginal peoples in Canada* (pp. 178–195). Vancouver, Canada: University of British Columbia Press.

Niezen, R. (2015). The Durkheim-Tarde debate and the social study of Aboriginal youth suicide. *Transcultural Psychiatry, 52*(1): 96–114.

Ozawa-de Silva, C. (2008). Too lonely to die alone: Internet suicide pacts and existential suffering in Japan. *Culture, Medicine, and Psychiatry, 32*(4): 516–551.

Ozawa-de Silva, C. (2010). Shared death: Self, sociality and Internet group suicide in Japan. *Transcultural Psychiatry, 47*(3): 392–418.

Pariser, E. (2011). *The filter bubble: How the new personalized web is changing what we read and how we think*. New York: Penguin.

Phillips, D. (1982). The impact of fictional television stories on U.S. adult fatalities: New evidence on the effect of the mass media on violence. *American Journal of Sociology, 87*(6): 1340–1359.

Pilkington, E. (2011, May 4). Former nurse jailed for aiding suicides over the Internet: William Melchert-Dinkel posed as woman in chat rooms and made fake suicide pacts. Guardian.co.uk. Retrieved from www.guardian.co.uk/uk/2011/may/04/william-melchert-dinkel-suicide-internet

Prass, S. (2002). *Suizid-Foren im World Wide Web: Eine neue Kultgefahr* [Suicide forums in the World Wide Web: A new danger of cults]. Jena, Germany: IKS Garamond.

Ruder, Thomas, Hatch, Gary, Ampanozi, Garyfalia, Thali, Michael, & Fischer, Nadja. (2011). Suicide Announcement on Facebook. *Crisis, 32*(5): 280–282.

Ryan, C. (2009). Out on a limb: The ethical management of body integrity identity disorder. *Neuroethics, 2*: 21–33.

Scherees, J. (2003, June 8). A virtual path to suicide: Depressed student kills herself with help of online discussion group. *San Francisco Chronicle*. Retrieved from www.sfgate.com/cgi-bin/article.cgi?f1/4/c/a/2003/06/08/MN114902.DTL

Schmidtke, A., & Häfner, H. (1988). The Werther effect after television films: New evidence for an old hypothesis. *Psychological Medicine, 18*(3): 665–676.

Statement of purpose. (n.d.). Retrieved from www.sanguinarius.org/purpose.shtml

Sueki, Hajime. (2013). The effect of suicide-related internet use on users' mental health: A longitudinal study. *Crisis, 34*(5): 348–353.

Sunstein, C. (2006). *Infotopia: How many minds produce knowledge*. Oxford: Oxford University Press.

Sunstein, C. (2009). *Going to extremes: How like minds unite and divide*. Oxford: Oxford University Press.

Takahashi, Y., Hirasawa, H., Koyama, K., Senzaki, A., & Senzaki, K. (1998). Suicide in Japan: Present state and future directions for prevention. *TransculturalPsychiatry, 35*(2): 271–289.

Tam, J., Tang, W., & Fernando, D. (2007). The Internet and suicide: A double-edged tool. *European Journal of Internal Medicine, 18*: 453–455.

Welcome to AFF. (n.d.). Retrieved from www.aspiesforfreedom.com

Welcome to Aspie Affection. (n.d.). Retrieved from www.aspieaffection.com

Yalom, I., & Leszcz, M. (2005). *The theory and practice of group psychotherapy* (5th edition). New York: Basic Books.

Part V
Conclusions

11 Beyond law

Protecting victims through engineering and design

Nicole A Vincent and Emma A. Jane

Children groomed by online predators, revenge porn victims extorted by unscrupulous internet entrepreneurs, Muslim community members targeted for racialised cyberhate.... Many of the contributors to this book have painted a grim picture of the various ways victims of cybercrimes are suffering, and the multiple ways law is failing to assist. Clearly something is not right here. However, while it is one thing to identify new problems, it is quite another to figure out what to do. Especially when the domains in which these problems are playing out are novel, complex, and extremely volatile.

It could be argued that those victimised online are currently being neglected because insufficient attention is being paid to their plight. Yet the existence of this book is testimony to the fact that – while victims of crime and other problems online may not be receiving as much recognition as they need and deserve – they are not entirely invisible. Continued awareness-raising is essential for bringing attention to the plight of victims in online spaces. This might help address the relative lack of knowledgeability on the part of front-line respondents such as police and prosecutors (Citron, 2014, pp. 83–91), as well as the sorts of victim-blaming outlined in Chapter 3. But sensitisation and education strategies alone will not constitute a remedy.

Others might make the case that it is legislators who are dropping the ball, and that what is urgently needed are new or revised laws. We are not so sure. Implicit in Chapter 1 is a provocative question. Namely: are the sorts of social problems outlined in this collection best understood as having come about as a result of *deficits in* law, or are they more to do with a surplus of *unrealistic expectations of* law? Our view is that both the first and second part of this question can be answered in the affirmative. That is, we agree that some new and improved legislation is required to better reflect the realities of the cybersphere (laws relating to horse-drawn carts only retaining utility for so long after a dirt track becomes a six-lane highway). But we also suspect there is overconfidence in exactly how much can be achieved by law – particularly when it comes to meeting the needs of victims.

Given that the focus of this collection is international, we will not here be offering specific suggestions about which laws in which nations are deficient or non-existent, and therefore require attention from policy makers. Neither will we be providing precise details about exactly how these laws should be written or revised. While we acknowledge that law reform is important, the staggeringly large number of jurisdictions and legislative contexts involved in cybercrime scenes means that meaningful research, critique, and recommendations must be situated at the local level (even if what are ultimately required are inter-jurisdictional responses). Attempting to sketch all the cybercrime-related legislative change that might be beneficial for all people in all nations of the world is beyond the scope not only of this single text, but, we would argue, of *any* single text. Instead, we urge our colleagues to prioritise research in this area, and to communicate with and lobby policy makers as a matter of urgency. By the same token, we urge policy makers to take these matters seriously and begin the processes necessary to determine what changes might be required in law – both in terms of regulating the conduct of individuals, as well as of service providers and platform managers.

While law might offer some benefits for some victims of some crimes in some jurisdictions, however, our overall argument is that these must be supplemented by a multitude of non-legislative responses in order to truly make a difference. In this final section of the book, therefore, we return to the two harsh, legislative realities detailed in Chapter 1. First, that criminal law – by its very nature – does not make a good ally for victims of any crimes. And, second, that the special features of online environments present yet another set of obstacles to the prosecution of those who have committed cybercrimes (these relating to jurisdictional issues, the identification of offenders, and the high standards of proof required to secure criminal convictions).

While we do acknowledge that the legislative odds are stacked against the victims of cybercrime, we also explain why this does not mean we should give up in despair. Specifically, we outline a non-legislative approach which shifts the focus away from the slow-moving mechanisms and blunt instrumentality of the criminal justice system, and towards a focus on – among other strategies – designing technology in a way that 'nudges' people towards better behaviour online.

In a nut shell, our proposal is that criminologists, social scientists, and ethicists work alongside engineers and technology experts in designing, deploying, testing, and engaging in the ongoing re-evaluation of information communication technologies so as to produce better 'moral technologies' – that is, devices, platforms, and systems that encourage ethical conduct and provide fewer opportunities for unethical behaviour. Such approaches are guided by work in political philosophy, philosophy of technology, and ethics of technology, and have a number of advantages. Unlike changes in criminal law, for instance, technological interventions can be devised and implemented swiftly. Technology-based approaches are also unconstrained by state borders which greatly inhibit legislative responses. As such, rather than being a runner-up or second-best to legislative responses, we argue that such approaches are *as* or even *more* important than legal responses for assisting the victims of cybercrime in a timely, sensitive, and effective manner. Further, they are approaches which are likely to be extremely useful for many other social problems stemming from technological innovation.

Cybercrimes or cyberwrongs?

To set the stage for this discussion, we revisit the broad concern that, technically-speaking, it is an open question whether the sorts of things we have in mind when we speak of 'cybercrimes' are indeed even *bona fide* crimes. We then argue that trying to get them recognised *as* crimes may be very difficult. Even if we recognise that serious things are at stake in cybercrimes, it could be (and indeed very often *is*) argued that these are things involving acts that are not as unequivocally serious as threats to life and limb. As such, progressives and conservatives are both likely to be disinclined to accept the curtailment of liberty that recognising these as criminal offences would necessarily entail. To further spell out this argument, we return to the case studies of sextortion and cyberhate, and make use of the discussion of John Stuart Mill's harm principle (1859, I.9) from Chapter 1.

As explained in the Introduction and Chapter 3, sextortion involves obtaining sexually explicit pictures of a victim, and then threatening to post them onto public fora unless the victim provides yet further sexually explicit material, thus exposing themselves to even greater potential to be sextorted by the offender in the future (Wittes et al. 2016). Currently, although offenders who commit sextortion can be charged with and prosecuted for such offences as computer hacking, wiretapping, stalking, paedophilia, and harassment, they cannot actually be charged and prosecuted specifically for sextortion-specific offences because (at least in the US) no such offence is currently defined within state or federal criminal statutes. Benjamin Wittes and colleagues thus observe that, as a consequence:

> There is no consistency in the prosecution of sextortion cases. Because no crime of sextortion exists, the cases proceed under a hodgepodge of state and federal laws. Some are prosecuted as child pornography cases. Some are prosecuted as hacking cases. Some are prosecuted as extortions. Some are prosecuted as stalkings. Conduct that seems remarkably similar to an outside observer produces actions under the most dimly-related of statutes.
>
> (2016, pp. 4–5)

This state of affairs is arguably bad for everyone involved. The public has no guidance about what conduct is prohibited, victims lack certainty about whether and what kind of protection and remedies they might seek and obtain, and people found guilty of essentially identical conduct receive punishments of widely divergent kinds and severities. From an economic perspective this ad hoc approach is also tremendously inefficient since, for each case, state prosecutors' and defence attorneys' time is taken up in debate that may have simply been avoided with better-formulated laws that function effectively as guides and deterrents. To remedy this problem, Wittes and colleagues thus recommend that:

Given that these cases are numerous, many are interstate in nature, and most being prosecuted federally anyway, Congress should consider adopting a federal sextortion statute that addresses the specific conduct at issue in sextortion cases and does not treat the age of the victim as a core element of the offense.... [T]his statute should combine elements of the federal interstate extortion statute with elements of the aggravated sexual abuse statute and have sentencing that parallels physical-world sexual assaults.... State lawmakers should likewise adopt strong statutes with criminal penalties commensurate with the harm sextortion cases do.... In our view, states should both criminalise the production and distribution of nonconsensual pornography and give victims of it reasonable civil remedies against their victimisers. In combination with a federal statute, this would create a number of avenues for victims to pursue.

(2016, pp. 26–27)

The case that Wittes and colleagues are making is that because sextortion is harmful, legislation should be enacted so that courts can recognise this cyber*wrong* as a cyber*crime*. Similar reasoning could presumably also be used to support a case in favour of criminalising other cyberwrongs, for instance like the gendered cyberhate discussed in Chapter 3. At present, women and girls worldwide are not uniformly protected from explicit, sexualised vitriol, rape threats, and revenge porn by the criminal justice system *qua* 'gendered cyberhate' because no crime of gendered cyberhate currently exists. Individual cases of rape threats have been successfully prosecuted, as have jilted lovers who posted sexually explicit photographs of their ex-partners on revenge porn web sites. However, the cases are prosecuted under the banner of existing criminal offences, not specifically under the banner of 'gendered cyberhate' offences. Thus, extending Wittes and colleagues' reasoning, it could be argued that because gendered cyberhate is also harmful, legislation should be enacted to enable courts to recognise *this* cyber*wrong* as a cyber*crime* too.

We share Wittes and colleagues' view that sextortion is harmful (as is cyberhate, cyberbullying, racialised abuse, and other examples discussed in this volume). As Chapter 1 argued, however, appeals to harmfulness as a basis for criminalising conduct are likely to strike unhelpful hurdles. After all, laws that protect people from cyberhate and/or other cyberharms wouldn't *just* make some people (i.e. potential victims) better off. They would *also* make other people (namely, those who would otherwise engage in that conduct) worse off. For instance, cyberhaters routinely insist they are actually cyber*commentators* who are harmlessly exercising their right to freedom of speech. If laws were created that removed their freedom to engage in this conduct, they – alongside staunch supporters of free speech as an ideal – would likely strongly object to the state taking steps that would deprive them of their current freedoms. For this reason, when the state contemplates creating legislation that prohibits certain conduct for the benefit of one group of people through the mechanism of the criminal law, it must also consider how much harm this course of action would inflict

Conclusion beyond law 213

onto another group of people whose liberty would be curtailed by such legislation.[1] But since the degree of harm in cyberhate is not as *unambiguously* great as, for instance, murder, attempts to gather broad public support for such legislation will likely get mired in lengthy, murky, and ultimately unproductive debate; for instance, over whether what is at stake for potential victims is truly harmful as opposed to merely offensive,[2] and, if harmful, over whether the degree of harm is sufficiently great to warrant inflicting the correlative harm of restricting potential cyberhaters' liberty.[3]

Regardless of whether *we* think cyberhate is harmful, and regardless of whether *we* think that the freedom to engage in cyberhating conduct is not a freedom that anyone should be entitled to exercise in the first place, the state (which creates laws that govern everyone) must adopt an impartial position and thus consider opposing views if such exist. Unfortunately, what this means in practice is that if others don't see things our way, and if they can present a sufficiently plausible case to warrant further inquiry, then the debate that is likely to ensue is bound to be long and unproductive. Abstracting away from the example of cyberhate, our point is that the *criminalisation* of cyberwrongs is not a promising strategy for cases which are likely to generate murky debate about whether the conduct in question is sufficiently harmful, whether victims can mitigate their harm just by choosing to not take offence,[4] and whether it is more harmful than curtailing the liberty of those whose conduct would be criminalised.

Furthermore, it is also important to keep in mind that law reform is a very slow and resource-demanding process because of the built-in legal inertia which favours the status quo over the new and reformative. It may be tempting to view this legal inertia as a fault with how the law functions. However, when considered against the backdrop of constant political pressures to accept change in this or that direction driven by populist appeal to views *du jour*, this inertia may actually be a source of comfort even to progressive folks, since it offers protection from potentially reactionary changes being made to society. Finally, given that internet phenomena are often fast-paced and short-lived, reform of the criminal justice system has little chance of keeping pace with technological changes. This includes keeping pace with responding to new ways in which online fora may create opportunities for cyber-victimisation, and thus taking adequate account of the interests of victims of cybercrime.

For such reasons, investing much effort into criminal justice system reform so that it can take better account of the harms suffered by victims is not an ideal plan, at least not if this is the only thing we plan to do.

Civil remedies

But if not (only) through criminal law reform, then how else could we respond to cyberwrongs, cyberharms, or cyberoffences (or whatever other terminology we adopt to recognise the plight of those who have been victimised – though not necessarily as the result of a criminal offence)? Wittes and colleagues also recommend providing 'victims … reasonable civil remedies against their victimizers' (2016, p. 27). As argued in Chapter 1, civil remedies do indeed give plaintiffs more explicit recognition, control, and pride of place than what the criminal law does. Furthermore, the threat of being sued is likely to have some general deterrence effects, as long as potential offenders know they may be sued and they are in a situation to think far enough ahead before they act, to stop themselves from doing what they would otherwise regret (see below for further discussion).

There are, however, problems with civil remedies, too. One is that civil litigation is costly (Willging and Lee, 2010), and this can create barriers to entry for plaintiffs who cannot afford up-front fees to finance litigation. This costliness is also likely to present a barrier to victims of relatively more minor cyberharms. For instance, in potential cases that would involve defendants who inflict many tiny cyberharms on many separate victims (Wall, 2007), no individual plaintiff would ever have sufficient financial incentive (in the form of a prospect of receiving compensation from a successful lawsuit) to warrant litigating.[5] Furthermore, for the civil law approach to work, we would still need to build up society's recognition of the way in which things like gendered cyberhate and sextortion genuinely harm their victims, and thus why they should be treated as potentially compensable harms. Admittedly, the barriers to recognition here, by comparison to those present in the context of the criminal law, are likely to be smaller. After all, recognising that these are genuine harms will not result in anyone being prohibited from engaging in the respective conduct, but only potentially open them up to being sued. However, the decision to protect people by offering them the remedy of pursuing a lawsuit, rather than by outright prohibition of the harmful behaviour, is problematic too because it converts objectionable behaviour into de facto permissible behaviour – permissible, that is, as long as whoever engages in it is prepared to compensate their victims. The prospect of converting objectionable behaviour into in-effect, retrospective judge-brokered financial transactions, where people can commit offences with impunity as long as they subsequently compensate their victims, is distasteful and wrong.

What is needed is for these offences to simply not happen in the first place, and, given the concerns we expressed above regarding the effectiveness and propriety of legal approaches (i.e. criminal sanctions and civil law remedies), it might be tempting to suppose that perhaps another way to change people's behaviour is through better education campaigns targeted at potential offenders. However, although we do not wish to discourage such efforts – just as we do not intend to discourage efforts to reform the law – our concern with this suggestion is that educating people about the consequences of their actions still has limited capacity to effect behavioural change. After all, people may simply remain unconvinced. But even when people are genuinely convinced, they still often fail to act in accordance with their own considered judgments (see below).

For this reason, in the next section we will consider two groups of theories from political philosophy and ethics of technology regarding how to effect behavioural change through smarter design of environments and technologies –

namely, so-called 'nudge' techniques and value sensitive design (VSD), both of which fall under the broader umbrella heading of 'moral technologies'. Instead of trying to change people's minds at the conscious level through reason-giving practices – for example, by creating threats of criminal sanction or of being sued, or by trying to convince anyone through explicit education (and then hoping that convincing them to *think* differently will lead them to *act* differently) – these moral technologies aim to alter people's behaviour and its outcomes by changing the environments in which people act. Specifically, they aim to change environments and artefacts in order to prompt better behaviour, to foster better outcomes, and to promote the values that we as a society wish to promote.

Enter nudge

To understand what nudge techniques are and why they might be useful, we shall begin by considering an example from the political domain (concerning retirement savings plans) developed by Richard Thaler and Cass Sunstein (2009), as discussed recently by Jeremy Waldron (2014). After the example is presented, we will then comment on the core ideas that nudge techniques employ, and indicate how we think these same ideas could also be deployed to foster better behaviour and better outcomes in interactions in online environments. We will finish by considering some objections to nudging.

Here is Thaler and Sunstein's (2009) example. Presumably, few people would savour the prospect of being poor in their old age, and, from this perspective, it makes sense to put a small portion of our income away into a retirement savings plan dedicated specifically to providing adequately for our financial needs in our old age. However, despite this, and despite the fact that governments go to considerable lengths to educate and entice the public to subscribe to better retirement plans, many people still fail to do this. Why? Evidently, not because they remain unconvinced that this is what would serve their own best interests, but for such mundane and all-too-human reasons as because they get distracted and fail to sign up for a savings plan, or because their resolve to do so weakens in the face of temptations (for example, purchasing airfares for a luxurious holiday), or because they lack the relevant knowledge and thus under-estimate their future needs or over-estimate the minor proximal costs of making slightly larger contributions to their retirement savings plans to finance the distal outcome of having an adequate income in their old age.

A consequence of this is that many people have woefully inadequate retirement savings plans. Not because they want things that way, but because the way things are currently arranged is such that, unless people explicitly choose to save up for their retirement, by default they will be saving nothing (or not enough). This outcome, in other words, is not a consequence of people's express choices – it is not what people genuinely want and what they explicitly choose – but it is rather just a consequence of the way that things are currently set up, so that *by default*, nothing (or not enough) is put away for retirement. However, things could be set up differently: by default, more money could automatically be set aside from people's incomes, and, if some people really do object to this, then there is nothing preventing us from giving them an option to alter their contributions (i.e. an option to opt-out from the default setup). At least setting things up this way would ensure that *by default* (i.e. even if nobody makes any decisions whatsoever) everyone would have sufficient income in their retirement. Furthermore, to ensure that people do not make weighty decisions whimsically, we could also set things up such that to lower one's retirement plan contributions, a person must go through a more complicated and involved process. Not to prevent anyone from lowering their contributions if that is what they truly desire, since that would be paternalistic and objectionable on grounds that it would infringe on individual liberty. But just to give them time to fully think through this weighty decision.

At the core of nudge techniques are three closely-linked ideas. One, that people generally act in predictable ways, and that the mind sciences and social sciences – for example, psychology and anthropology – can be used to illuminate this. Two, that all actions, including inaction, have some outcome by default, and that this outcome is not an immutable fact of nature, but something that it is in our power to set as we see fit. And, three, that for liberty to be respected, nobody should be forced to engage in any action, nor to pursue any particular outcome, though they should be given sufficient opportunity to consider the ramifications of their decisions. Interplay between these three ideas explains why Sunstein and Thaler suggest that governments should set up default retirement savings plans from which people can, by going to some effort, withdraw, in order to ensure that citizens get a better outcome vis-à-vis retirement incomes through a liberty-preserving process – i.e. one that nudges people into doing what they would most probably want to do anyway, but that at the same time also enables anyone who wants to resist the nudges to do so.

In summary, 'nudge' techniques make use of research in the mind and social sciences to reveal how people behave as a general rule and what factors can influence people's behaviour. This information is then factored into the design of environments in which people live and interact. And the intention is that, by default, people's interactions would then take desirable rather than undesirable forms, and generate desirable rather than undesirable outcomes. While the option to pursue undesirable forms of conduct would still remain, engaging in these forms of conduct would take additional effort (since they would be a departure from the default) and thus would be less attractive (but not impossible) to pursue.

Turning now to our re-deployment of this idea, as a first approximation to what this might look like vis-à-vis the design of online interactive environments, consider a computer interface deliberately formulated to encourage the use of standardised responses. That is, the fastest and easiest method of using this interface to interact with other people would be to express opinions through likes, favouriting, re-tweeting, thumbs-ups, +1s,[6] and so on, and presumably also through negatively-valenced variants such as dislikes, thumbs-downs, and −1s. Users would still have the option of entering text responses, but this option would require a greater investment of time and effort, perhaps because permission would be required from the post's author for the comment to appear, or perhaps because entering text would simply require a more convoluted and time-consuming procedure which would discourage users from engaging in that mode of interaction. A minor variant on this approach might be to create a more nuanced dictionary of iconic expressions which still give people the option of expressing a wide array of disapproving sentiments, but which remove some of the sting involved in highly-personalised textual comments. These particular suggestions are untested, and they are only intended to convey some initial ideas, rather than to solve concrete problems. As such, we strongly encourage further empirical studies to ascertain precisely which methods of shaping human conduct in online environments might have the potential of reducing the incidence and/or severity of cyber-victimisation and cyberharm.

Critiques of nudge

Nudging is a *subtle* form of influence, and this gives rise to at least two distinct forms of criticism.

On the one hand, one disadvantage of *subtle* techniques is their fallibility – i.e. that it is quite possible to resist them. In other words, internet users who wish to be vile and harmful will still be able to do so with relatively little effort. However, it is precisely the subtlety of the verb 'to nudge' that makes this technique easier to defend (at least from a perspective that is mindful of infringements on liberty) than, say, something along the lines of a 'coerce technique' or a 'shove technique'. Yes, internet users intent on being vile and harmful would still be able to act in these ways. But, given the incidence of violent crime throughout the world, those who strongly wish to be vile and to do harm to others will (unfortunately) probably always find ways to do so. Consequently, we think it is more realistic to aim not at 100 per cent compliance or 100 per cent eradication of cyberoffences, but rather at a significant reduction of their occurrence through the design of interactive environments in such ways that they discourage undesirable conduct and guide users into pro-social interactions. Again: the aim of our earlier critique of legal responses to cyberharms in this conclusion was not to discourage efforts to reform the legal system altogether, but only to highlight the limits of these approaches so that we do not end up relying solely on those strategies. Hence, even if nudging does not provide a fool proof method for completely eradicating cyberharms, we do not see this as a problem since our ultimate aim in this chapter has been to draw attention to other remedies we could also develop in order to ensure that this group of victims is catered for more adequately, as opposed to finding one, single fool proof strategy.

On the other hand, a less obvious but perhaps more troubling form of criticism of subtle forms of influence, by comparison with more overt forms of influence, is that they can be more difficult to notice, insidious, and thus difficult to resist. This makes them more akin to sinister forms of manipulation and social engineering, not unlike that depicted in George Orwell's *Nineteen Eighty-Four* (1949). In this famous dystopian novel, language was itself fashioned and crafted in line with the political ideology of the fictional totalitarian government of Oceania in an attempt to make not only the expression but potentially the very thinking and conceiving of certain things impossible. The way in which Sunstein (2015) deflects the accusation of Orwell-like totalitarianism in relation to nudge is to point out that the aim is not to make it *impossible* for people to express themselves in violent ways, but only to make it *more difficult* for them to do so. By creating an outlet for cyberoffending – albeit a difficult or awkward one to use – we do sacrifice 100 per cent effectiveness or 100 per cent compliance. However, we also avoid the dilemma faced by the criminalisation of cyber-conduct that sits at the penumbra of harm and offence. People retain the ability to do what is wrong, but they are provided with disincentives to exercise that ability, as well as incentives (for example, in the form of ease of interaction through pre-fabricated responses) to engage in pro-social conduct.

In summary, at the core of nudge techniques are two closely linked – and perhaps somewhat odd-sounding – ideas. These acknowledge: (1) the power of people doing nothing; and (2) the importance of ensuring people still have the option of behaving badly. The first idea recognises that even doing nothing will generate some outcome by default. Thus one way of improving outcomes in any given sphere of human conduct is to alter what comes about by default. (In other words, to change what happens if people do nothing.) The second idea responds to libertarian objections about the use of state force. It notes that compelling people to behave in this or that way violates liberty, even if those violations are supposedly in the name of good. One way to preserve liberty and avoid the charge of compulsion is to give people the option of behaving in ways that go against what is otherwise deemed right. This option should, however, be discouraged by designing-in hurdles that make that conduct more difficult and less attractive.

Taken together, the design of default choice architectures (the first idea) and the deployment of insights into human psychology to discourage bad conduct and encourage good conduct (the second idea), potentially provide a liberty-respecting approach to the design of all kinds of environments. If it is used to fashion interaction in pro-social ways in online environments, it is plausible that this method could reduce the incidence of cyberoffending by funnelling people's behaviour in pro-social directions. This would not be a fool proof approach, but it could stem the number of offences and even create more opportunities for positive encounters.

Value sensitive design

Nudge is a technique intended to shape how humans behave by modifying their environments. Its potential to better respond to the needs of victims and their harms relies on the idea that shaping human interactions in online environments through better design of those environments might reduce cyberoffending.

Another, similar approach is what Batya Friedman *et al.* refer to as 'value sensitive design' (VSD), that is, 'a theoretically grounded approach to the design of technology that accounts for human values in a principled and comprehensive manner throughout the design process' (2008, p. 70). Like nudge techniques, the value sensitive design approach recognises the fact that the way we design technology strongly influences how that technology is used. Thus it is possible to influence usage patterns if we think carefully at the design stage about the types of behaviours we value, and to craft our new devices and systems in a way that supports these.

Given the popular misconception that technology is ethically neutral (and that humans are the source of moral and social problems when they use technology in unethical ways), it is helpful to consider two examples which illustrate the way values are built into the technologies that we make and use. Consider a touch-screen combination lock by the side of a door, and a closed circuit television camera monitoring system.[7] Both examples involve the value of *security* in one sense or another. However, the first device might score poorly in regards to the value of *equality*. After all, visually impaired people may have trouble using touch screens. On the other hand, the second device may compromise the value of *privacy*, perhaps by inadvertently recording the identities of people engaged in normal but private affairs, rather than just those engaged in prohibited conduct. Thus, if the value of equality is also important, then a different security lock might need to be fitted (not one that relies upon its user being sighted). And if the value of privacy is important, then maybe a new security camera system will need to be developed and fitted – for instance, one that automatically blurs the faces of all people and maybe any other identifying markers or private information, unless an incident happens, in which case a supervisor with a sufficiently high security clearance can view the footage without the blurring filters applied.

The point of these examples is twofold. One, to highlight the way in which three particular values – namely security, equality, and privacy – might manifest themselves in different implementations of two kinds of security devices. Two, to highlight how deployment of some technologies rather than others can generate ethical problems, though not because any specific humans use the technologies in unethical ways, but because the technologies were designed in ways that failed to adequately accommodate important values. However, there are other values we could consider such as *sustainability* and *efficiency*. It is notable that the more values we consider and try to accommodate in the design of technology, the more we may discover tensions between different values at the design stage. Imagine, for instance, that we do also care about efficiency. A proximity detector-based lock might be very efficient, but it might come at the cost of the value of security. Importantly, we are not here asserting which of these values is more important than the others. Rather, we are pointing out that the values that are embedded into technology – technology that we design – can come into conflict with one another and this conflict among values embedded in technology may be in need of resolution.

When used as a methodology, value sensitive design requires that we make explicit the values we wish our technologies to promote (rather than leaving it up to accident and just hoping for the best). It is also demands that we treat these *ethical requirements* as sitting side-by-side with *functional requirements* at the stage when technology is designed. So, from this perspective, instead of bemoaning the fact that a proximity-activated locking device cannot satisfy both of the values we wish it to satisfy (for example, security and efficiency), this *ethical dilemma* is turned in the eyes of a value sensitive design engineer into a *technical problem*. Namely, the challenge is to design an artefact that not only satisfies the strict functional requirements of locks, but also the ethical requirements we want locks to meet. Something similar can be said about the CCTV security camera example. If privacy and sustainability are also as important as security, then what we should ask our engineers to design are security cameras that will achieve all three of those moral aims in order to accommodate all of those values.

So how might this work in the context of cybercrime and its victims? The first step would be to use the methods described in value sensitive design literature to identify the kinds of values that are compromised when cyberoffenders harm cybervictims – not least by identifying the harms involved. The next step would involve working alongside software engineers to develop technologies that would safeguard and promote those values. One example of this kind of effort is Mireille Hildebrand's discussion of a 'proactive technological infrastructure' – a 'so-called "vision of Ambient Law"' which builds 'legal protection into the ICT architecture, to safeguard our rights and freedoms within the various cyberspaces we inhabit' (2011, p. 223). A more recent example is provided by Maryam Al Hinai and Ruzanna Chitchyan (2015) who describe their design of a software system that caters for the value of equality (even though we personally find their particular suggestions vis-à-vis gender objectionable).[8]

Closing thoughts

Taking a step back from the important question of precisely how environments and artefacts could be designed to better secure the interests of victims of cybercrime, we can make the following observations. One way to view the moral problems that we encounter in this book – the harms that some people inflict on others through interactions in online environments – is as human-created problems for which solutions should be sought in the human domain. For instance, through the law, which, through its system of rules and punishments and so on, addresses itself to people at the conscious level by creating incentives and disincentives to certain forms of behaviour, with the hope of providing people with consciously salient reasons to act in some ways and desist from other ways of acting. Another way to address these problems, though, is to view these as design flaws (that is, that the environments we live in and the artefacts we use have been designed in a manner which permits and maybe even promotes troublesome interactions). Conceptualising these problems in this way – as challenges to design better moral technologies – means that these problems can potentially be *designed* out of the equation. Designed, that is, in such a way that it becomes impossible or at least more difficult to engage in undesirable conduct in the cybersphere, and easier and more inviting to engage in desirable conduct.

None of this needs to carry with it the connotation that cyberoffenders are not agents who choose to inflict harm on cybervictims. People can still be blamed for what they do wrong. Rather, the suggestion is simply that if certain uses of information and communication technologies result in forms of harm that we would rather avoid, then one of the methods at our disposal to reduce the incidence of this harm is to investigate how the values that need to be protected from this harm can be secured through the design of better moral technologies. This, to us, is what it would mean to have a truly *victim*-focused response, rather than an *offender*-focused one. Just as cyberoffenders should not be treated as devoid of their agency when they commit offenses against their victims, so, too, it is helpful to notice that the technology we create and use is not a value-neutral part of the environment. It is not a piece of nature which, like a hurricane, cannot be blamed when destruction occurs.

Instead of designing artefacts and environments that create, encourage, or enable social problems to occur, and only afterwards stopping to think about how those artefacts could have been designed better to avoid creating those problems,[9] it would be better to think ahead about how these technologies – that is, either the artefacts that we use, or the environments that we inhabit – could be designed in better ways. Lest this sounds vague and fuzzy, consider that even explicitly harmful technologies like guns can these days be designed in ways that make them less likely to be used in prohibited ways – that is, so-called 'smart guns' (Sebastian, 2016). As such, there is no in-principle reason why the design of the software through which we engage in internet-mediated interactions with one another could likewise not be designed to be less harmful, that is, to leave less scope for it to be used to harm victims.

In conclusion, our argument is that the best response to cybercrime, and its victims, is the careful deployment of criminal law, alongside: civil litigation; the education of the public and police; the lobbying (and perhaps even the nudging) of internet platform providers to develop their own policies so they are more sensitive to the needs of those who would otherwise be cybercrime victims; and – especially – approaches such as nudge and value sensitive design. This sort of broad, multifaceted response is, we think, the most effective and savvy way to work around the limitations of law so as to address the very real suffering being experienced by victims of cybercrime around the world.

Notes

1 As Wesley Newcombe Hohfeld (1975) famously pointed out, all rights are underpinned by correlative duties. Consequently, the legal protection of one group's rights invariably comes at the cost of curtailing another group's liberty. For example, the right to be free from cyberhate imposes a correlative duty on others to not speak to people in ways

that upset them. This curtailment of liberty, rightly or wrongly, is likely to be viewed by potential cyberhaters as a harm.
2. Producers of cyberhate, for instance, claim that what they produce is merely a form of 'speech', and that, as words rather than sticks, stones, or bullets, what is occurring is not the *infliction* of genuine harm but only the *taking* of mere offence (Jane, 2017, pp. 109–110). Some opponents of such legislation also argue that the harm suffered by victims of revenge porn and cyberhate could be mitigated *by victims* if only they chose to not be embarrassed, humiliated, and threatened. Please note that we do not endorse these arguments, but are simply mentioning them as examples of those prosecuted by others.
3. To proponents of minimal government who view state restrictions of individual liberty as paradigm cases of state wrongdoing, criminalisation of actions that do not involve sticks and stones but only words and hurt feelings (as it would likely be viewed from their perspective) falls into the category of very serious wrongs.
4. This begs the question regarding whether this is indeed something that people can just *choose* to not take offence at, though, for brevity, we set this aside.
5. And a class action may likewise not be attractive for victims to join for precisely the same reason, namely, because the administrative overhead involved with becoming a party to the class action may not be warranted by the small compensation payment one is likely to receive.
6. The +1 feature allows users of certain internet platforms to either +1 or –1 a comment or a solution in order to up-rate or down-rate the quality of the various responses.
7. We borrow the second example, and the general shape of the discussion, from Jeroen van den Hoven's (2014) presentation of the topic. See also van den Hoven (2007) and van den Hoven and Manders-Huits (2009).
8. Our affront relates to Hinai and Chitchyan's proposal for *how* to ensure gender equality in their system. They write, 'Some values, such as gender equality, can be indirectly supported through ICT by ensuring that gender is not revealed, or is actively hidden when participation or remuneration is concerned' (2015, p. 35). To our minds, covering up signs of one's gender on the internet in order to secure equality is almost an expression of the very problem of misogyny online rather than a way of confronting it and securing equality. This is not intended as a criticism, but as an invitation to feminist scholars to engage with those who attempt to secure important values to ensure that patriarchal modes of oppression are not reproduced in the process of trying to secure gender equality.
9. Or, even less helpfully, asking who is to blame for misusing that technology, which simply pulls focus away from victims and their harms, and redirects it to offenders.

References

Citron, D.K. 2014, *Hate Crimes in Cyberspace*, Harvard University Press, Cambridge, Massachusetts, London, England.

Friedman, B., Kahn Jr, P.H. and Borning, A. 2008, 'Value Sensitive Design and Information Systems', in K.E. Himma and H.T. Tavini (eds), *The Handbook of Information and Computer Ethics*, John Wiley & Sons, Inc., New Jersey.

Hildebrand, M. 2011, 'Legal Protection by Design: Objections and Refutations', *Legisprudence*, vol. 5, no. 2, pp. 223–248.

Hinai, M.A. and Chitchyan, R. 2015, 'Building Social Sustainability into Software: Case of Equality', *Proceedings of the 2015 IEEE Fifth International Workshop on Requirements Patterns (RePa)*, IEEE Computer Society, Washington, D.C., pp. 32–38. doi: 10.1109/RePa.2015.7407735

Hohfeld, W.N. 1975, 'Rights and Jural Relations', in J. Feinberg and H. Gross (eds), *Philosophy of Law*, 4th edition. Wadsworth Publishing Co., Belmont, California.

van den Hoven, J. 2007, 'ICT and Value Sensitive Design', in P. Goujon, S. Lavelle, P. Duquenoy, K. Kimppa and V. Laurent (eds) *IFIP International Federation for Information Processing, vol. 233, The Information Society: Innovations, Legitimacy, Ethics and Democracy* (pp. 67–72). Springer, Boston.

van den Hoven, J. 2014, 'The Dutch Approach to Responsible Innovation and Value Sensitive Design', *MVIcommunity*, 5 June, viewed 20 July 2016, www.youtube.com/watch?v=u5BYjD1Gn4g

van den Hoven, J. and Manders-Huits, N. 2009, 'Value-Sensitive Design', in J.K.B. Olsen, S.A. Pedersen and V.F. Hendricks (eds), *A Companion to the Philosophy of Technology*, Blackwell Publishing Ltd., West Sussex.

Jane, E.A. 2017, *Misogyny Online: A Short (and Brutish) History*. Sage, London.

Mill, J.S. 1859, *On Liberty*. Library of Economics and Liberty archive. Viewed 16 July 2016, www.econlib.org/library/Mill/mlLbty.html

Orwell, G. 1949, *Nineteen Eighty-Four*. Penguin Books Ltd., Middlesex, England.

Sebastian, D. 2016, 'What Makes a "Smart Gun" Smart?', *The Conversation*, 11 January, viewed 20 July 2016, https://theconversation.com/what-makes-a-smart-gun-smart-52853

Sunstein, C.R. 2015, 'Nudges, Agency, and Abstraction: A Reply to Critics', *Review of Philosophy and Psychology*, vol. 6, pp. 511–529.

Thaler, R.H. and Sunstein, C.R. 2009, *Nudge: Improving Decisions About Health, Wealth, and Happiness*, Penguin Books, New York.

Waldron, J. 2014, 'It's All For Your Own Good', *The New York Review of Books*, 9 October 2014, viewed 29 October 2016, www.nybooks.com/articles/archives/2014/oct/09/cass-sunstein-its-all-your-own-good/

Wall, D.S. 2007, *Cybercrime: The Transformation of Crime in the Information Age*, Polity Press Ltd., Cambridge, UK.

Willging, T.E. and Lee III, E.G. 2010, 'In Their Words: Attorney Views About Costs and Procedures in Federal Civil Litigation', *Federal Judicial Center*, March, viewed 20 July 2016, www2.fjc.gov/sites/default/files/2012/CostCiv3.pdf

Wittes, B., Poplin, C., Jurecic, Q. and Spera, C. 2016, 'Sextortion: Cybersecurity, Teenagers, and Remote Sexual Assault', *Brookings Institution*, May, viewed 12 May 2016, www.brookings.edu/research/reports2/2016/05/sextortion-wittes-poplin-jurecic-spera

Index

Page numbers in *italics* denote tables.

9/11 149, 156, 159; attacks 148, 150, 152, 158; auto-immune disorder precipitated 157; before 136; political and media discourse 151; reporting 153; *see also* post-9/11

Aboriginal Canadian community 190
abuse 6, 10, 54, 62, 64, 67, 133, 142; aggravated sexual abuse statute 212; child and young people 103, *112–13*, 115–16, 123, 124n1; contact 110; cyber 66; cycle of 111; directed against minorities 14; disclose 104; emotional 16, 95; expect 74; human rights 103; image-based 68; inciting 70; internet-facilitated 104; intimate partner 83; offline 115–16; online 7, 15, 51, 53, 66, 71–3, 108, 115, 118–19, 138; online victim 117; peer-perpetrated 123–4; protection from 196; racialised 212; report 115; sexual 18, 95, 110–11; of transgender people 39n12; on Twitter 73; underestimated 123; victims 69, 80; virtual 123; *see also* child sexual abuse, images of children
abusers 13, 109, 110, 119, 121–2
abusive 53, 62, 70, 124; pattern 110; situations 120
actus reus 30, 39n11
Adam, A. 50–2
Adler, P. 195, 201
Ahmad, M. 148
Ahmed, S. 160–1
al-Qaida 154
Alao, A. 192
Albury, K. 43, 51, 80, 82–4, 87, 89
alcohol use 173; parental 95

Allen, C. 131–2, 138, 140
alt.suicide.holiday 200
Aly, A. 153, 159
Aly, Waleed 67
America, North 152
American: adolescents 117; African Americans 171; Law Institute 39n10
anorexia 187, 195; pro-anorexia websites 200
anti-Muslim 157; narrative 138; rhetoric 150, 159
anti-suicide web sites 192
Ashley Madison *see* Madison, A.
Aspie Affection 195
Association for Progressive Communications 71
at risk 16, 46; of being persuaded to remain silent 120; children 95, 116–17; girls 115; heightened 66; individual 192; of suicide 192; of trafficking 101; women 103; young people 123
Australia 19, 150; advice on sexual consent 46; Cyber Friendly Schools Program 180; federal police assistant commissioner 73; high ranking police officer 62; legal scholar 13; Model Criminal Code 39n10; Muslim extremists 158; Muslim minorities 159; public anxieties over Islamic extremists 149; radicalised youth 152
Australian: authors on radicalisation 156; campaign group 70; Childhood Foundation 119; collective identity threatened 159; Criminal Intelligence Commission/Crime Commission 7; cyber victimization 171, 173–4; English language suicide prevention web sites

193; fat activist 72; government funding 75n1; government website on radicalisation 158; high school sexting 83; law on grooming 114; media personality 67; women 64, 84
Awan, I. 131, 133, 138, 144

Ball, J. 8
Banks, J. 131, 133
Barker, C. 2, 4, 8–9, 12
Barlow, J.P. 2–3
BBC News 133
Beech, A.R. 11, *112*
Bergelson, V. 28, 38n4
Bethel School District v. Fraser 178
Betterton, R. 86
Black, C. 66–7
Black women 53; female sexuality 52
blackmail/blackmailed 9–10, 18, 94, 96; pornographic films/photographs of victims 97; rape video 63, 69; *see also* sextortion
block/blocked content 47; pornographic websites 48; sites 8; *see also* content blocking
Boni, W.C. 3
Bonilla-Silva, E. 134, 138
Borradori, G. 150–1, 157, 159, 161
Bouché, V. 97, 99, 103–4
Bourdieu, P. 133–4
Bradley, P. 8
Brayley, H. 95
Brennan, T. 153, 160
Brickell, C. 18, 48
Britain 134, 136–7, 142
British 137; adolescents 172; bank notes 67; culture 137, 144; government 137; Labour MP 67; Muslims 136; National Party (BNP) 134–5; nineteenth-century philosophers 29; OFCOM research 116; police 133; Social Attitudes Survey 138; society 134; United British Alliance 135; values 140
British-based charity organization The Samaritans 192
Britons 138, 142
bullied students 173, 178
bullying 7, 108, 197; based on disability 177–8; dynamics of 49; freedom from 178; gendered attacks online 64; homophobic 89; impact on individuals 174; laws 179; off-campus 176; online and textual 167; reluctant to report 50, 169; research 88; scenes in school 65; society 134; staff members 179; traditional 168–74, 180; using technology 79, 167; victimization 174
bullying prevention 175, 181; intervention programs 180; in UK schools 179
Burkett, M. 82, 88
Busher, J. 132, 137
Butler, J. 157, 160

Callinicos, A. 149
Carmody, M. 46, 88–9
Cawson, P. 119
chat rooms 51, 97, 192, 198; cyberbullying 167; fantasy users 114; forum moderators 197; friend 120–1; gay male users 54; heterosexual male frequenters 52; minimum standards of acceptance 196; multiple participation 199; student safety and security 177; suicide 200
Child Exploitation and Online Protection Centre (CEOP) 116
child images *see* images of children
child pornography 97, 211; websites 7, 13
child sexual abuse (CSA) 17, 108, 110, 122; compliance induced 121; contributory factor for perpetration 122; intra-familial 120–1; literature 116; non-physically violent nature 120–1; online 10, 111, 115–16; reports 119, 123; under-reporting 118–19
ChildLine 121
Children's Bureau and Department of Health and Human Services 116
Children's Internet Protection Act (CIPA) 177
Children's Online Privacy Protection Act (COPPA) 175
Citron, D.K. 11, 13, 64, 66, 70, 209
civil rights 189; Department of Education Office for (OCR) 177–8
Cleland, J. 18, 131–3, 138–41, 144
coercion 121; perpetrators 12–13; sexting 83; technology-facilitated 7
community 29, 108, 134, 180–1, 203; of affirmation 195–6, 199; Aspie 195; building 52; Building Resilience to Violent Extremism 158; Canadian aboriginal 190; education and awareness 74; groups 15, 17; heart of 123; Internet 194; Muslim 159, 209; network-based 201; offender re-integration into 40n15; online 187, 189, 193, 196–9, 201–2; of online peers 194; protection of 40n15; of regular participants 187;

community *continued*
  responses 63; self harm 197; services 14; of strangers 202; threatened with change 140; Usenet 188; vampiric 198; white 139; wider 159, 161
ConRed Program 180
content blocking 48; mechanisms 192
Conway, M. 155–6
Copsey, N. 132, 135
Cornell, D. 177–8
Couldry, N. 79–81, 86
counter-terrorism 149, 154, 157, 159–60; experts 150, 156
counter-terrorist measures 149
Crampton, J. 44, 53
criminal law 13, 212, 214, 221; addressing social problems 38; Amendment Act 2013 40n12; changes 210; coercive force 41n23; Contemporary 4; cybercrime victims 37; high evidentiary standards 36; interest in the offender 32; reform 213; victim-disregarding 18, 27–8, 30–1, 33–4
Criminal Law Amendment Act 2013 40n12
Crofts, T. 80
Cross, D. 173–4, 180
crowdsource harassment 7; crowd-sourcing internet properties 155
cyber violence against women and girls (cyber VAWG) 63–4, 71, 74
cyberbullying 4, 19, 49, 88, 110, 168, 176, 212; behaviour/behaviour 173, 181n1; frequency 170; impact on psychological and physical health 174; intervention program 180–1; interventions 50; involvement 171; legislation related to 175, 178–9; perpetration 172, 175; rates 169, 171, 181; reported incidents 170, 177; research 64; towards staff member 179; traditional definitions 65; victimization 170–4; victims 167–9; UK Anti cyberbullying 180; victimization 175, 181; victims 180
cybercrimes 3–6, 8, 10, 13, 31, 33, 37, 211–12, 220; best response to 221; Budapest Convention on 40n19; convictions of perpetrators 32; defining 41n23; equivalents of traditional crimes 7; interventions for 14, 17; location of 35; prosecute 36; recognizing and adjudicating 27; regulatory and non-regulatory responses to 12; related arrest 14; related legislative change 210; responding to 34; targets of 11, 15; violence involved in 15
cyberharms 212–13, 217
cyberhate 53, 64, 72, 75n1, 211–13, 221n1, 222n2; racialised 209; *see also* gendered cyberhate
cyberhaters 212–13, 222n1
cyberspace 1, 6, 15, 220; anonymous intimacy 201; declaration of independence 2; dwellers 2; interactions 5; new terrain for traffickers 18, 94, 103; offers opportunities 111; part of environmental system 104, 108–10, 119; sex offending 124n1; utopian or dystopian framings 3
cyberstalkers 51, 70
cyberstalking/cyber-stalking 4, 51, 63, 69, 97, 167; targets 66
cyberwrongs 6, 12–15, 17, 31, 211–13

Dalla, R.L. 95, 98
Dank, M. 97–9
dark web 8–9, 102
Dark Web Social Network (DWSN) 9
Davidson, J. 114–17
Davis v. Monroe County Board of Education 177
deep web 8, 102
Deibert, R. 48
Dempsey, A.G. 174
denial-of-service attacks (DoS) 7, 11, 20n4; distributed denial-of-service attacks (DDoS) 20n4
Devlin, P. 39n8
digilantes 54; tactics 17
digilantism 11, 53–4
Discovery Early Career Researcher Award (DECRA) 75n1
Dobson, A.S. 18, 80, 83–9, 90n1
domestic violence 7, 10, 69, 95; hotline 16
doxing 68
Doyle, S. 65, 67
Drouin, M. 79, 83
drugs 95–6, 173; addiction 38n2, 98, 187; adult users 8; manufacture for one's own use 38n2; online trade 8; parental use 95; recreational 28; synthetic 8; user 38n4; *see also* substance use
Duff, R.A. 30, 32–3
Duggan, M. 13, 66
Durkheim, E. 189
Dworkin, G. 39n8

e-bile 53–4; gendered 67

Edelmann, N. 175
Egan, M. 8–9
Englander, E. 168, 170
English Defence League (EDL) 132, 134–5; contributors 136–7, 142–3; message board 139–44; supporters 132, 135
enmeshment tactics 95
entrapment 9, 120
ethnic cleansing 142–3; cousins 138; distinctions 144; domination 131; friends 139; groups 158; minorities 136, 157; multi-ethnic societies 152–3; multi-ethnic public-sphere 151; residents 140
Europe 142; anti-immigrant sentiment 150; antipathy towards Muslim men and women 148; Council of Europe 40n19; home grown extremist attacks 156; Islamic extremists 19, 149, 158; radicalised youth 152; threat from outside 158; victims of online dangers 117
European birth rates 136; Commission Directive 115; cyber victimization rates 171; home-grown Islamist political violence 149; sexual grooming criminalized 114–5; structural linguistics 63; values 151; women 71; women trafficked 96, 102
Evans v. Bayers 179
exclusion 136, 140, 167, 196, 198; exclusionary practices 134
exploit/exploited/exploiting 95–6, 101, 153; latest technologies 154; opportunities to 18, 94; women at risk 103
exploitation 50, 120; Californians Against Sexual Exploitation Act 101; CEOP 116; commercial *112*; corporate 11; of the media 154; opportunities for 98; sexual 10, 17–18, 38n4, 95, 108; technology-facilitated 94

Facebook 4–5, 99, 131, 143, 187; adolescents falsify age 175; blocked in China and Iran 48; deceased people's pages vandalized 35; EDL supporters 135; harassment 179; LYC safer-sex promotion campaign 46; messaging 104; page 72; policies 71, 109, 133; privacy 196; profiles 12; sexual health campaigns 47; support and empathy mobilized 201; text-based harassment 67; users 52, 144n1, 174

Featherstone, B.A. 121
feminist 64, 66, 86; activist 67; blogger 65; cultural critic 68; performers and artists 87; pornography 51; scholars 222n8; video blogger 69; writer 72; writing 50
fetishism 155, 195
Finkelhor, D. 79, 81, 111, 115, 119
First Amendment rights 176
First World 151, 153
flaming 53, 64–5, 167, 181n1
FoMO (fear of missing out) 167
Foucault, M. 44, 49
Frey, B.S. 40n20
Functional, Overlapping, and Competing Jurisdictions (FOCJ) 40n20
Furedi, F. 123

Gallagher, B. 120
GamerGate 16, 65–8
Garland, J. 132
Gehl, R.W. 9
gendered cyberhate 18, 62–7, 73, 212, 214; impact of 74; targets of 70–2
Gerassi, L. 95
Gill, R. 90, 90n2
Girl on the Net 17
Giroux, H. 152
Giumetti, G.W. 19, 65, 174
Gjoni, E. 16
Goffman 86–7, 90n2
Gottschalk, P. *112–13*
Gould, M. 189
government 1; addressing human trafficking 102; agency 10; Australian 75n1; Australian 2016 inquiry 73; British 137; Chechnya 142; employees 13; minimalist 39n6; national 137; purposes 3; regulations 153; responsibility 101; self 49; Singaporean 48; snooping 9; Syrian soldiers 154
government 159; Australian website 158; fictional totalitarian 218; minimal 222n3; role 156
Gradinger, P. 180–1
grooming 110, 114–15; behaviours 95–6, 111; internet offenders 111; online 7, 110, *112*, 117, 120, 123; online sexual 17–18, 108, 110–11, 114–15; process 119; techniques 95

hacker 3; world's creepiest 9
hacking 7, 20n6, 69, 211
hacktivism 11, 20n2
harass/harassing 7, 37, 49, 69, 82

harassment 6, 10, 43, 50, 70, 108, 167, 211; crowdsourced 7; cyber 52, 64; disability-based 178; electronic 175, 179; expect 74; federal or state laws 177; image-based 68; Internet 171; offline 52; online 49, 66, 71; sustained online 13; technology-facilitated 79; text-based 67; towards a staff member 179; UK Protection from Harassment Act 180; victims of 80; *see also* sexual harassment
Harindranath, R. 19, 157
Hart, H.L.A. 39n8
Hasinoff, A.A. 79–81, 87–9
hate speech 143; online 4, 133; racial 131, 141
Henry, N. 64, 70, 80
Hess, A. 72
Hickle, K. 18, 98, 103
Hinai, M.A. 220, 222n8
Hinduja, S. 50–1, 169–71, 173–5, 178
Hoff, D.L. 170
home grown terrorist 153; extremist attacks 156
Home Office 138
homophobia 90
homophobic 4; attacks on male peers 49; bullying 89; communication 133; hate speech 131
homosexual 28; suspected 154
homosexuality 87; criminalization/de-criminalization 39n8
Human Rights Watch 39n12
human trafficking 94, 100–2, 104; investigations 95; networks 97
humiliate/humiliated 7, 35; choose not to be 222n2; online 52
Hussein, Saddam 158

I-Way 3
identity theft 7, 20n1, 70, 167
images 49, 51, *112–13*, 118, 155; of body parts 82; digital sexual 18, 79; explicit 52, 86; gendered media 89; grisly/gruesome 150, 154; of horrific violence 153; image-based abuse 68; inappropriate 175; Internet memes 75n4; intimate 10, 13, 69; jihadi 156; macabre 151; of male bodies 87; media 149, 152; obtained without consent 69, 84; pornographic 79; produced 86; self-produced 86–7; sexual 80–1, 83–5, 88–9, 124; sexually explicit 81; sharing apps 116; social media 150, 159–62; of suicide 189; as target of violence 68; televised 159; *see also* self-images
images of children: child abuse 8, 13; indecent 108, 110, 124n1
images of female bodies 87; of Black women 52–3; sexualised 80; too attractive or unattractive 74
impersonation 167; of former partner 66; obtaining material for blackmail 69; online 70; on Twitter 35; *see also* identity theft
Innocenti Research Centre (IRC) 114
institutional control of the internet 47; responses 63
institutionalised/institutionalized discourses 134; feature of online life 52; regulatory power 48; victimisation 137
International Communications Union (ITU) 116
internet 1–6, 8, 34, 52, 73, 117, 122, 131, 144, 222n8; abuse amongst young people 115–16; access 48, 50, 103, 117, 123; accounts with feminine usernames 66; anonymity secured 36; antagonists 68; attacks on women 62–5; changes in design and use 75n7; channels 45; child safety 108; child sex offenders 111; children's access 48; communities 19; connection 7; crowd-sourcing properties 155; early years 53; entrepreneurs 209; fora 108; grooming 114–15, 119; historiography 63; infrastructure monitored 13; leak 16; new technology 74; open 14, 47; penetration in developing world 116; phenomena 213; pioneers 9; platform providers 221; platforms 222n6; pornography 50–1; portable 43; pre-internet age laws 14; racist communications 133–4; regulation 48; relations 54; researchers 44; scammers 20n3; service providers (ISPs) 48; services 48; settings 44; sex offenders 110; sexuality 49, 54; take a break from 71; threats 69; university policies 48; Watch Foundation 119
internet platform 222n6; providers 221
Internet suicide 189, 193; forums 192
Internet Users 7
internet users 4, 7, 9, 11, 37, 48, 187, 217; female 63, 71; international 131; user-friendly 3
internet-based challenges 40n20; discourses 54; society 47

internet-enabled devices 7, 117; technologies 114
internet-facilitated child abuse 104; child pornography production 97; normalisation of suicide 19; sexual exploitation 18, 98, 103
internet-mediated interactions 34, 221
Islamic 136; extremism 135, 143, 161; extremists 19, 148–9; identity subversion fear 159; State 153; values 151
Islamism 161
Islamist 151; home-grown political violence 149; movement 135
Islamists 142–3; Radical defeat 143
Islamophobia 131–2, 136, 139
Ivie, R. 151, 158

Jackson, L. 132, 138, 143
Jane, E.A. 1–4, 6, 8–9, 11–12, 15–19, 34, 52–4, 65–8, 70–3, 222n2
Japan youth suicide 191–2
Jason, Z. 16, 68, 72
jihad/jihadi 136, 150; anti-jihad groups 135; images 156; milieu 155, 157
jihadisphere 155, 158
jihadists 156
Jones, A. 98
Jones, C. 141
J.S. v. Bethlehem Area School District 178

Karaian, L. 80, 87
Kassimeris, G. 132, 138, 143
Klump v. Nazareth Area School District 179
Kotrla, K. 95
Kowalski, R.M. 19, 65, 167, 168–77, 180–1
Kral, M. 189–90
Kundnani, A. 149, 156
Kushner, D. 9

La Fontaine, J. 119–20
Lamont, T. 1617
Lanning, K. 119–20
Latonero, M. 94, 98–100, 104
Laughlin, G. 48
Laville, S. 15
Lenhart, A. 81, 169
Lester, L. 173
LGBTQI 88, 90; *see also* transgender people
Lillie, J. 54
Limber, S. 168–70, 173, 177–8, 181
Lippman, M. 4, 28, 38n1, 84, 87

Index 229

Livingstone, S. 84, 117, 122
loners 201
Love Your Condom (LYC) 46
Lucy Faithfull Foundation 119–20
luring 115; *see also* grooming

McDonald, M. 134
MacKinnon, C. 50
Madden, M. 174
Madison, A. 16–17
malicious 102; circulation of intimate images 10, 79; damage 7; edits 68; intent 72, 176; intentionally 41n23
Mantilla, K. 64, 70
Martellozzo, E. 1, 7, 10, 13, 15, 17–18, 81, 109, 111, *113*, 114–17, 119–20, 122
Martin, J. 8, 99, 103–4
Martin, L. 99, 103
Media Heroes Program 180
Mendel, J. 94, 102, 104
mens rea 27, 30, 32, 36–7, 39n11, 40n13, 41n23
Mill, J.S. 29, 39n5, 39n6, 39n8, 211
Miller-Young, M. 51
Mishna, F. 4950
Mitchell, A. 79, 81
Mitchell, S.N. 170
Mitchell, W.T.J. 154–5
Modood, T. 138–9, 144
Moseley, G.L. 12
Mulvey L. 86, 90n2
Muslim 136–7; anti-Muslim attitudes 157; anti-Muslim narrative 138; anti-Muslim rhetoric 150; asylum seekers 150; community members 209; culture 140, 143; extremists 158; immigrants 148; immigration 138; minorities 149, 157, 159–60; Other 132, 135, 140–1, 153, 161; religion 141; woman 148, 162n1; youth radicalisation 149, 154, 159
Muslims 132, 135–7, 139, 141–3, 158; deep hatred towards 144; living in Western societies 148; online abuse of 138; popular belief about 159; stereotyping of 140
Musto, J.L. 100–2

Naito, A. 191
National Geographic 194–5
Niezen, R. 19, 189–90
non-consensual: image production/distribution 84; media practices 79; sex 51; sex between two men 39n12; sexting practices 83; sexual intercourse 30

non-Muslims 142; bias against 137; presentation as victims 132, 135, 137, 144, 157
NSPCC 121–2

Oaten, A. 132, 142
obesity: Australian fat activist 72; morbid 195; pro-obesity sites 195, 200
O'Brien, S.A. 72, 122
OCC (Office of the Children's Commissioner) 118
OFCOM 116
Office for National Statistics 136
O'Keeffe, G.S. 175
Ólafsson, K. 116
Olweus, D. 168–9, 173
online abuse 7, 15; children traumatised/ harmed by 119–20; children at risk of 118; directed towards Muslims 138; targets of 53; victims of 108, 115–16, 123
online grooming 7, 110, 117, 120, 123
online suicide 19, 41n22; pacts 191
Orwell, G. 218; Orwell-like totalitarianism 218; Orwellian 72
Ostini, J. 7, 64
Otherkin Alliance Web site 203n5
outing 89, 167

Palfrey, J. 47–8, 50, 53
parental: consent lacking 175; drug and alcohol use 95; involvement 123; lack of monitoring 172
Parliamentary Counsel's Committee 39n10
Pascoe, C.J. 8890
Patchin, J. 50–1, 169–71, 173–5, 178
Patel, N. 1
Payne v. Tennessee 30, 33
perpetrator-exculpation 63, 73–4
Perren, S. 174
Perry, S. 134
Phillips, P.A. 13
Phillips, W. 65
Phippen, A. 81, 108
phishing 7, 20n1
pimps 97, 100
platform 119, 131, 134, 136, 194; access for older children 116; affective 153; changes 5; different frameworks 40n16; digital 156; expression of racist thoughts 144; internet 221, 222n6; internet providers 221; managers 6, 15, 17–18, 62, 71, 210; multimedia 149, 155; operators 71, 74; publically accessible 99; racial discriminatory discourses 18; social media 4, 62, 64, 79, 99, 133, 175, 187; technological 118; Usenet 187
Plummer, K. 43–5, 47
Polder-Verkiel, S.E. 41n22
police 7, 10, 61–2, 69, 121, 135, 142–3, 188, 209, 221; awareness campaign 124; biggest challenge is Internet 98; dispatchers tricked 68; failing to address cyberhate 71; failure to address cyber VAWG 74; inadequate responses 18; lack resources 14; London HTCU 111; practice in the area of child sexual abuse 17; presence on trafficking sites 100; response on revenge porn 73; seeking assistance from 72; service 15; standard response 71; sting operations 104; undercover operation 111; warning 67
police officers 61–2, 68, 109, 117; Australian federal assistant commissioner 73; British 133; Chief Officers in England and Wales 133; undercover 117
porn/pornography 44–5, 50, 84, 195; access filtering system 48; commercial 81–2, 85; exposure of victims to 95, 97; female porn-makers 51; feminist 51; internet 50–1; mob attack 68; nonconsensual 212; online 51; *see also* child pornography; revenge porn
pornographic 82; commercial media 85; films/photographs of victims 97; images of children 79; media 82, 85; pictures 51; threats to share films/photographs of victims 97; websites 48, 51
post-9/11 162; American politics 152; era 16; changes 138; racial politics of affect 157; war of appearance 153
postfeminist cultural and media environment 82; media discourses 83
Potter, C. 51
Powell, A. 51–2, 64, 70, 80
Powell, Enoch 134
Power, M. 8
power relations 43, 49–50, 52–3
prostitute 38n4
prostitution 28–9; criminalization/ de-criminalization 39n8; street-based 97–8

Quayle, E. 13, 114, 116, 118–19, 122

Race, K. 48

Index

racism 90, 131–2, 134, 138, 140; anti-immigrant 149; casual 141; cultural 136; embedded 144; online 133
racist 11, 64; attacks on minorities 150; comments 4, 34, 132; communication 133, 141; discourse 131–3, 138, 140–1, 143; hate speech 131; language 65; messages 133; thoughts and beliefs expressed 144; violence 161
raids 65, 75n5
rape 31; at gunpoint 67; inciting 66, 70; rapeability appraisal 67; threats 18, 64, 68, 72, 212; transgender people 39n12; video blackmail 63, 69
re-victimisation 13, 50
Reid, J. 95
reluctance to report 14, 50, 115, 119, 123, 172
report/reported/reporting 202; of 9/11 153; abuse 115; advertising online 98; blackmailed not to 69; cheating in marriage 16; CSA 123; cyberbullying 50, 169–73, 177; cybercrimes 36, 40n19; death threats 72; discriminatory hate speech 133, 148; hate crime 133; media 8; mental health problems 96; negative impact of religious diversity 138; new marking opportunities for pimps 97; Pew Research 174; provision of appropriate means 177; sex work experiences 98; sexting coercion 83; sextortion 12; of sexual abuse 10; solicited for online sex 117; success of prevention/intervention programs 180; trusting of traffickers 99; underreporting of CSA 118–19, 122; victimization 169, 173; violence against women 71; *see also* reluctance to report
Retort 152–3
revenge porn 10–13, 18, 63, 69; police response 62, 73; sites 35, 52, 212; victims 209, 222n2
Rice, E. 81, 117
Rice, R. 81, 117
Ringrose, J. 80, 82–5, 87, 89
risk/risks online 5, 45–6, 62, 180; associated with new drugs 8; of being accused of fetishism 155; of being ghettoized 51; of being persuaded to remain silent 120; for children and young people 108, 115–18; credibility 198; digilantism 11, 17; factors 18; gendered 82; high 73; incurred 104; invisible 123; low 94; management 45;

minimise 50; of radicalisation 161; for reoffending 124n1; of sex trafficking 94–5, 98, 101; sex work 100; of sexting media practices 18, 79–82, 89–90; sexual abuse 115–16; of suicide 192; taking 121, 123; *see also* at risk
Rivers, I. 88, 131
Roe-Sepowitz, D. 95, 98, 103
Ronson, J. 11
Runnymede Trust 136
Ryan, C. 195

Sallaz, J. 134
Salter, M. 80, 84, 87
Sandoval, G. 67–8
Sarkeesian, A. 68–9
scam-baiting 11, 20n3
scammed online 14
Schmid, A. 156, 158
School Standards and Framework Act 179
self-destruction 19, 188–93, 195, 199, 202
self-harm 187, 195, 197
self-images *see* sexual self-images
self-inflicted death 19, 188–9, 194, 200, 202
self-injury 192; SIFriends 197; web sites 197, 201; *see also* self-harm
Selkie, E. 44–5
Seto, M. 110, 124n1
sex offenders 111, 122; anonymity benefits 119–21; internet 110–11; online *112–13*, 116; psychological characteristics 124n1
sex trafficking 94–5, 97, 102; internet-facilitated 103; networks 100; role of technology 101; survivors of 96; victims 98–9, 101, 103
sexting 108, 124, 167, 181n1; coercion 83; media practices 18, 79–84, 8790
sextortion 9, 10, 12–13, 63, 69, 96, 123–4, 211–12, 214
sexual harassment 48–9, 51–3, 66, 83; online 54; student-on-student 177
sexual identity 44, 47
sexual media practices 82, 85–6, 89; socially transformative 87–8
sexual power 86; in online settings 55
sexual self-images 85
sexual violence 11, 18, 46, 66; continuum 52; prevention 88; technology-facilitated 64
Shariff, S. 4950
Sharland, E. 122
Slonje, R. 169–70
Smith, L. 7, 74

232 *Index*

Smith, P.K. 167–70
Spain 114, 138, 172–3, 180
Staksrud, E. 109
stalking 7, 10, 66, 70, 211
standard of intentionality 41n23
Stokes, C. 50, 52–3
substance use 124n1; misuse 95–6
suicide 17, 28, 38n2, 192, 197; advocacy forums 201; alt.suicide.holiday (a.s.h.) 187–8, 200, 203n1; attacks 148; attempt 13, 38n3; bombings 150; forums 19, 187–8, 192, 194, 199, 200, 203; imitative 190; incitement to 67; Internet 189, 192–3; Internet-based advocacy 192–3; intervention 192–3; methods 192, 203n2; militants 150; Net 191–2; Net-based provocations 196; normalization of 188–90, 202; note 201; obsession 187; oriented web sites 203n3; pacts 191, 200, 203; partner 187–8; positive value 195; prevention web sites 193; pro-suicide sites 202; rate 189–90; rate in Japan 191; youth 191; *see also* online suicide, self-inflicted death
Suler, J. 109–10, 168
Sullivan, J. 111, *112*
Sunstein, C. 194, 215–16, 218
survivors 192; emotional abuse 16; of sex trafficking 96
Suzor, N. 13
swatting 68
Sydney Criminal Lawyers 38n3

Tam, J. 192, 203n2
Taras, R. 138, 144
Taylor, M. 13
technology-facilitated: abuse, harassment, and coercion 7; sexual violence 64
teen/teenaged/teenagers 46, 118; chatrooms 119; dangers online 88; Facebook/Twitter users 174; female 123; gay or lesbian 48; girls 9; sexting 79, 81–4; views on social networking sites 44–5
terrorism 110, 135, 149, 156–8, 160, 162n2; contemporary forms of 152; global 150–1; media representations of 153; media responses to 159
terrorist 149; activity 153; acts 148, 155, 157; attacks 136, 154, 156, 161; home-grown 153; incidents 150, 156–7; organisations 154; potential 159; violence 148, 154
terrorists 16, 151; attacks on soft targets 150; exploit latest technologies 154; potential 161; techno-terrorists 3
Thakor, M. 97, 100, 102
Thaler, R.H. 215–16
threat/threats 3, 14, 68, 70, 74, 178; to Australian collective identity 159; of being sued 214–15; credibility 72, 133; death 67, 72; to democratic freedoms 152; explicit *112*; to integrity 199; of Islamic extremism 143; to life and limb 211; to masculinity 115; Muslim 135, 159; from outside 158; perceived 135, 137, 144; physical 13, 66; posed by terrorist acts 157; potential 150; racial Other 161; rape 18, 64, 212; to remove child from family 121; to safety and security 180; sexualized violence 53; social 134; toward teachers 179; of violence 133; from within 135
threaten 15; with change 140; inquirer's sense of self 45; internet regulation 48; position and privilege 138; suicide 13; victims 54, 69, 222n2; violence 72
threatening behavior 179; cohesion of multicultural communities 149; discourse 66; internet messages 66, 70; offline world 45; portrayal of Muslim culture 143; to share photos or videos 96, 211; with total destruction 151
Thrift, N. 153, 160
Tinker v. Des Moines Independent Community School District 178
Tokunaga, R.S. 64, 170
totem 194; totemism 155
traffickers 18, 94, 98–9, 102–4; control of victims 95–6; legislation intended to penalize 100; network 101; utilize social media 97; *see also* pimps
transgender people: abused or raped 39n12; indecent assault 31; transphobic online hostility 64
Treadwell, J. 132
trickery 167; tricked by traffickers 102; swatting 68
trolling 64–5, 196–7, 200, 203; anti-trolling defences 197; gendertrolling 64
trolls 133, 196, 200
trust 45, 104, 120; child's 111, 120; lack of 193; the wrong men 11
trusting 172; relationships 95; traffickers 99
Turner, H.A. 170–1
Twitter 11, 131, 155–6, 187; abuse 73; blocked in China and Iran 48; clogging 66; death threats 72; impersonation 35,

Index 233

70; policies 71, 133; text-based harassment 67; trending 62; users 67, 138, 144n1, 174

United Kingdom (UK) 142; abuse on Twitter 73; bullying prevention in schools 179; child abuse 118–19; ChildLine 121; children sexually abused 118; cultural racism 136; ethnic distinctions 144; government snooping 9; grooming techniques 95; immigration 138; Lucy Faithful Foundation 119; perceived social decline 137; Protection from Harassment Act 180; sex education 122; sexting media practices 83; sexual grooming legislation 115; Sexual Offences Act (SOA) 2003 114; women 7; Women's Aid 7; see also Britain, British, Britons
United Kingdom (UK) police forces 133; chief constable 14
United Nations (UN) 64, 66, 71, 74; Broadband Commission for Digital Development 73; Protocol to Prevent, Suppress, and Punish Trafficking in Persons, Especially Women and Children 94; Women 2016 66
United States (US) 9/11 attacks 150; anti-immigrant sentiment 150; anti-trafficking campaigns 100–2; Army 155; assault on Arab, Muslim, and South Asian immigrants 148; black adolescent girls' homepages 52; child sex trafficking 97, 99; child sexual abuse 118; classified information leak 16; commercial sex economy 97; cyberbullying 174; cyberstalking 66; enemy within 158; external threat 149; government snooping 9; hacker 9; home-grown Islamist violence 149; human trafficking 95; Islamic extremists 19, 149; luring 115; policies on bullying prevention 175; revenge porn 12; sex trafficking 94–5, 102; sexting 88; sextortion 10, 211; Twitter and Facebook platforms hosted 133; victim impact statements 30; women 72, 83
US Department of Education Office for Civil Rights 177–8
US Department of State Victims of Trafficking and Violence Protection act (TVPA) 94–5
Usenet platform 187; suicide community 188

user-generated content 75n7, 155; pictures 83

Valenti, J. 72
van den Hoven, J. 222n7
van Dijk, T. 131, 140
van Doorn, N. 84
Vanden Abeele, M. 81, 85
victim-blaming 11, 14–15, 63–4, 71, 73–4, 209
victimisation 6; of children and adults 18; collective 137; complicit in 18; cyber 213, 217; cycle of 13; of minorities 19; new forms 4; online 2–5, 10–11, 17, 116; at risk of 116; suffering 6; see also re-victimisation
victims of cybercrime 6, 12, 19, 28, 33, 38, 210, 213, 220–1; marginalised by criminal law 18, 27, 37, 209
Vincent, J. 117, 138
Vincent, N.A 6, 18–19
viral 75n4, 160
ViSC Social Competence Program 180

Wang, J. 170–1
Waskul, D. 44–5, 47
webcams 9, 69, 108, 119
Webster, S. 108, 111, *113*, 117, 120
Weeks, J. 43, 54
Welcome to AFF 195, 198
Wetherell, M. 144n2, 160
Whittle, H. 110, 115–17
Willard, N. 48, 167, 177, 181n1
Williams, K.R. 170, 172
Williams, M. 40n17, 40n18
Wittes, B. 9–10, 12–13, 69, 96, 211–13
Wolak, J. 79, 81, 115–16

Yaffe, G. 28, 38n1
Yalom, I. 202–3
Yar, M. 4–5
youth 65; cyber safety education 90; digital natives 169; hours online 116; likelihood of involvement in bullying 181; marginalised 87–90; Muslim 149, 159; pre-pubescent 116–17; radicalised 149, 152, 154; at risk of trafficking 101; sext education films 83; sexting 79, 82, 88; sexual image production and distribution 80–2; social media profiles privacy settings 174; suicide in Japan 191–2

Zhao, S. 47, 54
Zizek, S. 151

Taylor & Francis eBooks

Helping you to choose the right eBooks for your Library

Add Routledge titles to your library's digital collection today. Taylor and Francis ebooks contains over 50,000 titles in the Humanities, Social Sciences, Behavioural Sciences, Built Environment and Law.

Choose from a range of subject packages or create your own!

Benefits for you
- Free MARC records
- COUNTER-compliant usage statistics
- Flexible purchase and pricing options
- All titles DRM-free.

Benefits for your user
- Off-site, anytime access via Athens or referring URL
- Print or copy pages or chapters
- Full content search
- Bookmark, highlight and annotate text
- Access to thousands of pages of quality research at the click of a button.

REQUEST YOUR **FREE** INSTITUTIONAL TRIAL TODAY

Free Trials Available
We offer free trials to qualifying academic, corporate and government customers.

eCollections – Choose from over 30 subject eCollections, including:

Archaeology	Language Learning
Architecture	Law
Asian Studies	Literature
Business & Management	Media & Communication
Classical Studies	Middle East Studies
Construction	Music
Creative & Media Arts	Philosophy
Criminology & Criminal Justice	Planning
Economics	Politics
Education	Psychology & Mental Health
Energy	Religion
Engineering	Security
English Language & Linguistics	Social Work
Environment & Sustainability	Sociology
Geography	Sport
Health Studies	Theatre & Performance
History	Tourism, Hospitality & Events

For more information, pricing enquiries or to order a free trial, please contact your local sales team:
www.tandfebooks.com/page/sales

The home of
Routledge books

www.tandfebooks.com